Artisans Abroad

Artisans Abroad

British Migrant Workers in Industrialising
Europe, 1815–1870

FABRICE BENSIMON

OXFORD
UNIVERSITY PRESS

OXFORD
UNIVERSITY PRESS

Great Clarendon Street, Oxford, OX2 6DP,
United Kingdom

Oxford University Press is a department of the University of Oxford.
It furthers the University's objective of excellence in research, scholarship,
and education by publishing worldwide. Oxford is a registered trade mark of
Oxford University Press in the UK and in certain other countries

Published in the United States of America by Oxford University Press
198 Madison Avenue, New York, NY 10016, United States of America

British Library Cataloguing in Publication Data
Data available

Library of Congress Control Number: 2022947320

ISBN 978-0-19-883584-4

DOI: 10.1093/oso/9780198835844.001.0001

Printed and bound by
CPI Group (UK) Ltd, Croydon, CR0 4YY

Acknowledgements

This book has been a long time in the making and I have incurred many debts during the research and the writing.

I must first thank Margot Finn who gave advice at all stages of the project and was most helpful and inspirational. I am also most grateful to Constance Bantman, Julian Hoppit, Sandrine Parageau, Rachel Rogers, Callie Wilkinson, and an anonymous reader for reading the text, and for their valuable comments and corrections.

Other friends and colleagues have provided useful advice on specific chapters and issues, especially Jane Humphries on the economy, Colin Pooley and Marjory Harper on migration patterns, Robert Poole and Katrina Navickas on politics, Chris Whatley on linen and jute workers, Arnaud Page on food and drink, François Bourmaud on sports, Nicola McLelland on language issues, Anaïs Albert and Manuela Martini on female labour, and Maurizio Gribaudi on 1848. This book has most benefited from exchanges with all of them. Of course, all remaining errors are mine.

This research profited greatly from exchanges with Malcolm Chase (1957–2020), who is sorely missed. Over the years, many other friends and colleagues have given valuable advice: Joan Allen, Richard Allen, Sylvie Aprile, Jean-Claude Caron, Laurent Colantonio, Alain Corbin, Michel Cordillot, Mark Crail, Martin Crawford, Pierre-Jacques Derainne, Delphine Diaz, Caroline Douki, Claudine Ducol, Chris Evans, Rainer Fremdling, Alexandre Frondizi, Nancy Green, Emma Griffin, Louis Hincker, Joanna Innes, Alvin Jackson, François Jarrige, Philippe Minard, Jeanne Moisand, Paul Pickering, Iorwerth Prothero, Philippe Rygiel, Jean-Claude Sergeant (1943–2014), Ann Thomson, David Todd, and Julien Vincent.

A Marie Sklodowska-Curie fellowship at University College London (2016–2018) enabled me to carry out this research. At UCL, the feedback of Catherine Hall, Keith McClelland, Florence Sutcliffe-Braithwaite, and especially Margot Finn, was also appreciated. Jane Humphries, Mark Greengrass, Miles Taylor, and Frank Trentmann have been helpful in turning the research into a book.

I have benefited from the advice of many archivists and historians in various places: Ian J. Kerr (1941–2020) and David Brooke (1935–2013) on the railways; Stanley D. Chapman and Sheila Mason on lace in Nottingham and Ilkeston; Serge Chassagne on cotton masters; Marie-Pierre Cariou in Landerneau; John Barzman in Le Havre; Jean-Pierre Emo in Malaunay; Nicole Duboc in Pissy-Pôville; Eric Geerkens in Liège; Noël Gavignet, Anthony Cadet and Mary Wood in Calais; Gillian Kelly and the Australian Society of the Calais Lacemakers in Australia;

Philip Emerson, Richard Gaunt, Dawn Whatman, Christopher Richardson (1947–2020) and Rosie Wileman in Nottingham; Audrey and John Carpenter in Loughborough; Michel Croguennec in Grand-Quevilly; Thérèse Boulanger in Grand-Couronne; Maureen Morris in Brighton; Natalia Da Silva Pereira in Brussels; Alexandra Cransac in Aveyron; Yannick Marec in Rouen; Carol Morgan and Mike Chrimes at the Institution of Civil Engineers in London; Annie Laurant on Fourchambault; Annick Michaud on the Carmichael business in Ailly-sur-Somme; Bénédicte Meurice on John Leavers; Jarmo Peltola on Finland; Rosalind Frogley on George Good; Maureen Morris in Brighton; Gérald Mennesson in Dunkirk; Christine Proust and Céline Van Lierde-Carbon in Coudekerque-Branche.

Some of this work was presented at seminars and conferences and I am grateful to the convenors of these events and to all those who offered comments and questions, like Owen Ashton, Joan Allen and Richard Allen in Newport, Rachel Hammersley in Newcastle-upon-Tyne, Catriona Macdonald in Glasgow, Matthew Roberts and Antony Taylor in Sheffield, Chitra Joshi in Delhi, Christina de Bellaigue and David Hopkin in Oxford, Marianne Amar, Nancy Green and Paul-André Rosental in Paris. This work has also benefited from exchanges with colleagues in the *Revue d'histoire du XIXe siècle,* in the Centre d'histoire du XIXe siècle, in the British history seminar in Paris, as well as with some students, especially Anh-Dao Bui Tran, Léa Leboissetier, Leila Raffiee and Béatrice Robic.

Some parts of book are excerpted from articles I have published over the years: "British workers in France, 1815–1848", in *Past and Present* (n° 213, November 2011, pp. 147–189); with Christopher A. Whatley, "The thread of migration: a Scottish-French linen and jute works and its workers in France, c.1840–c.1870", in the *Journal of Migration History* (n° 2, 2016, pp. 120–147); "The emigration of British lace makers to continental Europe (1816–1860s)", in *Continuity and Change. A Journal of Social Structure, Law and Demography in Past Societies* (n° 34.1, April 2019, pp. 15–41); «"À bas les Anglais!" Mobilisations collectives contre des Britanniques, de la monarchie de Juillet à la révolution de 1848», in *Diasporas. Circulation, Migration, Histoire* (n° 33, 2019, pp. 75–90); "Women and children in the machine-made lace industry in Britain and France (1810–1860)", in *Textile. Cloth and Culture* (vol. 18, 2020, pp. 69–91); and "John Leavers (1786–1848)", *The Nottinghamshire Historian*, No.109, Autumn/Winter 2022, pp. 34–47. To the editors of these journals go my thanks for their permission to use the material presented here.

Thanks also to Miles Irving at UCL for the maps, to the various colleagues and institutions that have provided pictures, and to Cathryn Steele and Kalpana Sagayanathan at OUP.

My personal thanks go to my aunt Florise L'Homme. This book is dedicated to my parents, Ariane L'Homme (1939–2018) and Paul Bensimon.

Contents

List of Figures

List of Tables

List of Maps

Introduction

When railway contractor William Mackenzie and engineer Joseph Locke undertook to build a line between Paris and Rouen in 1841, they faced a major challenge. Four large tunnels and five viaducts over the Seine had to be built. To complete the project, Mackenzie and Locke brought in thousands of British itinerant masons, miners, and navvies to assist them. The railroad was inaugurated in 1843 and then extended to Le Havre by 1847. Many of the migrant construction workers remained in France over those years, and some later worked on other continental lines. In addition to the men who built the railways, many of the early train mechanics were also British, as well as those who made the trains themselves. These emigrants were some of the thousands—possibly tens of thousands—of British workers and engineers who journeyed to the Continent for work during the period 1815–70 and played a decisive part in European industrialisation. They came from across Britain, but especially from industrialised areas such as South Wales, Staffordshire, Lancashire, Nottinghamshire, and the city of Dundee in Scotland. They worked in linen, cotton, lace, wool combing, the iron industry, machine-making, steamship manufacturing, and railway building. These were sectors in which Britain, in the first phase of European industrialisation (1780–1850), enjoyed a technical advantage.

These British workers had different motivations for journeying abroad to work. Some moved because their British employers, like Mackenzie, sought to make the most of their technical lead by establishing businesses abroad. Some emigrated on their own initiative because they could market their skills at good value. Some were artisans who could avoid protective tariffs by plying their trade on the Continent. Most workers went to France, while others went to Belgium and the German states, or to Holland, Scandinavia, Austria and the Habsburg dominions, Switzerland, Russia, and southern Europe. Some stayed just a few years—the time it took to build a railroad—and then went elsewhere, while others settled on the Continent permanently. In consequence, although European countries followed different paths to industrialisation, British workers and engineers contributed decisively to each of their distinctive trajectories. For instance, early industrialisation in Belgium was shaped by the contribution made by British workers at Cockerill's factory. William Cockerill was a Lancashire worker who wandered through Sweden and Russia before ending up in a textile factory in Verviers, Belgium. He and his son John built machines for textile production before expanding to other industries and opening the first vertically integrated

Artisans Abroad: British Migrant Workers in Industrialising Europe, 1815–1870. Fabrice Bensimon, Oxford University Press.

factory on the Continent in 1817, with its own mines, coke ovens, and machine construction sites and a workforce of over 2,000 people by the late 1830s. The expansion of French iron, textile, and railways cannot be understood without taking into account the important contribution of skilled British artisans.

The principal aim of this book is to explain the reasons for such industrial mobility from Britain to and across Europe and to understand how it was experienced by the workers themselves. It contributes to the social history of migration and early industrialisation, as well as the broader social, cultural, and political history of the period. It diverges from a top-down approach in that it does not consider only the part played by entrepreneurs and companies but also that by workers. It argues that the emigration of thousands of British workers to the Continent during the industrial revolution is a crucial part of the history of both the United Kingdom and Europe in the industrial era and beyond. With the exception of large numbers of Irish immigrants, Britain was first and foremost a country of emigration rather than immigration during this period. The flow of migrant workers was an integral part of Britain's industrial transformation and explains the profound impact of the latter across Europe. Retracing the stories of British migrant workers can help us better understand how industrialisation took place on the Continent by demonstrating how technical expertise was spread through the crucial input of British skilled workers.

The emigration of British workers to Europe parallels Britain's colonial impact in the nineteenth century, but is much less studied and not so well understood. Although research on the history of emigrants has expanded over the past thirty years, studies on the global diaspora of British engineering are usually limited to the 'Anglo-world' of the United States and the settler colonies (Canada, Australia, New Zealand, and South Africa).[1] This is partly because the numbers of British emigrants to these places were larger, especially after 1850, but also because most research on British emigration has been conducted by English-speaking historians from the UK, the settler colonies, and the United States. The emphasis on long-distance migration has also been shaped by archival considerations: passenger lists, traditionally an important source for historians of migration, were only kept for long-haul voyages to destinations outside Europe. In the colonies and the United States, most migrants settled for good, and therefore produced more sources than the often-temporary migrants who went to the Continent, some of whom were itinerant workers who moved on regularly from their employment.

As a result, only selected aspects of the flow of British emigrants to Europe have been studied. Most research has focused on specific technologies or trades

---

[1] Daniel Headrick, *The Tools of Empire: Technology and European Imperialism in the Nineteenth Century*, New York, 1981; Daniel Headrick, *The Tentacles of Progress: Technology Transfer in the Age of Imperialism, 1850–1940*, Oxford, 1988; Ian Kerr, *Building the Railways of the Raj, 1850–1900*, Delhi, 1995; Shelton Stromquist, 'Railroad Labor and the Global Economy: Historical Patterns', in Jan Lucassen (ed.), *Global Labour History: A State of the Art*, Bern, 2006, pp. 623–47.

(particularly iron puddlers) or the diffusion of specific manufacturing techniques.[2] Workers are understudied in comparison to manufacturers and entrepreneurs.[3] The social and cultural dynamics of British labour migration to Europe remain little understood. Given this relative paucity of scholarship on British industrial migration outside the borders of the country, there is scope for further study of this phenomenon to broaden our understanding of the European dimensions of this history of transnational technical exchange. Through an analysis of the continental dimensions of Britain's globalising workforce, this book will assess the nineteenth-century roots of some of the present-day connections and disconnections between Britain and the rest of Europe.

Beginning with an analysis of the economic parameters of these migration flows, which were often related to gaps in technological knowledge, this study expands to include their social and cultural dimensions, covering the practicalities of migration, the links cultivated by migrants with local populations, and their cultural, associational, and political practices overseas. It addresses the distinguishing features of these flows in industrial sectors as diverse as lace, linen, iron, and the railways. At the same time, it also considers what the migrants employed in these different industries had in common.

What economic, social, and cultural factors enabled British capital to fund continental enterprises, allowed British skills to shape labour processes in Europe, and prompted British male and female labourers to seek and find continental employment? What were the practicalities of labour migration? Did migrant Britons make up isolated or relatively integrated communities? How and why were they targeted by xenophobic protests? What can be said of their religious and cultural lives? Were they involved in trade unions or political associations? These are some of the secondary questions addressed in this book.

1. Period

The period under consideration is 1815–70. By 1815, the industrial revolution was well underway in Britain but still in its infancy on the Continent. During the eighteenth century around 1,000 British artisans had already emigrated to France to market the skills they had acquired, especially in textiles—a mobility which has

---

[2] W. O. Henderson, *Britain and Industrial Europe 1750–1870: Studies in British Influence on the Industrial Revolution in Western Europe*, Liverpool, 1954; Patrice Bret, Irina Gouzévitch, and Liliane Pérez (dir.), 'Les techniques et la technologie entre la France et la Grande-Bretagne XVIIe–XIXe siècles', *Documents pour l'histoire des techniques*, 2010, no. 19; Rainer Fremdling, 'The Puddler: A Craftsman's Skill and the Spread of a New Technology in Belgium, France and Germany', *Journal of European Economic History*, vol. 20, no. 3, 1991, pp. 529–67.

[3] Henderson, *Britain and Industrial Europe*.

been well documented by J. R. Harris.[4] Channel crossings were made more difficult by the protracted wars between France and Britain (1793–1802 and 1803–15) but were not completely interrupted. When normal traffic resumed in 1815, it shared certain aspects with the eighteenth-century pattern of migration of skilled textile- and machine-making artisans. But at the same time, post-1815 migration was different. Migrant workers arriving in Europe after the end of the Napoleonic wars took up employment in new sectors of manufacturing that had developed over the preceding years, such as machine-made lace or iron puddling. While eighteenth-century migrants were mostly artisans, a distinctive feature of post-1815 mobility was that it involved increasing numbers of industrial workers. Artisans arriving from Britain in the eighteenth century did not have legally recognised status, were vulnerable to the repercussions of economic warfare, and were often accused of 'industrial espionage'. However, by the early nineteenth century free-trade doctrines gained ground, especially in Britain. British bans on the emigration of artisans and on the exportation of machinery were lifted in 1824 and 1843, respectively. In the 1820s, the 1830s, and the 1840s, the numbers of British industrial workers arriving in the rest of Europe swelled to thousands.

By the 1840s, the number of sectors in which British workers gained employment had expanded. In linen and then jute, a series of continental ventures using British machinery resorted to taking on workers from across the Channel, especially from Dundee. In these sectors, male carders and female spinners were hired alongside mechanics. In the railways, after a decade of frantic growth and development in Britain, capitalists such as Mackenzie and engineers like Locke crossed the Channel to undertake the building of modern lines on the Continent. They took with them thousands of workers to undertake the construction. Many of these men were navvies, a very different workforce from the skilled British artisan who had traditionally migrated in the eighteenth century. In wool, lace, cotton, iron, and even in some mines, the flow of skills persisted until the 1860s, interrupted only by the 1847–8 crisis and the 1848–9 European revolutions.

Every country followed its own trajectory and advanced at different rates, with industrialisation beginning in Belgium by the 1820s, in France after 1830, and in Germany after 1850. From mid-century, all European governments had supported an industrial economy and fostered industrial expansion. Ending this study in 1870 might seem arbitrary, as British engineers and workers have continued emigrating to the Continent to this day. Yet, by 1870, industrial Europe was very different from what it had been in 1815. Britain was still the leading industrial nation: by 1860, while it accounted for 2 per cent of the world's population, it controlled 40–45 per cent of the world's modern industrial capacity. Its energy consumption of coal, lignite, and oil was five times that of Prussia and six

---

[4] John Raymond Harris, *Industrial Espionage and Technology Transfer: Britain and France in the Eighteenth Century*, Aldershot, 1998.

times that of France. But the gap with Germany was shrinking. By 1870, some continental sectors of manufacturing were starting to compete with British businesses for markets. The French and German railway networks began to rival those of the British. While in 1820 German coal output was one eighth of the British, by 1870 it was one third. French and German steam power increasingly rivalled that of the British, as did cast-iron output. Considering the total manufacturing output of Britain, France, Germany, and the United States, Britain's share shrank from 45 per cent in 1825–34 to 35 per cent in 1875–84.[5] Local workforces had been trained, and British engineers were no longer a crucial asset in western Europe. The nature of the manufacturing workforce had also changed, with increasing numbers of unskilled workers in lieu of the apprenticed artisan. In France, which was the main European destination for British migrant workers, the proportion of British people among the foreign population was shrinking, and many who immigrated after this date belonged to the middle and upper classes. At the same time, growing numbers of British engineers made their way to the settler colonies of Australia, Canada, New Zealand, and South Africa, and also to Russia and South America.[6]

2. Sources

This book will try to both quantify and map these labour migrations, and use 'qualitative' material to understand the cultural, religious, social, and political dimensions of migrants' lives. Such an approach is fraught with difficulty because, although the nineteenth century witnessed the publication of unprecedented numbers of newspapers and autobiographical writings as well as an expansion of state and administrative record-keeping, many migrants left few traces. The migrants studied here were mostly workers, and workers left little printed material behind them. On top of that, migrants were, by definition, elusive, and even today establishing precise figures is difficult and results are often contested. They left little trace of themselves at their point of departure. When they crossed the Channel or the North Sea, passenger lists were not drawn up, and those making the journey were not even counted. When they reached the Continent, they were usually not registered either. Few states recorded incoming and outgoing migrants. Prussia made various administrative efforts to register non-residents and changes of residence status. But until the end of the century and the

---

[5] Patrick Verley, *L'Echelle du monde. Essai sur l'industrialisation de l'Occident*, Paris, 2013, p. 112.

[6] R. A. Buchanan, 'The British Contribution to Australian Engineering: The Australian Dictionary of Biography Entries', *Historical Studies*, vol. 20, 1983, pp. 401–19; Bruce Sinclair, 'Canadian Technology: British Traditions and American Influences', *Technology and Culture*, vol. 20, January 1979, pp. 108–23; R. A. Buchanan, 'The Diaspora of British Engineering', *Technology and Culture*, vol. 27, no. 3, July 1986, pp. 501–24.

introduction of an alphabetical system for all residents past and present, records remained incomplete and fragmentary.[7] In France, a census was organised every five years from 1801 (except in 1821 and 1826); however, the nationality question was only asked for the first time in 1851 and then again only in 1872. For the first half of the century, one may make estimates at a local level of the number of British migrants on French soil by relying on names, but no national count was undertaken, and we must rely on irregular administrative surveys. Births, deaths, and marriages were registered, and this can be helpful to document life stories. But, again, this is not sufficient to assess the population at any given time: most migrants probably neither married, nor had children, nor died on the Continent. 'Livrets de travail' (employment booklets) theoretically listed the different occupations of workers in France, but they were not always well kept, and most have disappeared.

However, a wide range of sources, both British and continental, do exist. They include the press, especially the local papers, at a time when they were thriving, first and foremost in Britain, but also on the Continent. Every significant town had at least one and sometimes two or three newspapers, and they were often interested in the life and work of outsiders.[8] Even the local British newspapers documented the lives of emigrants. In the Nottingham press in the 1840s, advertisements for jobs in Calais could be found, as well as surveys on mechanics in Saxony and letters from emigrants in Australia. With the gradual digitisation of the provincial press, historians are just beginning, 'over that great ocean of material' Lytton Strachey wrote about, 'to lower down into it, here there, a little bucket', hoping it 'will bring up to the light of day some characteristic specimen from those far depths, to be examined with a careful curiosity'.[9]

In the host countries, migrants were also scrutinised by the authorities, especially when there was trouble. The British authorities kept a trace of their nationals abroad. Such evidence of careful monitoring can be found in diplomatic and consular correspondence. In the nineteenth century, as British trading interests gained ground in Europe, the Consular Service developed. By 1848, in France, there were twelve consuls and twenty-five vice-consuls. Consuls were supposed to deal with business matters but they also addressed the requests of British subjects on other issues and could act as intermediaries with the British government and the local authorities. They reported to the ambassador and the Foreign Office, and this correspondence now offers another 'great ocean' of manuscripts. These records do, however, have several drawbacks. On the one hand, most of the letters dealing with workers' problems were written by men rather than women, by skilled artisans rather than unskilled operatives, and often by learned go-betweens

[7] James H. Jackson, Jr., 'Alltagsgeschichte, Social Science History, and the Study of Migration in Nineteenth-Century Germany', *Central European History*, vol. 23, no. 2/3, Jun. to Sep. 1990, pp. 242–63.
[8] Andrew Hobbs, *A Fleet Street in Every Town: The Provincial Press in England*, Cambridge, 2018.
[9] Lytton Strachey, *Eminent Victorians*, London, 1918, preface.

rather than by workers themselves. Another source of bias is that people wrote to consuls when they had problems, for instance to seek help when they were laid off by their employers or targeted in xenophobic attacks. As a result, diplomatic correspondence often fails to capture the daily routine and lives of workers.

The records of a few companies have also survived. When they include lists of staff, the information about workers is usually limited to wages and output. Yet here and there some insight can be gleaned into their social lives. Some managers also kept diaries and exchanged letters that have survived. In an age when captains of industry and skilful engineers were worshipped as heroes, some had their biographies written by relatives or by writers, sometimes using material they had composed, like letters or diaries. However, all these sources share the common feature that the lives of migrant workers are reported by non-workers, be they journalists, businessmen, diplomats, or civil servants. Occasionally, some texts by skilled workers have survived, for instance those written by machine fitters or foremen to their employers.

Some sources, however, partly elude the pitfall of middle-class bias towards workers, namely working-class autobiographies. This body of texts, written by workers themselves, was inventoried in the 1980s by John Burnett, David Vincent, and David Mayall.[10] Many autobiographies which were previously unknown and inaccessible have been republished and have found a new readership. Over the past twenty years, these texts have been the object of several studies, for example by Jonathan Rose, Jane Humphries, Emma Griffin, and Julie-Marie Strange.[11] This book will also use the memoirs of a few migrant workers who wrote about their lives on the Continent. They were mostly skilled artisans who were upwardly mobile, such as printer Charles Manby Smith, goldsmith William Duthie, mechanic Timothy Claxton, and train mechanic Henry Dove.[12] One of them, John Colin, was a reformed alcoholic leather-dresser.[13] All of them therefore fit into a pattern of upward social mobility, and by the time they wrote about their working-class youth, they had sometimes changed their social milieu. For the period 1815–70, none of the migrants whose writings have reached us was a woman

[10] John Burnett, David Vincent, and David Mayall (eds.), *The Autobiography of the Working Class: An Annotated Critical Bibliography*, Brighton, 3 vols., 1984–9; David Vincent, *Bread, Knowledge and Freedom: A Study of Nineteenth-Century Working Class Autobiography*, London, 1981.

[11] Jonathan Rose, *The Intellectual Life of the British Working Classes*, New Haven, 2001; Jane Humphries, *Childhood and Child Labour in the British Industrial Revolution*, Cambridge, 2010; Emma Griffin, *Liberty's Dawn: A People's History of the Industrial Revolution*, New Haven, 2013; Julie-Marie Strange, *Fatherhood and the British Working Class, 1865–1914*, Cambridge, 2015; Emma Griffin, *Bread Winner: An Intimate History of the Victorian Economy*, New Haven, 2020.

[12] Charles Manby Smith, *The Working Man's Way in the World*, London, 1853; William Duthie, *A Tramp's Wallet; stored by an English Goldsmith during his Wanderings in Germany and France*, London, 1858; Timothy Claxton, *Hints to Mechanics on Self-Education and Mutual Instruction*, London, 1839. Henry Dove's memoirs can be found in Edward Blount, *Memoirs of Sir Edward Blount*, London, 1902, pp. 75–82.

[13] John Colin [pseud.], *The Wanderer Brought Home. The Life and Adventures of Colin. An Autobiography*, London, 1864.

and none was unskilled, as many British migrants were; therefore, they do not necessarily reflect the experience of the full range of British workers. Another source where the words of the workers could be kept and transcribed were parliamentary papers. There were various public inquiries for which some workers were interviewed. But even when the committees debated matters relating to artisans and labourers, workers giving evidence were scarce in comparison with capitalists, social scientists, and managers. The voice of the workers sometimes emerges from judicial archives, but these have seldom been well preserved, and are usually not indexed. Lastly, some insight can be found in private documents. Many of the migrants whose lives are mentioned in this book went on to have children. Some of their descendants have researched their ancestry, and some have also inherited objects, artefacts, or letters. Amateur family history is now a thriving field and should not be dismissed by academic historians. This book has relied on many encounters with family historians and genealogists as well as local antiquarians to gain a more comprehensive and accurate picture of the lives of migrant workers in industrial Europe. Its historiographic background is not to be found only in *Past and Present* and the *English Historical Review* but also in the *Clwyd Historian* and the *Annales de Normandie*. Local historians go through sources such as birth, marriage, and death registers and municipal records and make them accessible to others. 'Amateur' family and local historians are sometimes the keepers of objects and artefacts that cannot be found in museums, such as an 1800 King James Bible inherited from a family ancestor in Calais; a large headstone for two Welsh railway builders in a small village in Normandy; the medallion of lace machine-maker John Leavers and his second wife after their marriage in 1826 in Grand-Couronne; a nineteenth-century prosthetic hand inherited from an injured foreman in the Carmichael linen factory in Ailly-sur-Somme. These various artefacts also document the material history of migration.

All in all, however, because of the elusiveness of the words of the workers themselves, one is confronted with the usual challenges when trying to write about the lives of nineteenth-century workers. For most ironmasters, textile factory managers, or railway entrepreneurs, workers were a burdensome cost. For the local authorities, they were a potential source of disturbance. The local newspapers were rife with stereotypical visions of the British, some of which had been inherited from the period of the wars or were related to continental visions of the British 'character'. This book tries to circumvent the obstacle of the various biases of middle-class sources and draws upon the scattered and often rare testimony of the migrant workers themselves to document their lives.

3. Methodology

To gain an insight into migrants' lives, *Artisans Abroad* has relied on the traditional methods of social and cultural history. It aims to be a history both from below and from above. The history from below is indispensable when one wants to grasp workers' experiences, while history from above is needed to understand why and how ironmasters, textile manufacturers, and railway entrepreneurs organised the migration of so many workers, and why governments and parliaments could find this useful—in the case of the receiving countries—or acceptable—in the case of Britain. *Artisans Abroad* is a book firmly anchored in labour history, a field which was once thought to be in decline but is now being rejuvenated by a series of new methods and studies. While labour history is traditionally confined within national boundaries, this book tries to overcome such limitations, relying on the methods of transnational labour history, which considers not just international labour organisations but also the movement of workers and activists.[14] It is also anchored in the booming field of migration history.

As much as possible, biographical texts have been drawn upon. It is assumed that biography can help us understand larger historical processes, for example in the way that Clare Anderson has used biography to reflect on the experience of convicted criminals and document the penal experience in the colonial context of the Indian Ocean.[15] In labour history, biography has become a central discursive strategy. As Malcolm Chase has argued, it helps overcome the division between empiricism on the one hand and cultural history marked by the linguistic turn on the other.[16] It can help relate the personal to the social and the political. It can also help bridge the gap between academic historians and the wider public, as life history can be an engaging way of prompting interest in larger, complex historical processes. In Britain, the *Dictionary of Labour Biography* has long tried to compensate for the relative absence of figures of the labour movement in main-stream history. The *Oxford Dictionary of National Biography* (*ODNB*) (since 2004) has gradually been trying to incorporate some of them into its records. In France and Belgium, the *Maitron* has become an impressive dictionary accounting for the lives of tens of thousands of labour activists and is being both used and contributed to by many non-professional historians. *Artisans Abroad*, however, evokes the biographies not so much of labour activists as of workers who often had no known political involvement, and who are not mentioned in either of these dictionaries. It uses these biographical trajectories to illuminate larger issues.

The focus of this book is labour migration from Britain to the Continent, especially to France and Belgium. Yet it is important to emphasise that British workers did not insulate themselves from other workers, both local and foreign, and did not form a separate, watertight community when abroad. They worked

---

[14] See, for example, Gopalan Balachandran, *Globalizing Labour? Indian Seafarers and World Shipping, c. 1870–1945*, New Delhi, 2012; Neville Kirk, *Comrades and Cousins: Globalization, Workers and Labour Movements in Britain, the USA and Australia from the 1880s to 1914*, London, 2003; David Finkelstein, *Movable Types: Roving Creative Printers of the Victorian World*, Oxford, 2018.

[15] Clare Anderson, *Subaltern Lives: Biographies of Colonialism in the Indian Ocean World, 1790–1920*, Cambridge, 2012.

[16] Malcolm Chase, 'Labour History's Biographical Turn', ed. Fabrice Bensimon, *History Workshop Journal*, vol. 92, 2021, pp. 194–207.

alongside local workers as well as migrants from other countries, for example Italians, Swiss, Belgians and Germans in France. Moreover, moves to the Continent were seldom unique and definitive, as many of the British migrants to the Continent either returned to Britain, or went elsewhere, or both. The period 1815–70 was not only one of huge industrial transformation, it was also one of major changes in transport that brought the Americas and Australasia closer to Europe. Between the loss of the American colonies and the 'new imperialism' of the late nineteenth century, the 'imperial meridian' was also a period of expansion for Britain, whose Empire gained about 100,000 square kilometres each year.[17] As Catherine Hall, John MacKenzie, and other new imperial historians have argued, and as economic historians have long discussed, the Empire was not just relevant for those who lived in the colonies. Being an imperial nation had many economic, cultural, and political consequences for those who stayed in Britain. As is well known, the industrial revolution thrived on sugar produced in the colonies and cotton produced by slaves in the United States. It is likely that some of those who invested, for instance, in the railways had benefited from slave compensation in the mid-1830s, and this could have been true of some bankers as well.[18] The cotton used by migrant lacemakers came from the United States, via Liverpool and Manchester, to the East Midlands and northern France. Continental destinations formed part of a range of options for migrant workers, and increasingly so as overseas emigration continued rising from the 1820s, when it was marginal, to the 1860s, when it had become massive. Hundreds of the lacemakers who had moved from Nottingham to Calais eventually made it to Australia. British horizons included both the Continent and the Empire. In brief, focusing on Europe does not obscure imperial connections; it places them in context.

There are contemporary echoes to this research. One is Brexit, and the rift between the UK and the European Continent. After all, the agenda of the Brexiteers was premised on the idea that Britain's past and future lay further afield rather than with Europe. Supporters relied on a vision of history that argued that the economy of Britain had traditionally been orientated towards its Empire and the United States. As this book argues, things were not so clear-cut in 1820. Long before the successful comedy-drama television programme *Auf wiedersehen, Pet* (1983–2004), some British construction workers went to the Continent for work purposes. By 1840, Calais was not seen as the symbol of a major immigration crisis or a closed door into Britain, but as an entry point to the Continent.[19]

---

[17] Chris Bayly, *Imperial Meridian: The British Empire and the World, 1780–1830*, Harlow, 1989.

[18] Catherine Hall, Nicholas Draper, Keith McClelland, Katie Donington, and Rachel Lang, *Legacies of British Slave-Ownership: Colonial Slavery and the Formation of Victorian Britain*, Cambridge, 2014, pp. 91–3.

[19] Fabrice Bensimon, 'Calais: 1816–2016', https://www.historytoday.com/calais-1816-2016, 24 October 2016.

Not many in Britain wanted to move to France or Belgium, but even fewer wanted to emigrate to Australia.

Brexit was also about 'taking back control' of the borders of the UK. In the nineteenth century, these borders were open to flows to and from the Continent. The UK governments were also arguing for free trade with the rest of Europe because this benefited the British economy. Considering the human intercourse of the mid-nineteenth century may help us better understand the flows of today. Migration is a major feature of the modern-day world. In 2019, 272 million people—that is, 3.5 per cent of the world's population—lived in countries where they were not born, the United States housing more than 50 million of them.[20] This figure does not even take into account the hundreds of millions of migrants who live and work far away from their birthplaces, for example in India or China. In most receiving countries, xenophobia has been prevalent, and it has sometimes become a major feature of domestic politics. But long before the 'yellow peril' was denounced, long before 'British jobs for British workers' and 'La France aux Français' were demanded, cries of 'À bas les Anglais!' could be heard in France. By addressing the origins of modern-day labour migration, this book considers some early forms of contemporary xenophobia.

4. Outline

This book assesses the quantitative parameters of migration trends from Britain to Europe in this period and sketches the economics of these flows. It examines the practicalities of migration and addresses the issues of gender specialisation and wages. It retraces the cultural, educational, and religious activities of migrants and then moves on to consider their associations and their politics. Last, it explores how migrants cultivated links with and integrated into local populations and tries to assess xenophobia and conflict. It is divided into six chapters organised along the following lines.

Chapter 1 addresses the political economy of British emigration to the Continent. After all, the emigration of workers, technicians, and engineers from the dynamic economy of a country that was fully involved in the industrial revolution to the Continent, where industrialisation was still in its infancy, may sound counter-intuitive. Throughout the eighteenth century, about 1,000 engineers and artisans crossed the Channel. After the end of the Napoleonic wars, however, this flow dramatically increased. As free-trading ideas gained ground, as mentioned earlier, British bans on the emigration of artisans and on the exportation of machinery were lifted in 1824 and 1843, respectively. Parliamentary

---

[20] International Organization for Migration, *World Migration Report 2020*, Geneva, 2019.

reports and British newspapers provide evidence of the reasons why thousands of workers left Britain for the Continent.

In most cases, skilled migrants could rely upon the technological gap between Britain, which had begun its industrial revolution in the late eighteenth century, and the Continent, which lagged behind. In several sectors (e.g. linen, iron, railway building), employers played a crucial part in the hiring of British artisans. Given the superiority of British technology, both continental entrepreneurs and British investors preferred to use British machinery, and to employ British workers who knew how to operate it. In lace, by contrast, workers themselves were the primary agents of migration. Their movement to the Continent was mostly at the behest of British artisans who crossed the Channel to have access to continental markets without having to pay duties or the cost of smuggling. The press, information passed by word of mouth, and in some cases recruitment agents could also play a part in prompting the move.

In most cases, migrants expected these moves to be temporary, and aimed to return home eventually. In many respects, these flows thus resembled domestic migration more than long-distance and definitive departures for the United States, Canada, or Australia. However, temporary migration often ended up becoming long term. Similarly, middle-distance migration could lead to longer, unplanned journeys. For instance, around 1839 George Stubbs (1806–66) from Quorn (Leicestershire) emigrated with his family to Calais, where he was employed as a lacemaker. Following the economic crisis in 1848, they emigrated to Australia alongside 641 other Britons resident in Calais, for which their passage was paid. In New South Wales, George took up joinery again, which was his first trade skill. This chapter thus discusses the interconnection between continental and long-distance migration, between temporary and long-term mobility.

Chapter 2 specifically addresses the sectors migrant workers joined, because most migration flows were organised within individual industrial sectors. Four sectors were especially important and are the focus of this chapter. The first was iron and steel. South Wales had developed a dynamic iron and then steel industry, and several continental ironmasters set up 'forges à l'anglaise' for which they were willing to hire Welsh puddlers or rollers, despite the high costs of such labour. The second major sector that shaped continental labour migration was machinery. British expertise in steam-powered machinery was unrivalled. For instance, Aaron Manby (1776–1850), a Staffordshire engineer who patented steam engines suited to marine use, opened the first steamship company on the Seine in 1822. He then set up an engineering works, a forge, and a foundry in Charenton, near Paris, in business with Daniel Wilson, a chemist. They soon employed 250 British workers and British mechanics were also hired on the Continent in all sectors of industry. The third major sector was textiles. William Cockerill set up a thriving woollen industry in Belgium, while thousands of lace workers from the East Midlands, especially Nottinghamshire, went to northern France, especially to the Calais area.

This craft-based, hand-worked industry shifted to factory production in the 1850s, but British input persisted until the 1870s. From the 1840s, there was significant migration into the linen and jute trades, as several works relied on British machinery and workers, especially women from Dundee. The fourth and final sector considered in this chapter is railways. British engineers and investors were instrumental in the early stages of European railway construction, in France, Belgium, Italy, and Spain. More modest numbers of railway mechanics also came for longer periods. In other sectors, for example mining, some smaller-scale recruitment was also organised. This chapter addresses the diversity and specificities of labour migration flows. Iron, steel, and machinery involved small numbers of migrants and relied on the technological gap between Britain and the Continent. In linen and jute, the workers included not just mechanics but also dozens or even hundreds of operators, usually hired by manufacturers. In lace, labour migration flows differed markedly, as most of the emigrants were artisans or small-scale lacemakers. In the railways, numbers swelled to thousands of itinerant navvies at a time when British entrepreneurs contracted to build long lines on the Continent. Such migration brought together workers from different regions and prompted settlement in an array of different areas.

Chapter 3 addresses a hidden group within the migrant population: women and children. While in some sectors such as railway building a large part of the workforce was made up of single male workers, in others emigrants moved with their families. Many female linen workers also emigrated while young and single. This could mean having to cope with local opposition to female labour. This chapter explores the gendered dimensions of migration. While the occupational structure of work in Britain at the time has been well researched, this chapter considers whether these patterns were replicated when workers emigrated or whether they underwent transformations. It specifically deals with women in the linen industry, and with women and children in the sector of machine-made lace. Following Heathcoat's 1809 bobbin-net invention, the formation of a machine-made lace industry in the East Midlands and elsewhere was driven by the men who operated the machines, the 'twisthands'. But they were assisted by boys, who were expected to replace and refill the bobbins. Women and girls did most of the mending, embroidery, finishing, dressing, bleaching, and dyeing of the lace, much of it in the dark and damp rooms of the home. Working hours were long, and toil was exhausting from a very early age. Although female lace workers featured prominently in local struggles, and were often highly skilled, they were neverthe-less restricted to low-paid positions in the trade because of gendered notions of skill and occupation.

When in 1841 Parliament discussed child labour, the regulation of hours was rejected for lace because of its domestic nature and because of competition from across the Channel. In the Calais area, British lacemakers had developed an industry, much like that in Britain. But France was a different country, with a smaller-scale economy, and as a result was characterised less by the separation between home and work and the male breadwinner model. This chapter examines machine-made lace in view of the historical literature on the part played by women and children in industrialisation in both countries. It focuses on the gendered segregation of the work and the respective wages of men, women, and children on both sides of the Channel.

Chapter 4 concerns the cultural and religious history of the migrants. When they left Britain, British workers usually spoke only English; interpreters, however, were only available for a few engineers. The rest of the workers had to manage for themselves. 'Not one of us [. . .] is able to speak more than a few words of the language', desperate Scottish linen female workers complained in 1848, when their employer in northern France laid them off.[21] Apart from the case of individual artisans, many of the interactions of emigrant British workers were with fellow countrymen and women and could therefore be sustained in English. By examining language, this chapter gauges British workers' level of integration into their new local communities. Regardless of whether they learned to communicate in a new language, British workers came to continental Europe with their own culture and built new institutions to bolster their British identities. English-language newspapers were set up and British games and sports were practised on the Continent, including the establishment of long-lasting clubs from the 1870s onwards. Although 'irreligion' and the decline in churchgoing in the new industrial towns were widely denounced in Britain, most migrant workers who settled in Europe shared a Protestant culture. English schools were opened with clergymen as well as Anglican churches and Methodist chapels. When they wanted to marry in Catholic areas, migrants were confronted with the denominational differences with their brides. This chapter also examines national representations of workers. Many stereotypes prevailed, for instance that the British were stronger and more hard-working than local workers (partly because they ate meat), and that they drank too much. Continental republican newspapers could also present the migrants as embodiments of the detested English materialism, as if they were merely human machinery.

Chapter 5 addresses migrants' history of political engagement. When they emigrated, British workers were confronted with political situations that could be very different from those they experienced in Britain. Between 1825 and 1870 in Britain, workers could create trade unions, organise meetings and processions, and join associations or parties—activities that were seriously curtailed or completely forbidden in most continental countries. In the period 1830–48, hundreds of thousands of British workers were involved in the movement for reform,

---

[21] The National Archives [hereafter, TNA], Kew. FO 146 350. Letter of Scottish linen female workers in Haubourdin (northern France) threatened with expulsion, to British ambassador in Paris, Lord Normanby, 21 March 1848.

Chartism, or the early trade unions. Adjusting could thus be a challenge for those who set out to make a living outside Britain. However, far from being a docile population, British workers knew how to market their skills in individual or collective negotiations. In iron or machinery, they bargained on the length of their employment and of the working day, on their wages and the refund of their travel expenses, and on the quality of housing for them and their families. These demands were sometimes accompanied by different forms of rebellion, especially against discipline, rules, or shrinking wages.

When they were present on the Continent in large numbers, migrants also set up friendly societies and masonic lodges. In France, as early as 1825, some founded trade unions and organised strikes, at a time when both were forbidden in France. In the 1840s, during the Chartist movement, France was the only country outside Britain where branches were set up, and in Normandy and Pas-de-Calais more than 100 emigrant workers subscribed to Feargus O'Connor's Land Plan, while a Chartist agitator toured areas with a substantial British presence. The Chartist *Northern Star* was read aloud in a linen workshop in Brittany, thus echoing Scottish working-class practices of the collective reading of radical texts. Focusing on the rare case of a British insurgent in Paris, the chapter also considers how 'British' political opinions could translate in the context of a French revolution.

Chapter 6 addresses issues of integration and rejection. For migrants, although moving to the Continent sometimes involved travelling short distances, often not much further than going to the other end of the British Isles, the environments they encountered could be very different from their places of origin in Britain. Overall, they were welcomed by local authorities, provided they did not become involved in local religious, political, or social disputes. We still know little about the interactions between British migrants and local populations. The social history of these encounters has traditionally pointed to a dichotomy between Anglophilia and Anglophobia. Migrants, however, are an ideal population for the study of 'diplomacy from below'. This chapter addresses British labourers' different interactions with the local populations, at work, in the localities where they lived, or in places through which they passed (harbours, etc.). There is some evidence of friendly relations between migrant workers and the local people, with whom they could work, share lodgings, worship, play, drink, and associate.

While most sources document the absence of real antagonisms with local communities, several outbursts of xenophobia can be identified. This chapter specifically addresses the 1848 crisis in France, when the combination of the economic crisis and the fall of the July Monarchy led to several demonstrations against British workers. Some had been living in France for years but now, faced with unemployment and local animosity, had no choice but to leave. This chapter assesses this flashpoint of hostility, exploring what it can tell us about xenophobia, including its modern-day forms.

1

'Taking their labour and art to the best market'

The Political Economy of British Emigration to the Continent

Georges Dufaud (1777–1852) was one of those ironmasters who benefited from the changes introduced by the French Revolution and the Napoleonic Empire (Figure 1.1).[1] He belonged to the first intake of students at the Ecole polytechnique in 1794 and went on to become an iron engineer. Bankruptcy in 1808 did not prevent him from enjoying later success, with the backing of senior officials and perhaps of the freemasonry. He established several iron businesses in the following years, as well as pioneering new methods of refining iron by replacing increasingly sparce and expensive timber with coal. Peace in 1815 resulted in a more favourable economic context for the iron industry. In 1817 he went to Wales on behalf of his employers, where iron could be purchased more cheaply than in France. There he met William Crawshay I (1764–1834), the 'uncrowned Iron King', and his son Richard Crawshay (1786–1859). The Crawshays invited him to visit their works in Glamorgan. The Crawshays were by then the most successful ironmasters of South Wales and the Cyfarthfa ironworks were the largest in Britain.[2] Guided by George Crawshay (1794–1873), another of William's sons, Dufaud was able to observe the various stages of production and was impressed by the quality and the quantity of irons, as well as the refining process, the power of the mill, and the railway that connected the pit and the forge. Unlike in France, steam, rather than water, provided a reliable source of power. British technology in iron was at that point probably some thirty-five years ahead of the French, and in the Taff valley thousands of ironworkers worked in around twenty works. Forty per cent of Britain's iron exports originated from Merthyr Tydfil, which was becoming the largest town in Wales. When George Crawshay was invited to Grossouvre (Cher) by Dufaud, he found that the works Dufaud managed were comparable to theirs, refining and rolling iron, producing items that were very

---

[1] The quote in this chapter's title is from Joseph Hume, House of Commons debate on artisans and machinery, 21 May 1824.
[2] J. P. Addis, *The Crawshay Dynasty: A Study in Industrial Organisation and Development, 1765–1867* (1957); Chris Evans, 'Crawshay, William (1764–1834)', *ODNB*, Oxford, 2004.

Artisans Abroad: British Migrant Workers in Industrialising Europe, 1815–1870. Fabrice Bensimon, Oxford University Press.
© Fabrice Bensimon 2023. DOI: 10.1093/oso/9780198835844.003.0002

G. DUFAUD,

Conseiller de Préfecture, Officier de la Légion d'Honneur.

Figure 1.1 Georges Dufaud (1777–1852) (photo B. Imhaus, Wikimedia Commons).

similar to those produced in South Wales: 'Vous nous l'avez volé' ('You stole it from us'), he told Dufaud.[3] Crawshay senior feared he had been spied upon, particularly as Dufaud had asked for puddlers to be sent to work for him in France. However, the relationship between the two families did not turn sour but instead became a partnership: in 1818, George Crawshay (1794–1873) married Dufaud's daughter Louise (1802–83) and they had eleven children, who lived on both sides of the Channel. In the next generation, two more marriages strengthened the links between the Crawshays and the Dufauds.

From 1819, Dufaud started to apply what he had learned in Wales by developing modern works at Fourchambault (Nièvre). He soon asked for and obtained from his masters, the Boigues brothers, permission to hire foreign workers: 'we would give each of [the British puddlers] alone one of our most intelligent workers to second them, so that by this means, we would have a sufficient number for puddlage'.[4]

---

[3] Guy Thuillier, *Georges Dufaud et les débuts du grand capitalisme dans la métallurgie, en Nivernais, au XIXe siècle*, Paris, 1959, p. 29.

[4] 'Parce que nous donnerions à chacun d'eux pour second un de nos ouvriers les plus intelligents et que par ce moyen nous aurions bientôt un fonds suffisant de puddlage'. Annie Laurant, *Des fers de Loire à l'acier Martin*, vol. 1, *Maîtres de forges en Berry et Nivernais*, Paris, 1995, p. 110. All translations, unless otherwise mentioned, are by the author.

In 1820 the first wave of workers arrived. All in all, some fifty mechanics, blacksmiths, chippers, cutters, and above all puddlers came over the following years.[5] The Dufauds were exasperated by the cost and demands of these workers. In 1823, Dufaud's son Achille wrote from London that Wales and Cyfarthfa admittedly had the best puddlers in the world, and that an ordinary and careless worker could not work there—'unfortunately we get the scrap': 'We can't conceal that we are paying and shall long be paying for all workers far more than in Wales . . . added to that are the huge expenses entailed by the importation of the workers'.[6] 'As for other English workers, I believe we have enough of them. Importing them is a costly trade, which must cease. Those we have cannot escape us. They are dependent on us', Achille Dufaud added in a letter.[7]

These disparaging remarks remind us of the problem of using the sources produced by the masters when attempting to uncover the experience of the workers. In many ways, for the Dufauds and other ironmasters, the workers were just a means of production, and relying on their written testimony prevents us from accessing the lives of those who worked for them. We know that the working conditions of ironworkers at the time were harsh. Puddlers endured long hours in extreme heat, or in very low temperatures in wintertime, and ran the risk of injury caused by burns or explosions. Puddlers seldom worked beyond the age of forty. If Dufaud was prepared to grant the Welsh workers wages which he thought were excessive, it was because he absolutely needed them. Later in the 1820s, the French government investigated the iron industry to decide whether the high duties on imports of British iron which had been passed in 1822 should be maintained. Dufaud explained the key role of British workers in the early years of the works:

A: The French workers have less experience and dexterity and because of the greater consumption of fuel and greater waste of cast iron we make a loss despite paying them less.

Q: Do you believe the French workers could develop the same qualities?

A: Workers who have been trained since they were children have acquired a skill from which they can profit . . . When the children of French workers acquire the strength to

[5] On the links between the Dufauds and the Crawshays and the emigration of British workers to Fourchambault, see Thuillier, *Georges Dufaud* and Laurant, *Des fers de Loire*; on the puddlers, see Fremdling, 'The Puddler'.

[6] 'Et malheureusement, c'est le rebut qui nous vient . . . 'Nous ne pouvons donc dissimuler que nous payons et payerons longtemps toutes les main-d'œuvre beaucoup plus cher qu'en Galles . . . ajoutons à cela les dépenses énormes que nous coûte l'importation des ouvriers'. Letter from Achille Dufaud, 19 June 1823, in Thuillier, *Georges Dufaud*, pp. 225–6.

[7] 'Quant à d'autres ouvriers anglais, je crois que nous sommes suffisamment garnis. Ce commerce d'importation nous coûte cher, il faut le cesser. Il est impossible que ceux que nous avons nous échappent. Ils sont dans notre dépendance'. Letter from Achille Dufaud, 19 June 1823, in Thuillier, *Georges Dufaud*, p. 226.

do this work they will be just as good workers as the English. But those we have employed in this work were 22 to 25 years old when we hired them.[8]

By the mid-1840s, the Société Boigues managed by Dufaud was the fifth biggest iron producer in France. In 1846, it was visited by the duc de Montpensier, one of the king's sons. By 1856, the ironworks employed 2,000 workers (see Figure 1.2). The factory played a key role in French steel production, later producing components of the Eiffel tower. In the early decades of the firm, the technological input of the British had proved critical. As for Dufaud, he became one of the great French ironmasters of the first half of the nineteenth century.

In many ways, the Dufaud–Crawshay connection is emblematic of a transition in the economic relations between Britain and the Continent. In eighteenth-century Britain, the struggle against industrial espionage was the defining feature of this relationship. Yet in the wake of the Napoleonic wars, the continental quest

Voyage de Leurs Majestés. — Vue des forges de Fourchambault.

Figure 1.2 'Voyage de Leurs Majestés.—Vue des forges de Fourchambault', *Le Monde illustré*, 12 July 1862.

[8] 'R. Oui; les ouvriers français, ayant moins d'habitude et de dextérité, nous font perdre, en consommation plus grande de combustible, et en plus grand déchet de fonte, au-delà de ce que nous leur donnons en moins.
D. Croyez-vous les ouvriers français propres à obtenir les mêmes qualités?
R. Les ouvriers venus d'Angleterre, ayant été élevés dès l'enfance ont acquis, en se jouant, une habitude qui leur profite. Quand les enfants d'ouvriers français auront la force de supporter ce travail, ils seront aussi bons ouvriers que les anglais. Mais ceux que nous avons appliqués à ces travaux avaient de 22 à 25 ans lorsque nous les avons pris'.
Ministère du commerce et des manufactures, *Enquête sur les fers*, 1829, p. 65.

for British innovations became even more important than it had been before, and for the British the Continent increasingly appeared not as a threat but as a new sphere of opportunity. The countries were no longer at war and borders were no longer blockaded. The expansion of trade and manufacturing was full of promise, especially for those who saw themselves as pioneers, and free-trading ideas were gaining ground. For the export of machinery and technology to be possible, workers who could operate the machines were crucial.

This chapter addresses the political economy of this transition, beginning with the protective tariffs and legal restrictions that prevailed in the wake of the Napoleonic wars. It addresses the topic of this book from above, from the viewpoint of manufacturers. This perspective helps us understand the trajectories of many workers in this period. These movements were organised to meet specific manufacturing needs (section 1). The chapter focuses on two moments of change: the 1824 debate and reform relating to the emigration of artisans, and the 1843 discussions on the exportation of machinery, which paved the way for the beginnings of free trade between Britain and the Continent (section 2). It then addresses a specific sector, machine-made lace, which, though new, expanded rapidly in the aftermath of the Napoleonic wars (section 3). It then tries to assess the numbers of emigrants who crossed the Channel (section 4), before considering some of the main features of this emigration in terms of the distance travelled and the duration of stays (section 5). Lastly, it discusses migrants' wages in the context of the controversy over workers' pay during the industrial revolution (section 6). Section 7 concludes.

1. The Conflicting Imperatives of Trade and War (c.1710–1824)

In the eighteenth century, the British state was geared to defend the technical progress of proto-industrialisation from continental, especially French, espionage. The resulting pieces of legislation, starting in the 1710s, against the emigration of skilled artisans and the export of machinery were consistent with this aim in an age of mercantilism. Historian Linant de Bellefonds suggested that an estimated 400 technicians and 1,000 workers emigrated to France between 1715 and 1815.[9] J. R. Harris refined this picture in a detailed history of industrial espionage and technology transfer between the two countries in the eighteenth century. Harris traced some 1,000 British artisans and manufacturers who went to live in France between 1710 and 1800.[10] Under Colbert, France took an interest in the technical

---

[9] Xavier Linant de Bellefonds, 'Les techniciens anglais dans l'industrie française au 18ᵉ siècle', thesis, Paris, 1971.

[10] John R. Harris, *Industrial Espionage and Technology Transfer: Britain and France in the Eighteenth Century*, Aldershot, 1998, p. 552.

and industrial progress of Britain. 'Observation' voyages, industrial espionage, the smuggling of machinery, and the recruitment of artisans were all strategies devised to compete with Britain, as illustrated by the case of John Holker (1719–86). A Jacobite soldier, Holker had escaped to France and been introduced to Daniel-Charles Trudaine, the 'Directeur du commerce', head of the French department of trade. In Rouen, where he settled in 1751, Holker was meant to bring the cotton industry up to English standards. He illegally arranged for the transportation of English workers from his native Lancashire, as well as the transfer of some machinery. For over a quarter of a century he was a senior advisor to the French government and in 1766 he acquired French nationality. In 1774 he was granted *lettres de noblesse* for his services to industry. Holker had poor written English and his command of French was limited even in the 1770s. But he had introduced Hargreaves's spinning jenny and Arkwright's water frame into France, and he played an important part in the proto-industrialisation of the country, especially in textiles; this made up for his literary deficiencies.[11]

In the face of such organised industrial espionage, the British government banned the emigration of artisans and the export of British machinery. The first piece of legislation against the suborning of workers by bribery or inveigling was passed in 1719, after John Law had recruited a large group of 200–300 (including wives and apprentices) to work in France. Under such laws, trespassers were liable to fines and imprisonment. In 1750, an Act prohibited the export of 'tools and engines' before further Acts in 1774, 1782, and 1785 targeted cotton, linen, calico, and tools. No systematic study of the implementation of these acts has been undertaken, but we do know that the suborning of British workers by recruiters was a risky business. Harris argues that 'laws had not been a dead letter', listing several French industrial spies who were very worried about their situation, who feared apprehension, and whose relatives or suborned workers were sometimes arrested.[12] However, by the 1780s attitudes had become more mixed. Some export merchants who were influential in London tried to obtain the repeal of the 1785 Tools Act. In 1786, an Anglo-French Commercial Treaty was signed, the purpose of which was, in Britain, to promote the export of cotton, hardware, and pottery manufactured goods. However, its consequences were feared by other British manufacturers. In the seventeenth and early eighteenth centuries there were anxieties around the export of raw wool to France, on the grounds that it was superior and that, with it, France might potentially out-compete British manufacturers of woollens and worsteds, which were widely viewed as the most important goods manufactured in Britain. This anxiety flared up from time to

---

[11] Harris, *Industrial Espionage*; John R. Harris, 'John Holker (1719–1786)', *ODNB*, Oxford, 2004; Philippe Minard, *La France du colbertisme*, Paris, 1998, pp. 212–17; Renaud Morieux, 'Diplomacy from Below and Belonging: Fishermen and Cross-Channel Relations in the Eighteenth Century', *Past and Present*, vol. 202, 2009, pp. 83–125; Henderson, *Britain and Industrial Europe* Ariane Fennetaux and John Styles (eds.), *Album Holker. The Holker Album*, Paris, 2022.

[12] Harris, *Industrial Espionage*, p. 465.

time and was acute in the 1780s.[13] If the 1786 treaty introduced foreigners to good-quality English yarn, wasn't there a danger that they might then try to manufacture it themselves, using machinery imported from Britain?

This more liberal atmosphere ended with the conclusion of the wars which raged between both countries from 1793 to 1802, from 1803 to 1814, and again in 1815. Overall, the period between the 1790s and 1824 saw the implementation of tight restrictions. On the British side, economic protection was increasingly associated with military might. In 1798–9, French businessman and engineer Lieven Bauwens (1769–1822) and his British associates were tried for industrial espionage and for having suborned British workers to come and work in France. They were accused of deceiving workers by telling them they were going to Hamburg when they were actually intended to go to France. During the hearing the judge emphasised the wartime circumstances: 'The great resources of the country are our manufactures, and the general commerce of the kingdom. If these are to be invaded, and taken from us,—Alas, all is over'.[14]

Penalties for infringing the rules were particularly severe. Artisans or manufacturers who emigrated lost their nationality and property, and recruiters could be fined £500 and sentenced to a year's imprisonment as well as further imprisonment if the fine was not paid. The export of machinery was sanctioned with the seizure of items, a £200 fine, and a year's imprisonment. In this period, especially during wartime, the government sought to enforce the ban. The most effective means of doing so was to try and prevent recruiters from suborning workers in Britain. Preventing skilled workers from emigrating was another issue, as emigration overseas was becoming increasingly common. For example, between 1783 and 1812, 100,000 people, an average of 3,000 a year, left Ulster alone for the United States. The government received reports of British workers who had gone abroad, but there was little it could do to counter such migration flows. In an emigrant harbour, assessing who was a skilled artisan—as opposed to an unskilled labourer—was fraught with difficulties. Moreover, if an artisan wanting to return risked prosecution, this would not entice him to come back. In 1812, when unemployed arms workers in Birmingham wanted to emigrate to America with their tools, the Board of Trade suggested that the Board of Ordnance be asked to find work contracts for them.[15]

As for the prohibition on the export of machinery, it was even more difficult to enforce. Smuggling across the Channel was very common. In 1817, the British consul in Calais, Thomas Fonblanque, reported to Foreign Secretary Lord Castlereagh 'that an extensive Contraband trade is successfully carried on with

---

[13] Julian Hoppit, *Britain's Political Economies: Parliament and Economic Life, 1660–1800*, Cambridge, 2017, ch. 7.

[14] *Manchester Mercury*, 19 March 1799, quoted in Harris, *Industrial Espionage*, p. 476.

[15] David J. Jeremy, 'Damming the Flood: British Governments Efforts to Check the Outflow of Technicians and Machinery 1780–1843', *Business History Review*, vol. 51, 1977, p. 10.

England from the coast of my Consulate', the traffic 'being now usually carried on in a larger class vessel than those formerly employed in illicit trade'.[16] In 1821, an Englishman in Lille wrote to Home Secretary Lord Sidmouth that 'there [was] a person in Nottingham continually sending Machines into this country' and that 'the last machine that came is to make Bobin nett [sic] lace'.[17] Again in 1822, an informer named 'Bill', who was on the books of the Board of Trade, detailed a smuggling route to the Continent: 'the means practiced for conveying off machinery is by concealing it in different Packages and sending them to Rye and other places from when they are taken to the Continent by Fishermen.'[18] Renaud Morieux has shown that even during the Napoleonic wars fishermen on both sides of the Channel came into contact with one another.[19] In the early development of the lace industry, machinery was smuggled throughout the wars on *smoggleurs*, a French word, adapted from the English, for long thin boats specialising in this activity.[20] On top of this, many exemptions were granted by the Board of Trade, such as for steam engines. During the French wars, Boulton and Watt were able to export their machinery regularly. David Jeremy has noted that although the Board did make limited efforts to enforce prohibition until about 1807, it subsequently gave up blocking the emigration of artisans and the export of machinery.

On the French side, attitudes were flexible. On the one hand, a continental blockade was enforced against Britain from 1806, and the British in France were to be imprisoned in prisoner-of-war camps.[21] On the other hand, this did not totally stem the flow of machines and artisans. British machinery was still smuggled into France. Some Britons were jailed or detained, but others found employment.[22] William Haynes, a Nottingham tulle-maker, came to Paris during the Amiens peace (1802–3) to set up a tulle importation network, stayed when the war broke out again, and was supposedly asked by Napoleon to develop a tulle industry in France. He continued smuggling instead until his goods were seized and burnt in 1809, and he had to run away.[23] Henry Sykes, the British owner of a cotton-spinning factory in Saint-Rémy-sur-Avre (Eure-et-Loir) from 1792, employed

---

[16] TNA. FO 27/166. Consular correspondence. Fonblanque to Castlereagh, 17 February 1817.
[17] TNA. HO 44/10/79, ff. 268–9. Samuel Butler to Lord Sidmouth, 24 December 1821.
[18] TNA. BT 1/169, bundle 26, quoted in Jeremy, 'Damming the Flood', p. 14.
[19] Renaud Morieux, 'Diplomacy from Below and Belonging: Fishermen and Cross-Channel Relations in the Eighteenth Century', *Past and Present*, vol. 202, 2009, pp. 83–125.
[20] Christian Borde, 'Le contrebandier, le tulliste et le négociant: Calais, relais européen de l'industrie dentellière, 1802–1832', in Stéphane Curveiller and Laurent Buchard, *Se déplacer du Moyen âge à nos jours*, Calais, 2009, pp. 291–302.
[21] Elodie Duché, 'L'otium des captifs d'honneur britanniques à Verdun sous le Premier Empire, 1803–1814', in Nicolas Beaupré and Karine Rance (eds.), *Arrachés et déplacés. Réfugiés politiques, prisonniers de guerre, déportés (Europe et espace colonial 1789-1918)*, Clermont-Ferrand, 2016, pp. 117–44; Linant de Bellefonds, 'Les techniciens anglais'; Harris, *Industrial Espionage*.
[22] Henderson, *Britain and Industrial Europe*, pp. 31–4 and Harris, *Industrial Espionage*, p. 552.
[23] Samuel Ferguson fils, *Histoire du tulle et des dentelles mécaniques en Angleterre et en France*, Paris, 1862, p. 62.

about 200 workers by 1800 and obtained French nationality in 1807; his business became large and prosperous.[24] William Cockerill, a mechanic from Lancashire, lived in Verviers from 1798, where he was joined by his sons who also came from England. In 1807, in Liège, he set up a workshop to produce wool-carding and spinning machinery. At the time, Liège was French and Cockerill was granted French nationality in 1810. This position gave him unique access to the continental—especially French—market which was protected from British com- petition by the war and the continental blockade. The company underwent a major expansion during this period. In other words, although the French govern- ment was wary of the enemy within, it was aware of the importance of the economy in wartime and was keen on making the best use of foreign skills. The · post-war period would offer further opportunities.

2. Emigrant Artisans and Exported Machinery: From Prohibition to Liberalisation (1824–43)

The end of the Napoleonic wars paved the way for a more liberal atmosphere. Economically, the post-war years were very difficult for Britain, with a series of poor harvests, the loss of wartime economic stimulus, and the demobilisation of 300,000 to 400,000 men in the years following Waterloo. The second and third censuses (1811 and 1821) made it clear that the population was growing rapidly. The circulation of people and goods not only resumed but also reached unprece- dented levels. Free-trade economics had also made significant progress. Early in 1824, Ricardian economist John Ramsay McCulloch published an essay condemn- ing the 'unjust and oppressive restraints laid on workmen by the combination laws' which had been passed in 1799–1800 against the trade unions.[25] The end of his *Edinburgh Review* article focused on restrictions on the emigration of work- men. His argument was a classic liberal one: 'Why should [an artisan] be forced to remain in this country, if he supposes he can improve his condition by removing to another?'[26] McCulloch pointed to the inefficiency of controls and added that 'the lowness of wages in the Continental States, the difference of customs and habits, and above all of language' were obstacles to emigration anyway. He also remarked that legislation only prevented the 'poor and ill-educated class of artificers, whose emigration would be equally advantageous to themselves and the country', from leaving.[27] Against the ban on the export of machinery, he put

---

[24] Geneviève Dufresne-Seurre, *Les Waddington, une dynastie de cotonniers en Eure-et-Loir: 1792–1961*, Chartres, 2011.

[25] 'Draft of proposed Bill for repealing several Acts relating to Combinations of Workmen, and for more effectually protecting Trade, and for settling Disputes between Masters and their Work-people', *The Edinburgh Review*, vol. 39, no. 78, January 1824, pp. 315–45, p. 340.

[26] Ibid., p. 342.   [27] Ibid., p. 344.

forward similar arguments of inefficiency, unfairness, and counter-productivity. Radical MP Joseph Hume soon pressed for a Select Committee, which the president of the Board of Trade, William Huskisson, agreed to. Hume argued that the legislation was unfair and cited the example of the 'gentleman of property' who 'might go over to France, or to any other country, and there spend his whole substance, or he might annually draw his income from England, Scotland or Ireland, and disperse it abroad without the slightest responsibility', whereas the 'the poor man, whose whole wealth consisted in the art he had learned, and the strength he enjoyed, was unable to apply that art and that strength to the best advantage'. As for machinery, another argument was put forward:

> Why... instead of clandestine exportation, should not this country become the great manufacturer of machinery, thus adding to the rest a most important application of ingenious industry?[28]

Huskisson concurred with another argument that matched McCulloch's: 'many of the individuals so engaged abroad, would, in the fluctuations to which their trade had been exposed, have willingly returned to England, had they not considered themselves proscribed by this very law'.[29]

The 1824 Select Committee on artisans and machinery examined the three issues of the combination laws, the emigration of artisans, and the export of machinery. The manufacturers it interviewed were divided. The Committee recommended the repeal of the ban on combinations and on emigration so that artisans could 'take their labour and art to the best market', and the law was repealed on 21 June 1824. However, large-scale opposition against lifting the ban on the export of machinery was voiced by textile manufacturers. The case was postponed and in 1826, in the context of economic depression, and despite Joseph Hume's efforts, the campaign to repeal the ban was dropped. This may seem contradictory: British workers and machines often went together, as artisans were needed to build and fit the new equipment, train the local workforce, and often operate the machines in the early stages. Hume had pointed to the contradiction between the free emigration of artisans and the ban on the emigration of machinery: 'it would be more wise to send the machines abroad, and to keep the workmen at home', he said.[30] But as Jeremy suggested, this reflected 'differing assumptions about the locus of technology'.[31] For free-traders like Hume, who drew his observations from the London machine-building sector, new tools would soon make it possible to build machines in Paris as well as in Britain. For Manchester machine-makers, the division of labour was reaching new levels, with several

---

[28] Parliamentary Debates in the House of Commons (hereafter HC Deb.), new series, vol. 10, 12 February 1824, col. 143.

[29] Ibid., col. 147.   [30] HC Deb., 11 May 1826, vol. 15, cc. 1118–22.

[31] Jeremy, 'Damming the Flood', p. 20.

Figure 1.3 'Here and there: or Emigration A Remedy', *Punch*, 15 July 1848. By the 1840s, mainstream papers were promoting emigration.

specialised sub-trades now being needed to make machines, so that the free emigration of artisans did not endanger the British monopoly on technology.

More broadly, in the second quarter of the century, attitudes to emigration were changing. Whereas the state had traditionally been reluctant to allow emigration, except for the 'residuum' of society—felons, paupers, or prostitutes—a new paradigm was emerging. It was widely assumed that Britain was overpopulated, and that emigration could act as a safety valve limiting social unrest (see Figure 1.3). The 1834 New Poor Law allowed parishes to elicit funds to underwrite the emigration of destitute people to British colonies. Notwithstanding the traditional reluctance of governments to intervene in such matters, in 1836 an Agent-General for Emigration was appointed and in 1840 the office was superseded by a formal Colonial Land and Emigration Commission (CLEC). Several assisted emigration schemes were also set up, while the UK now connected its imperial expansion with the peopling of the colonies.[32] John Stuart Mill summarised the new approach:

---

[32] Eric Richards, *Britannia's Children: Emigration from England, Scotland, Wales and Ireland since 1600*, London, 2005.

The exportation of labourers and capital from old to new countries, from a place where their productive power is less, to a place where it is greater, increases by so much the aggregate produce of the labour and capital of the world. It adds to the joint wealth of the old and the new country, what amounts in a short period to many times the mere cost of effecting the transport. There needs be no hesitation in affirming that Colonisation, in the present state of the world, is the best affair of business, in which the capital of an old and wealthy country can engage.[33]

Mill and other political economists were not thinking of the Continent when they outlined their rationale, but of the British colonies. However, it was not possible to favour emigration to Australia, whose image was poor until the discovery of gold in the early 1850s, while deterring people from moving to nearby France or Belgium. Of course, assisted emigration schemes were also set up for colonial emigration, but the official relaxation of rules on migration was a general one, which also made moves to the Continent easier.

During the following period (1825–43), exporting machinery was therefore submitted to the discretionary powers of the Board of Trade, which could license the export of some machines and refuse that of others. Between 1825 and 1843, 2,098 applications for licences were submitted, a large proportion of which involved textile machines that were bound for Europe.[34] Only 10 per cent were denied licences. There was some coherence in the licensing policy, as the interests of British manufacturers were always taken into account. Exports to areas that were not seen as posing a competitive threat—for instance, New Zealand, Egypt, or India—were usually licensed, whereas those to Europe and the United States were tightly controlled. However, there were many ways to circumvent the law, especially when it came to exports to the Continent. Guarding the extensive coastline of Britain and Ireland proved a hard task. Smuggling was common across the Channel, and became even more so with the advent of steamboat services. Coastal trade could also be used. Machinery could be exported in parts, or it could be shipped under a false description, while the transfer of drawings could not be prevented. Seizure even in the ports proved limited, to the point that risk of confiscation was scarce, especially if exporters used lesser-known routes.

By the early 1840s, bolstered by the efforts of the Anti-Corn Law League, free-trading ideas had gained ground among textile manufacturers. In February 1841, Manchester MP Mark Philips presented a petition for the 'free exportation of machinery'.[35] A Select Committee was appointed and voted in favour of repealing the prohibition. The usual arguments were put forward: artisans could emigrate freely. Coal could be exported more or less freely, as could machine tools. More

---

[33] John Stuart Mill, *Principles of Political Economy*, London, 1848, vol. 2, p. 540.
[34] Jeremy, 'Damming the Flood', p. 27.   [35] HC Deb. 16 February 1841, vol. 56, cc. 670–92.

and more machines were now made on the Continent and in the United States. New inventions could easily be circulated, and the ban harmed British inventors. Although it took another two years, Parliament eventually adopted a Machinery Exportation Bill introduced by William Gladstone, who was president of the Board of Trade at the time. By August 1843, all British machines could be exported freely without sanction.

In many respects, this change echoed the shift from the dominance of mercantilist doctrines to those of free trade; it was no coincidence that it happened in the same period as the repeal of the Corn Laws (1846) and that of the Navigation Acts (1849). It can also be argued that by the early 1840s, the technology gap had already shrunk. Increasingly sophisticated machines were being made on the Continent, and British manufacturers sought to ensure that their designs sold well in Europe rather than sitting back while imitations were developed. Moreover, conflicting interests were at play in Britain between those who made the machines and were keen on exporting them and those manufacturers who used them, and who feared more intense competition resulting from a lifting of the ban. Lastly, allowing the free circulation of artisans meant that machines had to be exported freely, as is well illustrated by the case of lace.

3. A Case Study: Machine-Made Lace

In the early nineteenth century, lace was hand-worked by women and children exclusively. In Britain this sizeable sector of employment was concentrated in the traditional rural areas of Bedfordshire, Buckinghamshire, and Northamptonshire.[36] Mechanised lacemaking did not grow out of this industry but out of hosiery, the stronghold of which was the East Midlands, particularly Nottinghamshire. The hosiery industry was relatively prosperous until about 1810, when men's fashion shifted from stockings to trousers. This change provoked a major crisis, exacerbated by the free hand given by the government to the manufacturers, which manifested itself in the Luddite crisis over the adoption of textile machines in 1811–16. It took the industry about thirty years to recover and it was not mechanised until the second half of the century. Meanwhile, framework knitters—or 'stockingers'—tried to imitate hand-worked lace, a valuable commodity which was then still only a craft luxury industry. Many framework knitters, frame smiths, and mechanics of the East Midlands devised small inventions which improved the stocking frames. In 1809, Loughborough manufacturer John Heathcoat (1783–1861) patented a bobbin-net lace machine which made him a leading lace entrepreneur. While the hand of the

---

[36] Pamela Sharpe and Stanley D. Chapman, 'Women's Employment and Industrial Organisation: Commercial Lace Embroidery in Early Nineteenth-Century Ireland and England', *Women's History Review*, vol. 5, 1996, pp. 325–50.

Figure 1.4 Model of an early single-tier twist-net machine claimed to have been made by John Levers. © City of Nottingham Museums.

lacemaker could make five meshes per minute, Heathcoat's machine made 1,000. By 1836, improved machines produced 30,000 meshes per minute. When Heathcoat's patent expired in 1823, an unprecedented level of capital and manpower was invested in the bobbin-net machine, which had been improved in 1813 by mechanic John Leavers (1786–1848) and would be named the 'Leavers' (see Figure 1.4 and Chapter 6). The Leavers machine became very successful from the 1840s, with the use of the Jacquard technique of punched cards which further transformed the technology. Mechanisation revolutionised the sector with machine-made lace competing with and gradually replacing handmade lace.

Although most of the lace was not produced in Nottingham itself, the city maintained a central position in the trade, akin to that played by Manchester in the cotton industry. Until the advent of factory production in the 1840s and 1850s, the sophisticated lace machines were operated by feet and hands, and not all framework knitters managed to make the transition from hosiery. Most machines were operated in the upper storeys, including attics and garrets, or in the cellars of houses whose other storeys were occupied by shops and lodgings, while even 'stables, kitchens and the most unlikely buildings were accommodated'.[37] Machines were expensive (£200, £300, and up to £1,000 per unit; i.e., £17,000–£85,000 in 2021 real prices, or £182,000–910,000 in 2021 labour value), and most artisans did not own one. It was common practice to rent them, to purchase them on credit, or to buy them second-hand in the crisis of the late 1820s to early 1830s. This still left room for small-businessmen, many of whom had originally been framework knitters themselves, to ply their trade. We have a fairly reliable knowledge of the structure of ownership in the Midlands in 1829, as a trade committee tried to get signatures from the owners of the 4,000 existing machines to enforce a restriction of the working hours of the machines from eighteen or twenty daily, which was then common, to twelve. What emerges from this list gathered by William Felkin, then one of the key figures in the Midlands industry and the first historian of the trade, is that 46 per cent of the net machines in the East Midlands were owned by small entrepreneurs who owned one, two, or three machines.[38] They usually operated one of these machines and then let the others to middle-men called 'machine-holders' who hired the workers and paid a rent to the owner; occasionally the machine-owners hired the workers themselves. An overwhelming proportion of owners were men.[39] The position of these small entrepreneurs was unstable. Over the following years, capital was increasingly concentrated. The size, the cost, and the sophistication of the machines continued to increase.

By the 1840s, steam power was used, which meant concentrating machines in a single large building where one or several capitalists owned machines operated by steam, as in the cotton industry. It was also from this point forwards that the

---

[37] Stanley D. Chapman, 'The First Generation of Nottingham Lace Makers: The Restriction of Hours Deed of 1829', in J. B. Bailey, *Nottinghamshire Lace Makers: The First Generation of Nottingham Lace Makers—Including 700+ Names of Lace Machine Owners in 1829*, J. B. Bailey, Melton Mowbray, 2003, p. 2. The archive ('Signatures to agreement for execution of restriction of hours deed in bobbin net trade in Nottingham, etc; with explanatory note, 1829') is at the Nottinghamshire Archives (shelf mark M/351); see also Honeyman, *Origins of Enterprise*, ch. 8.

[38] Chapman, 'The First Generation of Nottingham Lace Makers', p. 4.

[39] Among the 700 or so lace machine owners who signed (including a tiny proportion of +/− 5 per cent for whom sex cannot be determined), owning some 4,000 machines, five women owning six machines can be strictly identified: Eliza Barrett (one machine in New Radford); Ann Palfreman (one machine in Sneinton); Elizabeth Slack (two machines in Hyson Green, Nottingham); Harriett Haughton (one machine in Castle Alley, Nottingham); and Mary Wells (one machine in Sussex Street, Nottingham). Chapman, 'The First Generation of Nottingham Lace Makers'.

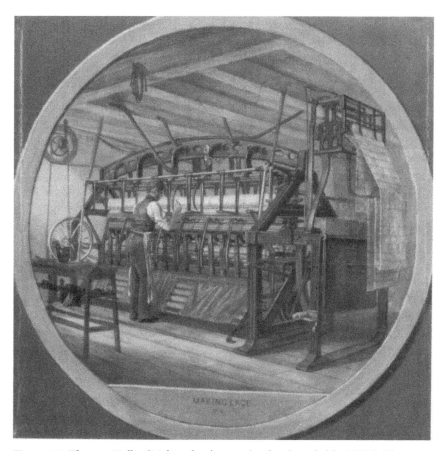

Figure 1.5 Thomas Hollis, 'Making lace', no. 4 (undated, probably 1850s). The Leavers machine was by then a large one, water or steam-powered and using the Jacquard technology (to the right). © Stanley Chapman.

application of the Jacquard attachment to Leavers lace machines allowed patterned lace to be entirely mechanically made (see Figure 1.5). Between 1840 and 1860, the 'stall system' developed as capitalist machine-owners built factories in which not only their own machines were operated but also those of other lacemakers who rented space and power. In Britain, the bulk of this transition from craft to industrial stage was completed by 1860; the number of lace manufacturers shrank from 1,400 in 1829 to 250 in 1865. By then, Nottingham had achieved a position of global dominance, which Felkin could celebrate in his *magnum opus*.[40] The city would retain this ascendancy in the production of lace and in the making of machines until the mid-twentieth century.

[40] William Felkin, *A History of the Machine-Wrought Hosiery and Lace Manufactures*, London, 1867.

Some of the female lace 'runners' (embroiderers) may have started in hand-worked lace, but most of the early male lacemakers had a background in framework knitting. This was very much a family-based, domestic industry. At the same time, the dominance of large merchant companies which employed up to thousands of stockingers, combined with the intensification and increased division of labour, along with the resulting deskilling tendencies, undermined this strong artisan culture. By the early nineteenth century, framework knitters were independent in theory, but although they were paid a price for a commodity, rather than for working hours, they were in effect wage-earners. Many tried to preserve some independence and form trade union associations.[41] Their champion was Gravener Henson (1785–1852), whom E. P. Thompson portrayed as one of three 'truly impressive trade union leaders' alongside contemporaries John Gast and John Doherty, arguing that he 'challenge[d] comparison with Francis Place'.[42] A self-taught man, Henson also wrote a *History of the Framework Knitters.*[43]

Machine lace workers were highly skilled and supposedly better paid than framework knitters, although this changed over time: while the 'twisthands' who operated the machines might have earned 30–40 shillings a week in 1824, this fell to 24 in 1828, 18 in 1833, and an average of 15 in 1857, which was not much more than the average 12 shillings earned by framework knitters. It was common practice for lace machines to be worked in two shifts, with one being operated from 4 a.m. to 2 p.m. and the other from 2 p.m. to midnight. In total, each man worked ten hours a day. They worked all of Friday night, ending the working week at 6 p.m. on Saturdays. As in hosiery, women and children worked with male adults. Children replaced and refilled the bobbins—working for up to ten hours a day from an early age. Women and young girls bleached, dyed, and dressed the lace. There were more women and children than adult men in the trade and the plight of these low-paid workers became a matter for public debate in the 1840s (see Chapter 3). When parliamentary committees investigated and discussed child labour in 1833 and 1841, two major arguments were put forward against the regulation of working hours in the lace industry. One was that female and child labour was mostly domestic. The other was the fear of foreign competition. Indeed, by then France had become a serious competitor for Nottingham lace, and the emigration of the Nottinghamshire lacemakers had played a key part in this.

[41] James Epstein, 'Some Organisational and Cultural Aspects of the Chartist Movement in Nottingham', in James Epstein and Dorothy Thompson (eds.), *The Chartist Experience: Studies in Working-Class Radicalism and Culture, 1830–60*, London, 1982, pp. 221–68.

[42] E. P. Thompson, *The Making of the English Working Class*, Harmondsworth, 1968 [1963], pp. 541, 851.

[43] *Henson's History of the Framework Knitters*, a reprint with a new introduction by S. D. Chapman, London, 1970.

Indeed, while the mechanised lace industry made huge progress in the East Midlands, it could not easily penetrate the French market which was also the largest market for lace on the Continent, as well as the main country in which handmade lace was produced.[44] At 30 or 35 per cent, tariffs were high and protective until the 1860 free-trade treaty between Britain and France. Smuggling was common across the Channel, but it also came at a cost of about 10–15 per cent. In 1816 three Nottingham lacemakers reputedly smuggled a bobbin-net machine to Calais. They were making a strategic move: they could sell their lace in France at no additional cost and remained close to Britain, where many of their relatives lived and where their resources in terms of cotton, machine parts, information on technical improvements, and patterns were located. There were legal obstacles but, as we have seen, the law was often breached, and once they were overseas the British artisans could not be arrested. For all these reasons, Calais became the hub of this French machine-made lace industry. It was as close as one could be to British shores while also being quite close to Paris, which was the centre of European fashion and the primary market for lace in France. When the expiry of Heathcoat's patent in 1823 resulted in a boom and declining wages, more lacemakers went to Calais, and this pattern persisted for decades. By the 1830s, the French lace industry, with Calais at its centre, was competing with its East Midlands ancestor.[45] It was less concentrated than in Britain, but the number of frames was rapidly rising. Henson was involved in various attempts to fight this French competition. He said he knew more about the trade in Calais than in Leicester and was often consulted for his expertise in the trade.[46] He advocated the establishment of certain institutions which already existed in France, such as local chambers of commerce, *conseils de prud'hommes* (courts for labour disputes), and schools of design. But in Britain, calls for protection failed.

Because of the British ban on the export of machinery, and because of French tariffs, the smuggling of cotton thread, lace, and machines persisted until the 1850s. Smugglers' premiums between Calais and Kent varied, reportedly from 10 per cent on lace to Calais, 15 to 20 per cent on machines to northern France, and 33 per cent on cotton to Lille in 1824.[47] The attitudes of the authorities were mixed. Such smuggled imports were viewed leniently by the French local authorities. It seems that British custom-house officers also allowed such smuggling to the Continent. Smuggling worked both ways, with finished lace also being

[44] Felkin, *A History of the Machine-Wrought Hosiery*, p. 402.

[45] A text suggests there were 603 machines in Calais in January 1851: *Notice historique et statistique sur l'industrie tullière à Calais et à Saint-Pierre les Calais présentée avec un album des échantillons de ses produits à monsieur le ministre de l'agriculture et du commerce, sur sa demande, par la chambre de Commerce de Calais*, Paris, Imprimerie Bénard, February 1851.

[46] UK Parliamentary Papers (hereafter PP). Select Committee on Postage, vol. 1 (1837–8), 221, q. 9250.

[47] PP. Select Committee on Artizans and Exportation of Machinery, 1824, evidence of Mr Alexander (2 March, 107) and Gravener Henson (28 March, 283).

introduced into Britain.[48] However, as David Todd has argued, the French national authorities insisted on preserving the prohibitive system which had been set up during the Empire. Under the Restoration, the customs administration was large, with some 25,000 officials, and it wielded significant power.[49] This power may account for why smuggling premiums remained high, and why competition remained less cut-throat in France than in Britain. But while premiums were high on cotton imports, the influx of foreign machinery and skilled workers went unopposed. Some advocates of tariff protection like Friedrich List, who derived his *National System of Political Economy* (1841) from his observations in France in 1837–40, argued for the importation of capital and skilled labour and against that of agricultural produce and raw material. This was basically what France did in the period 1815–48.

As for Britain, the 1824 repeal of the ban on the emigration of artisans signalled that Westminster was turning its back on its traditional mercantilism. Changes in 1834, 1841, and 1846 paved the way for free trade to flourish. Still, obstacles remained.[50] For instance, when in 1834 the French government allowed the import of thin cotton yarns from Britain, while other yarns remained banned, Nottingham manufacturers were alarmed at the boost it would give to France. But because of the high duties on them (about 50 per cent), 'an Old Townsman' of Calais rightly remarked that English anxiety was not justified:

> The French manufacturer, because the duty is to be so high, can get it cheaper from the smuggler!... Consequently, the idea of the alteration being detrimental to the interests of Nottingham is a bugbear, and nothing else.[51]

Far from being an anomaly, smuggling was an integral part of the Channel economy. It is impossible to assess it accurately. But the figure of half a million pounds a year, just for lace, was mentioned in the debate on the exportation of machinery.[52] For the British lacemakers in Calais, it remained critical, especially for acquiring the interior parts of machines. This infuriated Nottinghamshire competitors, including Henson, who waged a determined campaign to ban the evil trade. In 1824, when interviewed by a Select Committee, he denounced smuggling, against which 'His Majesty's government would never interfere'.[53] He later wrote:

---

[48] 'Female smuggling', *Nottingham Review* (hereafter *NR*), 11 July 1834, p. 4.
[49] David Todd, *Free Trade and Its Enemies in France, 1814–1851*, Cambridge, 2015, pp. 34–5.
[50] On the tariff policy of the July Monarchy, see Todd, *Free Trade and Its Enemies*, especially ch. 4.
[51] 'The Lace trade [Letter from 'an Old Townsman', Calais, June 26, 1834]', *NR* (11 July 1834), p. 2.
[52] Observer [Anon.], 'Exportation of Machinery', *NR* (4 October 1833), p. 1.
[53] PP. Select Committee on Artisans and Machinery, evidence given by Gravener Henson, 275.

While the English were thus totally losing the silk lace trade, the French were rapidly gaining the cotton lace trade, though they affected to prohibit both; the former being really and rigidly prohibited, the latter only speciously in order to encourage English workmen to establish machines in France, and to make one piece and smuggle another, thus completely outwitting us, in which the original patentee [Heathcoat] unfortunately took the lead.[54]

Meanwhile, machinery continued to be exported. In 1832, manufacturer William Morley toured France and Belgium, and estimated that there were about 2,000 machines.[55] In 1833, Henson was involved in a campaign waged by some of Nottingham's leading men against French lace competitors. In a context of economic depression, manufacturers targeted the Board of Trade. Henson accused the latter of not reciprocating the high French duties at a time when free-trade ideas were gaining ground in Britain. Appointed assistant secretary to the committee which he himself set up, Henson conducted his own crusade against the export of machines. He made his case against free trade after persuading thirty-two lace manufacturers to sign his petition. Then he set out on a long journey around the ports to discover who the machine smugglers were, and during his tour seized machinery being embarked for France by a London merchant.[56] When this merchant sued for the recovery of his property, Henson conducted his own defence. The Nottingham Committee, embarrassed by this turn of events, broke up. Henson lost in court, and his defeat marked the collapse of the campaign to oppose machine exports to France.[57] Still, in 1838 Henson complained that 'Calais [was] rising upon the ruins of Nottingham'.[58] A few years later, the Nottingham lace manufacturers complained that thirty-four warp and bobbin machines had been exported in a month: 'So bold has this trade been carried on, that machines were openly packed at a neighbouring village, and taken to a wharf in open day'.[59]

The failure of Henson and other protectionists can be explained by various factors. Practically speaking, enforcement was difficult in a context where many of the propertied wanted the central state to be smaller and less intrusive. Fighting against smuggling came at a cost for the state, and the most serious convictions in Britain were against smuggling into the country, not out of it: after all, smugglers to the Continent marketed British goods. But there was another factor at play: whereas the export of lace machines was seen by Nottingham lace manufacturers

---

[54] *NR*, 3 June 1831. [55] Felkin, *A History of the Machine-Wrought Hosiery*, p. 353.
[56] Ibid.; Chapman, 'Introduction', *Henson's History . . .* p. xvii.
[57] Roy A. Church and S. D. Chapman, 'Gravener Henson and the Making of the English Working Class', in E. L. Jones and G. E. Mingay (ed.), *Land, Labour and Population in the Industrial Revolution*, London, 1967, p. 153.
[58] PP. Select committee on postage, 1837–8, vol. 2, p. 217, q. 9192.
[59] 'Hosiery and Lace Trades', *Nottingham Journal* (hereafter *NJ*) (17 June 1842), p. 3.

as a threat, it was profitable for its machine manufacturers. Moreover, the prohibition seemed pointless since the emigration of artisans had been legal since 1824. In 1833 an anonymous 'Observer', who obviously produced lace machinery, argued in the Nottingham press:

> In Calais alone are 150 men employed in building carcasses ... The greater part of the machinery now in Vienna were built in Calais and Lisle; and machines are now building in France for exportation.... There are probably 300 workmen of all descriptions, now or lately employed in England in the same manufacture of lace machinery for exportation: if such exportation is prevented, it is clear that these workmen will be discharged ... And it will be borne in mind, that a removal to France is not now the kind of affair it was thought some years ago: so many workmen have passed and repassed, that the road has become perfectly familiar; and too many are now living there for any to fear the want of society.... The sole question to be determined therefore, is whether it is better to export machinery, or the makers of machinery![60]

In other words, because workers could freely emigrate, prohibiting the export of machines would simply undermine British machine-making. This free-trading argument would strike a chord in 1841 when a new select committee investigated the practice at length. In 1843 the export of machinery became legal. Free-traders had won the upper hand and the final blow would come with the 1860 Cobden-Chevalier treaty.

The structure of the Calais lace industry resembled that of Nottinghamshire, albeit on a smaller scale: small entrepreneurs, with just a couple of machines which they often bought on credit. Although most innovations originated in the Midlands, some techniques devised in France were also imported by the British; for instance, from the early 1840s the Jacquard technique of punched cards which, combined with the Leavers machine, transformed the technology once more. The market expanded massively: lace was 'now within the reach of all purses', as an Anglo-French historian of the trade wrote.[61] Zola expressed this passion in a department store:

> But the ladies had still kept hold of the bits of lace, fascinated, intoxicated. The pieces were unrolled, passed from one to the other, drawing the admirers closer still, holding them in the delicate meshes. On their laps there was a continual caress of this tissue, so miraculously fine, and amidst which their culpable fingers fondly lingered.[62]

---

[60] Observer, 'Exportation of Machinery', NR (13 September 1833), p. 3.

[61] Samuel Ferguson, fils, *Histoire du tulle et des dentelles mécaniques en Angleterre et en France*, Paris, 1862, p. 3.

[62] Émile Zola, *The Ladies' Paradise*, English translation by E. A. Vizetelly, London, 1886 [1883], p. 100.

The plummeting prices, from 45 francs per metre in 1815 to less than 0.5 francs in 1850 (i.e. a price cut to one ninetieth), may account for the difficulty in accumulating capital. At the same time, it enabled the Calais lacemakers to cope successfully with the competition from craft lace, as in Britain. Until the 1870s, hand-worked lace was often preferred to machine-made lace, and by 1851, 240,000 women still crafted lace manually in France.[63] The shift to steam-powered factories took place between the 1840s and 1860s, with some delay in comparison to the British trajectory. This is usually attributed to the higher cost of coal and spun cotton—which were then imported from Britain—but time allowing for the transfer of technology may also have played its part. By then, Calais had begun to seriously compete with the East Midlands industry, which preserved its leadership, as we have seen. Visiting France in 1871, the Japanese Iwakura embassy praised the 'high reputation' of the lace of Calais.[64] Between the 1850s and 1950s, there were no major changes in the production of lace, but rather a series of improvements.

The production of manufactured lace and the making of machines now followed different patterns. Lacemaking gradually expanded to the Continent. By 1842, the *Nottingham Journal*, which voiced the demands of lace manufacturers against the export of machinery, estimated that while 5,500 out of the 7,390 world's lace machines were in England in 1832 (74 per cent), this had now dropped to 2,000 out of 5,473 (36 per cent), while 2,800 machines were in France, mostly in Calais, and others in Switzerland, Saxony, Russia, Austrian dominions (Moravia), and Prussia.[65] Henson's nightmare had come true. The first historian of the French lace industry, Samuel Ferguson, estimated that there were 3,200 machines in England in 1844 versus 1,800 in France.[66] And even when carcasses of the machines were made on the continental mainland, reputedly below the Nottingham quality, the internal mechanisms were still made in Nottingham and smuggled into France. By 1842, while only twelve men in Nottingham were making machines for the domestic market, 150 men were making them for France. By 1847, eighty workers were making bobbins and carriages for Austria.[67] In terms of machine-building, the Nottingham area remained at the forefront of the industry.[68]

Fundamentally, despite duties and the costs of transport and smuggling, what was taking place was the creation of an integrated northern European market of lace and knitting. When in 1837–8 a parliamentary committee discussed postage,

---

[63] Stéphane Lembré, 'Les écoles de dentellières en France et en Belgique des années 1850 aux années 1930', *Histoire de l'éducation*, vol. 123, 2009, pp. 45–70.

[64] Kume Kunitake, *Japan Rising: The Iwakura Embassy to the USA and Europe*, Cambridge, 2009, p. 215.

[65] *NJ* (23 September 1842).   [66] Ferguson, *Histoire du tulle et des dentelles mécaniques*, p. 159.

[67] *NJ* (17 June 1842).

[68] Sheila A. Mason, *Nottingham Lace 1760s–1950s*, Ilkeston, 1994, p. 61.

one of the central concerns was that its high cost hindered the circulation of business information. Committee members wanted to know about wage levels overseas and the kind of patterns being produced. The information conveyed in newspapers was considered insufficient. Henson corresponded with many across Britain and Europe and argued for the importance of cheap postage.[69] At the same time, large quantities of information about lace already circulated between the East Midlands and Calais. Nottingham newspapers gave detailed accounts of machine and worker numbers both at home and overseas. This news was supplemented by hearsay, by letters and probably by professional agents. Another feature of this integration was the great fluidity of labour between both areas: emigration fostered more emigration, as studies on chain migration have often noted.[70] At a time of economic depression, it was reported that in Calais 'a number of the English workmen have lately gone to England, being unable to obtain work'.[71] Printer Charles Manby Smith remembered that, when he crossed the Channel in 1826,

> [there] were a party of Nottingham weavers, who, having been starved out of their native place through want of employment, were going over to Calais in search of it. Most of them had left wives and families behind; others had left their parents. The entire luggage of each was packed up in a cotton handkerchief, and some had not even that.[72]

Throughout this period, communication and exchange between the Midlands and northern France was lively and dynamic. While some emigrants ended up being Anglo-French, many maintained connections with their native land and went back and forth between both areas. In the Nottingham papers, trade news on France and personal information, such as obituaries of Calais residents, were published (see Figures 1.6 and 1.7).[73]

As Colin Pooley has argued, other motives (marriage, family, health...) could also play an important part in what seemed, on the surface, to be simple labour migration.[74] All in all, we can infer from the local press and other sources that in the Midlands information about the French lace industry was available, while the Nottingham papers were subscribed to in Calais and were distributed in some taverns. As a result, regardless of how long they lasted, most moves between the

---

[69] PP. Report of the Select Committee on Postage (1837–8), vol. 2, p. 207, q. 9091.

[70] Dudley Baines, *Migration in a Mature Economy: Emigration and Internal Migration in England and Wales, 1861–1900*, Cambridge, 1985, p. 280.

[71] 'The Lace Trade', *NR* (11 November 1836), p. 3.

[72] Charles Manby Smith, *The Working Man's Way in the World*, London, 1853, p. 46.

[73] Obituary of John Briggs, 25, *NR*, 6 January 1832, p. 3; John Fisher, *NR*, 12 October 1832; George Taylor, *NR*, 14 February 1834, p. 3.

[74] Colin Pooley, 'Using Life Histories to Explore the Complexities of Internal and International Migration', *Continuity and Change*, vol. 36 no. 1, May 2021, pp. 111–31.

Twist Hands wanted.

WANTED, a few good Hands to work in Ma-
chines: Width, Eight-Quarter and upwards.
The Price given is One Penny per Quarter, and One
Penny the Dozen Breadths.
Apply to Mr. ATKINS, Union Hotel, Calais, France.

Figure 1.6 'Twist Hands wanted', *Nottingham Review*, 24 August 1827, p. 2. By the 1820s, the hiring of Nottingham workers by the Calais industry was already well organised.

At her father's house in Milton-street, in her 25th
year, Caroline, the wife of Thomas Mather, now of
Calais, leaving two children the loss of an affectionate
mother.

Figure 1.7 Obituary, *Nottingham Review*, 2 October 1840, p. 4. As this obituary testified, migration could cause family separation, or result from it.

two areas were reasoned and well informed—a conclusion that Dudley Baines made about English and Welsh transatlantic emigration in 1860–1900.[75]

4. Counting Labour Emigrants

How many British artisans emigrated to the Continent between 1815 and 1870? It is impossible to give an exact figure because of a lack of sources. Even today, at a time when states are concerned about and sometimes obsessed with migrants, counting them is difficult. In Britain, only passenger lists for long-haul voyages to destinations outside Britain and Europe have been kept at the National Archives (BT27 series), and until 1852 they distinguished neither between 'British' subjects and 'aliens' nor between migrants and other passengers.[76] Still, migration to the Continent was not insignificant. For instance, in the sample studied by Colin Pooley and Jean Turnbull, 12.3 per cent of the 146 emigrant families in the 1750–1839 period went to western Europe, and so did 6.8 per cent of the 459 families in 1840–79; that is, in a period when possibly 4 million British people emigrated overseas.[77]

What kind of sources are available at the point of destination? In the United States, in Canada, and in Australia, there are detailed records of incoming passengers, but in most European countries these records were deemed

[75] Baines, *Migration in a Mature Economy*.

[76] Marjory Harper and Stephen Constantine, *Migration and empire*, Oxford, 2010, p. 1.

[77] N. H. Carrier and J. R. Jeffery, *External Migration: A Study of the Available Statistics 1815–1950*, London, 1953, pp. 93, 95–6; Colin Pooley and Jean Turnbull, *Migration and Mobility in Britain since the Eighteenth Century*, London, 1998, p. 280.

unnecessary for short-distance trips. Working-class migrants were seldom counted as such by the local authorities. For instance, a witness to the 1824 Select Committee on Artisans and Machinery argued that 16,000 workers had emigrated to France in the years 1822 and 1823 alone.[78] However, he admitted this was second-hand information and Tory MP Charles Ross, a leading member of the Select Committee, contested this, arguing on the basis of information from the French police that there were only 1,300 or 1,400 in all, and his figures are supported by a case study.[79] In France, which was the principal destination for immigration in nineteenth-century Europe, the first census in which foreigners were counted was in 1851: there were then 20,357 British nationals (i.e. 5.4 per cent of the 379,289 foreigners), including many middle- and upper-class residents who settled in France for their leisure or for their health.[80] In 1861, the British government asked Belgium to provide figures on the number and gender of the British in the country. The reply was 4,092, including 1,766 men and 2,326 women (governesses in particular), but again with few details on their occupations.[81]

Assessing the nature and scale of British migration is easier at the level of local communities. Whereas the British who lived in Cannes, Pau, Biarritz, Chamonix, or later Nice were mostly middle-class and domestic servants, those who lived in the manufacturing towns of Landerneau (Finistère), Sotteville-lès-Rouen (Seine-Inférieure), or Saint-Pierre-lès-Calais were mostly working-class. In Pas-de-Calais, the French département with the largest British population after Paris, Boulogne-sur-Mer housed a large British population of more than 3,000 in the 1840s. But although there were also British workers there, this population of British expatriates was mostly composed of genteel, middle-class residents, many with servants, some of them in debt. When British slavery was abolished in 1833, Boulogne housed about half of the seventy British slave-owners who lived in France and who applied for compensation.[82]

In manufacturing towns, the number of British workers seldom reached the thousands. For example, in Charenton, near Paris, where Manby and Wilson ran an ironworks, there were 248 British workers in 1824. With their families and a

---

[78] Evidence given by Mr Alexander, 2 March 1824, in PP. *Report from the Select Committee on Artizans and Machinery*, 1824, p. 108.

[79] Anon. [Charles Ross], '1st, 2nd, 3rd, 4th, 5th, and 6th Reports, from the Select Committee on Artizans and Machinery', *Quarterly Review*, vol. 31 (March 1825), pp. 392–3. Ross was probably close to real figures. For example, he stated that the Manby and Wilson ironworks in Charenton only employed 250 English, and not 500 to 1,200 as argued by some witnesses.

[80] Recensement de la population française, 1851, available at https://www.insee.fr/fr/statistiques/2653233?sommaire=2591397; Archives nationales, F/7/12338, Etats numériques du mouvement des étrangers; Gerbod, *op. cit.*, chs. 4 and 5.

[81] Archives royales de Belgique à Bruxelles—Inventaire F1075—Dossiers généraux—I 160. 321 Demande faite par le consul anglais à Bruxelles afin de connaître le nombre de sujets anglais habitant le pays. 1861.

[82] See the Legacies of British Slave-Ownership database, and Leila Raffiee, 'A Study of British Slave Owners in Boulogne-sur-Mer based on the Records of the Slave Compensation Commission Following the Abolition of Slavery in 1833', Master's thesis, Université Paris-Sorbonne, September 2016.

few other fellow Britons, this community, one of the largest in France, totalled about 640 people. By October 1825, the factory was reported to employ 350 British workers, alongside 350 French ones.[83] In Calais, there had been a continuous influx of British lace workers since the late 1810s. Calais itself was home to a few wealthy Britons, like James de Rothschild, and others in genteel poverty, like Emma Hamilton who died there. But those who lived in nearby Saint-Pierre-lès-Calais, where most of the workshops were based, were lacemakers and their families. Although it is difficult to arrive at a total number without the creation of a nominal database, census results show that thousands of British workers and their families lived there, while their proportion in the local population reached a peak in the 1840s, before the 1847–8 crisis. Although not all the British residents were lacemakers, as they included publicans and other trades, a large proportion were, including women and children. In Calais as in Britain, it was common in lacemakers' families for women and for children at an early age to work in the embroidery and the finishing parts of the process.

The British population in Saint-Pierre fluctuated, depending on trade cycles and other factors (see Table 1.1). The discrepancy between the ups and downs/peaks and troughs in the British population of Saint-Pierre and the slow growth of the British population in France can be explained by the fact that, in a general context of increasing mobility due to the improvements in transport and the beginnings of tourism, labour migration was heavily dependent on trade cycles. This is particularly evident when studying the impact of the 1847–8 crisis.

Large numbers of British workers were also employed in railway building, especially in the early stages when British engineers could not rely on a local workforce. When in 1846 the Select Committee on Railway Labourers 1846

Table 1.1 Population of Saint-Pierre-lès-Calais, including the British[84]

	1820	1831	1841	1851	1861	1872	1881
Total population of Saint-Pierre	4,007	6,802	9,128	11,325	14,779	20,409	32,958
British-born population			1,578	1,073	1,597	1,224	3,021
British proportion in Saint-Pierre			17.3%	9.5%	10.8%	6%	9.3%

[83] Jean-François Belhoste, 'Les forges de Charenton', in *Architectures d'usines en Val-de-Marne, (1822–1939), Cahier de l'inventaire*, no. 12, 1988, p. 29; *Gazette de France*, 24 October 1825, p. 1.

[84] Archives départementales [hereafter AD] du Pas-de-Calais, Recensements de population. For 1841, the number of Britons was assessed by Anne V. Fewkes, 'Protestant Families Extracted from the 1841 Census of St Pierre, Calais, France', *Nottinghamshire Family History Society*, vol. 121 (December 1998). Thanks to family historian Philip Emerson, who has compiled the occupations and addresses of these 1,578 British in a systematic way.

interviewed William Reed, one of the directors of the line, he said that about half of the 10,000 men employed at one time on the Paris and Rouen line (P&R) came from Britain. But the directors of the P&R in their report to shareholders of November 1841 claimed that French labourers were working well with 'the comparatively small number of Englishmen, whom the contractors have felt it necessary to send over to France, in order to show how works of this sort are conducted'.[85] Figures are partial; in 1842, in one district, out of 768 navvies, 203 (26 per cent) were British.[86] David Brooke considered that the most credible estimate probably appeared in the *Journal des Chemins de Fer* which reported that 2,000 of the 12,000 men on the line in the autumn of 1842 were British.[87]

Other sectors where the British could be numerous were the cotton and linen trades. In the late 1840s, Seine-Inférieure (Seine-Maritime), which boasted a large textile manufacturing sector, had, according to the British consul, '3000 or 4000 English workmen employed in the factories in the neighbourhood of Rouen'.[88] In Landerneau (Finistère), in a linen factory where the British played an important part, at least 400 Scots and Irish came for work in the 1840s and 1850s, although only 230 were actually hired (see Chapter 2, section 1.2).[89] In another linen factory in Haubourdin (Nord), 140–150 British were employed in 1848. At Dickson's in Coudekerque-Branche, 190 British workers at least came between 1837 and 1870.[90] And other examples could be quoted.

This—and other local data—does not enable us to draw any reliable conclusions about total numbers. If one adds up a few thousand workers in railway building, a few thousand in lace, maybe a thousand in linen, and a few hundred in cotton, iron, machinery, and mining, a very approximate estimate of 10,000 for the total cumulative number of British workers who worked in France in the 1840s can be proffered. If one extends this to the period from 1815 to 1870, 15,000 to 20,000 could be suggested, but again these are more like orders of magnitudes since, for instance, we still know little about the mobility of this workforce. At best

[85] PP. Select Committee on Railway Labourers, 1846. William Reed interviewed, 19 May 846, q. 327 and 328. *Railway Times*, 11 December 1841.

[86] AD Seine-et-Oise. 4 M I41: rapport sur la construction et l'exploitation des chemins de fer, 1842–1845: Arrondissement de Mantes. Surveillance des ateliers du chemin de fer—Tableau des communes dans lesquelles des ateliers sont établis, en renseignemens sur la nature et la composition de ces ateliers (undated).

[87] *Herapath*, 1 October 1842, 1025, ZPER 2/4.

[88] Featherstonehaugh to Palmerston, 1 March 1848, TNA, FO 27/818; Featherstonehaugh to Normanby, 4 March 1848, TNA, FO 146/350; Marquis of Normanby, *A Year of revolution. From a journal kept in Paris in 1848*, London, 1857, vol. 1, p. 231.

[89] Yves Blavier speaks of a total of 250–300 (*La société linière du Finistère. Ouvriers et entrepreneurs à Landerneau au XIXᵉ siècle*, Rennes, 1999, p. 90). But the records of the préfecture show at least 400 British and Irish applied for a 'permis de séjour' (AD Finistère, 4M 83 Surveillance des étrangers, undated).

[90] Odette Bonte, 'Coudekerque-Branche, les Dickson et la colonie d'Ecossais', *Revue de la Société dunkerquoise d'histoire et d'archéologie*, no. 26, November 1992, pp. 155–84.

we can get snapshots of migrant communities, but diachronic assessments have not been carried out. In Germany and Belgium, numbers were significantly below those of France, and may have reached a few hundred workers. In the rest of Europe (Norway, Finland, Italy, Spain, Russia, the Austrian Empire, the Ottoman Empire...), there were rarely more than a few dozen British workers.[91]

Were these migration flows large? In comparison with other flows from Britain in the same period, they were small. The whole period was one of huge population growth and increasing emigration. For example, in the 1815–52 period in Britain, 3.47 million passengers (including non-British) left UK ports for overseas destinations (excluding the Continent), and from 1853 to 1869, 2.68 million British left.[92] Labour emigration to the Continent was marginal, and as trans-oceanic emigration was becoming cheaper and easier, the relative share of those who went to the Continent was declining. This is substantiated by Pooley and Turnbull's sample study.

In the destination countries, the same could be said since the British accounted for a small, decreasing proportion of all migrants. Although the foreign popula-tion was not taken into account in the French census until 1851, other evidence suggests that the proportion of British-born workers reached a peak in the middle of the century. By 1851, France was home to 379,289 foreigners, including 57,061 Germans, 63,307 Italians, 128,103 Belgians, and only 20,357 Britons (5.36 per cent), many of whom were not workers (Table 1.2). In 1872, the British and Irish only totalled 26,003 (3.7 per cent) in a total foreign-born population of 740,668. In other words, the proportion of British people in the overall total of immigration to France was declining and would continue to do so. The British, although their gross numbers still increased, remained a tiny minority, unlike the Belgians, the Italians, and the Germans, those other neighbouring peoples who made up the bulk of the record-high numbers of immigrant workers in the late nineteenth century, before Portuguese, Spanish, and Algerian immigrants did so in the twentieth century.

However, if one considers not the gross number but the part played by immigrants in the industrial take-off of the places they settled in—that is, if one focuses on the economic dimension of this migration trend—British workers were crucial. As Sidney Pollard has already noted: 'There is no single important industry in any of the major continental regions that did not have British pioneers as entrepreneurs, mechanics, machine builders, skilled foremen and workmen, or suppliers of capital (and usually several of these combined) to set them going'.[93]

[91] Kristine Bruland, *British Technology and European Industrialization: The Norwegian Textile Industry in the Mid-Nineteenth Century*, Cambridge, 1989.

[92] H. Carrier and J. R. Jeffery, *External Migration: A Study of the Available Statistics, 1815–1950*, London, 1953; *Commission on Emigration and Other Population Problems, 1948–1954: Reports*, Dublin, 1956; Constantine and Harper, *op. cit.*, pp. 1–2.

[93] Sidney Pollard, *Peaceful Conquest: The Industrialization of Europe 1760–1970*, Oxford, 1981, p. 145.

Table 1.2 Population of France, including the British[94]

	1851	1861	1872	1881
Total population of France	35.8 m	37.3 m	35.4 m	37.7 m
British-born population	20,357	25,711	26,003	37,006
British proportion in France	0.56%	0.69%	0. 73%	0.98%
Number of foreigners in France	379,289	506,381	740,668	1,001,090
Proportion of foreigners in France	10.6%	13.5%	20.9%	26.6%
British proportion among foreigners	5.36%	5.08%	3.51%	3.7%

Historians of German industrialisation, such as J. J. Lee and Rainer Fremdling, have insisted on the importance of British labour to this process, especially in textiles.[95] In Norway, numbers were small—ninety-six British workers were employed in the textile industry up to 1870, not including those on short stays—but 'British workers and managers remained important beyond the early stages of industrialisation'.[96] The British labour migration of the half-century that followed the Napoleonic wars can therefore be summarised as small-scale, but high value. It bore some of the features of the mass migration of the industrial age, for instance in the case of the railways. But, above all, it involved skilled workers with high technological value.

5. Short or Long Distance, Temporary or Definitive: The Features of Migration

As early as 1885, geographer Ernst George Ravenstein argued that the bulk of all migration was made up of short-distance moves, including movement within national borders. He also developed a theory of step migration, according to which migration was often gradual and occurred step by step geographically.[97] Similarly, in his pioneering thesis on British labour migration, first published nearly a century ago, Arthur Redford argued that most migration flows were short distance. This insight has been expanded and elaborated by Dudley Baines and by the prosopography conducted by Colin Pooley and Jean Turnbull. Using

---

[94] Insee, 'Données historiques de la Statistique générale de France'.

[95] J. J. Lee, 'Labour in German Industrialization', in P. Mathias and M. Postan (eds.), *Cambridge Economic History of Europe*, vol. 7, part 1, Cambridge, 1978; Rainer Fremdling, 'The Puddler: A Craftsman's Skill and the Spread of a New Technology in Belgium, France and Germany', *Journal of European Economic History*, vol. 20, 1991, pp. 529–67; Rainer Fremdling, 'Transfer Patterns of British Technology to the Continent: The Case of the Iron Industry', *European Review of Economic History*, vol. 4, 2000, pp. 197–220.

[96] Bruland, *British Technology and European Industrialization*.

[97] E. G. Ravenstein, 'The Laws of Migration', *Journal of Statistical Society*, vol. 48, June 1885, pp. 167–235.

Redford's argument about the prevalence of short-distance (or short-wave) migration as a starting point, these historians discuss various types of migration and their relationship with each other, as well as trying to assess how internal migration and overseas emigration could be articulated.[98] During the industrial revolution, millions of Britons emigrated from the countryside to small towns, and from small towns to larger ones, in stages that seldom exceeded a few dozen miles.[99] For example, of the people who had moved to the three booming Lancashire towns of Manchester, Liverpool, and Bolton, a large majority came from Lancashire, Cheshire, and Ireland. The same was true for London, where most immigrants came from neighbouring counties. Hobsbawm's tramping artisan thesis focuses on a specific type of domestic migration: the organised 'tramping system' among the trades that worked through apprenticeship (compositors, brush makers, joiners, wool combers, masons, bakers...). By the middle of the century, however, institutional tramping was on the decline before it died out in the early twentieth century.[100] But domestic migration did not decline, and as the routes of several of the artisans mentioned in this book illustrate, tramping could easily extend to continental destinations.

There has also been a significant body of research on overseas emigration, to the United States (Charlotte Erickson), the Empire (Marjory Harper, Stephen Constantine), or both (James Belich, Eric Richards).[101] As a result, we know much more about flows previously studied mostly from the viewpoint of the receiving countries. British emigration has also been better understood in the context of European migration; that is to say, as part of the large transatlantic flows from the 1840s to the 1930s.[102] Although emigrating to America or to Australia could be the last stage of a series of shorter step-migrations, such a move definitely had distinctive features that made it a different experience. Until the 1870s, few expected to return from these journeys, although significant numbers eventually came home. In other words, emigrating across the ocean implied a break with a territory, with a community, and with loved ones. In Ireland, such departures were ritualised into 'wakes' known as the 'American wakes', even if the emigrants left for Australia—but not if they left for Britain or

---

[98] Arthur Redford, *Labour Migration in England: 1800–1850*, 2nd ed. revised by W. H. Chaloner, Manchester, 1964 [1926]; Dudley Baines, *Migration in a Mature Economy: Emigration and Internal Migration in England and Wales, 1861–1900*, Cambridge, 1985; Colin Pooley and Jean Turnbull, *Migration and Mobility in Britain since the Eighteenth Century*, London, 1998.

[99] See for instance Alison Light, *Common People: The History of an English family*, London, 2014.

[100] E. J. Hobsbawm, 'The Tramping Artisan', *Economic History Review*, vol. 3, no. 3, 1951, pp. 299–320.

[101] Charlotte Erickson, *Leaving England: Essays on British Emigration in the Nineteenth Century*, Ithaca, NY, 1994; Eric Richards, *Britannia's Children: Emigration from England, Scotland, Wales and Ireland since 1600*, London, 2004; James Belich, *Replenishing the Earth: The Settler Revolution and the Rise of the Anglo-World, 1783–1939*, Oxford, 2009; Harper and Constantine, *Migration and Empire*.

[102] Leslie Page Moch, *Moving Europeans: Migration in Western Europe since 1650* (Bloomington, IN, 2003); Klaus Bade, *Migration in European History*, Oxford, 2003; Dirk Hoerder, *Cultures in Contact: World Migrations in the Second Millennium*, Durham, NC, 2002.

Ireland. The process mirrored that of a funeral wake. After the emigrant made a round of visits to neighbours and talked with the priest, an all-night party was held with a mixture of joy and sadness in anticipation of departure to a far-off destination.[103] A convoy consisting of the family and members of the community would often accompany the emigrant to the boundary of the local area, which could later be a railway platform or the quayside of the docks.

As far as we know, no parallel ritual existed for migrants who went to the Continent. They often preserved many connections with their homeland. We have seen that lace workers often travelled back and forth, and the same applies to other groups. For instance, it took only a few days to travel to Landerneau from Dundee, where many of the flax workers came from. In the Société linière du Finistère, in the 1851 census, there were 116 Scots and Irish (including children) living in Landerneau and Pencran; in the 1840s and early 1850s, at least 400 applied for a temporary 'permis de séjour', while many came without applying, and children did not have to.[104] In May 1851 the director of the Société linière wrote to the director of the southwestern company of steamers, which operated ships between Southampton and Morlaix, asking for a discount: 'With all English and French companies, we obtain reductions on the ordinary fares for these workers, whose moves are quite important every year. We hope, Sir, that you will agree to the same discounts to those who will come with your company'.[105] As with domestic migration, there could be an important seasonal dimension.[106] Migrant workers formed an unstable population, with many making regular trips back and forth, or moving on to other places. The puddlers, who mostly came from South Wales, moved from ironworks to ironworks. So did the navvies, masons, and miners, who moved from one railway building site to another. Even the supposedly more sedentary lacemakers also travelled, as evidence from the routes they followed attests.

Were their moves temporary or permanent? As with internal migration in Britain, most of the moves to France were short-lived. In his major study on temporary migration in nineteenth-century France, Abel Châtelain showed the diversity of these flows, both to rural areas and increasingly to towns. They included Belgian harvesters who went to Normandy or later to the Paris area to harvest beetroot, masons from Creuse or Faucigny (Haute-Savoie), pedlars from Auvergne and

---

[103] Patrick Fitzgerald and Brian Lambkin, *Migration in Irish History, 1607–2007*, Basingstoke, 2008, pp. 17–18; Kerby A. Miller, *Emigrants and Exiles: Ireland and the Irish Exodus to North America*, Oxford, 1988, p. 556.

[104] AD Finistère. 4 M 48 (Étrangers) and 4 M 83 (Surveillance des étrangers).

[105] 'Avec toutes les compagnies anglaise et française, nous obtenons pour ces ouvriers, dont le mouvement est assez important chaque année, des réductions sur les prix ordinaires des places; nous pensons, Monsieur, que vous accorderez les mêmes avantages à ceux qui viendront par votre administration'. Archives municipales de Landerneau. AS35. Letter of 25 May 1851.

[106] Abel Châtelain, *Les migrants temporaires en France de 1800 à 1914*, Villeneuve d'Ascq, Publications de l'Université de Lille III, 1976, 2 vols.; Paul-André Rosental, *Les sentiers invisibles: espace, familles et migrations dans la France du 19e siècle*, Paris, 1999.

Oisans in the Alps, chimney sweeps and grinders from Savoy, pit sawyers from the Loire, Côte-d'Or, and Aveyron, lumber raftsmen who went along the Seine from Clamecy (Nièvre) to Paris, railway navvies, lumberjacks, beggars and prostitutes, and so on. Every year from the 1820s to the 1960s onion growers from Roscoff in Brittany crossed the Channel to sell their produce to the British.[107] It appears that regional migration was the most prevalent form.

As for the British migrants to the Continent, most saw their moves as temporary, for a period of two, three, or even five years. In the construction industry, they went back home when the building work ended. But in manufacturing, many eventually stayed for good and migrants became emigrants, even if they had not originally intended to. In this respect as well, the movements of British workers to the Continent can be compared more aptly with the short-distance moves that were so common for the working classes of Victorian Britain, rather than with transoceanic emigration. At the same time, moving to the Continent could be a first step towards a move farther away, as we shall see.

6. Wages across the Channel

We have seen that the labour migration at stake in this study cannot be separated from the industrial revolution. An ongoing debate among historians has focused on wages. Robert Allen has argued that it was the high cost of labour in relation to capital that fuelled technological innovation: manufacturers invested in machines because labour was expensive.[108] Based on a case study of hand-spinning, Jane Humphries and Benjamin Schneider have criticised this approach and contended that widespread low-wage, low-productivity employment was at the core of the factory system.[109] Indeed, migrants provide interesting case studies for wage comparison and may offer a new perspective on this debate. In other words, did workers emigrate because they could improve their wages, or did they emigrate just to find work?

In several cases, such as that of lacemakers, the wages of migrants overseas, although they outstripped those of the local workforce, turned out to be lower than those of workers in Britain. Often, lacemakers were not hired, and were instead migrant artisans who tried to circumvent the high French tariffs that protected the French market. In other sectors, individuals also moved to the Continent, but based on information received by word of mouth (see pp. 93–102).

---

[107] Léa Leboissetier, 'Les colporteurs étrangers et perçus comme étrangers au Royaume-Uni (années 1820–années 1970)', thesis, Lyon, Ecole normale supérieure.

[108] Robert C. Allen, *The British Industrial Revolution in Global Perspective*, Cambridge, 2009.

[109] Jane Humphries, 'The Lure of Aggregates and the Pitfalls of the Patriarchal Perspective: A Critique of the High Wage Economy Interpretation of the British Industrial Revolution', *Economic History Review*, vol. 66, no. 3, 2013, pp. 693–714. Also see Jane Humphries and Benjamin Schneider, 'Spinning the Industrial Revolution', *Economic History Review*, vol. 72, no. 1, 2019, pp. 126–55.

The British usually received higher wages than continental workers since they often met needs that could not be met locally. In iron, migrant British workers were highly skilled. In South Wales, puddlers earned between three and 4.4 times as much as the unskilled. In France, this could be up to seven or eight times the wages of the French unskilled labourers in the same sector. Even on piece rates, British puddlers got better wages.

In Fourchambault, Decazeville, and Alais (Alès today), wages were as in Table 1.3.

Wage differences were resented by the local workforce and could prompt protest/be raised in disturbances, as shown in Chapter 5. In the Manby and Wilson ironworks in Charenton in the mid-1820s, similar wage differences could be observed, as shown in Table 1.4.

This meant that the British outflanked the French workers in terms of both productivity and piece rates. Wilson, who then ran works in Le Creusot, was asked about the wages in Charenton in the mid-1820s:

Q: Were the superior wages given to the English puddlers compensated by a profit resulting from their work, or by a better work?
R: The compensation was not a better job but less waste in cast iron, and less fuel consumption. The difference in waste, for instance, was one twelfth: we therefore lost 40,000 francs training French workers. Today the French workers are worth the English workers. In our works in Le Creusot, there is now a perfect equality between the wages of both.[110]

Table 1.3 Wages in French ironworks (in francs and converted into shillings)

			Wages		Wages	French: British Ratio
1828	Fourchambault (Nièvre)	British puddler	13 F (10.4 s.)/ tonne	French puddler	9 F (7.2 s)/tonne	0.69
1828	Fourchambault (Nièvre)	British roller	7 F (5.6 s.)/ tonne	French roller	5 F (4 s.)/tonne	0.71
1833	Decazeville (Aveyron)	British puddler	7 F (5.6 s.)/ tonne	French puddler	5–6.5 F (4–5.2 s.)/ tonne	0.71–0.93
1857	Alais (Gard)	British roller	12 F (9.6 s)/ day	Unskilled French labourer	1.25 F (10 s.)/day	0.10

[110] 'D. La différence de salaire donnée aux pudleurs anglais était-elle compensée par un bénéfice résultat de plus de travail ou d'un meilleur travail?
R. La compensation n'est pas dans un meilleur travail, mais dans un beaucoup moindre déchet de fonte, et dans une moindre consommation de combustible; la différence du déchet, par exemple, était

Table 1.4 Wages in the Manby and Wilson ironworks in Charenton in the mid-1820s[111]

	Wages/tonne	Daily production	Wage/day
British puddler	14 F	800 kg	11.2 F (8.96 sh.)
French puddler	10 F	700 kg	7 F (5.6 s.)
French:British ratio	0.71	0.88	0.63

Even by 1828, for the ironworks of Terre-Noire in the Loire, the director spoke of wages a third higher for the ten workers or so he employed. But he added that at the start of the works, in 1823–4, there were as many as eighty British workers, and they earned twice as much as the French, for the same reasons.[112] All of these employers also mentioned that as some French workers were trained and caught up with their British counterparts, their wages increased to similar levels, as they did in the Le Creusot ironworks by 1828, where Wilson admitted that it was the wages of the British which had decreased, for instance to 8 F/tonne for the puddlers (i.e. a 20 per cent decrease in just three or four years).[113]

Another interesting comparison can be drawn with Welsh wages. In 1823, Achille Dufaud argued that puddlers and rollers were better paid in France than in Wales where 'a good puddler or roller only earned now, while working hard, £1 to £1 and 2 sh. a week'.[114] In Charenton at the same time, a puddler earned £2.7 a week, and in Fourchambault about £2.5/week, which equated to at least twice as much. Comparing purchasing power is more difficult, but this substantiates the thesis according to which emigration could be a self-improving strategy. It also corroborates the low-wage economy thesis on the British industrial revolution.

In railway building, a large section of the migrant workforce was considered unskilled. The British received better wages because of their higher productivity, as on building sites undertaken by British entrepreneur William Mackenzie (see Table 1.5).

Thus, in railway building, the French:British ratio—that is, the proportion of wages received by French workers compared to their British counterparts—varied from about 60 per cent for skilled workers like the miners to 75 per cent for the unskilled. Even in more traditional trades like carpentry, the rate could be as high as 82 per cent, but there were no industries where equality was reached.

---

d'un douzième aussi avons-nous perdu 40,000 francs à former des ouvriers français. Aujourd'hui les ouvriers français valent les ouvriers anglais. Aussi, dans notre établissement du Creusot, y a-t-il maintenant parfaite égalité dans le salaire des uns et des autres…'.

Ministère du commerce et des manufactures, *Enquête sur les fers*, 1829, p. 71.

[111] *Ibid.*, p. 71.   [112] Ibid., pp. 143–4.   [113] Ibid., p. 71.

[114] 'Nous payons et payerons longtemps toutes les main-d'œuvre beaucoup plus cher qu'en Galles, un bon puddleur ou un lamineur n'y gagne maintenant, en travaillant ferme, que 1£ à 1£2 sh par semaine', letter from Achille Dufaud, 19 June 1823, in Thuillier, *Georges Dufaud*, p. 226.

Table 1.5 Wages in railway building in France in the 1840s

	British	French	French: British ratio
1842 Labourers on the Poissy railroad	4–5 F/day (3.2–4 s.)	2.5–3 F/day (2–2.4 s.)	0.6–0.63
1841 Carpenters in Bezons[115]	5.5–6 F/day (4.4–4.8 s.)	4.5 F/day (3.6 s.)	0.75–0.82
1848 Miners at Hardelot tunnel on Amiens and Boulogne railway	7 F/day (5.6 s.)	4 F/day (3.2 s.)	0.57
1848 Labourers[116]	4 F/day (3.2 s.)	3 F/day (2.4 s.)	0.75

When interviewed by the Select Committee on Railway Labourers, one of the directors of the Paris and Rouen railway concurred:

Q 329. Were they better workmen than the French?—They did more work.
Q 330. What was the proportion, do you know?—At first, I think the Englishmen did nearly double, and received double wages.[117]

We shall come back to this issue, but the question of the higher productivity of British workers is a difficult one. As in other sectors, the most skilled jobs were performed by British workers, for example mining the numerous tunnels:

Q 341. Who were employed upon this difficult work, the English or French?—English chiefly; the French labourers drew away the stuff or wound it up the shafts, but the mining was done by Englishmen.[118]

Joseph Locke, the engineer who conducted the works on the Paris–Rouen–Le Havre railway, also claimed that 'Three or four francs a day were then expended more profitably than two francs on a Frenchman'.[119] For less skilled jobs, where British workers were better paid, several factors could be mentioned. In terms of navvying, the British had a wealth of experience in canal-digging, meaning that they had developed a work culture in the sector with teams of workers who knew how to operate effectively with the right techniques. Also, 'tools in use abroad

---

[115] Pay sheets for work at Bezons, Maisons, Rolleboise, Villers and Mantes, October–December 1841, B2L3 and C2L2, and On the Poissy Contract, 12 March–8 April 1842, B4R 1/2/3, ICE, quoted in David Brooke, *The Diary of William Mackenzie*, pp. 12–13.

[116] David Brooke, *The Diary of William Mackenzie*, p. 237.

[117] PP. Select Committee on Railway Labourers, 1846. William Reed, 19 May 1846.   [118] Ibid.

[119] Joseph Devey, *The Life of Joseph Locke, Civil Engineer*, London, 1861, p. 167.

were of a most inferior description', the biographer of railway entrepreneur Thomas Brassey noted: 'The French used wooden spades. Their barrow was of a bad form, and they had very inferior pickaxes'.[120] Joseph Locke said something similar: 'Discarding the wooden shovels and basket-sized barrows of the Frenchmen, [the British labourers] used the tools which modern art had suggested, and which none but the most expert and robust could wield'.[121] Locke also explained differences in productivity with reference to workers' diets, an aspect we'll come back to (Chapter 4).

But some reasons for employing British workers were given less prominence. Locke had first tried to use French contractors, but they 'demanded prices nearly double those which were asked by Englishmen, and that the work when done cd not be half so much relied upon even for safety or durability'.[122] For later contracts, once a French workforce was trained, there was no recourse to British labour. When a very cheap workforce could be recruited locally, as in India, only engineers, foremen, and skilled workers came from Britain, while millions of workers were hired in the areas where the railways were built.[123]

In linen, two comparisons with the wages that the British migrant workers earned can be made: that with wages earned by the local workforce, and that with the wages in Britain. Whereas the wages of skilled British working men could be much higher than those of the local workforce, those of migrant women were much lower. The usual wage difference that could be observed in Britain also prevailed in France, for instance in linen in Landerneau (Finistère, in Brittany) (Table 1.6).

Although wage disparities between skilled British artisans and French ones should be noted (the French smith earned only 59 per cent of the wages of the

Table 1.6 Day wages in Landerneau (Finistère) in 1859[124]

Spinners (Scottish/Irish women)	1.25 F
Flax carders (British men)	4 F
Mechanics (British men)	4.25 F
Carpenters (French men)	2 F
Masons (French men)	2.25 F
Joiners (French men)	2.25 F
Smiths (French men)	2.5 F
Tailors (French men)	1.75 F
Tailoresses (French women)	1 F

[120] Arthur Helps, *Life and Labours of Thomas Brassey*, p. 80.
[121] Joseph Locke, 'Presidential Address of Joseph Locke, M.P., January 12, 1858', *Minutes of the Proceedings of the Institution of Civil Engineers*, vol. 17, 1858, p. 143.
[122] Devey, *The Life of Joseph Locke*, p. 164.
[123] Ian Kerr, *Building the Railways of the Raj: 1850–1900*, Oxford, 1995.
[124] AD Finistère, 6M 1039 Salaires industriels—1853–92.

Table 1.7 Wages in linen in England, Belfast, and Ghent, Belgium, in pence (for convenience, day wages are transcribed into pence)[125]

Description of workers	Day wages (11.5 hours) England	Day wages (11.5 hours) Belfast	Day wages (11 hours) Ghent	Ghent: England ratio
Spreaders	15–18	10	11.75	0.65–0.78
First drawing	12–15	8.5	8.5	0.57–0.71
Second drawing	12–15	8.5	8.5	0.57–0.71
Roving	13–18	9	9.25	0.51–0.71
Carding	12–18	7.5–9.5	9.25	0.51–0.77
Spinner	12–16	10	8.5	0.53–0.71
Doffer	8	5.5	4.75	0.59
Reeler (piece work)	12–17	10–11	9.25	0.54–0.77
Dyer	30–36	16	15	0.42–0.50
Bundler	30–36	17.5	17	0.47–0.50
Hackler (roughing for machine)	18	16	19	1.06
Overlooker	54	42	28.5	0.53

British mechanic), gender differences mattered even more: French tailoresses earned only 57 per cent of what French tailors earned. As for the Scottish and Irish female spinners, their wages were indeed 25 per cent above those of French female workers, but always remained inferior to those of men, both French and British. They only accounted for 31 per cent of those of the British carders, who were often their husbands or brothers.

The comparison with the wages of workers in Britain does not suggest that pay was superior overseas. James Emerson Tennent, a British politician and traveller who visited Belgium, noted that, in Ghent, the 'quantity produced, per day, was quite equal to that of English spinners, and their wages much the same as those paid in Ireland, and somewhat less than the English'.[126] Indeed, the wages of most Belgian linen workers ranged from half to three quarters of those of English workers, with the exception of hecklers (Table 1.7).

It could be argued that the British workers worked more, as they worked 11.5 hours instead of eleven in Ghent, but the wage gap between both countries cannot be explained by this 5 per cent difference. Differences could also be noted between Landerneau and Dundee. For instance, a female flax spinner earned 7.5 shillings/week in Dundee in 1856,[127] while a similar worker earned 7.5 F/week; that is, 6.7 sh./week in Landerneau (Table 1.6).

---

[125] Tennent, *Belgium*, vol. 1, p. 68.   [126] James Emerson Tennent, *Belgium*, vol. 1, p. 68.
[127] *Dundee Advertiser*, 26 December 1856, quoted in Bruce Lenman, Charlotte Lythe, and Enid Gauldie, *Dundee and Its Textile Industry*, Dundee, 1969, p. 107.

In addition, wages were dependent on economic cycles, especially for female spinners who could be replaced with local workers, as this example in Haubourdin showed: 'during the course of the last year, the Company have taken occation as opertunity [sic] served them, either when a French girl was thought to be sufficiently taught, or Fleamish girl could be had cheaper, to reduce their wages from 12 francs to 10 per week and even to turn many of them away altogether, without even paying them any portion of the 50 Francs which they have retained in their own hands of the wages of each one'.[128]

It is therefore difficult to draw conclusions from the comparison of wages. Such comparisons are problematic as similar wages could mean a better standard of living in France. The calculations made by Angus Maddison suggest that GDP per head was, by 1820, superior in the UK (1707 in 1990 international dollars) to that in Germany (1058), France (1230), or Belgium (1319).[129] But these are averages that do not help to provide answers regarding the situation of migrant workers. National averages also ignore regional differences, which could be important. On top of that, at issue presumably was the reliability of employment. The British economy was unstable in these years, and for a British worker lower wage rates overseas might not mean lower income overall if there was greater certainty of employment. Rather than significant and lasting differences between the wages of British workers in Britain and their wages on the Continent, what emerges from this survey is evidence of wage differences between skilled and 'unskilled' workers, and between men and women, regardless of their nationalities. We'll return to this when addressing the part played by women and children in the migration process.

7. Conclusion

In the early hours of 29 June 1816, Heathcoat's Loughborough factory was attacked by the Luddites, who destroyed fifty-five lacemaking frames and burned the supply of finished lace. Heathcoat, who had bought a six-storey textile factory in Tiverton, Devon, the year before, decided to move there with his family.[130] Several workers went with him: they walked the 200 miles along the Fosse way, an old Roman road (see Map 1.1)—one of the common domestic moves millions of workers made during the industrial revolution. From Nottingham, Calais was not much further than Tiverton, and some of the Loughborough workers also subsequently moved to Calais; some even went on to move to Australia. Heathcoat himself conducted business in Paris and Saint-Quentin in the 1820s while

---

[128] TNA. FO 146 350 (Consular Correspondence): Letter of British workers in Haubourdin to the ambassador in Paris, 21 March 1850.

[129] Angus Maddison, *The World Economy: A Millennial Perspective*, Paris, 2001.

[130] D. E. Varley, 'John Heathcoat (1783–1861), Founder of the Machine-made Lace Industry', *Textile History*, vol. 1, no. 1, 1968, pp. 2–45.

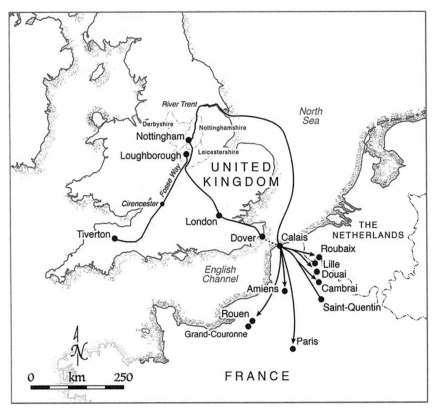

Map 1.1 The emigration of British lacemakers (1815–70).

managing his factory in Tiverton. This example and many others illustrate that there was no qualitative difference between moves within the country and from Britain to the Continent. Labour migration flows to the Continent in the period 1815–70 should be considered alongside other migration flows, especially domestic, short-wave flows. Temporary and seasonal labour migration also existed between Britain and the Continent in the first half of the century, much in the same way as they existed between Europe and the Americas in the later nineteenth century, or between the UK and South Africa, with Cornish miners moving back and forth, depending on the dynamics of each economy.[131]

Despite these parallels, there were important differences between moving to the Continent and moving to Dundee, Manchester, Merthyr Tydfil, or London. For small-businessmen and artisans, it could be a way to circumvent duties and get access to the continental markets. It could also be a way of palliating labour shortages in their home regions. Lastly, in some cases it might have been a way

[131] Philip Payton, *The Cornish Overseas: The Epic Story of Cornwall's Great Emigration*, Exeter, 2019.

to improve one's position and standard of living. For instance, as we have seen with the lacemakers, many went to the Continent to move away from the cut-throat competition and the crises in the Nottinghamshire industry. When they worked on the Continent, British workers were often paid more than local workers, but this was on account of their rare skills, and their continental wages seldom exceeded those they could make in Britain. Finally, such wages could fluctuate since they corresponded to what capitalists were ready to invest to stimulate industrial transition. In the longer term, wage differences tended to disappear: they were not set in stone, but rather represented small labour market adjustments. Thus, while most of the labour moves to the Continent were related to the technical lead of the UK at that time, each sector had some defining traits which should not be overlooked. These specific sectors of industry and employment will be examined next.

2

'The three principal manufactories at Paris are conducted by Englishmen'

The Sectors of Workers' Emigration

In Liège, a seemingly dull archival collection, the Mahaim Cockerill papers, became caught up in the turmoil of the twentieth century.[1] Ernest Mahaim (1865–1938) was an early professor at the University of Liège, where he taught law, political economy, and statistics. He was impressed by workers' rebellions in Liège and Charleroi and became interested in the legal protection of workers. His attention soon turned to the manufacturing history of the Belgian city, and the industrial empire that the Cockerill family had built in its suburbs. One aspect of this history that Mahaim wanted to understand was the practicalities of Cockerill's successful mechanisation in the early nineteenth century, in the early days of the venture.[2] The Cockerill firm lent Mahaim many records, some of which he kept at the university. When he died in 1938, he had had a long career not just as an academic but also as a diplomat. After the Great War, Maiham helped found the International Labour Organization, became a minister for labour in 1921, and participated in many organisations.[3] When Germany occupied Belgium in 1940, many records were seized: the Mahaim papers were transferred, probably to Berlin. In 1945, they were seized by the Soviet army and taken to Moscow, where they were discreetly kept in the Special Records of the Soviet Union (Osoby). The University of Liège had no knowledge of this until 1992, after the end of the Soviet Union, when a Belgian research mission in Moscow identified them. The university requested the documents from Russia. This process was completed in 2003, when Moscow returned the documents to the University of Liège, where they are now housed.[4]

---

[1] The quote in this chapter's title is from evidence given by John Martineau, engineer, to the Select Committee on Artisans and Machinery, 17 February 1824.

[2] Ernest Mahaim, 'Les débuts de l'établissement John Cockerill à Seraing. Contribution à l'histoire des origines de la grande industrie au Pays de Liège', *Vierteljahrschrift für Social- und Wirtschaftsgeschichte, 1905*, 4. Heft, pp. 627–48.

[3] Fabienne Kéfer, 'Ernest Mahaim: 1865-1892-1919-1938', February 2019, https://www.news.uliege.be/upload/docs/application/pdf/2019-02/ernest_mahaim.pdf.

[4] Eric Geerkens, 'Avant-Propos', in Nicole Caulier-Mathy and Nicole Haesenne-Peremans, 'Inventaire des archives Ernest Mahaim', Université de Liège, 2011, https://orbi.uliege.be/bitstream/2268/108622/1/Mahaim.pdf.

Artisans Abroad: British Migrant Workers in Industrialising Europe, 1815–1870. Fabrice Bensimon, Oxford University Press.
© Fabrice Bensimon 2023. DOI: 10.1093/oso/9780198835844.003.0003

In some ways, the collection's content is just as fascinating as its history. It relates to the very beginnings of the Cockerill works. William Cockerill (1759–1832) was a mechanic born in Haslingden, Lancashire, who made jennies; his wife was a spinner. In 1794 he went to St Petersburg to work for Catherine the Great. When the empress regnant of all Russia died in 1796, Cockerill was jailed for a minor infraction and escaped to Sweden, where he worked as an engineer and tried to build locks on a canal. Eventually hearing of the woollen industry in Verviers and Liège, he went there, probably in the hope of making machinery. In 1799, he began making machines for the spinning and the carding of wool in Verviers for cloth manufacturers Simonis and Biolley. They wanted exclusive access to Cockerill's machines, but William Cockerill Junior (1784–1840s) and Cockerill's son-in-law James Hodson (1768–1833) soon competed with Simonis and Biolley. By 1801, William Cockerill had devised his 'assortiment'; that is, a water-powered combination of engines including a scribbler for rough carding, a carder for fine carding, a roving-jack, and four jennies for spinning. Within a few years, Cockerill became a very successful producer of these 'assortiments', which he sold for 12,000 francs. These machines were sold across Europe under French domination, and Cockerill was protected from British competition by the war.[5] By 1812, Cockerill produced about half of the woollen textiles of the country and employed 2,000 workers to make highly successful machines.

In these early years of Cockerill's venture, Britain and France were at war. Ironically, this turned out to be crucial to the success of the Cockerill enterprise, which flourished under French, Dutch (1815–30), and then Belgian administration (from 1830). Verviers and Liège were part of the French annexations (1795), during which the British were banned. But Cockerill benefited from the fact that he was loyal to the French authorities and applied for French citizenship, which he got in 1810. During the fifteen years or so before 1815, Cockerill could thus market his machines in France and its Napoleonic Empire, while being protected from the competition of British manufacturers. During this period, he went from being a mechanic to an entrepreneur; when the war ended, his position was such that it could withstand British competition and foster further expansion. From 1815, Cockerill also made steam-powered machines. Cockerill senior withdrew and died in 1832. He was succeeded by his younger son John Cockerill (1790–1840), who took the company to a new level.

In 1817, the Cockerills acquired a castle in Seraing, near Liège, from which the Cockerill industrial empire was to grow. Within three years, William Cockerill produced his own raw material and owned a coalmine in Liège. By 1823, he had

[5]   Gérard Gayot, 'La classe ouvrière saisie par la révolution industrielle à Verviers, 1800–1810', *Revue du Nord*, vol. 4, no. 347, 2002, pp. 633–66; W. O. Henderson, *Britain and Industrial Europe*, Liverpool, 1954; Pierre Lebrun, Marinette Bruwier, Jan Dhondt, and Georges Hansotte, *Essai sur la révolution industrielle en Belgique, 1770–1847* (*Histoire quantitative*, 1ère série, t. II, vol. 1), Brussels, Académie royale de Belgique, 1979.

built a blast furnace relying on coke, supervised by a British engineer, Mushet. Cockerill specialised in steam machines, and after producing for coastal boats he began to supply huge machines to the Dutch Navy. By 1835 he had produced a first locomotive and rails. As a result, Belgium played a key role in the industrialisation of Europe, and until 1843 much of the cotton machinery that was sold across Europe was made in Belgium rather than Britain.[6] When Victor Hugo visited Liège in 1838, he wrote: 'Liège has no longer the enormous cathedral of the *prince-bishops*, built by the illustrious Bishop Notger in year 1000, and demolished in 1795 by—no one can tell whom; but it can boast of the iron-works of Mr. Cockerill'.[7] Hugo was impressed:

> A wild and violent noise comes from this teeming mass of workers. On stepping down from the coach, my curiosity led me to approach one of these dens. There, I gazed in wonder at the sight of industry. It provided a truly prodigious spectacle, to which the solemnity of the night hour lent an almost supernatural aspect. Under the action of steam, those monstrous contraptions made of copper, sheet-iron or bronze that we call machines burst into a sudden and horrific life. Wheels, saws, boilers, rolling mills, cylinders, scales—all gave out terrifying sounds—roaring, hissing, grinding, groaning, barking, yelping, their jaws chewing granite to pieces, twisting sheets of iron, tearing bronze apart. As the blackened workmen hammered away at them, they would let out the occasional howl of pain in the scorching heat of the mill, as if they were hydras and dragons tormented in hell by demons.[8]

To revert to the early days of the venture and the part played by artisans, the war between Napoleon and Britain did not prevent William Cockerill from returning to Britain between 1803 and 1806, and again in 1815.[9] The Lancashire mechanic had become a wealthy entrepreneur. As was usual with British industrialists in Europe, he preserved connections with his hometown and bought estate property in Haslingden in 1804 (£1,050) and 1819 (£2,500), as well as houses. These

---

[6] Pollard, *Peaceful Conquest*, p. 89.

[7] 'Liège n'a plus l'énorme cathédrale des princes-évêques bâtie par l'évêque Notger en l'an 1000, et démolie en 1795 par on ne sait qui; mais elle a l'usine de M. Cockerill'. Victor Hugo, *Le Rhin. Lettres à un ami*, vol. 1, Paris Librairie Olllendorf, 1906 [1842] (translation by Emmanuel Roudaut and Nigel Quayle).

[8] 'Un bruit farouche et violent sort de ce chaos de travailleurs. J'ai eu la curiosité de mettre pied à terre et de m'approcher d'un de ces antres. Là, j'ai admiré véritablement l'industrie. C'est un beau et prodigieux spectacle, qui, la nuit, semble emprunter à la tristesse solennelle de l'heure quelque chose de surnaturel. Les roues, les scies, les chaudières, les laminoirs, les cylindres, les balanciers, tous ces monstres de cuivre, de tôle et d'airain que nous nommons des machines et que la vapeur fait vivre d'une vie effrayante et terrible, mugissent, sifflent, grincent, râlent, reniflent, aboient, glapissent, déchirent le bronze, tordent le fer, mâchent le granit, et, par moments, au milieu des ouvriers noirs et enfumés qui les harcèlent, hurlent avec douleur dans l'atmosphère ardente de l'usine, comme des hydres et des dragons tourmentés par des démons dans un enfer'. Ibid.

[9] Henderson, *Britain and Industrial Europe*, p. 6.

connections probably facilitated the hiring of skilled staff. Though Cockerill recruited many local workers in Liège, he also relied on a few Britons. James Hodson, a Nottingham-born mechanic, arrived in 1802. He married one of Cockerill's daughters, Nancy (1782–1817), and made machines. Also in 1802, Cockerill's son John came to Liège and, aged twelve or thirteen, immediately started working as a mechanic.

So did Charles James (1787–1837), who worked as a mechanic for his father before withdrawing to Aachen where he enjoyed a bourgeois family life. In 1811, Charles James journeyed across France setting up the 'assortiments' (see Map 2.1). Through his correspondence with his family, we can follow his travels. Alongside considerations of health and complaints about not receiving letters, Charles James narrated the grandeur and hardships of his work. The job was difficult because France had no manufacturing industry and no industrial culture: 'I am in a strange country to set up machines in [sic] they know nothing of manufactory and to

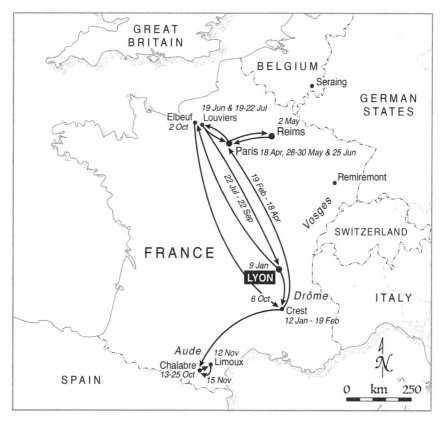

Map 2.1 In 1811, Charles James Cockerill travelled across France to set up 'assortiments'.

teach them is useless',[10] he wrote on 12 January 1811, while he was in Crest, a small village in very rural Drôme to set up an assortiment. The job was also full of glory because men like Charles James were bringing the industrial revolution and prosperity to destitute areas: 'I yesterday received all the honors intended for me'.[11] In another letter, he added:

> To set up machines in this Country, God knows, is no small object they ought to have learnt to manufacture ere they ordered machines. They do to be sure make as great an ado of me as if I was a prince, but I am either too weak or too humoursome to enjoy their kind favours. Wish they cd bestow them on yours and leave me a few moments' tranquility.[12]

After Crest, Charles James set off for Lyon, reached Paris, and went to Reims, then he went back to Paris, Louviers in June and July, and Lyon again in September. Such journeys could include many unexpected stages for repairs, for example in Elbeuf in October:

> Dear father,
>
> You will be astonished to hear from me at Elbeuf. I meant to write you the Day after my last but an extraordinary Letter from L'Ecalier, informing me that the machines wd not work any longer forced me to come here again, to put them to Rights. I remain a week with them.[13]

Cockerill then headed to Crest again before going to Chalabre near Carcassonne and Limoux in November. The area was again very rural, but Cockerill was competing with other machine-makers who made cheaper if probably inferior machines: 'I am surrounded with Mechanicks or better said Quacks', he wrote to his father.[14] Charles James was thus not just a mechanic who set up and repaired machines: he was also a travelling salesman. The correspondence kept by Cockerill helps us follow the routes of several 'monteurs de mécanique' (machine fitters) who travelled across Europe. The example of Cockerill shows that such artisans could spend many months very far from their base. They relied on a network of communications in which the post was central, with all its hazards: 'I don't know what to attribute your silence to, I scarcely know where to write you', Cockerill

---

[10] Fonds Mahaim Cockerill, Université de Liège, 295, letter from Charles James Cockerill in Crest (Drôme) to his mother, 12 January 1811.

[11] Fonds Mahaim Cockerill, Université de Liège, 292, letter from Charles James Cockerill in Crest (Drôme) to William O'Brien in Liège, 15 February 1811.

[12] Fonds Mahaim Cockerill, Université de Liège, 360, letter from Charles James Cockerill in Crest (Drôme) to his parents, 23 January 1811.

[13] Ibid., 400: letter from Charles to his parents, 2 October 1811.

[14] Fonds Mahaim Cockerill, Université de Liège, 292, letter from Charles James Cockerill in Chalabre (Aude) to William O'Brien in Liège, 25 October 1811.

wrote to his father, adding: 'I have twenty letters for you'.[15] Though Cockerill and his fellow machine fitters travelled in coaches and not on the tramp, their condition on the move was not a comfortable one. Like the puddlers and a few others, the machine fitters were seen as disposable despite being experts in their field. They were the indispensable artisans without whom the new techniques of the industrial revolution could not be circulated.

*

The Cockerills were pioneers in the industrialisation of the Continent. They innovated in the sectors that were most dynamic in the period 1815–48, and where British input was critical: textile and textile machinery, iron, the railways. These sectors are the focus of this chapter. The first major industry that shaped continental labour migration was Cockerill's initial sector: textile and textile machinery; that is, the main engine of the industrial revolution. As we have also seen, thousands of lace workers from the East Midlands, especially Nottinghamshire, went to northern France, especially to the Calais area (see pp. 28–39). This craft, hand-worked industry shifted to factory production in the 1850s, but British input persisted until the 1870s. From the 1840s, significant flows also took place in linen and jute, as several works relied on British machinery and workers, especially women from Dundee. A few workers, mostly foremen and mechanics, also worked in wool combing (section 1). The second sector where British input was critical was iron and steel. South Wales developed a dynamic iron industry. Several continental ironmasters set up 'forges à l'anglaise' for which they were willing to hire British puddlers or rollers despite high costs, as we have seen with Georges Dufaud. In mining, some smaller-scale recruitments were also organised (section 2). The third sector considered in this chapter is the railways. British engineers and investors were instrumental in the early stages of European railway construction, in France, Belgium, Italy, and Spain. More modest numbers of railway mechanics also came for longer periods (section 3). Lastly, this chapter considers the trajectories of individual artisans—a leather-dresser, a shoemaker, a gas mechanic, and a goldsmith—who did not work in the staple sectors of industrialisation but who emigrated to the Continent for various reasons, including economic ones (section 4). Section 5 concludes.

This chapter demonstrates the diversity and specificities of labour migration flows in the first two thirds of the century. Iron, steel, and machinery involved small numbers of migrants and relied on the technological gap between Britain and the Continent. In linen and jute, the workers included not just mechanics but also dozens or even hundreds of operators, usually hired by manufacturers. In lace, labour migration flows differed markedly, as most emigrants were artisans or

---

[15] Fonds Mahaim Cockerill, 2 May 1811, from Charles James Cockerill in Rheims to his father William in Remiremont (Vosges).

small-scale lace makers. In the railways, numbers swelled to thousands of itinerant navvies, at a time when British entrepreneurs were contracting to build long lines on the Continent. These specific flows also often entailed different geographical origins and different destinations.

1. Textile and Textile Machinery

It is known that textiles have played an important part in the making of trans-national networks of economic and cultural exchange.[16] No history of textiles can be wholly local. The part played by textiles, and especially cotton, as a driver in the British industrial revolution is also well known. It was likewise a driving force in the industrialisation of the Continent. The diffusion of British technology across the Channel has been addressed by W. O. Henderson and Sidney Pollard.[17] By the late eighteenth century there was virtually no modern machinery on the Continent. After the wars, the British started smuggling some, although legal exports gradually became the rule. Everywhere, British machines were bought. Whereas in linen, for instance, hundreds of Scottish and Irish workers were hired, in cotton and wool staff imports from Britain were usually limited to mechanics and foremen. However, each sector of the textile industry on the Continent was transformed by British input.

1.1 Cotton: The Engine of Industrialisation

The spread of the cotton industry from Lancashire and Cheshire to the Continent and the rest of the world followed some common patterns. As Pollard has argued, development took place regionally rather than on a national scale. These areas all had an early history of domestic manufacturing and cottage industries organised and mastered by merchants, for example in Saxony, Normandy, Holland, Alsace, Switzerland, Catalonia, and Lombardy. In some areas, cotton industrialised first through spinning; in others, it grew out of a printing industry. Everywhere capital was mobilised. 'Everywhere', as Sven Beckert notes, 'British entrepreneurs, British expertise, and British artisans played a crucial role'.[18]

The European businesses that were established before the blockade which, from November 1806 to April 1814, protected continental manufacturers from British competition usually took the lead. Even then, some British-born played a part. As

---

[16] Sven Beckert, *Empire of Cotton: A New History of Global Capitalism*, London, 2015; Giorgio Riello, *Cotton: The Fabric That Made the Modern World*, Cambridge, 2015; Beverly Lemire and Giorgio Riello (eds.), *Dressing Global Bodies: The Political Power of Dress in World History*, London, 2020.

[17] Henderson, *Britain and Industrial Europe*; Pollard, *Peaceful Conquest*.

[18] Beckert, *Empire of Cotton*, p. 153.

the cotton business set up in Saint-Rémy-sur-Avre in Normandy by Henry Sykes and the Waddingtons illustrates, Normandy, especially the area around Rouen, was one of these early clusters for the cotton industry (Chapter 1).[19] John Holker had introduced the mechanisation of cotton in the mid-eighteenth century, and by the middle of the nineteenth century there would be 110,000 handloom weavers and 40,000 in factories in the area. The Waddingtons were one of the early cotton businesses that developed there. Henry Sykes had set up a mechanised cotton mill as early as 1792 in Saint-Rémy-sur-Avre. By 1800 he employed 200 people and in 1807 he obtained French nationality. In 1788, Sykes's single daughter married William Waddington, a London banker who belonged to a Lancashire middle-class family. In 1812, the ageing Sykes managed to get his son-in-law William Waddington (1751–1818) and his grandson Thomas (1792–1869) to Saint-Rémy-sur-Avre, after he had been trained in a Lancashire spinning mill—a practice reminiscent of Cockerill's, though the middle-class background of Sykes and the Waddingtons differed from Cockerill's working-class origins. After Sykes's death the Waddingtons inherited in 1814 and Thomas ran the business with his brother Frederic. By 1828 their responsibilities had been distributed in the following way: Frederic ran the mill in Saint-Rémy, while Thomas settled in Rouen to ensure that they were supplied with good-quality cotton and to oversee the sale of their products. Thomas's sons William Henry (1826–94) and Richard (1838–1913) were partly educated in Britain but also made their careers in Normandy. At its peak, their company had four factories and a thousand workers—it was by far the first manufacturing business in their département. It still hired British workers to operate new machines and to train the domestic workforce (see p. 234). Waddington also became a paternalistic business, with a friendly society, a kindergarten, a primary school, working-class housing, a fire brigade, and a music band.[20] By the late nineteenth century, the Waddingtons belonged to the upper layers of the bourgeoisie. Under the Third Republic, William Henry and Richard became MPs and then senators. William was a minister in several governments and was briefly prime minister in 1879; he later acted as French ambassador in London. The Waddingtons stuck to their Protestant denomination. They remained bilingual until the twentieth century. Their business declined in the twentieth century and ended in 1961.[21]

There were families like the Waddingtons and the Cockerills in other parts of Europe, albeit often on a smaller scale. Kristine Bruland has researched the British

[19] Geneviève Dufresne-Seurre, *Les Waddington, une dynastie de cotonniers en Eure-et-Loir: 1792–1961*, Chartres, 2011.

[20] AD Eure-et-Loir. 6 J 13. Album souvenir des établissements Waddington, http://rdv-histoire.ac-orleans-tours.fr/php5/2007/departements/28/waddington-diaporama.pdf.

[21] Dufresne-Seurre, *Les Waddington*. The company records are kept by the Archives départementales d'Eure-et-Loir (6J 1–20).

businesses that settled in Norway.[22] Jarmo Peltola has done similar work on James Finlayson (c.1772–c.1852), a British engineer who first moved to St Petersburg in 1817 to found a textile factory before creating the cotton industry in Tampere in the Grand Duchy of Finland with the help of the Russian state. In all cases, they relied on artisans from Britain, often from Lancashire. In Sweden, John Barker (1791–1854), who established his engineering workshop in Tegelvick, Stockholm, in 1834, pioneering Sweden's modern cotton industry, had first been one of Cockerill's British artisans before leaving his business after 1830.[23] As these examples show, British input in the cotton industry was multi-faceted: it included entrepreneurship, capital, technology, and machinery. For technology to be conveyed and for modern machinery to be set up and operated, skilled workers were needed. Therefore, everywhere on the Continent, the spread of the cotton industry initially relied on Lancashire artisans.

1.2 Flax-Workers from Dundee and Ulster

Linen followed a different path to development.[24] It had been a traditional proto-industry in the Flanders, but local entrepreneurs did not improve the technology. Instead, it was in Britain that linen was first spun by machines—though innovation occurred quite late, in the 1830s. A wet spinning machine had been patented by Philippe de Girard in 1810.[25] But it was Peter Fairbairn, the engineer who modified Girard's innovations, and Marshalls, Britain's premier flax spinning firm, both of Leeds, that benefited most from Girard's work. Unlike cotton, flax was grown locally in many areas of northwest Europe, though the most successful businesses had to import some eventually.

In Scotland, Dundee's association with linen was long-standing, and had been consolidated over the course of the eighteenth century as part of the tendency in east-central Scotland—backed by the state-sponsored Board of Trustees for Fisheries and Manufactures—to specialise in the production of coarse linen cloth as opposed to cotton, which was eventually concentrated in the west of Scotland.[26] While Scotland was an important area for the growth of linen, Dundee specialised in the machine-made production of linen, and later jute.

---

[22] Kristine Bruland, *British Technology and European Industrialization: The Norwegian Textile Industry in the Mid-Nineteenth Century*, Cambridge, 1989.

[23] Jarmo Peltola, 'The British Contribution to the Birth of the Finnish Cotton Industry (1820–1870)', *Continuity and Change*, vol. 34, 2019, pp. 63–89.

[24] Fabrice Bensimon and Christopher A. Whatley, 'The Thread of Migration: A Scottish-French Linen and Jute Works and Its Workers in France, c. 1845–c. 1870', *Journal of Migration History*, vol. 2, no. 1, 2016, pp. 120–47. What follows about the linen industry, and specifically about the Ailly works, is borrowed from this co-authored article.

[25] Xavier Daumalin and Olivier Raveux, *Philippe de Girard ou l'invention de l'Europe industrielle (1775–1845)*, Avignon, 1999, p. 49.

[26] Alastair J. Durie, *The Scottish Linen Industry in the Eighteenth Century*, Edinburgh, 1979, p. 95.

This transformed the mercantile city into a major manufacturing centre, with the establishment of state-of-the-art mills at a time when elsewhere in Europe, not least in France, the linen industry was struggling to recover from the dislocation and in some places the devastation inflicted on it during the Napoleonic wars.[27] By 1826, Dundee had overtaken the port town of Hull as Britain's main importer of raw flax, and by the mid-1830s it was rivalling Leeds as the principal British linen manufacturing town.[28] The industry transformed Dundee from a modest town into an industrial heavyweight, with a population that doubled between 1820 and 1840 to reach 63,000. Exports of linen cloth from Scotland rose spectacularly, from an annual average of 26.6 million yards in 1813–17 to 79 million in 1845.[29] By this time Dundee was leading Europe in its capture of the world's markets for machine-flax and the coarse linen cloth woven from it, though initially the machinery was usually made in England.[30]

As in other sectors, the circulation of British machinery, technology, and workers across the Continent occurred in different ways. The links between the European and the British and Irish linen industries were not new: alongside other Huguenot artisans, the Frenchman Louis Crommelin (1653–1727), from Picardy, created a major linen manufacture in Lisburn (Ulster) from 1698, while French cambric weavers had been enticed to Scotland in the early eighteenth century to assist in improving the quality of Scottish linen cloth.[31] In France, spinning machine usage grew slowly and accounted for only a small fraction of French linen yarn output; even in 1844 only 10 per cent of France's yarn was machine spun.[32] Ambitious French linen manufacturers therefore had to resort to British technology if they were to establish larger-scale works. They tried to imitate British spinning equipment or to smuggle it into France, notwithstanding the British ban on the export of such machinery that remained in force until 1843. From that point on, machinery could freely be exported from Britain, and many continental businesses acquired the new technology—along with workers.

By 1837 France could only boast 14,000 spindles, compared to Britain's 250,000. French industry could hardly compete with the British linen imports, which were not controlled by tariffs until 1836 when a tariff on carded linen was

---

[27] Brenda Collins and Philip Ollerenshaw, 'The European Linen Industry since the Middle Ages', in Brenda Collins and Philip Ollerenshaw (eds.), *The European Linen Industry in Historical Perspective*, Oxford, 2003, p. 22.

[28] Gordon Jackson and Kate Kinnear, *The Trade and Shipping of Dundee, 1780–1850*, Dundee, 1990, pp. 2, 7.

[29] Christopher A. Whatley, *The Industrial Revolution in Scotland*, Cambridge, 1997, pp. 26–7.

[30] Louise Miskell, Christopher A. Whatley, and Bob Harris, 'Introduction: Altering Images', in Louise Miskell, Christopher A. Whatley, and Bob Harris (eds.), *Victorian Dundee: Image and Realities*, East Linton, 2000, p. 3.

[31] Brian Mackay, 'Overseeing the Foundations of the Irish Linen Industry: The Rise and Fall of the Crommelin Legend', in Collins and Ollerenshaw (eds.), *European Linen Industry*, pp. 99–122; Durie, *Scottish Linen Industry*, pp. 48–9.

[32] Collins and Ollerenshaw, 'European Linen Industry', pp. 21–2, 24.

imposed. The duties were raised in 1842 and again in 1847 and remained high until 1860 when a free-trade treaty was concluded. The effect of the impositions was a sharp decline in the imports of British yarns, which fell to a very low level.[33] The improved market environment in France prompted the erection of spinning mills in France, a process which continued until the late 1860s, with further benefits arising from the disruption of the UK cotton industry caused by the difficulty of obtaining raw cotton during the American civil war—with some cotton goods being substituted by linen and jute. By 1864 France had begun to close the production gap in relation to Britain, with 563,625 spindles, around one third of Britain's total of 1.7 million (in 1866).[34] Nevertheless, its industry was far less concentrated than that of Britain. By 1855, there were 5,576 factories in the flax and hemp manufacture in France, employing 56,167 persons, an average of ten people, while in Britain 440 factories employed 94,003 persons, an average of 213, although the extent to which the difference is accounted for by the way the statistics were recorded is not clear. It was the high tariffs during the period 1836 to c.1860 that largely accounted for the settling of several British textile firms in France.

As early as 1836, David Dickson established in Coudekerque-Branche (Nord) the first modern spinning factory for linen and hemp in the country, and later moved into jute.[35] By the mid-1840s, large linen factories could be found in Landerneau (Brittany), where the Société linière du Finistère was set up with 5,000 spindles (Figure 2.1);[36] in Petit-Quevilly, near Rouen (Normandy), with La Foudre (20,000 spindles) (Figure 2.2); and in Capécure (Boulogne-sur-Mer), with Hopwood and Borson. In Amiens (Picardy), a joint stock company for flax spinning had been established under the management of John Maberly (1770–1845), with a reputed 25,000 spindles, while a new mill was established by another partnership in the same place in 1838.[37] Despite having set up a large and highly profitable coarse linen manufactory—the Broadford works—in Aberdeen in the northeast of Scotland, Maberly had moved to France after going bankrupt in 1832.[38] All of these mills relied on British machinery: Maberly's works, for example, were driven by two 80-horse-power steam engines manufactured in France by William Fairbairn, Leeds's pre-eminent steam engine and boiler maker.

[33] Alexander. J. Warden, *The Linen Trade, Ancient and Modern*, Dundee, 1864, p. 306.
[34] Alfred Renouard, *Etudes sur le travail des Lins, chanvres, jutes, etc. Tome Premier. Histoire de l'industrie linière*, Lille, 1879.
[35] Odette Bonte, 'Les Dickson et la colonie d'Ecossais dans la région de Dunkerque', *Revue de la Société Dunkerquoise d'Histoire et d'archéologie*, no. 26, November 1992, pp. 11–75.
[36] Yves Blavier, *La société linière du Finistère. Ouvriers et entrepreneurs à Landerneau au XIXe siècle*, Rennes, 1999.
[37] *Mechanics Magazine and Journal of Science, Arts and Manufactures*, vol. 32, January 1840, p. 255.
[38] Durie, 'Government Policy', pp. 238–9.

Figure 2.1 The Landerneau flax mill, 1849 (*L'Illustration*, 27 October 1849, p. 140).

Figure 2.2 The linen factory 'La Foudre' (here in 1865–70) in Petit-Quevilly had been designed by engineer William Fairbairn (1789–1874) of Leeds. Fairbairn worked in Russia for the government and in Constantinople for the Sultan, as well as in Berlin, France, and of course Britain (Turgan, *Les grands usines*, vol. 3, Paris, 1874, p. 137).

Critically, however, because of the industry's proto-industrial origins, France had a limited pool of workers with the requisite skills to operate the new machines or the familiarity with or readiness to acquiesce to the steady work discipline demanded by water- or steam-powered mill production. Nor were there many mechanics to build and maintain the new machinery. Employers thus tried to import British workers along with British machines. Dundee, with its dynamic flax and linen industry and the start that had been made in jute production, as well as its sizeable skilled workforce that two decades earlier had started to become habituated to regular work in enclosed, supervised conditions, was an ideal location from which to recruit both managerial expertise and labour. We have seen that the population was rising fast, with an influx from inland Scotland but also from Ulster: by 1851, the Irish made up one fifth of the population of Dundee and perhaps half of the number employed in linen, a great majority of them women.[39]

Several sources document how the new workforce was hired in France. For the machines, the importation of British mechanics was common, especially before 1843. In the case of the Maberly factory in Amiens, for example, John Maberly's supplier of machines, Thomas Marsden, from Salford, answered a series of questions from members of the 1841 Select Committee on the export of machinery:

> 1146. Did you, in 1838, contract with Mr Maberly, as director of a large joint-stock company at Amiens, to make flax machinery to the amount of about 30,000l?—Yes...
>
> 1149. Did you contract to go over to France, taking with you all tools, workmen and raw material necessary for making the machinery?—Yes.
>
> 1150. Did you do so?—I did.
>
> 1151. How many men did you take with you for that purpose?—I took 100 from Manchester and other parts of England.
>
> 1152. Did you employ any Frenchmen besides?—I employed 30 or 40 French men, principally as inferior workmen and labourers to assist the English.[40]

As for the linen workers themselves, there were mostly two ways of recruiting them. One was to try and train a French workforce overseen by a few highly skilled British workers and foremen. A well-documented case was when two successful Dundee manufacturers, the Baxter brothers, secured a partnership with Parisian businessmen who were familiar with the market. When they set up a works in Ailly-sur-Somme (Figure 2.3), near Amiens, in 1845, they sent James Carmichael, an engineer-manager who worked for them. Carmichael got about two dozen workers from Scotland: male hecklers, mechanics, and some female spinners. But despite his early reservations about the quality of local workers—seven eighths of whom, he noted, came from 'the fields' and had 'never seen a spinning mill before'—within a few months he had managed to recruit spinners in France with some experience and who quickly adapted to the Ailly plant's technology.

[39] Louise Miskell and C. A. Whatley, "Juteopolis' in the Making: Linen and the Industrial Transformation of Dundee, c. 1820–1850', *Textile History*, vol. 30, no. 2, 1999, p. 179.

[40] PP. *Select Committee appointed to inquire into the Operation of the Existing Laws affecting the Exportation of Machinery*, 1841, 11 March 1841, questions 1146 to 1152.

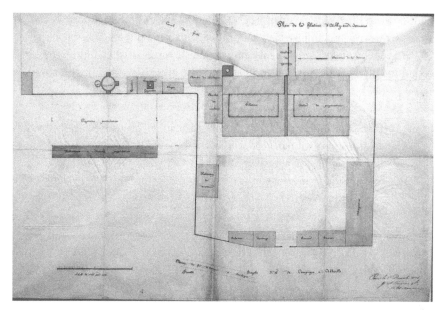

Figure 2.3 The Carmichael works in Ailly-sur-Somme, 1846. The preparing workshop, and the spinning, to the right near the diversion canal are close to the 'chambre des chaudières' (the boilers' room) and the engine-room. The manager's house ('habitation du directeur'), just below, is centrally located, not far from the workshops (Archives départementales de la Somme: Plan Masse de la filature d'Ailly-sur-Somme, 1846; 56.5 × 58 cm; scale: 1/200th; 99M_CP_81728).

Indeed, in March 1846 it was the 'Scotch people' with whom he was most exasperated, as he was later in the year when it was his own 'Countrymen' who pressed hardest for a wage rise.[41] The original Scottish female spinners did not stay long. By 1872, though the factory still produced linen, jute, and hemp cloth, there were only twenty British in Ailly, including Carmichael, a couple of mechanics and foremen, and their families. These British employees made up only a small proportion of the workforce, which was then about 500 employees and would grow to 1,500 by 1900.

Another industrial strategy was to import most of the workforce, at least initially. In Coudekerque-Branche, near Dunkirk, David Dickson (1811–69) created a works as early as 1836. Dickson's parents were farmers in Clocksbriggs, between Arbroath and Forfar, but he had learnt to be a master spinner in Dundee. From 1837 and as late as 1870, using British machines which they imported illegally, his company hired many workers and foremen from Dundee and the surrounding area.[42] In 1860, when the factory numbered 868 workers, Dickson

[41] University of Dundee Archive Services (hereafter UDAS), MS 102/9 (12), James Carmichael (JC) to Peter Carmichael (PC), 21 March 1846; MS 102/9 (23), JC to PC, 25 August 1846; MS 102/9 (26), JC to Baxter Bothers, 30 November 1846.
[42] Bonte, 'Les Dickson et la colonie d'Ecossais'.

continued to hire some Scottish workers, despite the cost of transport. When he was interviewed by a ministerial committte, he explained the higher productivity of the Scots by about 20 per cent not in intrinsic terms of skill, but by the large recruitment pool which prevailed in the Dundee area:

M. D'Eichtal: For linen, are your female workers as skilled as the English?

M. Dickson: Yes, I have some who are as skilled; but I must recruit them in England: I don't have enough good workers in the mill. [In Dundee, for the same number of spindles], one should employ, as I told you, only 44 or 45 workers where I need 54.... I am alone in my district, and I am compelled to train my workers: when they reach a certain age, they marry, sometimes change residency, and I'm always busy training new one....

M. the Chairman [the minister]: Do you find the female workers you train for linen as good as the English?

M. Dickson: There must be some bad ones in England as in France. But when there is a large cluster of factories, especially of the same factories, as in Dundee where only flax and jute are worked, the workforce is better skilled. In Lille, you have cotton, in Roubaix, you have wool: when workers move from one industry to another, they cannot be as good, as skilled as those who have always kept the same trade. In Dundee, they may well change mills, it's always the same industry. The nature of the work does not change, because there are neither cotton nor woollen spinning mills.[43]

Dickson was Scottish through and through: he maintained a detailed knowledge of the Dundee linen and jute industry thanks to many close relations there, including a brother-in-law manufacturer with whom he corresponded.

[43] 'M. D'Eichtal: Pour le lin, vos ouvrières sont-elles aussi habiles que les ouvrières anglaises?
M. Dickson: Oui, dans le nombre, j'en ai d'aussi habiles; mais je suis obligé de les recruter en Angleterre: je n'ai pas ici assez de bonnes ouvrières dans la filature. [...A Dundee, pour le même nombre de broches] on ne devrait en employer, je vous l'ai dit que 44 à 45 là où j'en mets 54, si l'on était dans de bonnes conditions de filature. Je suis seul dans mon arrondissement, et obligé de former mes ouvrières: arrivées à un certain âge, elles se marient, changent de résidence quelquefois, et je suis toujours occupé à en former de nouvelles....
M. le Président: Les ouvrières que vous formez pour le lin, les trouvez-vous aussi bonnes que les ouvrières anglaises?
M. Dickson: Il doit y en avoir de mauvaises en Angleterre comme en France; Mais quand il existe une grande agglomération d'industries, et surtout de mêmes industries, sur un point, comme à Dundee où l'on ne travaille que le lin et le jute, la main-d'œuvre est plus habile. Vous avez le coton à Lille, et la laine à Roubaix; quand les ouvrières passent de l'une à l'autre industrie, elles ne peuvent pas être aussi bonnes, aussi adroites que celles qui sont toujours restées au même métier. A Dundee, elles ont beau changer de filature, c'est toujours la même industrie; la nature du travail ne change pas, car il n'y a point de filatures de coton ni de laine'.
Conseil supérieur de l'agriculture, du commerce et de l'industrie, *Enquête: traité de commerce avec l'Angleterre*, Paris, vol. 5, 1860–2, p. 53.

But even businesses run by French manufacturers tried to hire Scottish workers. Another interesting case study in this respect is the Société linière du Finistère. Landerneau, in the far west of Brittany, had specialised in the making of linen cloth since the Middle Ages. By the early 1840s the local traders wanted to create a modern spinning mill which would be mechanised and concentrated. To this purpose, they set up the Société linière du Finistère in 1845. To conduct the works, they soon chose a man called Eastwood, who was the son of an English mechanic 'who had already set up several important spinning mills and whose acknowledged capacity should inspire confidence'.[44] Buying machinery in the UK then seemed logical: a scutching machine was bought in Ireland; cards were bought in Dundee, before a carding machine was purchased in 1850; spinning machines were bought from Peter Fairbairn in Leeds, and in Lisieux. How did the purchase of machines translate into the hiring of workers? The Landerneau managers asked Fairbairn for

a *very good* carder who could cleverly manage a large workforce, as you know we consume huge quantities of material and the heckling is, of all the preparatory works, the most important one.

We could offer him some honourable position and some prospects for the future, if we are satisfied with his management.[45]

The man was James Ogilvie, who had worked in Aberdeen in the choice of linen and the management of heckling. He was initially paid £130 a year and was asked to hire two good hecklers in Britain. Ogilvie then had to purchase flax in various places, like Riga. Instructions were given to him in two languages. That was not all: to operate the machines, a constant flow of workers between Dundee, Ulster, and Landerneau was initiated. By 1855, the factory employed 1,500 workers, mostly female spinners, on top of the male hecklers, carders, mechanics, and foremen, all of whom were British. Although it is impossible to number them exactly, there must have been at least 400 English, Scottish, and Irish workers, judging from the compulsory demands for permits of residence (*permis de séjour*) they had to make, not including married women and children (Figure 2.4).[46] In the following years, although the workforce was increasingly local, the influx continued. By the

---

[44] 'Qui a déjà monté plusieurs filatures importantes et dont la capacité reconnue doit imposer toute confiance', AD Finistère. 7M 247. Prospectus, 22 August 1845.

[45] 'Un très bon heckler et qui peut conduire avec intelligence un nombreux personnel, car vous savez que nous consommons des quantités considérables de matière et que le peignage (heckling) est de toutes les préparations la plus importante. Nous pourrions lui offrir une position honorable et de l'avenir, si nous sommes satisfaits de sa direction'. Archives municipales de Landerneau. 1 S 33: Copies de lettres. Letter to Fairbairn, 9 February 1846.

[46] AD Finistère. 4 M 83: Surveillance des étrangers—Permis de séjour.

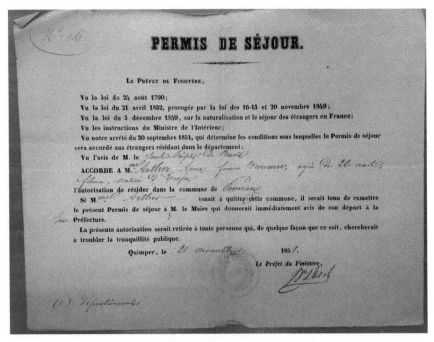

Figure 2.4 A 'permis de séjour' (licence to stay) for Anne Arther, a Scottish spinner at the Landerneau flax mill, 21 November 1851 (AD Finistère. 4M48. Etrangers).

mid-1850s, at a time when the company employed 1,500 workers, about 230 were still British. Even after the company had closed in 1892, some stayed.

1.3 The Holden Venture in Wool Combing

In wool, it seems the migration of workers was less systematic. As in cotton and linen, the mechanisation of the sector relied upon British machinery and technology, which were introduced from the middle of the century. In Bradford, entrepreneur Isaac Holden (1807–97), who had devised a new mechanical combing process, formed a partnership with combing manufacturer Samuel Cunliffe Lister to settle in France and to dominate the French market with combed wool produced on their own machines.[47] In 1849 they started business with a factory in Saint-Denis, and patented a series of techniques. From 1853 Holden then built two more factories: one in Croix (near Roubaix, Nord) and one in Reims, which became the most important of the Holden business. He was immensely successful

---

[47] Katrina Honeyman and Jordan Goodman, *Technology and Enterprise: Isaac Holden and the Mechanisation of Woolcombing in France, 1848-1914*, Aldershot, 1986.

in France. Between 1865 and 1895, Holden's two factories produced 25 per cent of the French production; during the 1870s, the two factories, which imported wool from across Europe, Russia, North Africa, Smyrna, Adrianople (Edirne), and Australia, made £4,000 a week in profits.[48] The Reims factory was managed by his nephew Jonathan (1828–1906), who had worked in Saint-Denis as a mechanic and a foreman. While Isaac the patriarch mostly stayed in Bradford, Jonathan lived and died in Reims, where he raised five children (who married British spouses). Holden became the largest manufacturer in Reims, employing 725 by 1864 and 1,200 by 1878. His factory was three times as productive as the local businesses. Holden's model was integrated: he did not just import British machines to penetrate the French market, he also patented and made machines that he used to produce combed wool (Figures 2.5 and 2.6).

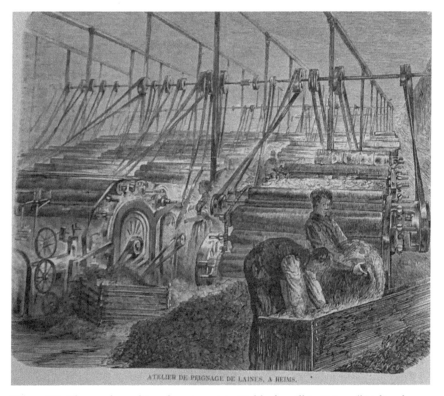

ATELIER DE PEIGNAGE DE LAINES, A REIMS.

Figure 2.5 The wool-combing department in Holden's mill in Reims ('Atelier de peignage de laines, à Reims', *L'Illustration*, 14 February 1863, p. 104).

[48] Katrina Honeyman, 'Holden, Sir Isaac, First Baronet (1807–1897)', *ODNB*, Oxford, 2004.

ATELIER DE CARDAGE DE LAINES, A REIMS.

Figure 2.6 The wool-carding workshop in Holden's mill ('Atelier de cardage de laines, à Reims', *L'Illustration*, 14 February 1863, p. 105).

Holden did not recruit massively in Britain, as several flax manufacturers did. Denis McKee has studied the Reims community that worked in 'l'usine des Anglais' ('the Englishmen's factory').[49] These British were a highly skilled minority, with only two mechanics and two foremen in Reims in 1856, and sixteen foremen and ten mechanics in 1866. Several of them first worked in Saint-Denis before moving to Reims and Croix, while others came from Britain—a pattern of mobility which also prevailed for other categories of workers, like the iron puddlers and rollers, or the railway navvies. For instance, foreman Jeremiah Baistow (1824–1907) worked in Saint-Denis from 1853, and then in Reims from 1855 to 1876. By the time he quit, he was a director. He later returned to Britain and died in Bradford. In a sample of identified British workers in Reims studied by McKee, 22 per cent were born in Bradford, 42 per cent within a 30-km radius,

---

[49]   Denis McKee, 'Jonathan Holden. 1828–1906. Industriel du peignage de la laine', in Gracia Dorel-Ferré and Denis McKee (dir.), *Les Patrons du Second Empire. Champagne-Ardenne*, Paris, 2006, pp. 141–4; Denis McKee, "L'usine des anglais' de Reims et Jonathan Holden (1828–1906): un succès industriel, un patron philanthrope', *Travaux de l'Académie nationale de Reims*, vol. 186, 2019, pp. 113–34; Turgan, *Les grandes usines. Etudes industrielles en France et à l'étranger*, Paris, vol. 8, 1868.

another 16 per cent within a 30–100-km radius, and 20 per cent came from further afield. Most had a working-class background, including Jonathan Holden himself, whose father John (1791–1847) was a wool-comber and had begun to work very early. When Holden came to France, two brothers, two sisters, and their four spouses came as well—a pattern of family migration that often applied in textiles. Most workers, including many female workers in both plants, were recruited locally.

Isaac and Jonathan Holden were paternalistic manufacturers. As early as 1860, Jonathan was involved in the building of workers' homes, and the 'cité Holden', with its small gardens, housed twenty British families that were involved in the management in 1876. There was an English school, a lecture and reading room, and a Wesleyan chapel. Holden had also bought a farm to provide the refectory with cheap food, and a land estate managed by his son John Edward (1854–91) in Boufarik, Algeria, to provide citrus fruits, wine, and olive oil for his staff. He created libraries which were later bequeathed to the city.

2. Iron, Machine-Making, and Mining

2.1 The South Wales Iron Workers across Europe

In iron, following the two key technological breakthroughs of Darby's smelting of iron with coke at Coalbrookdale in 1709 and Henry Cort's method of bar iron relying on puddling and rolling in 1783–4, the British acquired a significant lead in the sector, while on the Continent older techniques were still used. In the decades that followed the Napoleonic wars, the 'forge à l'anglaise', which combined puddling furnaces to produce wrought irons and rolling mills for shaping, was a must across western Europe. While only a quarter to a third of British pig iron was exported in the period 1815–30, this rose to 60 per cent in 1830–70, and continental ironmasters tried to cope with this competition.[50] In France, Belgium, and the west of Germany, a series of iron works were set up in this period, which marked the beginning of large-scale iron manufacturing on the Continent.[51] In each case, the technological input of British workers, especially Welsh puddlers and rollers, proved crucial.[52] Many economists, ironmasters, and engineers also went to Britain to learn more about the iron industry and to try to recruit

---

[50] Rainer Fremdling, 'Foreign Trade—Transfer—Adaptation: British Iron Making Technology on the Continent (Belgium and France)', in Chris Evans and Göran Ryden (eds.), *The Industrial Revolution in Iron: The Impact of British Coal Technology in Nineteenth-Century Europe*, Aldershot, 2005, p. 31.

[51] Bertrand Gille, *La Sidérurgie française au XIXe siècle*, Geneva, 1968.

[52] Evans and Ryden (eds.), *The Industrial Revolution in Iron*.

British workers.[53] In fact, the creation of all the great French iron works was preceded by technical trips to England and Wales.

Puddlers, whose job consisted of stirring molten iron in the furnace with rods to decarbonise it and make high-grade malleable wrought iron, were therefore the aristocracy of the trade. Puddling was a craft and, in a way, puddlers were artisans. As their historian Rainer Fremdling has highlighted, they endured extremely high temperatures and had to cope with the noise, smoke, and gases, as well as the glare of the iron.[54] During ten-hour-long shifts they also had to cope with the risk of burns and explosions. Concentration and strenuous work were both required, and puddlers seldom worked beyond the age of forty. They fascinated observers, who saw them as demiurges, as did Jules Verne in *The Begum's Fortune* (1879), who compared puddlers with 'half-naked Cyclops':

> When [the melted metal] acquires a certain consistency, the puddler, by means of his long hook, turns and rolls the molten mass, and makes it up into four blooms, or balls, when he then hands over to others.... To stir and knead four hundred-weight of metallic paste in that temperature, to see nothing for hours but the blinding glare of the furnace and molten iron, is trying work, and wears a man out in ten years.[55]

Because of their valuable skills, puddlers were in a good bargaining position, and could negotiate good wages overseas, as we have seen (Chapter 1). In Fourchambault they received ten-year contracts (Figures 2.7–2.9). There were about 2,000–3,000 puddlers in Europe, and they tried to preserve their secrets. However, they did have helpers, who were often their own sons, and when they were hired in continental works, they were asked to train a local workforce. The puddling process therefore spread, though this could take time. Productivity could vary among puddlers, depending on the amount of coal and pig iron used for the output of puddled iron and the time needed to produce a given quantity of iron, and with as little waste as possible. British rollers, balers, and shinglers also worked overseas. Most continental ironworks hired British iron workers. The part played by the British iron workers in the rise of the continental iron industry was major. The introduction of the techniques relied on them: on their gestures, their technical skills and secrets, their vocabulary. The input of the British iron workers

---

[53] Gille, *La Sidérurgie française*, p. 82.

[54] Rainer Fremdling, 'The Puddler: A Craftsman's Skill and the Spread of a New Technology in Belgium, France and Germany', *Journal of European Economic History*, vol. 20, no. 3, 1991, pp. 529–67.

[55] 'Le *puddleur* alors, du bout de son crochet, pétrissait et roulait en tous sens la masse métallique.... Pétrir à bout de bras, dans une température torride, une pâte métallique de deux cents kilos, rester plusieurs heures l'œil fixé sur ce fer incandescent qui aveugle, c'est un régime terrible qui use son homme en dix ans'. Jules Verne, *Les Cinq Cents Millions de la Bégum*, Paris, 1879, p. 46; translation: *The Begum's Fortune*, translated by W. H. G. Kingston, Philadelphia, PA, 1879, p. 72.

Figure 2.7 A British puddler in Fourchambault (late 1830s). This drawing is by François Bonhommé (1809–81), a Saint-Simonian and the first 'painter of industry' in France, as a preparation to his painting *Vue des forges de Fourchambault* (1840), where the worker can be seen on the left (Musée d'histoire du fer de Jarville).

Figure 2.8 François Bonhommé, *Vue des Forges de Fourchambault* (c.1840). Oil painting. 1600 × 700. The puddler can be seen on the left; on the right, Georges and Achille Dufaud are showing to the owners a map of the factory with changes they want to make. © Mairie de Fourchambault.

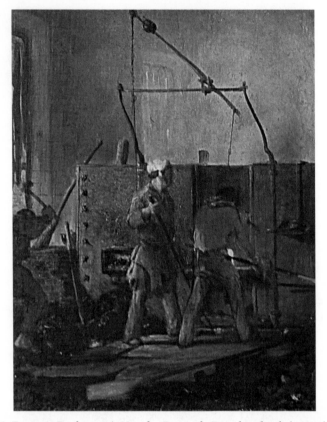

Figure 2.9 François Bonhommé, *Vue des Forges de Fourchambault* (c.1840) (detail).

probably reached a peak in the 1820s, when the new British technologies started to be used on the Continent.

How this influx of British workers was organised differed from one works to another. We have seen the case of Dufaud in Fourchambault, where a French manager arranged for the importation of British iron workers. The circulation of British iron workers could also be arranged by British manufacturers themselves when they conducted business on the Continent. Aaron Manby opened the first steam-ship company on the Seine in 1822 and created a firm which took a leading part in the gas lighting of Paris (Figure 2.10). With Daniel Wilson he set up and managed a modern factory in Charenton, south of Paris, from 1822 to 1828, gathering in one single place a foundry, a forge, and a mechanical construction workshop. By 1825 the Charenton works ranked second in France, and employed 248 workers who had come with their families to form a community of 640 people.[56]

---

[56] Archives municipales de Charenton. 5 I 3–1—Fonderie anglaise Manby Wilson; Jean-François Belhoste, 'Les forges de Charenton', in *Architectures d'usines en Val-de-Marne (1822–1939), Cahier de l'inventaire*, vol. 12, 1988, p. 29.

Figure 2.10 Manby and Wilson made this hallmark in the 1820s, celebrating their business, at a time when gas lighting was just starting in France. © CGB Numismatique Paris.

Staffordshire ironmaster Richard Harrison complained that fifty of his 200 workers, the 'best and most effective' ones, had been recruited by Manby.[57] Although he had to face some setbacks, notably in Le Creusot, Manby was a successful engineering businessman in France in the 1820s and 1830s, winning several prizes and securing important orders. The factory was visited by the future queen of the French, Marie-Amélie, who admired how 'a steam machine moved all the other machines'.[58] When in 1828 the government conducted an inquiry on the production of iron, Wilson in Le Creusot still relied on British workers exclusively for the rolling, and on half of them for the puddling; in Terrenoire, near Saint-Étienne, all the puddlers and rollers were British; Fourchambault still counted ten British puddlers and ten British rollers; in Charenton, though half of the puddlers were now French, all the rollers were still British.[59]

As late as the 1830s, 1840s, and 1850s, some works still hired British workers, albeit reluctantly. In Decazeville, all the ironworkers of the Société des Houillères et Fonderies de l'Aveyron were initially British: thirty-four, including women and children, came in 1832. Predictably, the managers disliked the British workers because of the higher wages they had to pay them. In 1833, after a master founder, Payne, had been hired, and the furnace had gone wrong under his deputy master caster, Payne was asked to restore it, which he accepted only for a bonus of 100 francs (£4). The manager wrote: 'It is with repugnance that I have yielded

---

[57] Evidence given by Richard Harrison, 5 March 1824, PP, *Report...*, p. 123.
[58] 'Une machine à vapeur met en mouvement toutes les autres machines'. *Marie-Amélie de Bourbon (reine des Français, 1782–1866), journal de*, présenté par S. Huart, Paris, 1980, p. 360.
[59] Ministère du commerce et des manufactures, *Commission formée pour l'examen de certaines questions de législation commerciale. Enquête sur les fers*, Paris, 1829.

to the need to bring caster Payne back to work with a bonus, but we have unfortunately no one to replace him'.[60] When a new director was appointed to manage the ironworks in 1838, he wrote: 'I have a pronounced antipathy for these overseas gentlemen, whom I acknowledge to be more skilful than our fellow-citizens only because they always manage to get paid three times as much as they are worth'.[61] Historians are dependent on management sources, which have often been preserved, and do not have at their disposal sources documenting the viewpoint of the workers. Ironmasters were not philanthropists, and the workers were not 'paid three times as much' as they were worth. A year later the manager in Decazeville had to send his engineer to Britain to hire a dozen good workers.

The same was true in the Société des Fonderies et Forges d'Alais (Gard), created in 1829. In 1836, one of the managers, Benoist, asked Aaron Manby, with whom he was on friendly terms, to send him 'a few English foremen, like a good puddler, a good caster to drive the furnaces, and an engineer to oversee the different machines', most of whom were British and whom he hired.[62] Other examples could be mentioned, such as the Indret works close to Nantes, those in Châtillon-sur-Seine in Burgundy, or those created by a Birmingham manufacturer, James Jackson, at Trablaine near Saint-Étienne and then Assailly (Loire).[63] François de Wendel also took British workers to Lorraine in 1824, Jean-Nicolas Gendarme to Boutancourt in the Ardennes in 1822; there were some British in the forges de Navarre in Evreux in 1843, and in Pont-Audemer in 1845. As a result of the need for a skilled workforce that was not available locally, British iron workers, especially the most skilled ones, had many opportunities to work on the Continent from the 1820s onwards.

It seems that many among them went from one works to the other. Rainer Fremdling studied the migration of eight workers employed by the Remys in 1824–5: all had worked in at least one other works previously. For example, R. Wills had worked in Plymouth, Châtillon, and Orban (Belgium), and most took another job after leaving.[64] Denis Woronoff and Jean-François Belhoste have noted that many of the workers in Le Creusot came from Charenton, and before

[60] 'C'est avec bien de répugnance, écrivit le directeur, que j'ai cédé à la nécessité de ramener le fondeur Payne au travail par une gratification, mais nous n'avons malheureusement personne...pour le remplacer'. Archives nationales du monde du travail. 84 AQ 18. Société des houillères et fonderies de l'Aveyron. Lettres du directeur au Conseil. Lettre du 1er février 1833. Thanks to Alexandra Cransac for pointing out this source to me.
[61] 'J'ai une antipathie bien prononcée pour ces Messieurs d'outre-mer, que je ne reconnais plus habiles que nos compatriotes que par ce qu'ils savent toujours se faire payer trois fois ce qu'ils valent'. Archives nationales du monde du travail. 84 AQ 21. Société des houillères et fonderies de l'Aveyron. Lettres du directeur au Conseil. Lettre du 27 septembre 1838; Gerd H. Hardach, 'Les problèmes de main-d'œuvre à Decazeville', Revue d'histoire de la sidérurgie, vol. 8, no. 196, 1967, p. 56.
[62] 'Quelques chefs ouvriers anglais, comme un bon puddleur, un bon fondeur pour conduire les fourneaux et un ingénieur pour la surveillance des diverses màchines'. Lettre de Benoist à Manby, 22 March 1836, in Robert R. Locke, 'Drouillard, Benoist et Cie (1836–1856)', Revue d'histoire de la sidérurgie, vol. 8, 1967, p. 284.
[63] F. W. Jackson, James Jackson et ses fils, Paris, 1893.
[64] Fremdling, 'Foreign Trade—Transfer—Adaptation', p. 566.

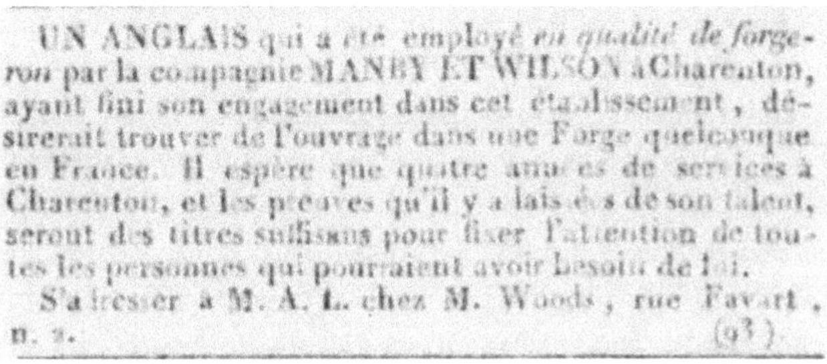

UN ANGLAIS qui a été employé en qualité de forgeron par la compagnie MANBY ET WILSON à Charenton,
ayant fini son engagement dans cet établissement, désirerait trouver de l'ouvrage dans une Forge quelconque
en France. Il espère que quatre années de services à
Charenton, et les preuves qu'il y a laissées de son talent,
seront des titres suffisans pour fixer l'attention de toutes les personnes qui pourraient avoir besoin de lui.
    S'adresser à M. A. L. chez M. Woods, rue Favart,
n. 2.   (93)

Figure 2.11 'An Englishman who has been employed *as a blacksmith* by the company of Manby and Wilson in Charenton... would like to find work in any forge in France' (*Journal du commerce*, 18 April 1827, p. 6).

that from Staffordshire where Aaron Manby was from.[65] The same names were also found at other times in Fourchambault, or Saint-Julien, Alais, Decazeville, or Rasselstein. Were workers transferred by ironmasters, from one place to the other, as between Crawshay and Dufaud? A small advertisement published in 1827 by 'an Englishman, who has been employed *as a blacksmith* by Manby and Wilson' for four years and 'would like to find work in a forge somewhere in France' suggests that workers moved on their own initiative, trying to improve their condition (see Figure 2.11).[66] In many respects, western Europe was thus an integrated labour market for Welsh and English iron workers.

During the period 1820–50, the British input was thus essential. In the second half of the century it was less crucial, as most continental works had managed to educate a local workforce. By the 1840s most British workers had probably left France, or were foremen, engineers, or maintenance workers. But still in the late 1850s, the ironworks in Alais employed British workers. In other parts of Europe, the trend would continue for much longer, as the Russian case testifies.

2.2 Cornish Miners in the Massif Central

From the 1850s, hundreds of thousands of Cornish miners emigrated and peopled the mining districts of the United States, South America, South Africa, and Australia. During the 1860s and 1870s, Cornwall was the only British region from which more migrants went abroad than to other parts of the country;

---

[65] Jean-François Belhoste and Denis Woronoff, 'The French Iron and Steel Industry during the Industrial Revolution', in Evans and Rydén (eds.), *The Industrial Revolution in Iron*, pp. 75–94.

[66] 'Un Anglais qui a été employé en *qualité de forgeron* par la compagnie MANBY ET WILSON à Charenton, ayant fini son engagement dans cet établissement, désirerait trouver de l'ouvrage dans une Forge quelconque en France. Il espère que quatre années de services à Charenton, et les preuves qu'il a laissées de son talent, seront des titres suffisans pour fixer l'attention de toutes les personnes qui pourraient avoir besoin de lui. S'adresser à M. A. L. chez M. Wood, rue Favart, n. 2', *Journal du Commerce*, 18 April 1827, p. 6. Thanks to Alexandra Cransac for directing me to this.

Baines notes that a net 118,500 people migrated overseas in the last quarter of the century—that is, 40 per cent of Cornwall's young adult males and over 25 per cent of its young adult females.[67] Most of these emigrants did not go to the Continent. One reason was that France was not a large mining country in the first half of the century, at a time when most of the coal was imported. It may also have been that French mine-owners found it difficult to hire British miners, although they knew about their skills. This is suggested by an 1847 report of directors of a mine in Grand-Combe (Gard), who tried to attract British 'workers of choice who could teach ours methods for felling [abattage] with which they could, while using their forces cleverly, manage to produce a lot without working more',[68] but were ultimately unsuccessful.

However, there were several exceptions to this, the most notable one being the employment of miners by railway entrepreneurs such as William Mackenzie and Thomas Brassey. There were also more local exceptions, like the Oberhof and Wildberg mines in Germany, the Tuscany Copper mines in Italy, the Linares lead mines in Spain, and the Dalecalia silver-lead mines in Sweden. In Pontgibaud, in the Puy-de-Dôme (Massif central), a silver and lead mine was run by Alphonse Pallu who visited Britain in 1845 to study mining techniques. Following an inspection by a mining consultancy firm, John Taylor Jnr, they formed a new company which relied on Cornish mining expertise. The new company, which began in 1853, was jointly owned by four French and four British directors, and was run by an English engineer.[69]

2.3 Suspension Bridges, Steamboats, and Locomotives: The Seguin Brothers

During European industrialisation, British machines were everywhere and in every sector of industry. While most were imported from Britain, the entrepreneurs who were based on the Continent also tried to make their own. We have seen how, in textile, Cockerill competed with others. In lace, some Calais mechanics soon made machines themselves. Ironmasters also made their own machines. They were also a few engineers who specialised in machine-making.

---

[67] Dudley Baines, *Migration in a Mature Economy*, pp. 157–9. Also see Pollard, *Peaceful Conquest* and Alessandro Nuvolari, 'Collective invention during the Industrial Revolution: the case of the Cornish pumping engine', *Cambridge Journal of Economics*, 2004, 28, pp. 347–63.

[68] 'Ouvriers de choix qui puissent enseigner aux nôtres les méthodes d'abattage au moyen desquelles, par un emploi intelligent de leurs forces, ils parviendront à produire beaucoup sans travailler plus'. AD Gard 18 J 21. Rapport du Conseil d'administration de la Compagnie de la Grand-Combe sur l'exercice 1847, in Fabrice Sugier, 'L'immigration européenne dans le bassin houiller de la Grand'Combe', *Causses et Cévennes, Revue bimestrielle du Club Cévenol*, no. 4, 1992, p. 266.

[69] Michael T. Kiernan, *The Engineers of Cornwall at the Mines of Pontgibaud in France*, Redruth, 2016.

Further south, on the Rhône River, the history of the Seguin brothers is significant, as historian Michel Cotte has shown.[70] Marc Seguin (1786–1875) and his brothers, who were engineers, devised a set of new techniques and works: they made an iron bridge across the Rhône in 1825, the first suspended bridge in continental Europe, and then a boiler for steamboats on the Rhône, which was used until a bad accident in 1827 in Lyon. Finally, they made a steam locomotive which ran from Saint-Étienne to Lyon in 1829, a few days before George Stephenson's Rocket travelled from Manchester to Liverpool. At every stage, and at least six times between 1823 and 1829, Marc Seguin—who was also inspired by US technology—and his associates went to Britain, including London, Darlington, Liverpool, and Glasgow. There they met engineers such as Humphry Davy, Marc Isambard Brunel, Thomas Telford, George Stephenson, Charles Babbage, Philip Taylor (who went to Paris in 1828 and founded engineering works), and John Martineau. They bought machines, asked for advice, investigated, and, as one might expect, hired British workers, although, as Cotte noted, they were reluctant to pay too high a wage to these workers.[71] However, in terms of railway building, they were outflanked by the British pioneers themselves.

3. The Railways

3.1 Railway Building: Navvies, Masons, and Miners

By the early 1840s, only ten years after the pioneering Liverpool to Manchester line was opened in 1830, Britain had already acquired a huge lead in railway building. In 1845, out of a total European railway network of 9,200 km, Britain alone comprised 4,900 km (53 per cent). France, whose surface was more than double, and whose population was also larger, had only 1,250 km (14 per cent) of track. When French banker Charles Laffitte contacted the shareholders of the London & South Western Railway in August 1839, he admitted that the French were 'children at the art of making railways'.[72]

The British lead was effective in several sub-sectors. For the building of the lines itself, Britain could rely upon existing expertise in canal-digging. For the locomotives and the steam-powered machines they worked with, the Stephensons were unrivalled. Britain was also ahead in terms of capital investment: by 1839, some £57 million had been invested in railway building in England—fifteen times as

---

[70] Michel Cotte, *Le choix de la révolution industrielle. Les entreprises de Marc Seguin et de ses frères (1815–1835)*, Rennes, 2007, pp. 93–114.

[71] Ibid., p. 99.

[72] David Brooke, *William Mackenzie: International Railway Builder*, London, 2004, p. 24.

much as in France; by 1846, the total subscriptions amounted to £230 million.[73] In the 1840s, Britain underwent a 'railway mania' of speculative schemes, which ended with a crash in 1846. In the meantime, however, railway entrepreneurs had started moving to the Continent. From 1840, they built a series of lines in different countries, starting with French railways (see Map 2.2).

In 1840, Joseph Locke was appointed engineer for the Paris–Rouen line. Comparing prices, he asked two rising entrepreneurs, Mackenzie and Brassey, to build the line. When it came to organising its construction, including four long tunnels and five viaducts across the Seine that were all technically challenging and required a large workforce, Mackenzie and Brassey made their calculations and resorted to British subcontractors for the several small contracts they negotiated, namely for gangers and workers. In total, 2,000 to 5,000 British workers, most of whom were itinerant navvies, crossed the Channel and moved along the line as it was built, or sometimes from one line to another.[74] Mackenzie and Brassey also imported shovels, pick rails, steam engines, wagons, and so on from Britain. The Paris–Rouen line was completed in 1843 and was then continued to Le Havre (1843–7), which also involved a series of difficult building sites. Despite the 1846 collapse of a viaduct in Barentin (Figure 2.12), the line was completed within deadlines.[75] This line, the first one between Paris and the sea, soon acquired a symbolic status. Writer Jules Janin commented:

> It was Emperor Napoleon who said so: Paris, Rouen, Le Havre are just one town, whose main street is the Seine. The image is noble, great, and true.... Time has been vanquished, distance has been overcome, space has been eliminated! Paris is at the door of Le Havre. Down the towers of Notre-Dame... the Ocean![76]

The Paris–Le Havre railway was represented in paintings by the impressionists Monet, Caillebotte, and Manet, who saw it as the incarnation of modernity. It formed the background of Zola's *La Bête humaine* (1890) and later Jean Renoir derived a film from it (*La Bête humaine*, 1938). To most observers, even if many of the workers had been French or from foreign countries, it was built by the British:

[73] Jean-Martial Bineau, *Chemins de fer d'Angleterre*, Paris, 1840, p. 10; this is based on the parliamentary returns of subscribers of railway contracts, in Hall et al., *British Slave-Ownership: Colonial Slavery and the Formation of Victorian Britain*, p. 91.

[74] Voir J. A. Durbec, 'Contribution à l'histoire du chemin de fer de Paris à la mer', in *Actes du 81ème congrès national des sociétés savantes, Rouen-Caen, 1956*, Paris, 1958; Virginie Maréchal, 'La construction des lignes de chemin de fer de Paris à Rouen et de Rouen au Havre (1839–1847)', *Revue d'histoire des chemins de fer*, no. 14, 1996, pp. 64–89; Hélène Bocard, *De Paris à la mer. La Ligne de chemin de fer Paris-Rouen-Le Havre*, Paris, 2005. Above all: Brooke: *The Railway Navvy*; Brooke, *William Mackenzie*.

[75] 'La construction du viaduc de Barentin', 1845, AD Seine-Maritime.

[76] 'C'est l'empereur Napoléon qui l'a dit: Paris, Rouen, Le Havre, sont une même ville dont la Seine est la grande rue. L'image est noble, elle est grande et vraie.... Le temps vaincu, la distance franchie, l'espace supprimé!—Paris, aux portes du Havre.—Aux pieds des tours de Notre-Dame...l'Océan!'. Jules Janin, *Voyage de Paris à la mer*, Paris, 1847, pp. 13, 17.

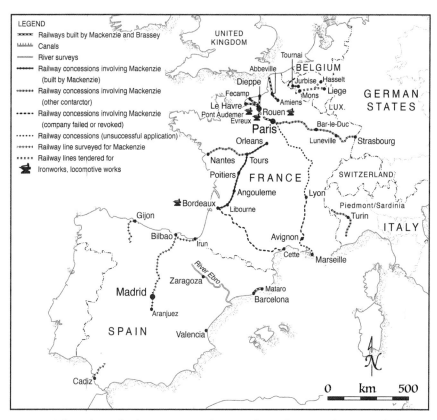

Map 2.2 The railways built in continental Europe by William Mackenzie and Thomas Brassey (adapted from Michael Chrimes, Mary K. Murphy, and Georges Ribeill (eds.), Mackenzie—*Giant of the Railways: William Mackenzie (1794-1851) and the Construction of the Early European Railway Network*, London, 1994).

part of the funding (Edward Blount) and most of the contracting and engineering (Joseph Locke) came from Britain.[77] The locomotives and carriages were built by William Buddicom and William Allcard in British workshops near Rouen and most of the stations were designed in the English style by architect William Tite (1798–1873), who designed the Royal Exchange in London as well as many railway stations and cemeteries (Figures 2.13 and 2.14). The train drivers were initially all British, and even coal for the locomotives was imported from Britain until 1867. Other smaller lines followed in France: an extension to Dieppe, and the Orléans–Bordeaux, Amiens–Boulogne, and Mantes–Cherbourg lines. Success in France also meant Brassey won contracts in Spain, Italy, the Netherlands, Belgium, Denmark, Norway, Austria, Poland, and Ukraine.

[77] Brooke, *William Mackenzie*; Brooke (ed.), *The Diary of William Mackenzie*.

Figure 2.12 'The Building of the Barentin Viaduct', a daguerreotype (1845 or 1846).
Several workers, on the scaffold and on the bridge itself, as well as a well-dressed
couple, are watching the camera, probably posing. The daguerreotype had been
devised in 1839, and photos of construction sites were a rarity at this early stage
(AD Seine-Maritime).

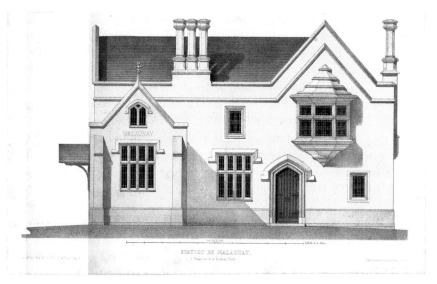

Figure 2.13 Malaunay railway station, designed by William Tite, 1843. Drawing by Victor Petit. Lithograph c.1850 (© Jean-Pierre Emo).

Figure 2.14 Malaunay railway station, designed by William Tite in 1843, here in 1917, is still erect today (© Jean-Pierre Emo).

After 1848, more continental railways were built by local entrepreneurs. Yet the British and Irish navvies had played an important part, and the Continent had boosted the businesses of the British entrepreneurs. After Mackenzie died in 1851, Brassey kept on building railroads in Britain, Norway, the Netherlands, Canada,

Crimea during the Crimean war, South America, Australia, India, Nepal, and Mauritius, as well as ships, drainage systems, sewerage systems, roads, embankments, and so on. At the peak of his business—that is, for about twenty years—he employed 80,000 men on four continents, and when he died in 1870 he left a legacy of £2 to 3.2 million (i.e. about 203–325 million in 2021 sterling)—which made him one of the wealthiest Victorian self-made men.[78] As for Joseph Locke, he left an estate worth more than £350,000 (i.e. about 35 million in 2021 sterling), also a considerable sum of money in the nineteenth century.

The lives of Brassey, Mackenzie, and Locke have been written, but those of their tens of thousands of workers have not and hardly could. When the Select Committee on Railway Labourers heard evidence in 1846, only three of the thirty-one witnesses were navvies. In Britain, a large workforce of navvies and miners had first been trained during the 'canal mania' of 1760–1830, when some 2,000 miles of waterways had been dug. When the railways came of age, this workforce was soon employed on its building sites. By 1846, at the peak of the railway mania, some 200,000 were employed in railway building in Britain.[79] They remind us of the fact that the industrial revolution created an army of jobs that relied on physical force, as Raphael Samuel argued.[80] In a way, these men even came to embody physical work, as in Ford Madox Brown's famous painting, *Work* (1852–65). The navvies were required to perform demanding labour, 'lifting twenty tons of puddle [their] own height in the course of the day'.[81] This took a horrifying toll, as the building of a single line involved the accidental deaths of dozens of navvies, especially in the building of the tunnels. One rare navvy autobiographer born around 1820 remembered working in a tunnel 'for about three months': 'It is rather chokey kind of work, all done by candle-light, and the smoke makes the air thick and misty'. He recorded a terrible experience in Dorset:

> I was in a tunnel that fell at both ends. There was only one man and me and some horses buried in it, and he drove a hole through the ground (he was about eight hours doing it), and then he and me got out, and left the horses in for three days and nights.[82]

No similar recollections for railway building in France have reached us, although the newspapers reported numerous accidents. For example, on 24 December 1841, in a tunnel, 'a landslide has occurred, a 9-metre-deep pit had to be dug in very

---

[78] David Brooke, 'Brassey, Thomas (1805–1870)', *ODNB*, Oxford, 2004; Diane K. Drummond, *Tracing Your Railway Ancestors: A Guide for Family Historians*, Barnsley, 2010, p. 101.

[79] Brooke, *The Railway Navvy*, p. 8.

[80] Raphael Samuel, 'The Workshop of the World: Steam Power and Hand Technology in Mid-Victorian Britain', *History Workshop Journal*, vol. 3, no. 1, spring 1977, pp. 6–72.

[81] Elizabeth Garnett, *Our Navvies: A Dozen Years Ago and To-Day*, London, 1885, p. 10.

[82] 'Autobiography of a Navvy', *Macmillan's Magazine*, vol. 5, 1861–2, p. 151.

Figure 2.15 The opening of the Rouen–Dieppe Railway, built by W. B. Buddicom of Penbedw, Nannerch (Flintshire), c.1848, possibly by Léon Oberlin. Varnished watercolour on board, 178 × 68 cm (Flintshire Record Office).

Figure 2.16 'Casket, presented to W.B. Buddicom by his grateful servants, the English enginemen of the Rouen, Havre and Dieppe Railways, 1852'—a medallion of Buddicom can be seen on the side (North East Wales Archives—D/B/254).

difficult ground, whose walls had to be buttressed. In thirteen and a half hours, the operation was completed and...the five men were saved'.[83]

Navvies were overexploited. Karl Marx called this nomad population 'the light infantry of capital, thrown by it, according to its needs, now to this point, now to that'.[84] Unlike other groups of male workers studied in this book, navvies were not trying to preserve a craft that was threatened by industrialisation; they were not artisans turned into workers. They were common labourers and had no skill they could rely upon in their collective bargaining with employers. As historian Peter Way has argued about canal diggers of the early United States, the navvies were more fully exploited than other workers, worse off economically, and socially fragmented; as a result, their cultures reflected their alienation as much as a sense of community. In the building of European railroads, navvies were often foreigners: British, Irish, and Belgians in France; Poles in Germany; Italians in Germany, France, and Switzerland. In Victorian Britain, by the 1840s, their professional identity was well defined (Figure 2.17). They had a poor reputation, associated with life on the tramp, virility, and strong drink. 'Whist with yer, or I'll give yer to a navvy', some mothers reportedly told their children.[85]

In larger patterns of migration from Britain to the Continent, navvies stick out: they were neither very skilled artisans from the viewpoint of employers, nor did they embody the industrial revolution. In some ways, they can more easily be compared with the unskilled migrant Italian, Belgian, or Polish workers of the late nineteenth century. They would move between countries and regions depending on where construction was ongoing and where jobs were available, and their flows followed that of British business ventures and expertise in railways across the globe. In some respects, navvying also required a series of specialised skills and knowledge. One of the rare navvies who wrote his memoirs, Albert Pugh, moved across occupations—stone breaking, operating a crane, point turning, tool carrying, engine cleaning, and so on.[86]

In 1846, the Select Committee on Railway Labourers asked one of the directors of the Rouen and Paris railway about the reasons for this organised flow. William Reed answered that out of 10,000 men employed for the building of the Paris–Rouen line, there were 'at one time as many as 5,000 Englishmen; but they afterwards decreased to about perhaps 1,000...chiefly navigators; a great many of them minors'. As for the reasons for such an organised and costly transfer of

[83] 'Un éboulement a eu lieu, et cinq hommes se sont trouvés isolés de toute communication. Pour les délivrer, il fallu creuser un puits de 9 mètres de profondeur dans un terrain très difficile, et dont les parois devaient être étayées. En treize heures et demie, cette opération a été terminée, et...les cinq hommes ont été sauvés'. La Presse, 29 December 1841, p. 3.

[84] Karl Marx, Capital, 1867, ch. 25, section 5 C.

[85] A threat said to have been used in the neighbourhood of the Leeds and Thirsk railway, quoted in Brooke, The Railway Navvy: 'That Despicable Race of Men', London, 1983, p. 108.

[86] Albert Pugh, 'I Helped to Build Railroads', ed. Charles Madge, Pilot Papers, Social Essays and Documents, 1/4 (November 1946), pp. 75–98, cited in Griffin, Bread Winner, p. 78.

SPADES ARE TRUMPS.

Navvy (to M——,) "NOW, OLD STICK-IN-THE-MUD, LET ME TRY IF I CAN GET YOU OUT OF THE MESS."

Figure 2.17 'Spades are trumps', *Punch*, 13 January 1855, vol. 28, p. 15.

workforce, he argued that they 'did more work' than the French: 'At first, I think the Englishmen did nearly double, and received double wage'.[87] On such a building site, the company did not employ the navvies directly but through subcontractors. They were paid on piece rates.

In a speech delivered in London to the Institution of Civil Engineers when he was elected president in 1858, Locke reported: 'often have I heard the exclamation of French loungers around a gang of navvies—"Mon Dieu, ces Anglais, comme ils travaillent!" ("My God, these English, how hard they work!")'. Locke mentioned the 'peculiarity of [the] Dress' of the navvies, 'their uncouth size, habits, and manners', using the picturesque image of 'the lawless and daring habits of this class of our countrymen'.[88] And in the literature, the emphasis was laid on their strength, as in the words of one of Brassey's time-keepers:

[87] PP. Select Committee on Railway Labourers, 1846. Evidence given by William Reed on 19 May 1846, questions 327–30.
[88] 'Presidential address of Joseph Locke, M.P., January 12, 1858', *Minutes of the Proceedings of the Institution of Civil Engineers*, vol. 17, 1858, p. 143.

I think as fine a spectacle as any man could witness, who is accustomed to look at work, is to see a cutting in full operation, with about twenty wagons being filled, every man at his post, and every man with his shirt open, working in the heat of the day, the gangers looking about, and everything going like clockwork. Such an exhibition of physical power attracted many French gentlemen, who came on to the cuttings at Paris and Rouen, and looking at these English workmen with astonishment, said 'Mon Dieu! Les Anglais, comme ils travaillent!' Another thing that called forth remark, was the complete silence that prevailed amongst the men. It was a fine sight to see the Englishmen that were there, with their muscular arms and hands hairy and brown.[89]

Both quotations add up to the stereotypical image of the navvy, which was, in a way, a kind of distant echo of the stereotypical John Bull, constructed in opposition to the French, and which continues to influence how navvies are portrayed in modern historical literature.[90] In other sources, explanations for their superior strength were predicated on their eating meat. However, more careful attention shows that even the seemingly elementary work of the navvies relied on industrialisation. As we have seen (p. 51), Locke noted that while the French had 'wooden shovels', the British could rely on metal ones; while the French wheelbarrows were 'basket-sized', those of the British were full size. A further reason for the organised flow may be related to the contracting system that prevailed in railway building. When he was appointed engineer, Locke had hoped for low costs; but French contractors demanded prices that were 'nearly double those which were asked by Englishmen'.[91] Locke thus chose to work with Mackenzie and Brassey, who could mobilise a large workforce; and transport costs were minimal, hence the choice for this unusual transfer.

3.2 Making and Operating Trains

The railway lines built by the British entrepreneurs did not just depend on an imported workforce for their construction. These lines also created the need for an industry devoted to the building of engines, a sector which was in its infancy on the Continent. For the Paris–Rouen–Le Havre railway, Locke relied upon William Allcard (1809–61) and William Buddicom (1816–87), two British entrepreneurs who set up works near Rouen in 1841 and produced machines and trains. Buddicom, who had begun as an apprenticed mechanic in Liverpool, had already worked with Cockerill and Locke. By 1849, he also provided locomotives for four

---

[89] Arthur Helps, *Life and Labours of Mr Brassey*, London, 1872, p. 72.
[90] Terry Coleman, *The Railway Navvies*, Harmondsworth, 1981 [1965].
[91] Joseph Devey, *The Life of Joseph Locke, Civil Engineer*, London, 1861, p. 164.

of the French railway companies and set up another construction workshop in La Bastide, near Bordeaux, for the requirements of the Midi (Southern) railway. After a difficult time in 1848, Buddicom went on to provide locomotives and carriages for other railways in France, in Italy, and in Prussian Rhinish provinces in the 1850s and 1860s.[92]

Other British workers continued working for continental railways. Little is known about their lives. For example, according to the 1851 census, a thirty-eight-year-old British 'employé au chemin de fer' (railways employee), 'George Heeley', lived in Valliquerville, a small rural village along the Paris–Le Havre line, where he was the only resident foreigner. We do not know any more about train drivers, many of whom were also initially British on continental railways, although their proportion declined in the 1850s and 1860s. Train mechanic Henry Dove left a brief memoir, which has reached us through the brokerage of banker Edward Blount: Henry Dove had begun as an office boy to Robert Stephenson in 1837 before becoming a driver in 1842 and moving to France in 1843. In the summer of 1848, after having been a witness to the February revolution in Paris, he 'ran five or six trains of deported insurgents', men who had been involved in the defeated insurrection of June 1848. He said he worked in France as an engine-driver until 1880, but no other trace of his life has been found.[93]

4. Four Artisans and Their Trades

In different sectors that had not yet been mechanised or were only beginning to be, some British artisans went to the Continent for a few years. Most of these moves were individual and driven by various motives, although most were related to labour rather than family or other considerations. Trying to understand why these artisans—here, a leather-dresser, a mechanic, a goldsmith, and a shoemaker—crossed the Channel and how they managed to work in Europe helps us understand the dynamics of some trades in the half-century which followed the end of the Napoleonic wars. Their sectors were not critical in the industrialisation of the Continent, but their moves were usually well informed, and in Europe they marketed skills acquired in Britain. Focusing on these individuals is also worthwhile because all four wrote about their own lives. In many ways, their narratives restore the agency of the migrant workers which is missing

---

[92] 'Obituary. William Barber Buddicom, 1816–1887', *Minutes of the Proceedings of the Institution of Civil Engineers*, vol. 91, 1888, pp. 412–21; George W. Carpenter, revised by Mike Chrimes, 'Buddicom, William Barber (1816–1887)', *ODNB*, Oxford, 2004.

[93] Edward Blount, *Memoirs of Sir Edward Blount*, London, 1902, pp. 75–82.

from many sources where they appear as the objects of entrepreneurial ventures run by others.

4.1 Colin, Leather-Dresser and Reformed Drunkard

Colin—the pseudonym of an anonymous autobiographer—was a leather-dresser in Saint-Denis, north of Paris, for nearly two years in the late 1810s.[94] Colin was born c.1794 in the east of Scotland and had been apprenticed there. Leather-dressers treated the hides, usually after the tanners had worked them. Colin enlisted in the Navy and was wounded in the battle of Algiers (1816) before sailing to 'Malabar and Coromandel'. While in La Rochelle, he deserted. In France tanning was mostly small-scale, with about 5,000 businesses numbering one to five tanners. Colin worked in Châtellerault and then for twenty-one months in Saint-Denis, which, because of its waterways and the proximity of the capital, had been a large production centre of leather (Figure 2.18). He had a relationship with one of his employer's daughters, Marie Antoine Longeville, but would neither become a Catholic nor swear an oath of allegiance to the French king, and he refused to marry. He returned to Britain, lived in different places, married, had a son, was jailed for debt, and did not see his wife and son for more than twenty years. The reason for this was that he was a 'drunkard' whose life had been plagued from childhood by his taste for alcohol. When Colin wrote his memoirs—or was interviewed about his life—he had met the Quakers, become 'reformed' and sober, and become a temperance advocate. Before being edited as a book, Colin's text was published in the *Bristol Temperance Herald*.[95] This type of uplifting narrative can be questioned as it was written with a purpose: the reformed drunkard exposed the damage caused by drinking, but also the possibility of redemption. As Colin was a pseudonym, the identity of the writer is uncertain. However, although the overnight conversion from drunkenness to successful abstinence is questionable, many of the details are reliable and the text cannot be wholly fictitious. The economic dimension of Colin's erratic itinerary is not obvious. However, he remembered learning to tan and dye Moroccan leather, which was not worked in Britain yet, but became popular to ladies' shoemakers, upholsterers, and bookbinders. His trajectory illustrates the importance of artisans, even in traditional trades, for the transnational circulation of skills, products, and techniques (Map 2.3), including from the Continent to Britain.

---

[94] John Colin [pseud.], *The Wanderer Brought Home. The Life and Adventures of Colin. An Autobiography*, London, 1864.
[95] *Bristol Temperance Herald*, August 1855 to July 1856.

Figure 2.18 This photo, taken in Paris in the late 1860s, shows tanners at work by the river Bièvre (Charles Marville, 'Cours de la Bièvre, près de la rue du Pont-aux-Biches, Paris 5ᵉ', 1865–8, 26.5 × 36.8 cm. Musée Carnavalet, PH691).

4.2 Timothy Claxton, Itinerant Gas Mechanic

Timothy Claxton (1790–1848) was born to the poor and illiterate family of a day labourer 'about a hundred miles from London' in Earsham, Norfolk.[96] From the age of twelve he was first apprenticed as a whitesmith in a workshop in Bungay, Suffolk, where, he wrote in his memoirs, 'we made or repaired every article of metal, which is used or about a house, together with mechanics' tools, and some work for mills'.[97] In 1810 he arrived in London where he went to a coffee-room which offered a selection of publications to their customers and enabled Tim Claxton to engage in auto-didactic pursuits. A whitesmith, he was later involved in the creation of the London Mechanical Institution when it was in its infancy. In 1812 Timothy married Hannah Stuniken (1780–1867) and it seems she followed him when, in 1820, he went to St Petersburg to work for the tsar putting up gasworks. There, Claxton was, for instance, involved in the making of a chandelier

---

[96] Norfolk Record Office; Norwich, Norfolk; Norfolk Church of England Registers; Reference: PD 519/3.
[97] Timothy Claxton, 'Memoirs', in his *Hints to Mechanics on Self-Education and Mutual Instruction*, London, 1839, p. 7.

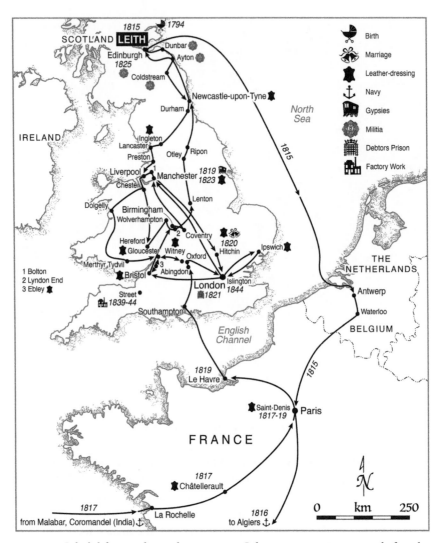

Map 2.3 Colin's life according to his memoirs. Colin was a tramping artisan before the railways. Though the complexity of his trajectory can partly be related to his alcoholism, such moves were not uncommon.

at the centre of a library, with 360 jets of gas. Interestingly, Tim was impressed by the Russian manufactures of iron, hemp and flax, paper, cotton, silk, and glass, as well as by their granite buildings. For some reason, he left Russia in 1823 and then went to Boston where he worked until 1836. He published his *Hints to Mechanics on Self-Education and Mutual Instruction* (1839), which is the main source we have on him (Figure 2.19). He was involved in the self-education societies which were then becoming so popular, like the Society for Promoting Practical Design,

Figure 2.19 Timothy Claxton, posing as a gentleman for his *Hints to Mechanics on Self-Education and Mutual Instruction*, London, 1839 (portrait by S. S. Osgood of Boston).

where he lectured on the 'Properties of Air'.[98] While in the United States in May 1836, he applied for US citizenship, but in July of the same year he returned to London for some unknown reason. He was then aged forty-six and lived in St Pancras, where he died and was buried in 1848 (see Map 2.4).[99] Claxton's trajectory is a reminder of how domestic, continental, and transatlantic migrations could be interwoven in complex patterns.

4.3 James Dacres Devlin, Political Shoemaker

James Dacres Devlin (1799 or 1800–c.1869) was a Dubliner by origin, an excellent shoemaker, and 'one of the very best boot-closers in early nineteenth-century London. He was able to do sixty stitches to an inch by hand'. 'Stitching is a handsome operation', he wrote.[100] He made a pair of riding boots wherein the tongue was designed to resemble a shamrock leaf. In 1836, Devlin went to Paris. He wanted to learn the techniques that made French shoes so popular in Britain. He wrote in *The Paris Sun-Beam* (1837–8) and later published a book on French shoe and boot-making.[101] In particular, he focused on 'blocking', the process whereby the leather on boots was shaped and tightened round the heels of boots. This, he thought, was superior in France because it was performed by specialist workmen called 'cambreurs' employed by the master curriers, whereas such workmen did not exist in Britain, where blocking was done by ordinary boot-makers—in the 1861 census, he was registered not as a shoe or boot-maker

[98] *Morning Advertiser*, 5 March 1838, p. 1; *The Sun*, 5 August 1838, p. 2.

[99] City of Westminster Archives Centre; London, England; *Westminster Church of England Parish Registers*; reference: STG/PR/7/62.

[100] Iorwerth Prothero, *Radical Artisans in England and France, 1830–1870*, Cambridge, 1997, p. 47.

[101] James Dacres Devlin, *The Boot and Shoe Trade of France*, London, 1838; James Dacres Devlin, *The Shoemaker*, 2 vols., London, 1839–41; James Dacres Devlin, *Critica Crispiana; or the Boots and Shoes British and Foreign of the Great Exhibition*, London, 1852; *Contract Reform*, 1856.

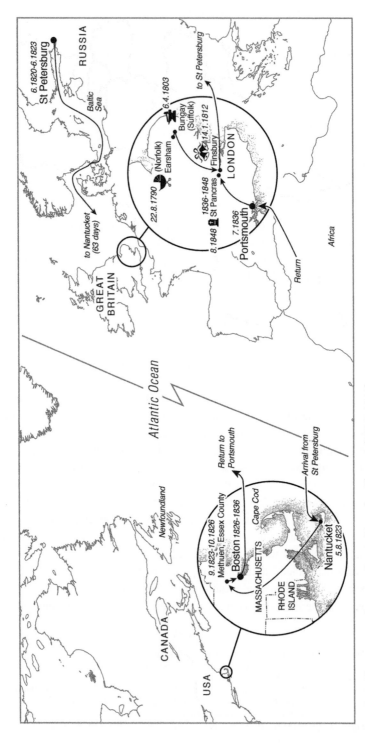

Map 2.4 The moves of gas mechanic Timothy Claxton (1790–1848).

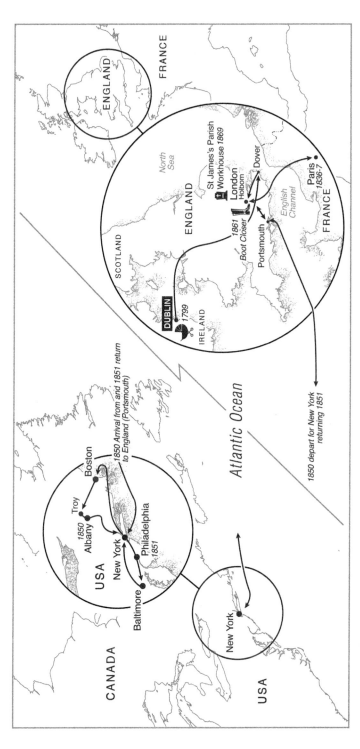

Map 2.5 From what can be inferred from the sources, James Dacres Devlin followed simple migration patterns, though including several steps.

but as a 'boot closer'. Devlin believed that shoemakers, instead of keeping their methods ('crans') secret, should share them with others in the trade. By the late 1830s, shoemaking was not yet mechanised, but was structured according to different specialities, such as clicking, closing, and making—that is, the various stages of the manufacture of shoes and boots. A 'political shoemaker' in his own right, Devlin was a Chartist.[102] In 1838 he was involved in an unsuccessful strike of the London shoemakers. In the 1840s he was part of a group of Chartists which included Thomas Cooper, Julian Harney, John Skelton, and Thomas Shorter.[103] A typical self-taught artisan, he was also a writer, who had contributed to Leigh Hunt's *London Journal* (1834–5). When, for some reason, he tried to emigrate to the United States in September 1850, he wanted to send to the London *Daily News* a series of letters on the condition of workers in the New World.[104] In one that was published, Devlin reflected on the fact that 'in the present year about 300,000 emigrants will probably have made their way from Great Britain to the States': 'Three hundred thousand men and women and male and female children, with all, either now or hereafter, single heads to plan and two hands to labour, passing from the dear "old country" to the "new" in the short space of, at most, about fifty weeks!'. Devlin provided a witty sketch of his 'companion voyagers' onboard the *Actress* which left St Katherine's Dock in London:

> I found myself most strangely commingled with adventurers of the most dis-similar taste, habits, and occupations, as also from very dissimilar localities; with the Irish hod carrier, and the Lincolnshire dyke digger; tailors, carpenters, coopers, and shoemakers, with young women in search of both 'situations' as servants and home-owners; of husbands leaving their wives, and wives going to their husbands; fathers and mothers with large appendages of children, and grandfathers and grandmothers flying from the dread of the workhouse to close their aged eyes in the presence of some beloved son or daughter...[105]

Devlin did not stay long in the United States. When he returned to London, his garret in Holborn was 'crowded with scarce and curious books'. However, Devlin was said to have ended his days in St James's parish workhouse—though this is not substantiated. He left no known autobiography, but several texts, which partly related to his own life, and through which his memory has survived.[106] Several of

[102] E. J. Hobsbawm and Joan Wallach Scott, 'Political Shoemakers', *Past and Present*, no. 89, November 1980, pp. 86–114.

[103] David Goodway, *London Chartism 1838–1848*, Cambridge, 1982, p. 16; p. 282, n. 81.

[104] James Dacres Devlin, *Strangers' Homes; or, the Model Lodging Houses of London*, London, 1853.

[105] 'Work in the West, in Letters from a British Emigrant', *Daily News*, 14 January 1851, p. 3.

[106] Thomas Wright, *The Romance of the Shoe: Being the History of Shoemaking in All Ages, and Especially in England and Scotland*, London, Farncombe, 1922, pp. 166–9; 1861 census (Devlin is listed as a widower, boot closer, aged 61, 2 George Street, in St George Bloomsbury); *Saint Crispin*, 20 March 1869, pp. 157–8, 2 October 1869, p. 160, 19 February 1870, p. 5.

these sources suggest that some of his moves, such as to Paris, involved the learning of skills that did not exist in Britain, for example 'blocking'. However, such skills were artisanal rather than industrial and do not contradict the overall features of cross-Channel technological transfers in this period.

4.4 William Duthie, Goldsmith on the Tramp

When William Duthie (1819–70) was born in London, his working-class father was in a debtors' prison (Figure 2.20). He was trained as a goldsmith at a mechanics' institute in London, and in 1841 as a journeyman he boarded a trading schooner to Hamburg, where he witnessed the great fire in the city on 5 May 1842. He then tramped for three and a half years with his knapsack to Altona, Leipzig, Vienna, and Paris. From Vienna to Strasbourg, he walked 500 miles, at an average rate of three miles an hour and 25 miles a day (see Map 2.6). He always worked in jewellers' and goldsmiths' workshops. Goldsmiths made brooches, bracelets, and necklaces, while jewellers made the mounts to set the gems. Duthie spent seventeen months in Paris, working in a workshop with three Russians, two Germans, two Englishmen, an Italian, and a Frenchman (Figure 2.21). Back in Britain, he married in 1847 and lived in Islington, where he had three children. He published an account of his travels across Europe in *Household Words*, a newspaper edited by Charles Dickens, before his memoirs were published in an extended version as a single volume.[107] The memoir was a well-documented account, with lists of wages and prices, some of which he had experienced personally, some of which he had obviously read about afterwards. A typical self-made, self-taught artisan, Duthie also published two novels.

Figure 2.20 William Duthie (1819–70), probably in his later years (courtesy Nancy Adams, descendant of William Duthie).

[107] William Duthie, *A Tramp's Wallet; stored by an English goldsmith during his wanderings in Germany and France*, London, 1858.

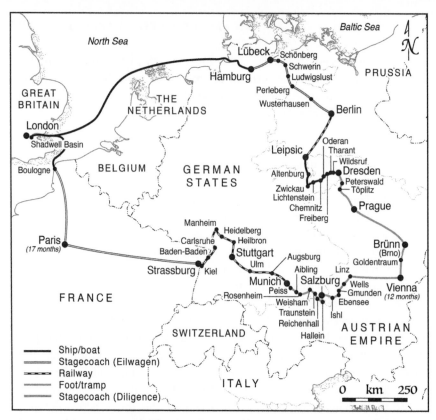

Map 2.6 The route of William Duthie across continental Europe in the early 1840s.

Figure 2.21 A goldsmith's workshop in Paris, 1822. Goldsmiths worked on different workbenches. In the back, the shop with a street entrance (François Barthélémy Augustin Desmoulins (1788–1856), *Vue intérieure des ateliers d'orfèvrerie de Monsieur Odiot*, 1822. Oil on canvas, 56.5 × 81 cm, Bremen, galerie Neuse).

5. Conclusion

The trajectories of these artisans illustrate the extent to which the Continent was perceived as a place of opportunity for British workers in the half-century that followed the end of the Napoleonic wars. As we have seen, most flows were organised by employers, but many workers moved on their own, responding to downturns in the economy of their sector, to word-of-mouth information, or to curiosity. In all these respects, these labour migrants shared the features of the pre-industrial migrant artisan. Yet at the same time, many of the moves we have seen were related to industrialisation. Some categories, like railway navvies, who moved in their thousands were more typical of the industrial age.

So far, most of the moves we have seen were initiated and organised by men. The figure of the 'tramping artisan' was a male one. Mechanics, engineers, iron and steel workers, foremen, factory managers, intermediaries, navvies, railway workers, and miners were all men. The sources that described these flows were also produced by men: newspaper articles, local public records, consular correspondence, parliamentary sources, and even autobiographies were written by men. However, women and children were not absent from these flows. Women moved as the wives of migrant workers, but also as workers in their own right, as we have seen in flax and jute. Children emigrated with their parents, and their entry into the world of labour could occur overseas. We now need to address the questions raised by the migration of women and children in terms of the different labour practices in Britain and France.

3

The Gender of Migration

Women, Children, and Textiles across the Channel

In 1826, Mary Bailey, a Nottingham lace embroiderer, published a collection of poems that mostly described her family life and work, often sadly, as here:

> O God! How hard's my lot
> Nor was a prison dreaded more
> Than entering my cot.[1]

Mary was one of the numerous 'lace runners' working in the new machine-made lace industry. These women and children, who were paid extremely low wages, worked for twelve to fourteen hours a day in darkened workshops in domestic settings, where they ruined their eyesight as well as their fingers because of the assumption that sun and light would damage the lace. Mary often contrasted the distress and occasional hunger she and her children experienced with the luxury of the pieces she embroidered and the indifference of the wealthy customers who purchased them. In a 'Petition to the British Fair', she wrote:

> You ladies of Britain, we most humbly address,
> And hope you will take it in hand,
> And at once condescend on poor RUNNERS to think,
> When dress'd at your glasses you stand.

> How little you think of that lily white veil
> That shields you from gazers and sun:
> How hard have we worked, and our eyes how we've strain'd,
> When those beautiful flowers we run.

> View the ball-room, where beauty beams round,
> And shines with such elegant grace,
> And think you in no ways indebted to us,—
> The RUNNERS of NOTTINGHAM LACE.[2]

---

[1] Mary Bailey, *Poems, Humorous and Sentimental*, Nottingham, 1826, p. 6. Dawn Whatman has found and transcribed one of the rare known copies kept at the Local Studies Library in Nottingham.
[2] 'Petition to the British Fair', Bailey, *Poems*, p. 11.

Artisans Abroad: British Migrant Workers in Industrialising Europe, 1815–1870. Fabrice Bensimon, Oxford University Press.
© Fabrice Bensimon 2023. DOI: 10.1093/oso/9780198835844.003.0004

Hardly anything else is known about Mary Bailey, except that she was the wife of a tailor. That her words have reached us at all is a matter of luck. It might also be the result of a kind of gender solidarity: at the end of her collection of poems, printed locally, there was a list of names of ninety-one subscribers. The practice was common but was mostly a product of male networks. Among Mary's subscribers, however, only twenty-two were men, while sixty-eight were women, and one was an unnamed 'friend'. Perhaps because Mary Bailey had published this 'small pamphlet of poems', an obituary was published in a local paper when she died in 1828 of an 'inflammation fixed on her lungs', 'too poor to employ medical assistance'.[3] She had learnt to read and write because she 'had been ladies' maid in a family of rank and title'. This skill led to her being in the habit of writing letters 'for females of inferior attainments'. She had given birth to at least eleven children, 'the eldest of whom [was] not thirteen' and the youngest just six weeks when she died; nine of them attended her funeral with her widowed husband, who had been sick and whose health was 'delicate'.[4]

Mary Bailey was not a migrant worker to the Continent. But she is one of the few female workers from this period whose words have survived, before the plight of women and children in the 'sweated industries' became a matter for public debate in the 1840s. Indeed, the lives of most of the workers in the nineteenth century, especially women, are unknown and mostly undocumented. For the later periods, historians can rely on some information from the improved censuses of 1841 and especially 1851. Civil registry also became more systematic, and the growth of the local press means that some sketchy information is sometimes available on shopkeepers and artisans. But for the first half of the century, and especially for women, whose occupations even went unrecorded, there is a big blank. Female home workers were a crucial though hidden sector of the workforce in the nineteenth-century economy. But for the workers of the 'sweated industries', who did not even figure in company records, the absence of sources is the rule. At most, a baptism, a death certificate, and a few census entries can be found.

The contribution of women to British industrialisation has been reassessed and addressed from various perspectives.[5] There has been substantial growth in a scholarly field which was, until the early 1970s, limited to Ivy Pinchbeck's

---

[3] 'Died', *Nottingham Review* [hereafter *NR*], 29 August 1828, p. 3.   [4] Ibid.
[5] Ivy Pinchbeck, *Women Workers and the Industrial Revolution, 1750–1850*, London, 1930; Judy Lown, *Women and Industrialization: Gender at Work in Nineteenth Century England*, Cambridge, 1990; Sonya O. Rose, *Limited Livelihoods: Gender and Class in Nineteenth-Century England*, London, 1992; Maxine Berg, 'What Difference Did Women's Work Make to the Industrial Revolution?', *History Workshop*, vol. 35, 1993, pp. 22–44; Sara Horrell and Jane Humphries, 'Women's Labour Force Participation and the Transition to the Male-Breadwinner Family, 1790–1865', *Economic History Review*, 2nd ser., vol. 48, 1995, pp. 89–117; Pamela Sharpe, *Adapting to Capitalism: Working Women in the English Economy, 1700–1850*, Basingstoke, 2000 [1996]; Katrina Honeyman, *Women, Gender and Industrialisation in England, 1700–1870*, New York, 2000; Jutta Schwarzkopf, *Unpicking Gender: The Social Construction of Gender in the Lancashire Cotton Weaving Industry, 1880–1914*, Aldershot, 2004; Joyce Burnette, *Gender, Work and Wages in Industrial Revolution Britain*, Cambridge, 2008.

ground-breaking work. Several trends have emerged. Women played a major, often unacknowledged, part in the industrial revolution. Until the 1840s, when mechanisation gained ground, various strategies on the part of employers and workers, as well as gendered notions regarding the different skills of men and women, resulted in the employment of many women in some sectors, primarily in the textile industry, and mostly in 'unskilled' or 'low-skilled', low-paid positions. At the same time, for many other occupations, including those for which corporations and trade unions played an active part, male exclusiveness was the rule. Protective labour legislation also contributed to the exclusion of women from the labour market. By the 1860s, the male breadwinner model prevailed. The two world wars excepted, it would be more than a century until women could work as mechanics, iron and steel workers, masons, carpenters, navvies, or engineers, or even simply remain in employment once married. What the historical literature shows is also a great degree of regional and occupational diversity with respect to employment opportunities as well as wage levels, with important inequalities between male and female workers.

Cross-border comparisons have helped us better understand the contribution of women and children.[6] Forty years ago, Joan Scott and Louise Tilly authoritatively compared female labour in France and England, with a focus on the cotton industry.[7] By 1850, women accounted for about 30 per cent of the total workforce in Britain, and slightly more in France. Until the 1960s, these rates rose little. Sex-typing and segregation in both countries adhered to similar patterns: women were concentrated in low-paid jobs, and seen as unskilled. In the first half of the nineteenth century, France remained predominantly agricultural and industrialisation was in its infancy. The employment structures of women on both sides of the Channel thus differed. In England in 1851, 45 per cent of all women workers worked in manufacturing; by 1866, when France was industrialising, only 27.3 per cent of working women were in manufacturing—mostly in textiles and the garment industry.[8] In production units where both men and women operated, women were often confined to the lowest-paid jobs. There was thus a major difference between both countries: because the French economy was characterised by small-scale organisation in the nineteenth century, the proportion of women in the workforce was higher than in Britain.[9] The persistence of small family farms and businesses in France made it possible to combine employment and domestic chores, unlike in Britain where factory production was predominant. Although

---

[6] Richard Biernacki, *The Fabrication of Labor: Germany and Britain, 1640–1914*, Berkeley, CA, 1995; Laura Lee Downs, *Manufacturing Inequality: Gender Division in the French and British Metalworking Industries, 1914–1939*, Ithaca, NY, 1995; Hugh Cunningham and P. P. Viazzo (eds.), *Child Labour in Historical Perspective, 1800–1985: Case Studies from Europe, Japan and Colombia*, Florence, 1996; Schwarzkopf, *Unpicking Gender*, 2004.

[7] Louise A. Tilly and Joan W. Scott, *Women, Work and Family*, New York, 1987 [1978].

[8] *Ibid.*, p. 69.   [9] *Ibid.*, p. 230.

studies of other sectors such as the garment industry have refined this view, showing that the evolutionary process from home to factory and from independent artisan to wage earner was more open-ended than previously thought, this distinction between France and Britain remains important for understanding changes in the economies of both countries.[10] However, in both countries, women were a major presence in the textile industry. This history is now well known for the British industrial revolution. In France, the textile industry was mostly located in and around Lille, in Saint-Quentin in Picardy, in Mulhouse in Alsace, and in the Rouen area of Normandy. The early textile factories, from the end of the eighteenth century, relied upon the participation of large numbers of women and children.[11] It was in this sector that wage-earning for women and children first became standard. Factory owners were indeed keen on such a cheap workforce, as we shall see. Sewing and textile work were constructed as female activities. Alongside men, women had tried to resist the progress of machinery which threatened their work in the domestic economy. But with the gradual concentration of textile output, they had to find work in factories. By the 1850s and 1860s, the textile industry employed most of the factory women. Their work was regarded as unskilled, even when, like the women in the Glasgow cotton industry or in the Dundee linen and jute manufacturing, they were spinners— while the male spinners in Lancashire and the male carders in linen managed to retain the status of skilled workers.

Tilly and Scott have also insisted on the importance of life cycles in female occupation. Andrew Ure remarked: 'it is known by the returns, and the factory commission inquiries, that very few women work in the factories after marriage'.[12] Women were often wage-earners before marriage, then withdrew from the labour market upon marrying, and then sometimes returned to it when children left the home or when the eldest child was old enough to mind younger siblings. In the home, other forms of income-related occupations prevailed, such as taking lodgers, doing laundry, or other forms of domestic labour.

Since Tilly and Scott, there has also been a large amount of research on domestic service, showing that although servants and unpaid housewives did not feature in the narratives of industrialisation, their work made it possible. It contributed to liberating middle-class men from domestic chores, while working-class housewives contributed to their husbands and sons getting paid work, often with long working hours. In Britain and then on the Continent, domestic service was the first occupation for working-class women. Migration was central in domestic service, from the countryside to the larger towns, from the provinces

[10] Judith G. Coffin, *The Politics of Women's Work: The Paris Garment Trades, 1750–1915*, Princeton, NJ, 1996, pp. 5–6.
[11] Madeleine Guilbert, *Les fonctions des femmes dans l'industrie*, Paris, 1966, p. 35.
[12] Andrew Ure, *The Philosophy of Manufactures*, London, 1835, p. 475.

to capital cities, and from abroad, with the Irish in Britain and the United States, or with German and Belgian servants in France. Some British servants also emigrated to the Continent, sometimes following their masters, like Sarah Cook, a twenty-two-year-old maid who in 1851 lived with the forty-seven-year-old widow of a rentier in Rocquefort, a small village in Normandy, where they were the only British out of 682 inhabitants.[13]

In manufacturing, however, the main female sector of employment on both sides of the Channel was textiles. How did migrant workers in this sector feature into the general picture we now have of the gendering of work? Did women play the same part as they did in Britain? Was the gender segregation that prevailed in British textiles the same overseas? Was the hierarchy in wages similar?

To address these questions, we can focus on two categories: the female linen and jute spinners and the female workers in machine-made lace. This chapter first focuses on the migrant female linen workers, who moved from Scotland and Ulster to the Continent (section 1). It then compares the parallel development of machine-made lace across the Channel and the ways in which this was mediated by the migration of capital, labour, and expertise. In both countries, machine-made lace competed with female-dominated hand-worked lace. In both countries, it initially relied on manpower and was largely produced domestically, until the shift to steam power and factory production. This chapter assesses whether this sector fits Scott and Tilly's overall model about gendered work patterns and life cycles (section 2). In so doing, unlike other chapters, it does not just focus on migrants but also compares the gender division of labour in textiles in Britain and France. It also compares child labour in lace on both sides of the Channel. As we shall see, the work of children was related to that of women as both categories were supposed to work in auxiliary parts of the production process (section 3). It focuses on wage hierarchies between men, women, and children in machine-made lace (section 4). Focusing on the two areas where the lace industry became most prominent, the East Midlands and the Calais area, this chapter argues that in machine-made lace, similarities were more important than differences. It relies on sources in both countries: official records (parliamentary and local enquiries such as those of the Calais Chamber of commerce and industry); local newspaper information; and, on occasion, ego-documents, though these are scarce. Section 5 concludes.

1. Linen and Jute Spinners across the Channel

From the late 1830s, several hundred young female workers in linen emigrated from Ulster and Dundee to the flax and jute works that were set up in the

---

[13] AD Seine-Maritime. 6M114 (2Mi 1004). Recensement de 1851. Rocquefort.

northwest of the Continent. In Dundee, female spinners played a critical part. As historians Louise Miskell and Chris Whatley have shown, they came either from the east-central textile region which Dundee had long served as a merchant centre or from Ulster. Irish immigration, which was evident from the late eighteenth century, accelerated after the mid-1840s: as the linen proto-industry declined in Ulster, migration was an attractive proposition, especially during and after the Great Famine. By 1851, the Irish made up one fifth of the population of Dundee and perhaps one half of the number employed in the town's textile trade. A great majority of these workers were women: they then accounted for 68 per cent of the textile workers in the town—that is, even more than in the rest of the country (53 per cent). The low wages Dundee manufacturers paid to these women gave them an advantage over their competitors outside Scotland.[14] As a result, Dundee women were, on average, more economically active (40.5 per cent in 1861) than the rest of Scottish women (33 per cent), and remained so until the Great War, while employment rates of women were declining across the country. Dundee was known as 'a woman's town', with about two thirds of the population being women. A correlated difference was that in Dundee a significant proportion of married women had paid work: while, according to the 1911 census, only 5 per cent of the women in Scotland and 9.6 per cent in Britain had paid work, the rate reached 23.4 per cent in Dundee—and was probably twice as much in reality, as historian Eleanor Gordon has shown.[15] At the same time, the industry in Dundee was cyclical, with booms and busts resulting in workers being laid off. Opportunities to work overseas, in France or Belgium, could therefore prove welcome.

As the flax industry was starting to become mechanised in the 1830s and 1840s on the Continent, British or continental employers were therefore keen on hiring young Dundee female spinners. They could operate the same machines they had operated in Dundee and for which continental manufacturers had no skilled workforce. In these factories, the structure of employment resembled that of Dundee and Leeds, the two main centres of British linen and jute, with male carders, mechanics, and foremen, and female spinners and winders (Figures 3.1 and 3.2). In Landerneau (Brittany), while the wages of male workers were higher than those of the local workforce, those of migrant women were much lower: by the late 1850s, Scottish and Irish spinners only earned 1.25 francs, while the male carders, who were often their husbands or their brothers, earned 4 francs, and mechanics 4.25 francs (see p. 52).[16] Single women usually lived in Landerneau, but most couples lived in nearby Pencran, where a 'Scottish village'

---

[14] Louise Miskell and C. A. Whatley, '"Juteopolis" in the Making: Linen and the Industrial Transformation of Dundee, c. 1820–1850', *Textile History*, vol. 30, no, 2, 1999, pp. 176–98.

[15] Eleanor Gordon, *Women and the Labour Movement in Scotland, 1850–1914*, Oxford, 1991, p. 20. In the 1911 census, married women were listed separately for the first time.

[16] AD Finistère, 6M 1039 Salaires industriels—1853–92.

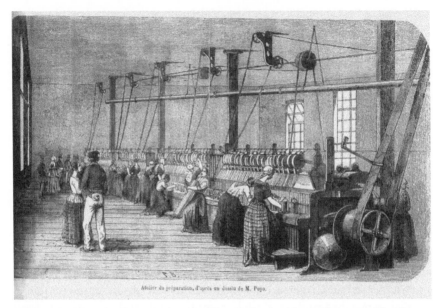

Figure 3.1 The preparing department of the Landerneau flax mill in 1849. This factory numbered many female workers. To the left, the man is probably a mechanic or a foreman ('Atelier de préparation', *L'Illustration*, 27 October 1849, p. 141).

Figure 3.2 The winding workshop in the Landerneau flax mill, operated by female workers and supervised by a man ('Atelier de dévidage', *L'Illustration*, 27 October 1849, p. 141).

was built. In Pencran, infant mortality was 262 deaths per 1,000 live births for the Scots in the period 1845–82, while the 1850 average was 150 in England and Wales, 120 per 1,000 in Scotland, and about 250 in France. Illiteracy was also high: 84 per cent of the women could not sign their employment booklets ('livrets de travail'); that is, below the average literacy rates in Scotland (see p. 145).[17] The Scottish spinners in Landerneau were nevertheless supposed to educate a local workforce which could gradually be substituted. A local newspaper reported:

> The attitude of the Scottish women with the children whose apprenticeship they had to monitor has always been admirable. Far from keeping them in ignorance for easily-understandable reasons, they were not only keen on teaching them, but they also showed affectionate proofs of their sympathy. Many times they were seen sharing their food with these young female workers whose wretchedness made them pitiful, before the company started feeding them.[18]

It is likely that these pictures of linen workshops were in some ways idealised, and that such relaxed attitudes in a clean and neat workshop were unlikely. Jules Simon—who opposed female labour—wrote:

> preparing hemp, linen, especially tow, produce an unhealthy and plentiful dust. They can only be carded and spun at a high temperature and with the addition of water. Nothing is more painful than a poorly kept flax spinning mill. Water covers the brick-paved floor; the smell of flax and a temperature sometimes above 25 °C spread an unbearable stench across the workshop. Most working women, compelled to get rid of most of their clothes, are there, in this stinky atmosphere, imprisoned between machines, close to one another, with their bodies sweating and bare feet, with water up to the ankles.[19]

---

[17] Yves Blavier, *La société linière du Finistère. Ouvriers et entrepreneurs à Landerneau au XIXᵉ siècle*, Rennes, 1999, p. 139.

[18] 'La conduite des écossaises particulièrement a toujours été admirable à l'égard des enfants dont elles ont été appelées à diriger l'apprentissage. Loin de les maintenir dans l'ignorance par des motifs faciles à comprendre ; elles se sont non seulement attachées à les instruire, mais elles leur ont donné souvent d'affectueuses preuves de sympathie. Maintes fois on les a vues partager leur nourriture avec les petites ouvrières dont la misère excitait leur pitié, avant que la société se fut décidée à les nourrir'. *Annuaire de Brest et du Finistère*, 1850, p. 153.

[19] 'Les préparations du chanvre, du lin, surtout des étoupes, dégagent une poussière abondante et malsaine. On ne peut les carder et les filer qu'à une température élevée et avec addition d'eau. Rien n'est plus douloureux à voir qu'une filature de lin mal entretenue. L'eau couvre le parquet pavé de briques; l'odeur du lin et une température qui dépasse quelquefois 25 degrés répandent dans tout l'atelier une puanteur intolérable. La plupart des ouvrières, obligées de quitter la plus grande partie de leurs vêtemens, sont là, dans cette atmosphère empestée, emprisonnées entre des machines, serrées les unes contre les autres, le corps en transpiration, les pieds nus, ayant de l'eau jusqu'à la cheville'. Jules Simon, 'Etudes morales. Le Salaire et le travail des femmes. II. Les femmes dans les filatures', *Revue des Deux Mondes*, vol. 28, 1860, p. 568.

Another way to address gender inequality at work is to focus on wages and to wonder whether the inequality that prevailed in Britain between men and women was echoed in France. Though Joyce Burnette and Janet Greenlees have argued that women's wages during industrialisation could be up to two thirds those of men, most studies have argued the proportions were from one third to one half.[20] Relying on the 1834 Supplementary Report on the Employment of Children in Factories, which was largely based on questionnaires returned by at least a quarter of textile factories, Paul Minoletti made a similar point regarding the cotton industry, adding that trends in the sex ratio of wages were similar in wool, silk, flax, and lace.[21]

Sonya O. Rose, Katrina Honeyman, Maxine Berg, Pamela Sharpe, and Paul Minoletti have argued that manufacturers based women's wages on custom and ideology, assuming their skills to be inferior to those of men. Burnette has argued instead that market forces regulated this differential: unequal wages reflected differences in productivity, which were determined by natural strength and the fact that only women were capable of giving birth and breast-feeding. The reasons for the gap are difficult to determine, however, since contemporaries seldom debated whether, and why, women's wages should be lower: manufacturers and workmen simply took it for granted that this should be the case. Occupational specialisation and wage differentials were often, though not always, the continuation of practices that were rooted in the pre-industrial economy.[22]

In Landerneau, as we have seen, while the wages of the British carders and mechanics could be much higher than those of the local workforce, those of migrant women were much lower. The usual wage difference that could be observed in Britain also prevailed in France (see Table 1.6). We have seen that, in some respects, gender mattered more than nationality (p. 51).

For the Dickson factory in Coudekerque-Branche (Nord), we do not know how wages varied according to nationality. But in 1859, when David Dickson

---

[20] Berg, 'What Difference Did Women's Work Make', p. 31; Pamela Sharpe, *Adapting to Capitalism: Working Women in the English Economy, 1700–1850*, Basingstoke, 2000, p. 146; Honeyman, *Women, Gender and Industrialisation*, p. 54; Burnette, *Gender, Work and Wages*, p. 73; Janet Greenlees, *Female Labour Power: Women Workers' Influence on Business Practices in the British and American Cotton Industries, 1780–1860*, Burlington, VT, 2007, pp. 80–3.

[21] Paul Minoletti, 'The Importance of Ideology: The Shift to Factory Production and Its Effect on Women's Employment Opportunities in the English Textile Industries, 1760–1850', *Continuity and Change*, vol. 28, no. 1, 2013, p. 127.

[22] Alice Clark, *Working Life of Women in the Seventeenth Century*, London, 1919; Susan Cahn, *Industry of Devotion: The Transformation of Women's Work in England, 1500–1660*, New York, 1987, ch. 2; Bridget Hill, *Women, Work and Sexual Politics in Eighteenth-Century England*, London, 1993.

Table 3.1 Wages in the Dickson factory in Coudekerque-Branche (Nord) in 1859[23, 24]

	Weekly wages	Day wages
Preparing department (women)	7.50 F	1.25 F
Spinners (women)	9 F	1.5 F
Winders (women)	6.6 F	1.1 F
Weavers (women)	12 F	2 F
Weavers (men)	15 F	2.5 F
Mechanics (men)	15 to 24 F	2.5 to 4 F

was interviewed by the French government about his position regarding duties with Britain, Scottish spinners represented a minority of the female workforce, while most of the mechanics and foremen were still British. Dickson thus explained the gender division of labour, which was the same as in Dundee: 'Men are employed…in all works demanding physical exertion'.[25] Dickson's practice was inspired by the values which traditionally differentiated men's work and women's work. But he also found obvious financial interest in this division and organisation of work. He employed 608 women (70 per cent) and 260 men (30 per cent), working seventy-two hours a week, for whom, in his written answers to the inquiry, he paid the wages shown in Table 3.1.

At first glance, differences between male and female wages were less important than they were in Landerneau, for instance with female weavers earning 80 per cent of the wages of male weavers. But when Dickson was interviewed by the Committee, he complained that it was difficult to find enough skilled female spinners in France, and that he had to hire more in Dundee. He gave details showing wages were often lower, and were not very different from those mentioned in Landerneau at the same time:

> The Chair [the minister]: Do your apprentice spinners earn less than your spinners?
>
> Dickson: The wages of the apprentices can be assessed from 0.6 to 1.2 francs per day; and when I have a good spinner, I give her 1.5 francs.[26]

---

[23] AD Finistère, 6M 1039 Salaires industriels—1853–92.   [24] Ibid.

[25] 'Les hommes sont employés au peignage et au tissage des toiles, voiles, dans tous les travaux qui exigent de la fatigue, tels que la préparation des fils, le débouillissage, le crémage, etc.', Conseil supérieur de l'agriculture, du commerce et de l'industrie, *Enquête: traité de commerce avec l'Angleterre*, Paris, vol. 5, 1860–2, p. 51.

[26] 'Le Président; Vos apprenties fileuses doivent avoir un salaire moindre que vos fileuses?

M. Dickson: Le salaire des apprenties peut être évaluée de 60 centimes à 1,20 f. par jour; et quand j'ai une bonne fileuse, je lui donne 1,50 fr.'. Ibid., p. 52.

This, and what Dickson said about the rare qualifications of the Dundee female spinners (see p. 70), reminds us that the skills of women workers were not inferior to those of men, although they were not acknowledged socially speaking or in terms of wages. As several historians have argued, skill was not an objective factor distinguishing between occupations, but a social construction.[27]

We do not know to what extent the Dundee female workers faced opposition to their employment. In France, in Catholic circles but also among some sections of the early labour movement, there was some hostility to female paid work. In Landerneau, the arrival of some female workers from Dundee had been publicised in the local newspaper, and L'Atelier (1840–50), which was an influential 'paper written by the workers themselves', in fact written by supporters of the Christian socialist Philippe Buchez, complained that:

It was not without deep sadness that we [L'Atelier] have read of an event publicized in nearly all the newspapers.

"The steamship the Finistère has recently disembarked in Morlaix thirty-eight Scottish women who are destined for the Landerneau mill. These women are intended to form the core of the workers of Société linière du Finistère. They have worked in manufactories since they were children; they obey any voice or sign, with a precision that would shame an elite battalion. When they left the steam-ship, they lined up on the wharf waiting for the order to set off. Although they were allowed to walk in Morlaix in the two or three hours before they departed, none had the curiosity to do so and all got into the carriages that were due to take them to Landerneau with the imperviousness and silence of a machine obeying its motor".[28] ...

If our Anglomaniacs have brought this sample of Britons to France with the aim of promoting and generalizing a similar result among us then they would do singular violence to our national spirit. To mould human nature to the point where it is reduced to the state of a machine, to reduce it to the passive role of a beast that one commands is repellent to this spirit. One can only speak with pity of the conditions of manufacturing workers on whom our modern lords of capital have practised for so long the disastrous

[27] Rose, Limited Livelihoods, p. 22; Anne Phillips and Barbara Taylor. 'Sex and Skill: Notes Towards a Feminist Economics', Feminist Review, vol. 6, 1980, pp. 56–79; Cynthia Cockburn, Machinery of Dominance: Women, Men and Technical Know-How, London, 1985, p. 4.
[28] L'Impartial du Finistère, 3 November 1847, is being quoted by L'Atelier, November 1847, vol. 3, p. 32.

theories of the English economists. Would one promote to the limit so abominable a system?[29]

L'Atelier reflected the French left-wing vision that Britain was a materialistic and self-interested society. In his 'Signs of the Times' (1829), Thomas Carlyle had also argued that British society had become mechanical in head and heart. And in 1845, Victor Hugo noted: 'If France is the victor, the world will be ruled by the 24 letters of the alphabet; if England wins, it will be tyrannised by the ten arithmetical figures'.[30] French anglophiles were usually liberals who were seen as wanting to import the inhuman factory system to France. Republicans and socialists for their part considered British emigrants as embodying this degrading system, and *L'Atelier*'s criticism may be related to its objection to female paid work. In fact, all direct evidence available contradicts *L'Atelier*: as we have seen, the Dundee workers employed in Landerneau were more skilled than the Breton workers recruited in this very rural area, which had no industrial tradition. They were generally well integrated. They trained their French fellow-workers, some of them married Frenchmen, and in 1848 there were no protests against them, though there were others in different parts of the country (see Chapter 6).

We lack information about individual trajectories. However, female workers sometimes feature in local records. In Coudekerque, while most of the workers seemed to have come in family groups to work for Dickson, some young Scottish

---

[29] 'Nous n'avons point lu sans un profond sentiment de tristesse le fait suivant, publié par presque tous les journaux:

'Le bateau à vapeur le *Finistère* a débarqué ces jours-ci à Morlaix trente-huit Ecossaises à destination de la filature de Landerneau. Ces femmes sont destinées à former le noyau d'ouvrières de la Société linière du Finistère. Elles travaillent dans les manufactures depuis leur enfance, obéissent à la voix, au signe même, avec une précision qui ferait honte à un bataillon d'élite. A leur sortie du bateau à vapeur, elles se sont rangées sur le quai pour attendre l'ordre de marcher. Quoique on leur eût laissé la faculté de se promener pendant les deux ou trois heures qui séparaient leur arrivée de leur départ, aucune d'elles n'a eu la curiosité de visiter la ville de Morlaix, et toutes se sont embarquées dans les voitures qui doivent les emporter à Landerneau avec l'insouciance et le silence d'une machine qui obéit à un moteur.'

Si nos anglomanes ont amené en France cet échantillon britannique dans le but de provoquer et de généraliser parmi nous un résultat semblable, il faudra qu'ils fassent singulièrement violence à notre esprit national. Pétrir la nature humaine au point de la réduire à l'état de machine et de l'abaisser au rôle passif d'une brute que l'on commande, est une chose qui révolte l'esprit. L'on ne parle qu'avec pitié de la condition des ouvriers de la manufacture, sur lesquels nos modernes seigneurs du capital ont expérimenté, par une longue pratique, les désastreuses théories des économistes anglais. Voudrait-on pousser jusqu'à ses dernières conséquences un si abominable système?'. *L'Atelier*, November 1847, vol. 3, p. 32.

[30] 'Si la France a le dessus, le monde sera gouverné par les vingt-quatre lettres de l'alphabet; si l'Angleterre l'emporte, il sera tyrannisé par les dix chiffres de l'artihmétique'. Victor Hugo, *Choses vues*, Paris, 1887 [1845].

women obviously came on their own, like Margaret, Helen, and Sarah Macfell (or McFale), three sisters aged twenty-one, seventeen, and fifteen, who came without their parents, suggesting some agency, though the sources reveal nothing more.[31] James Carmichael, in his linen and jute works in Ailly-sur-Somme, wrote in 1846 to his brother Peter that he dismissed one of his Dundee spinners—a 'poor Creature...brought almost to starvation'—an action he was gratified to find that was supported by the local court, causing him to reflect with some satisfaction that he had 'little fear from the remaining people I have'.[32] However, Carmichael lost a case in a 'prud'homme' (labour dispute) court versus a certain Jess Young— who was probably a Dundee woman worker—who refused to 'care for both sides of the spinning frame', arguing that she had only cared for one side in Britain. The court argued she had never cared for both sides of the machine, and that as a result there was no reason she should now be compelled to do so.[33] We know nothing else about Jess Young, who does not feature in the 1851 census record for Ailly-sur-Somme. She might be the 'Jessie Young', a linen spinner from Dundee who worked in 1848 at the La Foudre factory in Petit-Quevilly, from whence she had to leave with other workers in March 1848 (see Chapter 6).[34] After all, as we have seen, workers often moved from one factory to another, and Petit-Quevilly was only 70 miles from Ailly. Though the destiny of Jess Young is unknown, and her words are missing, her case shows that, even when they were on their own and far from home, young female factory workers retained their agency and could put up individual resistance to exploitative factory management.

2. Gender and the Transition to Machine-Made Lace

To assess how the gender segregation at work was translated overseas, machine-made lace is another relevant case. As we have seen, it gradually replaced pillow-lace, which was a female monopoly. Lace machinery was operated by men but relied on a large workforce of women and children with specific occupations. Pamela Sharpe and Stanley Chapman have discussed this division of labour and its changing contours: based on their analysis of lace embroidery in Essex, Limerick, and Nottingham, they insist on the part played by women, with a rising emphasis on the cleanliness and respectability of women's work in the

---

[31] Odette Bonte, 'Coudekerque-Branche, les Dickson et la colonie d'Ecossais', *Revue de la Société dunkerquoise d'histoire et d'archéologie*, no. 26, November 1992, p. 178; Archives municipales de Coudekerque-Branche, recensement de 1861 (they are listed as 25 route de Bourbourg).

[32] UDAS, MS 102/9 (14), James Carmichael to Peter Carmichael, 22 April 1846.

[33] James Carmichael's diary, in Jean-Paul Delahaye, 'La Filature d'Ailly-sur-Somme', Mémoire de maîtrise, Université de Picardie, 1976, pp. 14–15. Delahaye had access to family papers, including Carmichael's diary, which has since been lost.

[34] AD Seine-Maritime. 10 M 324. Mouvement et émigration de la main-d'œuvre...Renvoi d'ouvriers étrangers 1848.

nineteenth century.[35] This chapter aims to return to this question using the example of lace, during the transition from manpower in homes and small workshops to steam-powered, factory production. A significant dimension of this trade is, as we have seen, its transnational nature. We know that many lace runners from Nottingham like Mary Bailey emigrated with their husbands or their fathers, who were the 'twisthands' of the trade. The part played by children has also been the object of several reassessments. These point to the varied and multiple forms of labour, not just in the textile manufacture and the coal pit but also in the home, in the workshop, in the shop, or on the farm. In most cases, children contributed to family incomes even more than women. Not only did a large proportion of children work, but industrialisation was possible thanks to the expansion of child labour.[36] Children played a critical part in lace, often assisting their mothers, and they also emigrated with their parents, following them in their quest for work.

2.1 Britain

From the seventeenth to the nineteenth centuries, lace manufacture, Sharpe argued, was 'one of the only examples of enduring female-dominated occupational communities in English history'.[37] Those involved in production were mostly young women who were not yet victims of the reduced eyesight, back and neck pain, consumption, and dyspepsia associated with years of working in dark rooms and damp conditions. Those who stored the lace and sold it were also women. During the Napoleonic wars, when foreign competition was limited, the industry experienced a golden age. This ended with the invention of lace machines, from 1809, when, relying on a series of improvements, Loughborough hosiery manufacturer John Heathcoat patented a bobbin-net machine which produced a good imitation of handmade lace (see pp. 28–39). Hosiery was concentrated in the East Midlands, especially in Nottinghamshire, and it was being challenged by the mechanisation of the cotton industry.

Machine-made lace grew out of the hosiery industry, as we have seen, and it emerged in hosiery's traditional heartlands: Nottinghamshire, Leicestershire, and

[35] Pamela Sharpe and Stanley D. Chapman, 'Women's Employment and Industrial Organisation: Commercial Lace Embroidery in Early Nineteenth-Century Ireland and England', *Women's History Review*, vol. 5, 1996, pp. 325–50.

[36] Clark Nardinelli, *Child Labor and the Industrial Revolution*, Bloomington, IN, 1990; Sara Horrell and Jane Humphries, '"The Exploitation of Little Children": Child Labor and the Family Economy in the Industrial Revolution', *Explorations in Economic History*, vol. 32, no. 4, pp. 485–516; Peter Kirby, *Child Labour in Britain 1750–1870*, London, 2003; Jane Humphries, *Childhood and Child Labour in the British Industrial Revolution*, Cambridge, 2010; Nigel Goose and Katrina Honeyman (eds.), *Childhood and Child Labour in Industrial England: Diversity and Agency, 1750–1914*, Aldershot, 2013.

[37] Pamela Sharpe, 'Lace and Place: Women's Business in Occupational Communities in England 1550–1950', *Women's History Review*, vol. 19, no. 2, 2010, p. 301.

Derbyshire, with Nottingham playing a central role. An exception was Tiverton (Devon), which was an offshoot of the Midlands industry. Pillow-lace remained concentrated in its traditional rural areas of Bedfordshire, Buckinghamshire, and Northamptonshire. For decades, both sectors competed. Initially, machines could not produce the more complex types of lace, and customers were keen on the qualities of the craft which they saw as superior—wasn't the Queen's wedding dress made with hand-worked lace? However, by the late 1830s, the price difference between craft and the equivalent machine-made products was already estimated to be eight to one.[38] Handmade lace survived only because of the huge demand in the 1840s and 1850s among the middle class.[39]

The expansion of consumption was mostly achieved thanks to the growth of machine-made production. In the long term, the defeat of handmade lace was inevitable, and by the end of the century it had collapsed. From 1851 to 1881, the recorded number of hand lace workers fell from 32,819 to 14,134.[40]

At the artisan stage, lace machines were 'in the great majority' operated by men, usually assisted by boys. It was argued that 'the employment, especially in the wide machines, [was] very laborious, and, unless a wheel is used, require[d] the constant exercise of the hands and feet'.[41] As the width of the machines increased, more wheels were used. However, physical strength may not have been the single or even the determining factor, as young children sometimes operated the machines:

> Many boys, however, are employed either to assist the men, or where the machine is propelled by a wheel, then to take the entire charge of it. (N° 193, 194) Turning the wheel is very hard work: it is also liable to the objection of being carried at all hours of the night, no distinction in this respect being made in favour of the children (N° 192).[42]

Men were probably stronger than women, although we know that physical abilities are partly socially constructed; for instance, men had better access to nutritional resources.[43] However, prejudice regarding gender roles, rather than male physical strength, was a key reason for the exclusion of women from the machines. Framework knitters had traditionally been men, and so were the

---

[38] William Felkin, *A History of the Machine-Wrought Hosiery and Lace Manufactures*, London, 1867, pp. 360–5.

[39] G. F. R. Spenceley, 'The English Pillow Lace Industry 1840–80: A Rural Industry in Competition with Machinery', *Business History*, vol. 19, 1977, p. 72.

[40] Census figures cited in Spenceley, 'The English Pillow Lace Industry 1840–80', pp. 68–87.

[41] Royal Commission on Children's Employment in Mines and Manufactories. 1843. Second Report (Manufactures). Appendix, vol. 13, f. 3, 17.

[42] Royal Commission 1843: vol. 3, f. 3, 18.

[43] Jane Humphries, '"Bread and a Penny-Worth of Treacle": Differential Female Mortality in England in the 1840s', *Cambridge Journal of Economics*, vol. 15, no. 4, 1991, pp. 451–73.

twisthands who operated the lace machines. As Sonya O. Rose has argued, the ability to run large, complex machinery was believed to be a natural male attribute.[44] While domestic cotton spinning had traditionally been a female preserve, men operated the large self-acting mules; women often worked on the smaller power looms for weaving, which had been a male preserve in the proto-industry. When steam power was introduced into the lace industry, making the work far less physical, the operation of machines remained a male preserve. Rose noted that it was only at the end of the century that women were permitted to operate some machines, at which point special machines that made embroidered and braided laces were introduced by manufacturers as 'women's machines'.[45] But twisthands remained exclusively male. Occupational specialisation was a self-fulfilling prophecy: because they were not deemed good mechanics, women did not operate machinery; and because they did not operate machinery, they were not seen as technically competent. All overseers were men, as no adult man would accept to be supervised by a woman, even when this was not explicitly stated.[46]

At the same time, as Pinchbeck observed, 'while Machinery was one of the chief causes which deprived thousands of women of employment in the old lacemaking counties, it created at the same time an entirely new field of employment for an enormous number of women and children'.[47] Overall, Honeyman, Sharpe, and Chapman have confirmed this. The female workforce in lace was distributed between women working in their homes and those working in the workshops. Male lacemakers operating the machines were usually assisted by women and children who provided them with the bobbins of thread and took away the lace for further processing. A parliamentary committee reported in 1843 that in a temperature of 75–80 degrees Fahrenheit children from seven years old and women were employed twelve to twenty hours a day winding, threading, or taking lace off machines.[48] After a piece of net had left the machine, it underwent a series of operations which were usually carried out in other premises, especially homes, and were mostly performed by women like Mary Bailey and by children. First, there was the removal of the hairy filaments of the cotton. Then, some sorts of lace were embroidered by the 'lace runners' who, with the needle, imprinted a pattern on the net, which was stretched out horizontally, about 3 feet from the ground (Figure 3.3). Then the lace was sent back for mending; that is, removing the defects of the net. It was dyed or bleached and then 'dressed' with a mixture of gum, paste, and water, giving it some stiffness. Last, articles would be rendered suitable for marketing, by rolling, pressing, packing, and ticketing. Most of these

---

[44] Rose, *Limited Livelihoods*, p. 23.   [45] Ibid., p. 24.
[46] Minoletti, 'The Importance of Ideology', pp. 71–90.
[47] Pinchbeck, *Women Workers and the Industrial Revolution*, p. 209.
[48] Rose, *Limited Livelihoods*, p. 26.

[Lace-runners or Embroiderers at Work.]

Figure 3.3 'Our frontispiece ... was taken in a garret or attic in a house in an humble neigbourhood, in which seven or eight young women were a work. ... To eke out their earnings, the women in one room often have their meals in common ... There they sit, for twelve or fourteen hours a day, with the head stooping over their work, plying the needle, and driving off dull thoughts as well as they may be singing. ... It is not unfrequent for them to say—'If the great ladies of London knew how much work we have to do to their veils and capes for a shilling, they would pay better'. ('Lace-runners or Embroiderers at work'. 'A day at the Nottingham lace-manufactories', *Penny Magazine*, March 1843, vol. 12, pp. 113, 119.) © Private collection.

processes that followed machine production were seen as requiring less skill and training, and they were carried out by women and children (Figure 3.4).

Census enumerations did not properly report the occupations of the women and children, but some statistical attempts were made. Most machines were successively operated by two men, for a shift of ten hours each (e.g. 4 a.m.– 2 p.m. and 2–12 p.m.). Social enquirer R. D. Grainger reported:

> The most common time is 16, 18, and particularly 20 hours per diem; but if the trade is brisk, and 'when they can sell, the men work the machines all night and day'. Towards the end of the week it is also common to work all night, to make up the time which is lost by idleness on Monday and Tuesday.[49]

---

[49] Royal Commission 1843, vol. 13, f.3, 19.

Figure 3.4 'Lace Making. Engraved by T. Hollis from a daguerreotype' (undated, probably 1850s). While the twisthands were men, the other operations were performed by women and children, such as bobbin winding. © Stanley Chapman.

Long hours for machine operators meant long hours for children and women. In 1832 it was estimated that 'about 5,500 machines were fully employed in that manufacture, which required about 9,000 bobbin-net workmen, who, with other persons engaged, amounted in men and able boys to about 13,000 male persons; to which must be added, for ornamenting and preparing the lace, more than 20,000 women and children'. Ten years later, the industry was in crisis, and it was reported that only 2,000 machines were operated by 3,200 men, while 6,000 women and children—60 to 65 per cent of the workers—worked in the sector.[50] By 1831, Felkin estimated that the industry employed 180,000 women and children in their homes as regular workers—a figure one factory commissioner believed to be 'overstated'.[51] By the mid-1830s, after a crisis, Felkin still thought the industry employed 150,000 people, but this number was not substantiated.[52] In 1851 and 1861, parliamentary reports estimated that there were about 135,000 workers in the trade.[53]

2.2 France

In France as in Britain, hand-worked lace employed women. In Normandy and Le Puy, some 200,000 women produced handmade lace. It required years of

---

[50] 'Hosiery and Lace Trades', *Nottingham Journal*, 23 September 1842.
[51] Factory Commission, 1833, vol. 20, pp. C1, 187, C2, 24 (Power's Report).
[52] Felkin, *A History of the Machine-Wrought Hosiery and Lace Manufactures*, ch. 23.
[53] *Report addressed to Her Majesty's Principal Secretary of State for the Home Department upon the Expediency of Subjecting the Lace Manufacture to the Regulations of the Factory Acts*. London, 1861, p. 7.

apprenticeship but was not acknowledged as a skill proper: as we have seen, what mattered in terms of the value of work was not so much the skill and experience as the relative status of men and women in the family and in society. In the Calais area, although local workers were recruited and trained, the British still occupied a significant share of the jobs, especially the most skilled ones. By 1841, 1,578 of the people in Saint-Pierre-lès-Calais (17.3 per cent), mostly lacemakers and their families, were British. The British population level in Calais remained about the same until it shrunk in the early 1880s. All in all, thousands of lacemakers and their relatives crossed the Channel. Among them, women often belonging to the same families also played a key part in the industry right from the start. In 1821, while there were twelve lace businesses in Calais, all of them run by British artisans, out of a total of 248 workers, 195 were women (78 per cent), an even larger proportion than in Britain (see Table 3.2).

By 1834, the French lace industry was operated by approximately 50,000 people, two thirds of whom were women and children.[54] Following several petitions asking for the regulation of child labour, the French Académie des sciences morales investigated the issue. Doctor Louis-René Villermé, who had already published a famous study on the 1832 cholera epidemic and who had denounced the length of the working day in manufacturers, investigated industrial labour in 1835-7. In 1840 he published his inquiry. Regarding machine-made lace, he noted that 'more than two thirds [of the workers] were women and children in wheeling, winding, mending, bleaching, the finishing and the packing of the lace'. Nine people were employed per machine, six of whom at least were women or girls; that is, a proportion that was very similar to the British proportion of women and children employed in this way (60 to 65 per cent). Gender segregation in the occupations was also remarkably similar.

Table 3.2 The Calais and Saint-Pierre-lès-Calais industry in 1821[55]

Occupation	Gender	Numbers	Rate
Lacemakers	Men	53	21.3%
Lace runners	Women	112	45.2%
Menders	Women	60	24.2%
Winders	Women	23	9.3%
Total		248	100%

[54] Ministère du Commerce 1835; Louis-René Villermé, *Tableau de l'état physique et moral des ouvriers employés dans les manufactures de coton, de laine et de soie*, Paris, 1840, p. 132; 'Meeting of the Bobbin Net Trade, Nottingham', *NR*, 21 November 1834, p. 4.

[55] 'État des fabriques de tulle existant sur les communes de Calais et de St-Pierre-lès-Calais – 13 Septembre 1821'. Archives de la Chambre de commerce et d'industrie de Calais. 1ETP3130 (1819-1985): Tulles et dentelles: notes historiques, recensements des fabricants et métiers (1819-1960). Situation de l'industrie.

By 1851, following a major crisis in the industry, it was reported that in the Calais and Saint-Pierre workshops there were 1,201 men (57 per cent), 403 women (19 per cent), and 497 children (24 per cent). This obviously did not include the domestic side of production. A national inquiry was organised in 1860; that is, when the industry had largely moved into factories: in Saint-Pierre 475 out of the 550 machines were steam-powered. It was reported that within the factory alone, a machine required two male workers for twelve hours each and four women and children working ten hours a day for winding and so on. The standard proportion of one third men and two thirds women and children therefore persisted. Similar proportions were suggested in an 1868 census. The similarities in sex ratios across the Channel are easily explicable. As we have seen, in Calais the lace industry was set up by British artisans. Between 1815 and 1860, 270 Britons created some 230 different businesses. Some Frenchmen entered the trade, usually after a period of work in one of the British-owned workshops. By 1841, the fifty-nine Anglo-French firms still accounted for about 30 per cent of the total number of lace businesses. As is now acknowledged, gender is a critical characteristic in determining migration: women's trajectories were different from men's and most trajectories were gendered. At the same time, the mobility of men and that of women were linked. In lace, most of these migrants had either come as families or as young men, rather than as young women. This could be because lace runners or menders could more easily be recruited locally, whereas twisthands often came from Britain.

But what also made the structure of the Calais lace industry so much like the one in Nottinghamshire was that custom and prejudice respecting gender-related skills were similar on both sides of the Channel. Although women had played a critical part in the operation of domestic tools and machines during proto-industrialisation, men tended to occupy the skilled positions in the new sectors of industry. Again, what mattered was not so much skills per se. There were sectors of industry, such as hosiery, where women operated machines and eventually competed for jobs with men when production moved to factories. In lace this did not happen, as women did not operate machines at the putting-out stage of the industry. As we have seen, the skills of the female embroiderers were not inferior to those of the machine lacemakers—in both cases, it took years to acquire them. On his own account, when French manufacturer Narcisse Faucheur (1794–1875) set up a lace shop in Saint-Amand-les-Eaux (Nord), semi-mechanical and employing only eight workers, he carefully 'arranged for an English woman from Nottingham who was very skilled in embroidery work to teach' his workers.[56] Soon, he employed 300 workers. But when it came to the bobbin-net machines, it was assumed that only men should operate them.

---

[56] Narcisse Faucheur, *Mon Histoire à mes chers enfants et petits-enfants*, Paris, 1886, p. 360.

3. Children at Work in Lace

The reasons for the high participation rates of children during the industrial revolution have been much discussed. In the English case, studying family budgets, Sara Horrell and Jane Humphries have argued that their contribution was even greater than that of mothers.[57] While Pinchbeck and others argued that the contribution of children increased because of the rise of homework, it has also been suggested that early factory production, often located away from the main population centres, resulted in the hiring of many children because of the need for an expanded workforce. E. P. Thompson also insisted that industrialisation meant more intense child labour in factories, mines, and outwork.[58] It has also now been acknowledged that the exploitation of children in the proto-industry of Europe was just about as intensive and as pervasive. Hand-worked lace may have been one of the most notorious nineteenth-century employers of child labourers (understood here, as in Victorian census returns, as being under fifteen years old). However, it was industrialisation that raised child labour as an issue for public debate. By the 1830s, in Britain, it was widely discussed and was part and parcel of the 'condition of England' debate, inspiring pamphlets, newspaper articles, public inquiries, and parliamentary debates.

The 1833 Factory Act which regulated child labour in the larger cotton manufacturers was preceded by a parliamentary inquiry which circulated questionnaires to lace manufacturers. Manufacturers usually argued that their workshops were healthy, that children were happy to work in them, and that their employment reduced their families' pauperism. More pragmatically, the cheapness of child labour was often mentioned: 'Having a great deal of very light work, such as winding, reeling, &c. &c.', J. Strutt from Belper (Derbyshire) argued, 'children from nine years old to twelve are very suitable for it, as they can do it quite as well as older hands, and at less cost'.[59] Moreover, manufacturers were keen on workers being trained from their infancy. Asked about the 'difference in skill and general character of those employed in the works who have been employed from infancy, as compared with those who have been taken into employment at later periods', employers often insisted that 'the difference [was] immense'.[60] From their multiple self-justifying answers, the harshness of child labour can sometimes be inferred, for instance when they reported on working hours, or on corporal punishment.

[57] Sara Horrell and Jane Humphries, '"The Exploitation of Little Children": Child Labor and the Family Economy in the Industrial Revolution', *Explorations in Economic History*, vol. 32, no. 4, pp. 485–516.
[58] E. P. Thompson, *The Making of the English Working Class*, London, 1963, pp. 306–9, 331, 335.
[59] Royal Commission on the Employment of Children in Factories Supplementary Reports. 1834. Part I and II, 1834, D1, 96, J. Strutt, Belper and Milford, Derbyshire, A. 11.
[60] Royal Commission 1834, C1, Fisher and Co, Radford, Nottinghamshire, A. 66.

In 1840–1, while the French Parliament was debating child labour in the manufacturers, another parliamentary committee inquired into it in Britain.[61] The outcome of the debate was a ban on child and female labour in the mines. The committee also investigated lacemaking in the Midlands. At this stage, factory reformers, Evangelicals such as Lord Ashley, trade-unionists, and Chartists denounced child labour, and the findings of the parliamentary committee further substantiated their grievances. It appeared that children often worked from a younger age than in other sectors, partly because the trade required little physical strength, partly because of its domestic nature. Already in 1833, a cotton manu-facturer in Belper, Derbyshire had reported that

> the parents not being allowed by act of parliament to send their children to a cotton factory under nine years of age, send them to lace-running or tambouring at a much earlier age, where numbers are shut up in small ill-ventilated rooms for twelve or thirteen hours a day, or even longer, at an employment more injurious to health, and particularly to eye-sight, than any employment they would be put to in a well-regulated cotton factory.[62]

Grainger's interviews of workers substantiated this:

Dec 10, 1840—Elizabeth Sweeting, 29 years old:
Is a 'lace runner'; has worked at the trade twenty-one years; when she first began it was a very good business; begins at 7 a.m., and leaves off about 10 p.m. but oftener later than earlier; often works till between 11 and 12, has done so all the winter round; in the summer generally begins between 5 and 6, and works as long as it is light, often till 9 p.m.; often does not go to the bottom of the yard for a week; can earn by working hard 7 d. a day; is working for Mr Fisher, lace warehouse, Nottingham. She has now a little girl helping, and together they can earn a shilling. Finds her sight very much affected, so much that she cannot see what o'clock it is across her room; the work affects the stomach and causes a pain in the side; often makes her light-headed; general the lace runners are crooked, so that the right shoulder is higher than the other. After a few years, five or six, the sight is so much injured that they are unfitted for any work where the common use of the eyes is required. Great debility and indigestion are also caused.

Girls begin about seven or six years, some as early as five or six; the hours depend greatly on the mistress... The mistresses who employ the children often work them very hard, has known children kept at it from 6 A.M. till 10 at night, sometimes not going out of the room, but eating their meals as they sat at work.

---

[61] Royal Commission 1843, vols. 13 and 14.   [62] Royal Commission 1834, D1, 96, Answer 11.

Mr Tivey, who employs many girls in Chevril-Street, used to sit in the room with his cane, and not allow any one to speak or look off if he could help. After sitting some time at lace-work, the fingers get stiff, and in cold weather benumbed for want of circulation; this would cause the work to go on slowly, and then the children were beaten; has known children to drop and faint at their work; many go off in consumption. The lace-runners seldom receive any other education than what they get at the Sunday schools.[63]

The Committee insisted on the plight of the children in lace: their education, their health, and even their morality were harmed as a result. Evangelical motives may have been central to the enquiry. Grainger unequivocally castigated the prevalence of sexual misbehaviour and abortion within the industry, which was obvious in the way he elicited responses from witnesses and exposed evidence.[64] He insisted that the mixing of girls (winders) and boys (threaders) was 'a most fertile source of immorality. There can, in fact, be but few states more immediately leading to vice and profligacy'.[65]

But no further restriction was imposed in manufacturing until the 1844 and 1847 Factories Act (Ten Hours Act). Ultimately Grainger was unsuccessful: Parliament decided not to legislate on domestic child labour. One argument was that 'a large proportion (above half) of the lace machines were worked by hand and in private houses. To that extent it was a domestic manufacture and could not be reached by legislation'.[66] And as in 1833, foreign competition was invoked. Manufacturers usually argued against regulating child labour on the grounds of foreign competition: 'Any material reduction of the working hours by legislative restriction in this branch of manufacture would have the certain effect, at no distant period, of causing its entire removal to foreign countries', Boden and Morley in St Peter, Derby, complained alongside other manufacturers.[67] During the inquiry, lace manufacturer William Astill, who had worked in France in 1824-6, argued that 'if practicable, [he was] most anxious that the children and young persons should have shorter hours of work', but 'that foreigners would, if such a change took place, immediately work longer hours, and so interfere with the demand for English goods'.[68] Astill successfully insisted on the fact 'that if the labour of children and young persons in the lace trade were to be regulated according to the provisions of the present Factory Act, that it would

[63] Royal Commission 1843, vol. 14, f. 5.
[64] Evidence no. 138, given by 'Y.Z.' on 20 February 1841.   [65] f 9 XII Moral Condition, no. 72.
[66] 'Lace Factories: Report addressed to her Majesty's Principal Secretary of State for the Home Department upon the Expediency of Subjecting the Lace Manufacture to the Regulations of the Factory Acts; with Appendix of Evidence'. PP. 1861 House of Lords Papers; Report, vol. 56, p. 6.
[67] Royal Commission 1840, D1, no. 79, A. 37.
[68] Royal Commission 1843, Appendix, 1843, q. 838, 24 February 1841.

give so great an advantage to the foreign manufacturer as seriously to injure the English'.[69]

Still, the ordeals of children in the 'sweated industries', including lace, had now been exposed. In some ways, as historian Sheila Blackburn has argued, Grainger, who had investigated the domestic textile industry in several areas, had revealed 'sweated labour' to the British public.[70] He argued that the functions of the upper and middle classes, such as festive events, weddings, and funerals, resulted in young girls working overnight to meet the orders. This was something Mary Bailey had already suggested in 1826; and in the early twentieth century, the advocates of moral consumption would argue that consumers should not promote sweated labour by buying cheap goods. Apart from being picked up by some papers and some famous *Punch* cartoons, Grainger's report inspired Thomas Hood's famous poem, *Song of the Shirt* (1843). Mary Botham Howitt, who lived in Nottingham, wrote a lively description in a short novel (1842).[71] In 1845, Friedrich Engels, relying on Grainger, described the exploitation of children in lace.[72] In 1849–51, Henry Mayhew resumed his investigation into the plight of domestic workers and published a series of letters on sweating in the *Morning Chronicle*, later to be found in *London Labour and the London Poor* (1851). In 1850, radical and popular writer G. W. M. Reynolds also contrasted the plight of the seamstress and the luxurious life of the upper class (Figure 3.5). Ernest Jones, the Chartist, published a series of articles entitled 'Woman's Wrongs' in his radical newspaper *Notes to the People*, and in 1855 he republished them as a novel which was 'hailed as his achievement'.[73] Karl Marx himself, in a section of *Capital* on the 'Branches of English industry without legal limits to exploitation', took the example of lace and denounced the fate of twenty-year-old milliner Mary Ann Walkley, who died in 1863 in a badly ventilated bedroom from over-work as she rushed to finish dresses destined for a ball organised by the Prince of Wales.[74]

Some autobiographical texts later evoked child labour in the sweated trades, including lace. William Jowett (1830–56) was born in Breaston (Derbyshire), about 10 miles away from Nottingham, where his father owned two lace machines, 'by which he was enabled to obtain a livelihood for himself and family'. However, because of an 'ebbing', he was compelled to sell his machines and in 1836 they moved to nearby Beeston (Nottinghamshire). As for William,

[69] PP. Royal Commission on Children's Employment in Mines and Manufactories. Second Report (Manufactures). Appendix (1843), q. 838, 24 February 1841.
[70] Sheila Blackburn, *A Fair Day's Wage for a Fair Day's Work? Sweated Labour and the Origins of Minimum Wage Legislation in Britain*, London, 2016, ch. 1.
[71] Mary Botham Howitt, *Little Coin, Much Care; or How poor men live. A tale*, London, 1842.
[72] Friedrich Engels, *Die Lage der arbeitenden Klasse in England* [*The Condition of the Working Class in England*], Leipzig, 1845: 'The Remaining branches of industry'.
[73] Ernest Jones, 1 November 1851 to 25 April 1852. 'Woman's Wrongs'. *Notes to the People* [republished as *Women's Wrongs: A Series of Tales*, London, 1855]; Miles Taylor, *Ernest Jones, Chartism and the Romance of Politics*, Oxford, 2003, p. 158.
[74] Karl Marx, *Das Kapital. Kritik der politischen Oekonomie*, Hamburg, 1867, vol. 1, ch. 10, section 3.

Figure 3.5 Illustration of the cover page of George W. M. Reynolds, *The Seamstress; or The White Slave of England* (London, 1850).

Before he attained the age of seven years, instead of going to school, to educate and prepare his mind for the business of life, he was put to the inhuman calling of 'jacking and threading'; turning his nights into days, and days into nights; thus inverting the order of nature, and preparing the little being for a downward instead of an upward course, by leaving no time for education or improvement except that which he obtained at the Sunday school.

A few years later he was working as 'a "sweater", or one who assists in turning a machine; a class of youths very numerous where steam is not applied thereto'. Then, when 'another fluctuation in the trade rendered him short of work', he was laid off, and left for London in 1846, where he soon became homeless. He later joined the army and served in Crimea.[75]

Future Baptist minister and politician John Clifford (1836–1923) was born in Sawley (Derbyshire), and his family moved to Beeston when he was three or four. His father was a Chartist lacemaker who had married a lace runner, at the time when hand-operated machines were yielding to steam-powered ones. He took little John with him to the factory where he worked from the age of eleven, sixteen hours a day, splicing the ends of cotton from bobbin to bobbin to keep the thread unbroken. 'I have worked', he remembered, 'from four o'clock on Friday morning

---

[75] William Jowett, *Diary of Sergeant William Jowett, of the Seventh Fusiliers. Written during the Crimean War. To which is added, a Brief Memoir*, Beeston, 1856, pp. v–vi.

all through the night to six o'clock on Saturday evening, and then run home glad and proud with my small wage of two shillings and sixpence to my mother—like a king'. Clifford was then employed as a threader, preparing 'carriages' and 'bobbins', and by the age of thirteen he helped a man to mind two machines. By the age of sixteen, he had been promoted to the position of book-keeper and head of the lace-mending department of Robert Felkin's factory, where he inspected the work of 150 women.[76] Although this type of promotion was rare, it reminds us that children's experience of work was gendered: although at a young age factory boys and girls were on an equal footing, their job prospects were different. Whereas boys and girls could have similar ancillary occupations, boys were to be trained as twisthands when they reached the age of thirteen or fourteen, while girls remained in low-wage occupations. Lown has observed the same pattern in silk, where although winding and spindle cleaning were performed by both boys and girls, mobility patterns were different.[77] 'Career ladders', as Rose noted, gave promotion opportunities to men because of the association between competence and masculinity.[78]

By 1861, not more than ninety out of 3,800–4,000 machines were still 'worked by hand in private houses'.[79] It is generally assumed that by then child labour was already declining, because of protective legislation or higher wages for fathers.[80] In lace factories, however, children were still employed, sometimes working over two successive divisions, perhaps intermittently for up to twenty hours.[81] In most cases, they were at least nine years old, unlike homeworkers. The dangers of factory work were an added consideration, including accidents, as in May 1851 in Saint-Pierre when a twelve-year-old child died from the mutilations he suffered after his blouse was stripped round a drive shaft.[82] But very young children were still employed in the finishing parts of the trade, much of which was still domestic. And women and girls from the age of nine upwards still accounted for 25 per cent of the factory workers, and boys aged nine to sixteen for 22 per cent.[83]

Opponents to legislation still argued about 'the advantages the French manufacturers have over the English manufacturers as regards the price and protection of labour'.[84] In France, a major Nottingham manufacturer, Heymann, complained that the 'Factory Act [was] far less stringent' than in Britain; and 'no combinations of workmen, such as our trades' unions, are allowed by law'.[85] However, Parliament chose to regulate the working hours of children and teenagers in factories. This did not apply to the homes, where much of the work was still

[76] James Marchant, *Dr John Clifford, C.H: Life, Letters and Reminiscences*, London, 1924.
[77] Lown, *Women and Industrialization*, pp. 53–6.   [78] Rose, *Limited Livelihoods*, p. 27.
[79] *Report*, 1861, p. 6.
[80] Nardinelli, *Child Labor and the Industrial Revolution*, p. 154, disputed by Horrell and Humphries, '"The Exploitation of Little Children"', p. 503.
[81] *Report*, 1861, p. 5.   [82] *Journal de Calais*, 14 May 1851.   [83] *Report*, 1861, p. 14.
[84] *Report*, 1861, pp. 19, 128.   [85] *Report*, 1861, pp. 92–3.

done. By the mid-1860s, Felkin complained there were still 'probably not much fewer than 40,000 [children] employed by mistresses'.[86]

In France, the issue of child labour had also been raised. After 1830, several riots and insurrections in Lyon and Paris testified to the extent of workers' discontent. The government organised debates on child labour. Villermé's public inquiry showed that in manufacturing most children were hired before the age of ten, usually aged eight or nine (1840). Between 1839 and 1845, children probably accounted for 15 per cent of the workforce in textiles, iron, or mining, not including the family sphere of the farms, the shops, and the home workshops. Villermé's pages on the topic soon became a classic text, along with Charles Dupin's *Du travail des enfants* (1840) and Eugène Buret's prize-winning *De la misère des classes laborieuses en Angleterre et en France* (1840). Villermé argued that children were the victims of torture, with working days sometimes stretching from the early hours of morning into the night; and while work was banned on Sundays, he added, this time was often used for maintenance or cleaning.

There was interaction between the debates on child labour in both countries. On 22 March 1841 a first piece of factory legislation was passed in France, which was inspired by the 1833 British Factory Act applying to textile manufacturing. However, the French Act (*Loi relative au travail des enfants employés dans les manufactures, usines et ateliers*) was even less restrictive: it provided that in workshops with more than twenty workers, excluding smaller workshops and family businesses, labour under the age of eight (under the age of nine in Britain) should be banned; it was limited to eight hours a day until the age of twelve (thirteen in Britain), and twelve hours until the age of sixteen (eighteen in Britain). Night work was forbidden below the age of thirteen (eighteen in Britain). The Act encountered opposition from many manufacturers. And as no professional inspectors were provided for until 1868, even these partial restrictions were not always enforced.[87] More restrictive legislation was passed only in 1874 and 1892, at a time when the state was trying to organise the systematic schooling of children. The same was true in Britain: the Elementary Education Acts of 1876 and 1880 and the Factory and Workshop Act of 1878 meant that full-time employment of children was no longer possible.

4. Men's, Women's, and Children's Wages in Lace

Humphries and Horrell have estimated the share of women's and children's wages in the family economy during the industrial revolution to be between 16 and 22

[86] Felkin, *A History of the Machine-Wrought Hosiery and Lace Manufactures*, p. 399.
[87] Yannick Guin, 'Au cœur du libéralisme: La loi du 22 mars 1841 relative au travail des enfants employés dans les manufactures, usines et ateliers', in *Deux siècles de droit du travail: L'histoire par les lois*, edited by Jean-Pierre Le Crom, Paris, 1998, pp. 29–44.

per cent, with high rates in sectors where outworking was standard.[88] Our study focuses on the relative importance of men's, women's, and children's wages in lace, apart from their impact on total family earnings.

In pre-factory lacemaking, wages were piece rate rather than time rate; that is, workers were paid per unit of output rather than per unit of time, so that daily wages are estimates based on regular working days. This also explains why a range of wages is often indicated, since wages depended on skill, speed, and productivity.

These wages should be taken as snapshots. In pillow-lace there was a steady decline from the late eighteenth century, when women could make up to 75 per cent of the earnings of men in agriculture, to the 1830s, when they only made 20 to 32 per cent of men's earnings, and when they could earn more in agriculture.[89] In machine-made lace, the instability of wages, depending on trade cycles, emerges from all the available evidence. Roy Church has argued that male lacemakers earned much more than framework knitters: 16 shillings was standard by 1837 and 20–35 shillings by 1860, while women earned on average 6 shillings by 1836 and 10–16 shillings by 1860. James Epstein has argued instead that the initial difference between the knitters and the lacemakers was reduced over time.[90] There is no evidence of women's wages being lower than men's for the same occupations: instead, the sex ratio of wages was dependent on segregated occupations. At artisan stage, it was common that women (e.g. lace runners) earned a third of what men (lacemakers) earned. In factory production, a 0.5 female:male ratio was more frequent, as can be seen from Figure 3.6.

Differences between wages may have been preserved by the fact that men were better organised. Since the 1810s, there had been repeated attempts at unionisation in lace. Some of these organisations had transnational connections, as was the case in 1825 with a 'Bobbin Net Committee at Calais, Lisle and St-Quentin', which was, according to the local authorities, inspired by 'the spirit of English workers' (see p. 181).[91] Several unions were organised afterwards, including a Lacemakers' Union (1831) formed by twisthands to strike against a twelve-hour working day which belonged to John Doherty's National Association or the Protection of Labour. A short-lived British Union of Plain Net Makers was formed in 1846 and managed to organise a noisy protest involving women and children against an employer who was reducing rates.[92] From 1850, more long-lasting 'new model' unions were created in the different sectors of the trade, including a Levers Lace Trade Society (1851); in 1874, they merged into an Amalgamated Society of

---

[88] Horrell and Humphries 'Women's Labour Force Participation', p. 101.

[89] Burnette, Gender, Work and Wages, p. 47.

[90] James Epstein, 'Some Organisational and Cultural Aspects of the Chartist Movement in Nottingham', in The Chartist Experience: Studies in Working-Class Radicalism and Culture, 1830–60, edited by James Epstein and Dorothy Thompson, London, 1982, pp. 221–68.

[91] Archives nationales, F7/9786.3. Le sous-préfet de Saint-Quentin au directeur général de la police, 25 September 1825.

[92] NR, 27 March 1846.

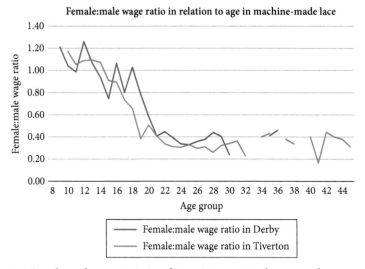

Figure 3.6 Female: male wage ratio in relation to age in two lace manufactures in 1833

This graph is based on answers provided in 1833 by Boden's lace factory in Derby (numbering 205 men and 241 women) and Heathcoat's factory in Tiverton (numbering 484 men and 333 women). In abscissa, the age of the workers; in ordinate, the female: male wage ratio. For instance, in both manufactures, the wages of 21-year-old women were about 40 percent of those of men (source: Royal Commission on the Employment of Children in Factories Supplementary Reports, Part 1 and 2, 1834, f. 31.).

Operative Lace Makers.[93] These male unions contributed to the rise of the wages of the twisthands. They made sure women were not substituted for men, though women were accepted in customary women's work; they opposed child labour.

Women also tried to organise, despite their dispersal and the absence of precedents. A strike took place in 1840 among the lace runners against the intermediary mistresses or agents who contracted with the capitalists and took their share.[94] Their address 'To the Lace-Runners of Nottingham' read:

> Are you thus to be robbed of your hard-earned pittance to maintain these cormorants [the mistresses] in idleness, and many of their husbands in drunkenness and profligacy;—no wonder that misery enters our dwellings—that we are in the depth of poverty, that our children are crying for bread, while there is a swarm of locusts hovering between us and the manufacturers, ready to devour one half of our hire, it is not enough that we have to compete with machines which, in many cases, supersedes needle-work; but are also robbed in the manner described above; is this state of things to exist? ... The Committee whom you appointed to manage

[93] Norman H. Cuthbert, *The Lace Makers' Society: A Study of Trade Unionism in the British Lace Industry, 1760–1960*, [Nottingham?], 1960.

[94] Papers relating to the turnout, quoted in *Children's Employment Commission*, 1843, xiv, pp. f. 43–4. Pinchbeck had noted this turnout (*Women Workers and the Industrial Revolution*, pp. 213–14).

your affairs, have agreed that there shall be a turn out on Monday next, against this most unjust of all practices, and we trust that the lace-runners will be at their post and show their oppressors, 'that their occupation is gone'.

We respectfully request, that the manufacturers will condescend to assist us in this just undertaking; we also trust that the male portion of society will assist us, as it is the cause of the poor working man as much as the females.

Committee: Mary Smith

Hannah Weatherbed

Mary Chapman

Ann Davis

SARAH HARGREAVE, Secretary.

The strike gathered between 440 and 600 lace runners. They walked in procession across Nottingham in rows of three, 'in boarding school order as [their oratress] Mrs Weatherbed said, that they must now consider themselves as being at a new school'.[95] After three weeks, they were defeated.[96]

Lace runners did not oppose twisthands, who often happened to be their own husbands, brothers, and fathers; but they were aware that as women they had specific grievances, such as lower wages and worse working conditions. Their claims resurfaced now and then. Chartism was strong among Nottingham women, many of whom worked in lace and formed a Nottingham Female Chartist Political Union.[97] And after the move to factory production, strikes would also occur, long before the 1888 London match women strike and the slow progress of female unionism. In 1871 when female lace-dressers at Nottingham struck for a 25 per cent wage-rise and a fifty-four-hour working week: 'The masters conceded all the time and half the money, and the majority have returned to work'.[98]

In France, while on average wages were lower than those in Britain, British workers could usually expect higher wages for themselves, especially in periods of sharp competition; such was the case for male puddlers or mechanics, who had better skills and productivity than the local workforce (see Chapter 1). However, economic downturns could affect this. In the early stages of the lace industry, it was reported that lacemakers could earn '15 to 20 francs' a day in 1823, but they were only making a tenth of this ten years later, as shown in Table 3.3.[99]

[95] *NR*, 4 December 1840, p. 2.   [96] *NR*, 11 December 1840, p. 3.

[97] Epstein, 'Some Organisational and Cultural Aspects of the Chartist Movement'; Christopher Richardson, *Socialism, Chartism and Co-operation—Nottingham 1844*, Nottingham, 2013.

[98] *Illustrated London News*, 25 November 1871, p. 494.

[99] *Mémoire et extraits de délibérations des Chambres de commerce et es chambres consultatives des arts et manufactures*, Paris, 1834, p. 396; also see Chambre de commerce et d'industrie de Paris, *Statistique de l'industrie à Paris résultant de l'enquête faite par la Chambre de commerce pour les années 1847–1848*, Paris, 1851, p. 354.

Table 3.3 Day wages in the French lace industry[100]

		From	To
Bleachers	Men	1.5 F	
Machine-makers	Men	2.5 F	5 F
Lace workers	Men	2.50 F	3 F
Lace runners (brodeuses au crochet)	Women	0.7 F	1 F

The incomes of the lace workers in France were thus comparable to those of their British counterparts (3 francs a day being about 14 shillings a week). Other evidence substantiates this, for example many press articles reported that people had gone to work in Calais because they were without employment, rather than in pursuit of better wages. The proximity between Calais and Nottinghamshire, the back-and-forth trajectory of many workers, the circulation of information through the press and correspondence, and the fact that northwestern Europe constituted an increasingly integrated economy meant that major wage differences for 'tramping artisans' could not survive long. Lace runners may have earned more in Calais than in Nottingham (1 franc a day being nearly 5 shillings a week), but even this is uncertain. In any case, this can be connected to another debate on the industrial revolution: Robert Allen has argued that it was the high cost of labour in relation to capital that fuelled technological innovation.[101] Studying hand-spinning, Jane Humphries and Benjamin Schneider have criticised this and countered that a widespread low-wage, low-productivity employment was at the core of the factory system.[102] By 1840, the lace industry seems to have become low wage across the Channel.

On average, a female lace runner in France earned at most a third of the male lace worker, a ratio that was essentially the same as in Britain. One interesting idiosyncrasy is that Villermé reported that in Lille bleachers were men (see Table 3.4). In Britain, bleachers were women, with wages as low as lace runners. In Lille, bleachers were clearly underpaid in comparison with the twisthands. But if Villermé was correct, the fact that they earned twice as much as the female runners substantiates the argument that custom and prejudice, rather than productivity, accounted for the gender gap. However, other sources suggest that at that point bleachers in Calais were women, and Villermé's observations should not be

[100] Villermé, *Tableau de l'état physique et moral*, p. 92.

[101] Robert C. Allen, *The British Industrial Revolution in Global Perspective*, Cambridge, 2009.

[102] Jane Humphries, 'The Lure of Aggregates and the Pitfalls of the Patriarchal Perspective: A Critique of the High Wage Economy Interpretation of the British Industrial Revolution', *Economic History Review*, vol. 66, no. 3, 2013, pp. 693–714; Jane Humphries and Benjamin Schneider, 'Spinning the Industrial Revolution', *Economic History Review*, vol. 72, no. 1, 2019, pp. 126–55.

Table 3.4 Day wages in the Lille lace industry, 1825–34 (minimums and maximums, in francs)[103]

Year	Bleachers (men)		Machine-makers(men)		Lacemakers (men)		Lace runners (women)	
1825	2	2.25	8	10	10	12	1	1.2
1830	1.5	1.75	3	5	4	6	0.9	1
1834	1.5	1.75	2.5	5	3	4	0.7	0.8

overinterpreted. By 1848, the poisonous effects of the lead carbonate used for bleaching were denounced.[104]

In other sectors of industry, the sex ratio varied: similar differences could be noted, though in some sectors, such as among cotton weavers in the Rouen area, female earnings reached 0.6 to 0.75 per cent of male earnings.[105] There could also be regional variations.[106] It is hard to interpret these aggregates, at a time when the mobility of the workforce was on the rise. Obviously, in the industry in Calais it was men's wages that had declined rather than women's and children's wages that had risen.

As we have seen, the shift from domestic to factory production did not end the practice of outworking: for new generations, lace finishing in the home would persist in both Britain and France. But this work was less commonly done by younger children, in line with the rise of elementary schooling in the 1870s and 1880s. By 1903, when the debate on the sweated trades had come to the fore, it was reported that much of the hosiery and lace-work in Nottingham was still done by women (Figure 3.7). An observer was struck by the 16,000 surplus of women (i.e. 6.6 per cent) in the population of Nottingham (239,743 in 1901), though in fact owing to lower death rates there was a 4 per cent surplus of women in the British population. And he added 'there [was] the unmitigated evil of child-labour after school hours. In home after home the children are kept out of the fresh air to do lace-work in one tiny "living room" of the back-to-back houses which are the shame of Nottingham'.[107]

In French factories, strikes and trade-union activity became legal in 1864 and 1884, respectively. When the Calais factory workers went on strike in 1890 against low wages, the dispute was reported in the Nottingham press and support was

[103] Villermé, *Tableau de l'état physique et moral*, p. 98.
[104] The 1835 edition of the *Dictionnaire de l'Académie française* mentioned the word in its female form ('blanchisseuse de dentelle'). On poisoning, see *L'Atelier. Organe spécial des ouvriers*, 12 April 1848, p. 122.
[105] Villermé, *Tableau de l'état physique et moral*, p. 144.
[106] Ministère des travaux publics, de l'agriculture et du commerce. *Statistique de la France, Industrie*, Paris, 1847, pp. 318–19.
[107] Arthur W. Hopkinson, 'Home Industries in Nottingham', *The Economic Review*, vol. 13, London, July 1903, pp. 334, 338.

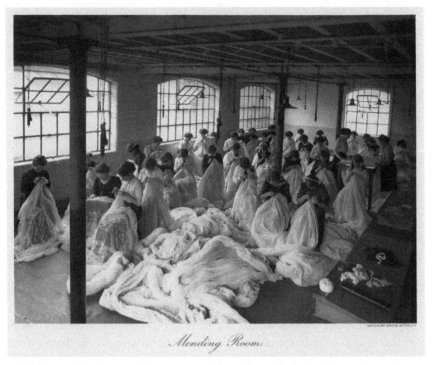

Figure 3.7 'Mending room' at Birkin and Co., New Basford, in Nottingham, c.1914. Some of the female workers were still children, such as to the right. © University of Nottingham Libraries, Manuscripts and Special Collections; BNN-1-10.

quickly requested: £257 was collected for the strike fund in Britain, mostly among the Nottingham lacemakers. Competition still prevailed between manufacturers but new forms of solidarity were being devised among workers, with the brokerage of some Anglo-French.[108]

5. Conclusion

This overview of the lace industry supports the hypotheses proposed by Scott and Tilly forty years ago. In lace as in linen, there was great homogeneity between the organisation of work in France and in Britain. This was reflected in the segregation of work, which was often comparable although it was not identical. National or religious differences did not play a significant part in the way the structure of the industry was transferred across the Channel. The more domestic nature of the

[108] *Nottingham Daily Guardian*, 18 October 1890; Michel Caron, *Trois âges d'or de la dentelle. 1860–1905*, Lille, 2003, pp. 51–63.

economy in France did not apply significantly to the lace industry. In lace, migrants played a key part: permanent imitation resulted in similar features of overseas technology and work organisation across the Channel. In both cases, occupations and wages complied with customs and prejudice with respect to abilities and skills, rather than just market forces.

The twisthands were exclusively male up until the point when the lace industry declined in Britain and France. As for the homework of women and children, it prevailed into the twentieth century, before the gradual increase of the school leaving age eroded child labour. The lives of the women and children who contributed so much to the dynamism of the industry and to the success of lace in nineteenth-century fashion and its mass consumption mostly survive through the scarce sources which have been examined here. And their names remain for the most part shrouded in obscurity, not unlike the dark rooms in which they worked.

4

'Not one of us . . . is able to speak more than a few words of the language'

Language, Cultural Practices, and Religion

Charles Manby Smith (1804–80) was born in Devon, on the banks of the Exe, in an 'honest, industrious, and God-fearing' family of seven children.[1] When he was thirteen his father, a cabinetmaker, 'suffered a loss', and the family left for Bristol. Charles was apprenticed as a printer there before working in London. But in 1826, printing and the book trade underwent a crisis, and he emigrated to Paris, probably based on information passed through word of mouth. His memoirs contain a wealth of details on his cultural integration in the French capital. Charles neither understood nor spoke any French on arrival. He remembered what a gendarme told him, that he 'had to gather his meaning from his gestures'. But 'In the course of a fortnight [he] could manage, with the help of a dictionary, to read the advertisements in the French newspapers'. Such skills, however, were not evenly distributed.

Smith lived in Paris for four years, only returning to London in the wake of the 'Trois Glorieuses', a popular uprising in July 1830 which toppled King Charles X and incidentally scared Smith, who was fairly conservative. In Paris he had first worked for Galignani, who published an English-language newspaper and owned a bookshop. It seems that Smith worked as a compositor for the book section of the business: he remembered a workshop with several Englishmen, three Frenchmen, and a Spaniard (see Figure 4.1). In his workshop, 'a Spaniard' spoke 'neither French nor English', while another English printer 'could read Homer in ancient Greek, Horace and Lucretia in Latin, spoke French fluently, could perfectly read Italian and expected to learn German in a year'. A few months later, Smith could teach some English, for which he used Cobbett's English grammar—a book which Cobbett had intended for popular use, and which remained used in schools into the 1930s. (Cobbett also published a *French Grammar* in 1824.)[2] Smith also used a French and English dictionary before transitioning to a French one.[3]

---

[1] Charles Manby Smith, *The Working Man's Way in the World*, London, 1853, p. 2. The quote in this chapter's title is from TNA. FO 146 350. Letter of Scottish linen female workers in Haubourdin (northern France) threatened with expulsion, to British ambassador in Paris, Lord Normanby, 21 March 1848.

[2] William Cobbett, *A Grammar of the English Language*, New York, 1818; Ian Dyck, 'William Cobbett (1763–1835)', *ODNB*, Oxford, 2004.

[3] Smith, *The Working Man's Way in the World*, pp. 38, 49.

Artisans Abroad: British Migrant Workers in Industrialising Europe, 1815–1870. Fabrice Bensimon, Oxford University Press.
© Fabrice Bensimon 2023. DOI: 10.1093/oso/9780198835844.003.0005

Un compositeur à sa casse.

Figure 4.1 'Un compositeur à sa casse' (Turgan, *Les grandes usines de France: tableau de l'industrie française au XIXe siècle*, Paris, 1860, vol. 1: 'L'imprimerie impériale', p. 97).

At Galignani's, Smith composed English books for cheap editions that were then exported to Britain: Byron, Shelley, Walter Scott, and James Fenimore Cooper were printed in Paris at about the same time as they were in Britain, and at a much lower price. This practice existed in Paris (Galignani and Baudry), Leipzig (Tauchnitz and Fleischer), and Brussels (Louis Hauman and Adolphe Wahlen). It relied on the fact that in Britain publishers still targeted a narrow market, with expensive multi-volume books. Moreover, copyright law did not operate internationally. In 1843, the novelist G. P. R. James denounced the precariousness of English publishing: books were more expensive and authors were less well paid and were not protected against 'piracy'; that is, the smuggling of books printed overseas.[4] When in 1850 a Franco-British agreement on copyright ended this practice, the catalogues of Galignani and Baudry numbered 450

[4] G. P. R. James, 'Some Observations on the Book Trade, as Connected with the Literature in England', *Journal of the Statistical Society of London*, vol. 6, 1843, pp. 50–60. William St Clair, *The Reading Nation in the Romantic Period*, Cambridge, 2004, p. 295; David McKitterick, 'Introduction', in *The Cambridge History of the Book in Britain*, vol. 6, *1830–1914*, Cambridge, 2009, p. 42.

one-volume books, including all recent novels such as those of Dickens.[5] In these cases, the British compositors such as Charles Manby Smith—and later George Good[6]—were marketing a skill for an economic niche.

Although printing was a staple sector of the industrial revolution, even in this industry the technological gap between Britain and the Continent resulted in technological transfers to the Continent. In the 1820s, steam-powered presses were introduced for newspapers in Britain and then in France. On 29 July 1830, during the 'Trois Glorieuses', some Parisian printers destroyed some of them, which had been made in Britain. Tension prevailed for the rest of the summer. On 2 September troops were sent to guard the main printing shops. A few days later, the préfet de police wrote in his daily report to the ministry of Interior that:

> English compositors did not dare print *Galignany's Messenger* [sic], Mr Galignany himself prayed the printer, Mr Delaforest, to use hand presses. But this weakness could have had regrettable consequences; authorities objected to Mr Galignany's request, English workers resumed working on their mechanic presses and no one thought of bothering them again.[7]

Printing was a transnational sector, not just in the early days when German printers spread the technology, but also in the Victorian era of mass migration. David Finkelstein has studied the circulation of English-speaking journeymen printers and compositors between Britain, the United States, Australia, New Zealand, Canada, and South Africa. He is interested in the 'typographical web' and how 'shared craft identities, creative endeavours, and trade press publications created a sense of moral community that linked the printing fraternity across space and time'.[8] Finkelstein argues that they created a 'printing diaspora' that helped construct political and cultural identities. As the example of Smith shows, the emigration of British printers was not limited to the English-speaking world. On the Continent, British compositors were in demand. As we have seen, books in English were printed and exported. And there were also English-language newspapers aiming at an audience of upper- and middle-class British residents, which required English-speaking compositors.

---

[5] St Clair, *The Reading Nation in the Romantic Period*, ch. 15, 'Those Vile French Piracies'; Diana Cooper-Richet, 'La librairie étrangère à Paris au XIXe siècle. Un milieu perméable aux innovations et aux transferts', *Actes de la recherche en sciences sociales*, vol. 12, March 1999, pp. 60–9.

[6] See pp. 171–8.

[7] 'Les compositeurs anglais n'osaient point imprimer le *Galignany's Messenger*, Mr Galignany lui-même priait l'imprimeur, Mr Delaforest, de se servir de presses à bras, mais cet exemple de condescendance eût pu avoir de fâcheux résultats; l'autorité s'est opposée à la demande de Mr Galignany, les ouvriers anglais se sont remis à leurs presses mécaniques & personne n'a songé à les troubler'. Archives Nationales. F7 3884. Bulletin de Paris, 7 September 1830.

[8] David Finkelstein, *Movable Types: Roving Creative Printers of the Victorian World*, Oxford, 2018, p. 5.

The case of Smith also raises several other cultural issues. When they emigrated to the Continent, British workers were confronted with a series of problems that were different from those they met with when they moved to a British manufacturing area or to London. Of course, even within Britain, a Geordie or a Scot could find it difficult to adjust to the way people spoke in the south. Attitudes, games, diets, and habits, could vary widely from one area to another, especially before the advent of a national railway network and a mass reading public. However, when they emigrated to the Continent, migrants had to cope with new challenges: relationships with the local populations, at a time of rising nationalism; language issues; legal constraints; food and drink; Catholicism; cultural differences. Did these differences have a significant impact? How did British workers integrate with the local populations of the countries they went to? Did they mix easily or were they rejected? This chapter raises issues that are still debated today about notions of identity and integration. It addresses language matters, as far as we can be aware of them (section 1), before moving to education and religion (section 2), two intertwined fields that mattered much for the authorities on both sides of the Channel. It then reflects on to what extent cultural practices could be transferred (section 3). Last, it considers the related issues of food and drink (section 4), which were part and parcel of the discourse both on work and on national identity, before concluding in section 5. This chapter considers not just the extent of cultural differences but also whether these mattered or not for the integration and relations with the local populations.

1. Coping with the Language Barrier

It is well known that language is a critical issue for integration. Unlike fellow-workers who went to the United States or the settler colonies of Canada, Australia, New Zealand, or South Africa, hardly any British migrants who went to the Continent had any knowledge of the vernacular languages. By the mid-nineteenth century, there was neither a public system of education in Britain nor any organised teaching of foreign languages. And in the host countries English was not widely spoken or understood. English played a relatively minor role and, even if things had changed since writer John Florio famously wrote that the English language was 'worthless beyond Dover' (1578), the Anglo-world was still a long time in the making.[9] By 1800, the population of Britain and the United States was still lower than that of France, and there were only 18 million English speakers in

---

[9] Florio, quoted in Richard Smith and Nicola McLelland, 'Histories of Language Learning and Teaching in Europe', *The Language Learning Journal*, vol. 46, no. 1, 2018, p. 3; James Belich, *Replenishing the Earth: The Settler Revolution and the Rise of the Anglo-World, 1783–1939*, Oxford, 2009, p. 2.

the world; by 1850 there were probably around 50 million. English was spoken and understood on the Continent by only small minorities, probably below 1 per cent. Among scholars, Latin as a lingua franca was declining. French rather than English remained the preferred second language of the aristocracy; that is, only among tiny minorities.

In 1858, when the universities of Oxford and Cambridge introduced public examinations for secondary school pupils, 'French and German were among the subjects offered', and modern languages became part of the university curriculum in the second half of the century.[10] Little is known about French-language teachers in Britain, except that they were mostly men, with a few women as well. They were only employed among the upper and upper-middle classes. After 1848, several continental refugees resorted to teaching French to make a living. French republicans and socialists Martin Nadaud, Pierre Leroux, and Gustave Lefrançais gave French lessons when they lived in London. Lacking even basic English, Lefrançais taught by using the various objects in his pupil's living room.[11] But the refugees had to compete with more respectable French-language masters. Immersion and imitation, such as with domestic servants, were also used to learn foreign languages, notably French.[12] Later on, some refugees of the Paris Commune had the same experience of losing their jobs as French teachers when their employers found out who they were.[13] In addition to studying languages at home, some young men learned languages abroad; travel was part of the education of the young man of the elite. A few middle-class Englishmen learnt French when they were young, like John Stuart Mill who spent a year in Montpellier when he was fourteen. But this was rare. When Thomas Paine was elected to the Convention in 1792, he could not speak French. When Robert Owen came to Paris in 1848 and addressed Étienne Cabet's club, he did so in English and was translated, maybe by Cabet himself who had spent five years in London. Ernest Jones was a German speaker, Bronterre O'Brien could translate from the French, but even Harney, the most internationalist of the Chartists, spoke no foreign language. And, for the International Working Men's Association (IWMA, 1864–72), language issues were serious: the major texts were published in French, English, and German, but this was criticised by sections speaking another language, and each conference required some of its members, often continental refugees in London, for the translation job. In 1867, some twenty years before

[10] Nicola McLelland, 'The History of Language Learning and Teaching in Britain', *The Language Learning Journal*, vol. 46, no. 1, 2018, 9.2.

[11] Gustave Lefrançais, *Souvenirs d'un révolutionnaire*, Paris, 1972, p. 164; Martin Nadaud, *Léonard, maçon de la Creuse*, Paris, 1998, p. 309; Pierre Leroux, *La Grève de Samarez, poème philosophique*, Paris, 1863, vol. 1, p. 237.

[12] Blaise Extermann, 'The Teaching of Modern Languages in France and Francophone Switzerland (1740–1940): A Historiographical Overview', *The Language Learning Journal*, vol. 46, no. 1, 2018, p. 41.

[13] See, e.g., the letter of Jenny Marx to Kugelmann, 21 December 1871, about Auguste Serraillier.

Esperanto was devised, the congress of the IWMA in Lausanne proposed the creation of an international language.[14]

However, from the end of the eighteenth century, long before modern foreign languages were introduced in school education, they featured better in adult self-instructional methods and benefited from the advances in printing and from the demand from learners.[15] Some books offered sentences to translate into and/or out of the new languages, such as J. C. Fick's *Praktische englische Sprachlehre* (1793). Some language textbooks were published, like *Une analyse raisonnée des langues française et anglaise: moyen facile pour apprendre l'une ou l'autre*, by Galignani in 1806.[16] As historian Diana Cooper-Richet writes, in Paris from the 1820s, in the heyday of Anglomania, there was even serious competition between English teachers, both for day and evening classes.[17] Shakespeare was performed in 1822 by English comedians, causing some uproar on the boulevards. Such classes, books, and plays could address only a minority of well-off learners. Stendhal, Delacroix, Mérimée, and Guizot might have been keen on learning English, but not everyone was.

For working-class migrants with no foreign-language education, emigrating to Belgium or Germany could therefore be more of a challenge than emigrating to New York, Toronto, or Sydney. Only a few businessmen and senior engineers could rely upon interpreters. Scottish manufacturer James Carmichael, after a week in Amiens where he went in 1845 to set up a linen and jute works, wrote to his brother: 'I find it to be a great drawback the want of the Language. I can only speak through an interpretation'.[18] Translating or interpreting did not exist as occupations. For instance, in Fourchambault, the Dufauds could rely on a former British prisoner of war, John or Jean-Baptiste Weiss, who had married a Frenchwoman, Jaquette Galy.[19] Mackenzie and Brassey could rely on interpreters, but the workers could not.[20] The situation was further complicated by the fact that society was multilingual. More than one language was spoken in Ireland, Belgium, and Switzerland, and even in France people spoke different regional dialects and *patois*, until the French state achieved linguistic unification through school

---

[14] Emmanuel Jousse, 'Les traducteurs de l'Internationale', *Cahiers Jaurès*, no. 212–13, 2014, pp. 181–94.

[15] A. P. R. Howatt and Richard Smith, 'The History of Teaching English as a Foreign Language, from a British and European Perspective', *Language & History*, vol. 57, no. 1, 2014, pp. 75–95; Blaise Extermann, 'The teaching of modern languages in France and francophone Switzerland (1740–1940): a historiographical overview', *The Language Learning Journal*, vol. 46, 2018, no. 1, p. 43.

[16] Salavy du Fresnoy, *Une analyse raisonnée des langues française et anglaise: moyen facile pour apprendre l'une ou l'autre*, Paris, 1806.

[17] Diana Cooper-Richet, *La France anglaise. De la Révolution à nos jours*, Paris, 2018, p. 122.

[18] James Carmichael to Peter Carmichael, 25 January 1845. University of Dundee Archive Services. Peter Carmichael of Arthurstone. MS 102-12-2.

[19] Annie Laurant, *Des fers de Loire à l'acier Martin*, vol. 1, *Maîtres de forges en Berry et Nivernais*, Paris, 1995, p. 110.

[20] Arthur Helps, *Life and Labours of Mr Brassey*, London, 1872.

education in the late nineteenth century. The British Isles had their own diversity of languages and dialects, including continental vernacular languages, even in early modern England.[21] Robert Owen noted that his speaking only English was a disadvantage when he arrived in New Lanark in 1800, affecting his ability to interact with the Scottish workers, 'many of [whom] knew only the Gaelic tongue'.[22] He used the silent monitors (or telegraphs) as an effective means of communication, especially with the Highlanders.[23]

There was great diversity among migrants when it came to their linguistic competence. Those who travelled on their own, and who were young and literate, could find it easy to learn a new language at a time when self-teaching was common among artisans. There is evidence that some managed to integrate and get the skills needed for basic communication in a few months, as we have seen with Smith, who learnt French easily. Goldsmith William Duthie (see Chapter 4.4) had comparable recollections: 'during a residence of seven months in Hamburg', he wrote, 'I had acquired enough of the German language to trust myself alone in the country'.[24] In Paris, Duthie worked in a workshop employing 'three Russians, two Germans, two Englishmen, an Italian, and a Frenchman; and sometimes a simple inquiry would have to pass through four languages before it received its answer'.[25] There were other examples of people who learnt foreign languages easily. Friedrich Engels remembered that in Paris among German artisans 'German was so much the prevailing tongue in this trade that I was acquainted there in 1846 with a Norwegian tailor who had travelled directly by sea from Drontheim to France and in the space of eighteen months had learned hardly a word of French but had acquired an excellent knowledge of German'.[26] Former Chartist and temperance lecturer Robert Lowery (1809–63) remembered a shoemaker named Thomas who had gone with him to Paris in a deputation 'to assure the French that the English people did not sympathise with the acts of Lord Palmerston', probably in the early 1840s:

> He could speak French fluently, which I could not. Considering his small opportunities he was a marvel at languages. He was a shoemaker, and acquired them all when following his trade. He was a native of Cornwall, was apprenticed to a shoemaker at Falmouth, where he acquired his French from mixing with the French boatmen who came there. This he afterwards improved by books. He was

---

[21] John Gallagher, *Learning Languages in Early Modern England*, Oxford, 2019.

[22] Robert Owen, *The Revolution in the Mind and Practice of the Human Race*, London, 1850, p. 9.

[23] Ophélie Siméon, *Robert Owen's Experiment at New Lanark: From Paternalism to Socialism*, London, 2017, p. 64.

[24] William Duthie, *A Tramp's Wallet; stored by an English Goldsmith during his Wanderings in Germany and France*, London, 1858, p. vi.

[25] Ibid., p. xxix.

[26] Frederick Engels, 'On the History of the Communist League', *Sozialdemokrat*, 12–26 November 1885, in Karl Marx and Frederick Engels, *Collected Works*, vol. 26, 1990, p. 315.

thus frequently called in to interpret at the principal hotel.... Afterwards a German ship with emigrants for America was wrecked near Falmouth in the autumn, and the Germans had to remain until the spring before they could proceed on their voyage, some of them lodged at his mother's and he became very intimate with one of the young women; he got the rudiments of the German from her, which he followed up by books until he could read, write and speak it fluently.... Although he had never been in France so perfect was his pronunciation that he was taken for a native.[27]

Beyond this rare case of unusual ability, the obstacles raised by a foreign language should not be underestimated. Smith suggested an explanation: 'Anybody who knows a language thoroughly may easily teach it to another knowing the principles of grammar; but to impart a correct knowledge of a foreign tongue to a man who does not his own is just one of the impossible things which none of the 'wondrous new machines of modern spinning' have been found competent to effect'.[28] Things were probably more nuanced, but most migrant workers had little formal instruction, usually only Sunday schools, where foreign languages were not taught. For instance, in 1856 in Landerneau, out of ninety-three Scottish workers, 51 per cent of the men and 84 per cent of the women could not sign their employment booklets ('livrets de travail'); that is, below the average literacy rates in Scotland.[29]

However, literacy was one skill and the ability to learn a foreign language another. In nearly all communities of migrants, including those with low literacy, like the Scottish female spinners in Landerneau, there were examples of marriages with local people, which suggests that language barriers could be overcome, at least partly. There were also several examples of isolated British workers living in foreign environments. As we have seen (p. 93), George Heeley, a railway employee, was the sole foreigner in the Norman village of Valliquerville. 'Marie Cusine', a thirty-one-year-old British female teacher, was the only foreigner living with 604 French people in Cliponville, another village.[30] Sources do not reveal anything of their lives, but we should assume that they had a working knowledge of French so as to communicate with locals.

While the autobiographies of learned artisans like Smith and Duthie point to easiness and success, other types of sources suggest difficulties, not just for groups but even for individuals. When James Emerson Tennent visited the prison in Ghent, Belgium, in the 1830s, he met an English inmate, Clarke, aged thirty-five or

---

[27] Brian Harrison and Patricia Hollis (eds.), *Robert Lowery: Radical and Chartist*, London, 1979, p. 164.
[28] Ibid., p. 113.
[29] Yves Blavier, *La société linière du Finistère. Ouvriers et entrepreneurs à Landerneau au XIX\u1d49 siècle*, Rennes, 1999, p. 139.
[30] AD Seine-Maritime. Recensement de 1851. 6M120 (2 Mi 1014): Commune de Valliquerville; 6M114 (2Mi 1004): Commune de Cliponville.

thirty-six, who had come over 'with his wife to seek for work as a machine-maker'. But Clarke had been unsuccessful, 'what became of his family he no longer knew', and he was now dying of consumption. Tennent was moved by 'his situation, surrounded by foreigners, to whose very language he was a stranger, far from home and England, and without a friend or relation to watch his dying bed'.[31]

More broadly, such sources suggest that the experience of not mastering the language was even more pressing than it would be today. The language barrier could be a major obstacle to the integration of British workers. And distinctions should be made between artisans who emigrated on their own, and therefore had to learn the language so as to be able to interact, and groups which could rely upon forms of sociability that enabled them to interact mostly with people who spoke the same language. When discussing emigration in 1824, political economist J. R. McCulloch, who argued for the repeal of the prohibition, added, after having interviewed some manufacturers:

> The unconditional repeal of the laws preventing emigration could not occasion any considerable influx of British artisans into the Continent. The lowness of wages in the Continental States, the differences of customs and habits, and above all of language, are obstacles to extensive emigration which it is almost impossible to overcome.[32]

A witness to the Select Committee on Artisans also noted that in France, 'common [British] workmen are very seldom able to speak the language'.[33]

In March 1848, a mechanic wrote to the British ambassador, on behalf of linen workers threatened with being laid off in Haubourdin (Nord), where most had worked for three years:

> To take our case in your consideration, there are about 140 or 150 of us in all men women and children not one of us excepting the before mentioned individual is able to speak more than a few words of the language, not one is able to ask a summons against this unjust company, many of the girls from the fines they are imposed and the reductions that have been made on their wages are in utter poverty and the company are constraining some of them to leave the work next week, having given them notice to quit telling them to get to Boulogne and that the British Consul there will send them home, the company always retaining their 50 francs, something must be done for us in this our miserable condition.[34]

---

[31] James Emerson Tennent, *Belgium*, London, 1841, vol. 1, p. 159.
[32] Anonymous [J. R. McCulloch], *Edinburgh Review*, vol. 39, no. 78, January 1824, p. 342.
[33] Evidence by Mr Taylor, 20 February 1824. PP. *Report from the Select Committee on artizans and machinery*, 1824, p. 36.
[34] TNA. FO 146 350. Consular Correspondence, Letter from Haubourdin (Nord), 21 March 1848.

Although it is hard to discern the role of rhetorical strategy in this plea for money, there is evidence that among migrant communities, adults could spend years in foreign countries without learning the language. The availability of English-language pubs and newspapers in areas where migrants clustered, like Calais, Rouen, or Boulogne, also made it easier for them to remain within an English-speaking community and to rely on English-speaking networks. Of course, there could be a great diversity of situations, even within the same groups: children and young people could learn the vernacular language more easily. We may also assume that male breadwinners had more practice than housewives, and there were also more or less keen or talented learners. Again, we are dependent on scarce sources to assess language skills.

A rare trace of a misunderstanding has survived. In central Nantes, a tall column now stands in the middle of a square, with a statue of Louis XVI at the top. The statue was erected in 1823 under the Restoration to celebrate the king guillotined by the French Revolution. On 30 July 1830, in the context of another revolution, a local confrontation resulted in several casualties nearby. A plaque was added on the pedestal of the column, which read in French: 'Near here, a bloody struggle between oppressors and oppressed took place on 30 July 1830. English workers and labourers [laboureurs] have had this inscription laid to testify of their admiration for the bravery, the value, and the fearlessness of the people of Nantes' (Figure 4.2).[35] However, the French 'laboureur' (ploughman) was an incorrect translation of 'labourer': there were no immigrant ploughmen, but British iron workers in Indret foundry, near Nantes. With this engraved mistake, a world of undocumented misunderstandings and uneasy communication emerges.

Perhaps the category about whom the language question was most discussed was that of the railway navvies. In Normandy, large numbers of them worked in gangs, as we have seen. They mostly worked with fellow-Britons, but also had to interact with French workers and other foreign navvies. In a biography of railway entrepreneur Thomas Brassey which partly relied on first-hand evidence, Victorian writer Arthur Helps reported that on the construction sites

> no fewer than eleven languages were spoken on the works. The British spoke English; the Irish, Erse; the Highlanders, Gaelic; and the Welshmen, Welsh. Then there were French, Germans, Belgians, Dutch, Piedmontese, Spaniards and Poles—all speaking their own languages. There was also one Portuguese, but he was a linguist in his way, and could speak some broken French.[36]

---

[35] 'Ici près a eu lieu une lutte sanglante entre les oppresseurs et les opprimés le 30 juillet 1830. Des laboureurs et ouvriers anglais ont fait poser cette inscription en témoignage de leur admiration pour la bravoure, la valeur et l'intrépidité nantaises'. Plaque laid in 1831 on the pedestal of the colonne Louis XVI (1823), Nantes, place Louis XVI (currently place du Maréchal Foch).
[36] Arthur Helps, *Life and Labours of Mr Brassey*, London, 1872, p. 63.

Figure 4.2 Plaque (1831) paid for by English workers, on the pedestal of the column Louis XVI in Nantes. © Emmanuel Fureix.

How did these workers interact? An article was published in the *Journal de Rouen* and then translated in *The Times*:

> A NEW 'TONGUE'—The *Journal de Rouen* of the 22d inst states that the best understanding exists between the numerous English and French workmen employed at the Paris and Rouen Railroad. They have organised a kind of language which is neither English nor French, but by means of which they are enabled to converse with each other.[37]

Helps discussed the language question at length:

> There was much difficulty for the English in a strange country, which their employer could not provide against....among the navvies there grew up a language which could hardly be said to be either French or English and which in fact must have resembled that strange compound language (Pigeon English) spoken at Hong Kong by the Chinese in their converse with British sailors and merchants. It must have had at least as much French in it as English, for it is stated in evidence that 'the English learnt twice as much French as the Frenchmen learnt English'. This composite language had its own forms and grammar; and it seems to have been made use of in other countries besides France; for afterwards there were young Savoyards who became quite skilled in the use of this particular language, and who were employed as cheap interpreters

---

[37] *The Times*, 27 May 1841, p. 5, col. 1; *Journal de Rouen*, 22 May 1841.

between the sub-contractors and the native workmen. One of Mr Brassey's agents speaking on this subject, says:—

'It was not necessary to understand a word of English, but to understand the Englishman's Italian or French. That I found in many cases. A sharp youth, for example, would be always going about with a ganger, to listen to what he was saying, and to interpret to his (the youth's) countrymen'.

It is pleasing to find that, after all, we have some power in the acquisition of languages, for several navvies did eventually acquire a considerable knowledge of French, not, of course, speaking it very grammatically, but still having acquired a greater knowledge of it, and a greater command of it than they had of their native tongue.[38]

Since then, the development of a new language on the building site has become a historical commonplace.[39] However, this is not unsubstantiated. Since the eighteenth century at least, building sites have been towers of Babel, filled with the various languages of migrant workers. Even in the late 2010s, French Conservative politicians were trying to impose the French language in French building sites.[40] In places where several native languages co-exist, basic communication can be facilitated through shared basics in the language of the home country. Marcus Rediker has been interested in language learning onboard transatlantic slave ships, which offers some scope for comparisons. He writes that slaves of different African linguistic groups were often grouped together, and the crew rarely spoke any of their languages. Some maritime languages were devised to facilitate interaction. In the west of Africa, these pidgin languages were often based on English or Portuguese, while some slaves learnt some English through interaction with seamen. Some seamen also used gestures and signs to communicate with slaves.[41] In South African diamond and gold mines, where workers came from a multitude of ethnic backgrounds and spoke multiple languages, Fanakalo emerged in the late nineteenth century as a contact language.[42] As for the British navvies overseas, in the absence of further evidence, we have to rely on the scarce sources available and assume that some form of communication between individuals

[38] Helps, *Life and Labours of Mr Brassey*, pp. 62–3.

[39] Terry Coleman, *The Railway Navvies*, Harmondsworth, 1981, p. 203. Virginie Maréchal, 'La construction des lignes de chemin de fer de Paris à Rouen et de Rouen au Havre (1839–1847)', *Revue d'histoire des chemins de fer*, no. 14, 1996, p. 102, Hélène Bocard, *De Paris à la mer. La Ligne de chemin de fer Paris-Rouen-Le Havre*, Paris, 2005, p. 16, and Julian Barnes ('Junction', *Cross Channel*, London, 1996) perpetuate this idea; David Brooke, *The Railway Navvy: 'That Despicable Race of Men'*, London, 1983, p. 128.

[40] 'La clause Molière imposant le français sur les chantiers publics, une disposition contestée', *Le Monde*, 10 March 2017.

[41] Marcus Rediker, *The Slave Ship: A Human History*, New York, 2007, ch. 9, 'Building Babel'.

[42] Bernardi Wessels, 'FANAKALO: Lingua Franca of the mining community', *Mining Survey*, vol. 1, 1986.

and people belonging to different linguistic groups was made possible. Among the children of migrants, a foreign language was no such obstacle. The 'sharp youth[s]' evoked by Helps were those through whom integration was completed. Children could thus be the brokers who facilitated the integration of migrants. Their education was critical and, in a period when education and religion could hardly be dissociated, it mattered not only to the migrants but also to their employers, the churches, and the authorities.

2. Protestant Worship and a Protestant Education

English-speaking migrant communities abroad soon made provisions for the education of their children. Among manufacturers, sending one's children to boarding schools in Britain was not unusual. For instance, James Carmichael, the manager of a Scottish linen and jute works in Ailly-sur-Somme (1845–70), sent his daughters to boarding schools in Scotland long after he had come to France.[43] The Waddingtons in Saint-Rémy-sur-Avre did the same. This expensive option was favoured by entrepreneurs who were keen on the assets of public schools and on preserving the link with Britain. Several English boarding schools were also set up in Normandy and northern France; that is, the areas where a significant number of middle-class British residents wanted to get their children educated.[44] But for working-class children, neither option was a viable prospect.

Among migrant workers, children often accounted for 30–40 per cent of the communities and remain a mystery, with so little being known about their lives. There are few instances of their being employed and sources are scarce on this. When it comes to schooling, religion remained a critical factor. The French Revolution had acknowledged both Protestant and Jewish worships, but since the 1804 Concordat, the Catholic Church had regained a dominant position in the religious life of the country. The 1814 constitution guaranteed protection to all denominations but made Catholicism the established religion. During the White Terror of 1815 many Protestants, who were likened to revolutionaries and Bonapartists, were killed. Under the Restoration until 1830, an authorisation was required for an Anglican school to be set up, and authorities were distrustful of British schoolmasters, who were assumed to be Protestant and liberal. In France, under the Restoration (1814–30) and to a lesser extent under the July Monarchy (1830–48), the denominational character of education was neglected neither by employers nor by the authorities. For instance, in 1826, the director of

---

[43] Fabrice Bensimon and Christopher A. Whatley, 'The Thread of Migration: A Scottish-French Linen and Jute Works and Its Workers in France, c. 1845–c. 1870', *Journal of Migration History*, vol. 2.1, 2016, p. 143.

[44] 'English Academy and Boarding School. At Bacqueville, conducted by M. Delahaye', *Norman Times*, 20 January 1844.

the police in the ministry asked the préfet in Rouen: 'I'd like you to inform me how the English practice their worship, whether they have a minister and, if they do, who he's paid by'.[45] The préfet investigated his department and the mayor of Rouen replied that those of the English 'who were Protestants attend the chapel devoted to this worship, that they are even relieved attached to it when they lived in poverty and that I am far from believing that they have special religious meetings'.[46] The sous-préfets in Dieppe and Le Havre gave similar replies. Under the July Monarchy, a more relaxed attitude prevailed: Catholicism was now the religion of the 'majority of French' people only, and Protestant François Guizot was the prime minister from 1840, while three of the king's children married Protestants.

Anti-Catholicism had also been strong in Britain, and the British had reasons for setting up their own schools. Some of them were set up by employers, who paid for the expenses incurred. It is hard to discern these initiatives' religious, moral, and educational purposes. In Charenton, where there were by 1825 some 624 British working-class people, including 248 children, an Anglican clergyman was soon sent. In Ailly-sur-Somme there was a local village school but in 1847 the master and priest had allegedly 'tried every means to get [the Scottish pupils] to Kiss the [Roman Catholic] Church', which had caused the Scots to withdraw their children from it.[47] Carmichael recognised the importance of getting a suitable teacher—his preference was for a Scot—and that a works school would need to be subsidised by the company. He seems to have been successful, having a 'class instruction school' in the mill complex and being able to offer free classes for boys and girls from the nearby villages.

With the building of railways, several schools could be opened. In 1844, an 'English national school' was set up in Rouen, and another at Malaunay, 'for the gratuitous instruction of children belonging to the English workmen employed on the railway from Rouen to Havre'. The Rouen school numbered eighty-nine children, the Malaunay one seventy-nine, and children were 'daily receiving lessons in all the useful branches of education, calculated to fit them for fulfilling the stations to which they may be called later in life'. Both were partly funded by Brassey himself and were under the control of the Church of England.[48] For instance, in April 1844 the bishop held a confirmation for 'the young persons

---

[45] AD76 Seine-Maritime. 4M 671. Lettre du Directeur de la police (ministère de l'Intérieur) au préfet de Rouen, December 1826: 'd'après les états des mouvements des étrangers, un nombre assez considérable d'anglais résident dans votre département. Je désire que ... vous me fassiez connaître comment les anglais célèbrent leur culte, s'ils ont un ministre et, dans l'affirmative, par qui il est rétribué'.

[46] AD Seine-Maritime. 4M 671. Lettre du maire de Rouen au préfet, 21 December 1826: 'que ceux qui sont protestans fréquentent le temple destiné à ce culte, qu'ils sont même secourus par le ministre qui y est attaché lorsqu'ils vivent dans l'indigence, et que je suis éloignés de croire qu'ils aient des réunions religieuses particulières'.

[47] UDAS, MS 102/9 (35), JC to PC, 4 September 1847.

[48] *Norman Times*, 13 January 1844, p. 1; 27 January 1844, p. 4 ('Advertisements'); 16 March 1844, p. 4; 20 April 1844.

on the railway, and the inhabitants of Rouen', in the premises of the school.[49] In Boulogne-sur-Mer schools were also set up from 1836. Children were admitted 'provided their parents are unable to educate them at their own expence, and that either their Father or Mother be a British subject'. The English language, writing, and arithmetic were taught, as well as needlework and knitting in the girls' school. A report mentioned that 'The great and fundamental truths of Christianity are diligently taught according to the Word of God, and every pains taken to instill into the minds of the children the only true principles of all moral rectitude and right conduct in life'.[50]

French authorities complied with the British children being taught by British teachers but could be suspicious. In Calais, in the late 1820s, the title 'gradué [graduate] de l'université de Dublin' of Revd. Palmer was not acknowledged as valid and a Mr Lloyds [sic] was also turned down, on account of his poor language skills.[51] In July 1844, the 'Recteur' who supervised education in the Rouen area had to interfere in a village conflict between a lady who had opened an English school for the girls of workers digging a railway tunnel and the mayor who, following a request made by the French schoolteacher, had closed it: 'if lady Peasneall has presented a certificate ascertaining her good life and behaviour delivered by the relevant authority', it should be tolerated, the recteur argued (Figure 4.3). He relied on an 1836 royal ordnance which provided for the subjects to be taught in girls' schools.[52]

During the Second Empire, authorities were also more lenient, and in 1850 the 'loi Falloux' on education provided that foreigners could be allowed to open up primary and secondary schools.[53] But in rural areas the Catholic aristocracy could dominate social and cultural life. In 1853, following the rise in the numbers of Scottish workers in Landerneau, the Scottish Kirk sent a clergyman to minister to the workers and for the 'religious and moral teaching of their children'. The British consul in Brest informed the préfet, adding that the new clergyman, Charles Frazer, 'could not speak French and his classes will entirely be dedicated to the instruction of English workmen and their families'.[54] The sous-préfet

[49] 'Anglican Confirmation', Norman Times, 27 April 1844. The 'bishop' may have been George Tomlinson, who was the Anglican bishop in Europe from 1842.

[50] TNA. FO 27/784. France: correspondence with Consul Thomas Pickford, Paris; Consul Edward Walter Bonham... The tenth report of the Committee of the British Free Schools, rue du Pot d'étain, Boulogne sur mer, for the years 1845 and 1846, 1847.

[51] Albert Vion, 'Aspects de la vie calaisienne aux XIXe siècle: la communauté britannique', Bulletin historique et artistique du Calaisis, vol. 80, December 1979, p. 520.

[52] 'Je suis informé qu'une dame Peasneall avait ouvert dans votre commune une école destinée aux enfants des ouvriers anglais du chemin de fer, et que sur la réclamation de l'instituteur français, vous avez cru devoir faire fermer cette école. Si la Dame Peasneall vous a présenté un certificat de bonnes vie et mœurs délivré par une autorité compétente, je pense qu'il y a lieu de tolérer temporairement cette école qui ne saurait être...aux prescriptions de l'ordonnance royale du 23 juin 1836'. Archives municipales de Pissy-Pôville (Seine-Inférieure), lettre du Recteur au maire, 22 July 1844.

[53] Article 78 of the 15 March 1850 law: 'Les étrangers peuvent être autorisés à ouvrir ou diriger des établissements d'instruction primaire o secondaire, aux conditions déterminées par un règlement délibéré en Conseil supérieur'.

[54] AD Finistère. 4 M 83. Consul britannique au préfet, 17 December 1853.

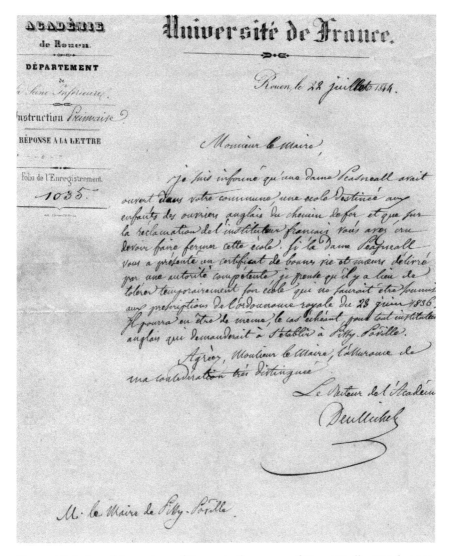

Figure 4.3 Letter of the recteur of Rouen to the mayor of Pissy-Pôville, 22 July 1844. Archives municipales de Pissy-Pôville (Seine-Maritime).

approved of the request, considering that 'his presence could have good effects on these foreigners whose morality had so far been far from blameless'. But he added a warning:

> The only drawback I would see in this creation would be if, because of excessive zeal, this clergyman tried to make converts outside the community, which could raise concern among the people. To avoid such a result, I think it would be good

to let him know that the administration insists on his staying within the object of the mission for which he's been called.[55]

So the préfet wrote to the consul, insisting on the fact that permission was granted because the Scottish children could not attend a French-language school, but did not imply that the clergyman could promote his faith more widely. Religious affiliations and national sensitivities were thus interrelated.

This also suggests that denomination played an important part in the migrants' lives. This could be because of their strong beliefs, although these were seldom formulated as such. Among the rare artefacts preserved by the Wood family in Calais today is a Bible of their ancestor, John Maxton Senior, who was born on 11

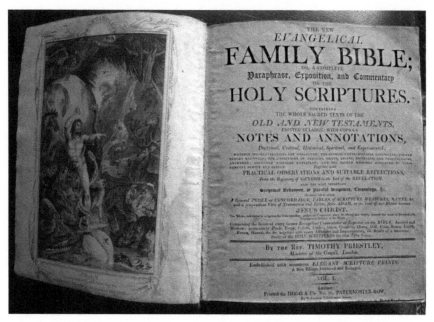

Figure 4.4 Bible that was brought to Calais by John Maxton Sr (1782–1846) and his wife Ann née Osborn (b. 1785), who came to Calais to make lace, at the latest in 1821. Four of the children became lacemakers. The Bible is the hands of Mary Wood, the widow of a fourth-generation descendant. © Mary Wood.

[55] AD Finistère. AM 83. Sous-préfet de Brest au préfet, 21 December 1853. 'L'établissement d'un ministre protestant dans la filature de Landerneau ne me paraît avoir aucun inconvénient, son action ne devant s'étendre qu'aux seuls Écossais, ses co-religionaires employés dans cette usine. Je pense même que sa présence pourra produire de bons effets sur ces étrangers dont la moralité a été jusqu'ici loin d'être à l'abri de tout reproche. Je ne verrais d'inconvénient à cette création que si, par un excès de zèle, cet ecclésiastique chercherait à faire des prosélytes au dehors ce qui pourrait porter l'inquiétude parmi les populations. Pour éviter un pareil résultant, je pense qu'il sera bien de lui faire connaître que l'administration tient à ce qu'il se renferme dans l'objet de la mission pour laquelle il a été appelé'.

November 1782 and emigrated to Calais c.1820 (Figure 4.4).[56] For working-class families, two dimensions of social life were particularly important where religion was concerned: education, as we have seen, and the family. Leather-dresser Colin, who lived in Saint-Denis in the late 1810s (see pp. 94–6), remembered his engagement to a local young woman, who was a daughter of his employer:

> After I had been there about a year, I and a Mdle. Longeville got intimately acquainted, and a marriage was agreed upon; but the priest would not marry us unless I would turn a Roman Catholic, and swear allegiance to Louis XVIII. I would not hear of turning my back upon the religion in which I was brought up, nor would I turn my coat against my King and country. I would rather part with Marie Antoine Longeville than do either.[57]

One may be dubious about such a narrative, delivered thirty years later for an Evangelical British newspaper, where anti-Catholicism would strike a chord. And there is evidence that such religious differences did not always have unhappy outcomes. In Pissy-Pôville, a small village in Seine-Inférieure where a British community lived during the building of a tunnel, James Handforth, a labourer from Hollingworth (Cheshire), and John Middleton, a navvying foreman from Leicestershire, married two local women, respectively Eugénie Fortunée Tougard, a laundress, and Onésime Eugénie Marc, a servant. Both weddings took place on 30 April 1846. And both bridegrooms renounced their faith and were baptised Catholics on that same day.[58] In Landerneau, some Presbyterian female workers married Breton workers, who were Catholics.

The nineteenth century was a golden age for Nonconformism, and in some migrant communities Methodists could be as numerous as Anglicans. In Calais, a Methodist chapel was opened as early as 1830. The Methodists were mostly workers, rather than manufacturers, and judging from the rates of mixed marriages with the French, it seems they integrated earlier than the Anglicans. While in the 1840s only 4 per cent of the seventy-one babies baptised in the Methodist chapel were born to mixed families, they reached 20 per cent in the 1860s. Rates also rose among Anglicans, although more slowly (10 per cent in the 1860s). By the end of the century, at a time when British immigration had slowed down, most marriages were mixed.[59] By then, Anglicans, Presbyterians, and Methodists had integrated into the French Protestant structures.

All in all, religion did matter for migrants, as it did for most people at the time. Moreover, education was not seen as distinct from religious instruction. At the

---

[56] Private records of Mary Wood, Calais.
[57] John Colin [pseud.], *The Wanderer Brought Home: The Life and Adventures of Colin—An Autobiography*, London, 1864, pp. 20–1.
[58] AM Pissy-Pôville, état-civil.   [59] Vion, 'Aspects de la vie calaisienne aux XIXᵉ siècle', p. 525.

same time, in an age when secularisation had begun, and in the decades that followed the French Revolution, the authorities were becoming more liberal regarding religious worship. In the interactions between individuals, the issue could weigh heavily, but sources suggest that denominations mattered less than class, occupation, or political leanings. Marriages between Protestant Britons and Catholic-bred French people became more common, and for second generations they were not problematic. At the same time, in some areas, some British migrants contributed to the blossoming or the consolidation of Protestant networks and communities. But even when they numbered many workers, Anglican and Presbyterian communities were often led by manufacturers and other entrepreneurs. These middle-class Britons, who also subsidised the schools, were likewise those who ran English-language newspapers and who eventually played a prominent part in the introduction of English sports to the Continent.

3. Newspapers and Games

Imperial history has now addressed many of the ways in which cultural practices could be conveyed by migrants, from schooling to newspapers, from sports to gardening. The migrants of the industrial revolution lived in an age when reading and writing became increasingly common. The most thorough source, marriage registers, suggests that literacy for adults in England and Wales had risen to 58 per cent in 1840, 50 per cent for brides and 67 per cent for grooms. By 1870, that is to say still before systematic elementary education was required by law, rates reached 73 and 80 per cent. Being able to sign a marriage register did not imply that workers were able to read lengthy newspaper articles and books. But a vast array of evidence suggests that these were present in the lives of migrants, as they were in Britain, even before the mass reading dailies of the late nineteenth century. The period 1815–70 was thus one of massive development of the press, due to rising literacy rates, falling prices, and the repeal of the stamp duties. By the 1840s, several weeklies sold 30–50,000 copies, and by 1863 *Lloyd's* sold 350,000.[60] There was a great diversity in the reading skills of the migrants, depending on occupation, gender, and educational background. We have seen that the literacy of linen workers, especially women, was below the average. But mechanics or train drivers could read and write and did so daily. We will examine the specific case of political literature in Chapter 5. What the Chartist press suggests, for instance, is that its newspapers were received in France, probably as they were subscribed to or as they were brought by travelling migrants. In a town like Rouen, the *Illustrated London News*, the *Weekly Dispatch*, and the *Northern Star* were available.

[60] Richard Altick, *The English Common Reader: A Social History of the Mass Reading Public 1800–1900*, Chicago, IL, 1957, pp. 394–5.

We have mentioned that some English newspapers were published in France, initially for upper- and middle-class readerships, but they could of course be bought or read in a *cabinet de lecture* or a tavern by migrant workers. *Galignani's Messenger* (Figure 4.5) was the most enduring of the English newspapers in France: it was a daily published between 1814 and 1890, and its readership consisted first and foremost of middle-class British residents in Paris, France and across Europe. *The Boulogne Gazette* was published from 1839 to 1863 (Figure 4.6). But there were several other more ephemeral newspapers, like the *Paris Monthly Review of British and Continental Literature* (1822–3), the *Paris Herald* (1835), the *London and Paris Courier* (1836), and *The Paris Sun-Beam* (1836–7),[61] and *The Norman Times* (1844) and *The Railway Advocate and Continental Express* (1844), both in Rouen, and even an early free weekly made with advertisements, *The Calais Messenger* (from 1827).[62] Some French newspapers, like the *Journal de Calais*, also published articles and advertisements in English. In Belgium there were also short-lived English-language newspapers, such as the *Brussels Herald* and the *British and Continental Gazette* (1848–9).

The Norman Times (Figure 4.7) and *The Railway Advocate and Continental Express* are interesting examples of newspapers that could address emigrants. Both were short-lived: they were published in Rouen in 1844, that is, during the building of the Rouen–Le Havre railway. They were weeklies, priced 0.5 francs, about the same as the *Northern Star* (4.5 d). They conveyed railway information, as well as local and British news. They celebrated Mackenzie and Brassey, who obviously funded the paper. They also included timetables of the trains to Paris and of the boats across the Channel. Advertisements also addressed the 'English Labourers' about employment, the English schools, church service, and administrative duties. Some articles were written in French, though most were in English. Accidents and deaths were reported, as were games and sports. Ads promoted hotels, tailors, newsagents and bookshops, physicians, Oddfellows' meetings, and a Chartist pub. With such sources, a historical bias can hardly be avoided: perhaps these short-lived papers were little read by navvies, if at all, while other publications were popular among them but have not survived. Historians have shown that there was an 'underworld' of British publications in the first half of the nineteenth century. But at least *The Norman Times* and *The Railway Advocate* help us understand what entrepreneurs wanted to circulate. All in all, the English-language newspapers in France may not have been sufficient to create

---

[61] Elizabeth Jay, *British Writers in Paris, 1830–1875*, Oxford, 2016.
[62] Diana Cooper-Richet, 'La diffusion du modèle victorien à travers le monde. Le rôle de la presse en anglais publiée en France au XIXe siècle', in Marie-Eve Thérenty and Alain Vaillant (dir.), *Presse, nations et mondialisation au XIXe siècle*, Paris, 2010, pp. 17–32.

Figure 4.5 *Galignani's Messenger* was published in Paris from 1814, daily from 1815, by the publisher and book-keeper Giovanni Antonio Galignani (1757–1821), and then by his London-born sons John Anthony (1796–1873) and William (1798–1882). Although the paper and the publishing business are over, the shop survives to this day at 224 rue Rivoli in Paris.

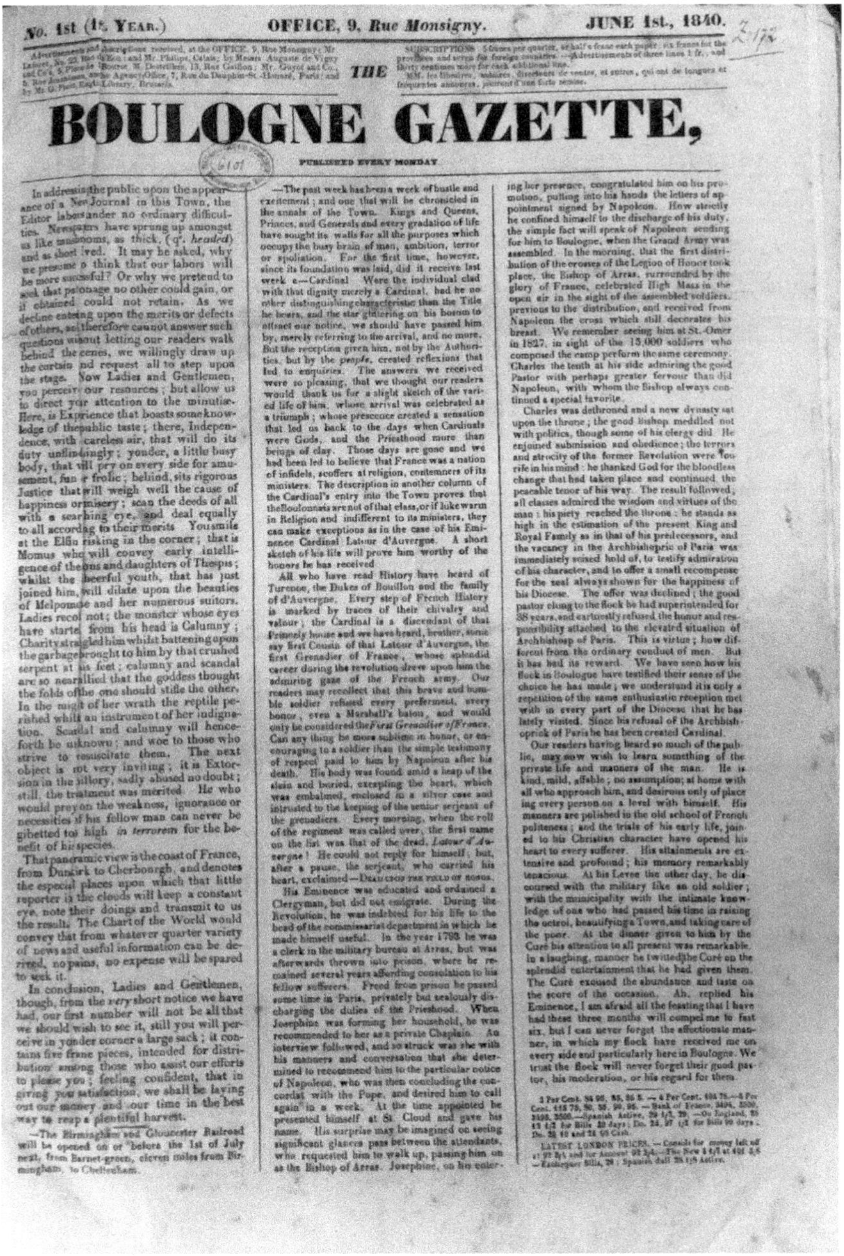

Figure 4.6 *The Boulogne Gazette* was published weekly from 1840 to 1869; its publication went on under different names until 1910 (here, the first issue on 1 June 1840. Archives municipales de Boulogne-sur-Mer).

Agents at

PARIS,
LONDON, Mr Barker, Fleet street.
BRIGHTON, Mr Wood, Gazette Office.
DIEPPE, Mr Huren, Messageries Royales.
HAVRE,
CAEN,
EVREUX,

THE

NORMAN TIMES

(A FRIEND TO ALL, AND AN ENEMY TO NONE.)

PUBLISHED EVERY SATURDAY, AT 13, QUAI DE LA BOURSE, ROUEN.

Subscriptions.

A single paper 50 centimes.

Paid in advance:
For three months........ 6 francs.
— Six — .... 12 —
— Twelve — .... 24 —

ADVERTISEMENTS.

First insertion, per line..... 75 c.
Second d°, d°...... 00
Each subsequent d°...... 50

ALL COMMUNICATIONS, AND ADVERTISEMENTS, TO BE ADDRESSED TO THE EDITOR, 13, QUAI DE LA BOURSE, ROUEN.

OUR FIRST BOW TO THE PUBLIC.

It has been customary for journalists to make a somewhat formal addres to their patrons at the commencement of the New year; but we, having just started into existence, may easily be excused such a formality. We have no friends to thank for favors conferred during the past, nor do we pretend to a more than ordinary power of peeping into the future, — we have however, the satisfaction of knowing, that our undertaking has met with the approbation of our countrymen of all classes; and, as we are determined to watch and preserve, as far as we are able, the interests of every Englishman, we look forward, with a confident hope of being able, at the commencement of the year 1845, to congratulale our neighbours and ourselves, in having jointly supported a journal for their advantage.

We refer our readers to the prospectus of this, the first number of the Norman Times, and plead, as an excuse for not addressing them further on the subject, the fact of our colunmns being already crowded with other matter.

THE ROUEN AND HAVRE RAILWAY.

The contract for the first *fourteen* miles of this line, from Rouen, taken by Messrs Mackenzie and Brassey, is the greatest ever entered into with the French goverment, either by English or French speculators. As the extent of the undertaking, and the extraordinary talent which must be brought to bear upon its completion are but imperfectly known to the public at large, or even by the English residents here, we propose to lay before them the following details, as the commencement of a series of articles, which cannot fail in general interest, from the fact that they will be drawn from the most authentic sources.

Although the whole extent of the line, from Rouen to Havre, has been finally determined, the exact position has not yet been traced farther than Barentin, a flourishing manufacturing town, situated about 14 miles from Rouen by rail.

The works will commence with a branch about one hundred yards below the Engine station at Sotteville, and will cross an extensive meadow (the Rouen race ground) frequently under water from the overflowing of the Seine, a circumstance which will render it necessary to cast up an embankment from 12 to 15 or 18 feet in height. From thence the rail will be conducted across the Seine by a bridge to the village of Eauplet, and, after traversing a hundred yards or so on the opposite bank, will enter a tunnel, to be excavated underneath St Catherine's mount. This spot is pregnant with interesting historical associations, which the length of this article will not permit us further to allude to, but which will form the subject of remark on a future day. This tunnel will measure in length about 1100 yards, and the average depth from the surface to the bore will be about 140 yards. From this termination the rail will pass along the valley of Darnetal by means of an embankment; cross the rue Darnetal by a bridge, and enter another tunnel of 130 yards long, under the rue Percée, describing a curve for the purpose of avoiding contact with expensive property, consisting of many respectable residences. The depth from the surface to the bore of this tunnel will be about 50 feet.

Before the line disappears again under ground, it crosses a space of 150 yards or so of open cutting; and then commences the tunnel underneath the boulevard St Hilaire, and the boulevard Beauvoisine. This tunnel, which will run exactly below the carriage road, and a very few houses, will be about 1700 yards in length, and 70 feet in depth, from the surface to the bore. The other extremity of this tunnel reaches to the rue Verte, which the rail will cross by means of a bridge, and, after traversing a distance of about 200 yards of open cutting, will enter another tunnel, the St Gervais, which will pass under the St Maur and St Gervais cemeteries.

Here we are constrained to pause for a moment, to call the reader's attention to this spot, which is justly considered as almost the cradle of religion. The history of the church (now a chapel of ease) dates as for back as 386; and we are told that the Archbishop worked with his own hands, and even helped to carry the stones on his shoulders for the erection of the sacred edifice. Here is to be seen an extremely curious and ancient monument, the crypt of St Gervais, deposited in a subturrenean chapel, where repose also the remains of the two first Archbishops of Rouen. St Mellon and St Avitien; and here also were discovered the only vestiges of Roman architecture which are to be found in the town of Rouen. It was at the Priory of St Gervais that William the Conqueror expired on the 9 of september 1087, having caused himself to be conveyed thither at the time when, on his way to Paris, he was mortally wounded by the pummel of his saddle.

The length of this tunnel, which will extend to the rue Chasselièvre, will be of about 1200 yards; and the average depth from the surface to the bore will not be more than 90 feet. On reaching the rue Chasselièvre, the rail, quitting Rouen and its environs, will traverse, for about 150 yards, an open country, presenting a gently undulating surface, entirely devoid of foliage, if we except the vegetable productions of the market gardeners to whom this land appears to be allotted. In this space there will be two cuttings and one large embankment. — The next point of attraction on this line will be a tunnel to be pierced at Déville, near the barrière du Havre, and to extend 340 yards. — the depth from the surface to the bore averaging 90 feet. — After emerging from this tunnel, the line will proceed in a parrallel direction with, and near to, the *route royale* to Dieppe, through an open country, and without any tunnelling, for about five miles. The surface of this country presents, however, many engineering difficulties, which will render it necessary to have several embankments as well as deep excavations. — At the termination of this distance the line will reach the village of Malaunay, where it will traverse a valley, of 3/4 of a mile in extent. — Having passed this place, the hardy miners will again be brought to operate upon the stubborn rock, which they will pierce to the extent of about 3000 yards. This tunnel is regarded as the principal one on the line. – The depth, from the surface to the bore, will average 70 yards. The line will then be carried forward by Clères, Duclair, and through the commune of Pissy-Pôville, a distance of 3300 yards or thereabouts until it reaches the hill overhanging the valley of Barentin. Owing to the nature of this country it will be necessary to cast up several embankments.

The giant effort for the completion of this portion of the line is reserved for its terminus. The bustling and thriving little town of Barentin lies snugly ensconced in a valley which, viewed from the opposite heights, has an imposing appearance, and connot fail to impress the beholder with an idea of the impossibility of any scientific effort being able to construct a means of crossing it. — Nevertheless, stupendous as are these obstacles, they will be overcome; — and the rail will be conducted from hill to hill by a viaduct, collossus like bestriding the valley. — When finished, this piece of architecture will rival the far-famed erection of the same kind at Stockport. The Barentin viaduct will consist of 27 arches, extending over a space of 430 yards, giving to each arch a span of nearly 20 yards.

— The piers by wich it will be supported, will be of solid brick work, of about 4 yards in thickness; and will measure 40 yards from the foundation to the springing of the arches. From the termination of the viaduct, the line will continue dbout 600 yards parrellel with the Paris and Havre route royale on the Havre side of Barentin, the greatest extent to which the company are at present warranted in going.

We cannot close this descriptive account of the line without adding a word of remark on the backward state of the works. When the final decision was given respecting this portion of the line, a period of four mouths was allowed to the proprietors of land, over which the rail would pass, to enable them to make as advantageous terms as they could with the company. Many of these proprietors have, by demanding a greater sum than the Company consider to be the value, prevented the la.ter from obtaining possession, and consequently retarded the works The period fixed by government will, however, expire in about *five* we ks from this day, when the company wil be empowerd to take possession of all the land on the line by the award of a jury. — When this has been accomplished, the number of Englishmen now out of employment, and, we regret to state, many of them in great distress will no doubt be immediately set to work. In the mean time, we have much pleasure in referring to two paragraphs in another part of our paper, as some proofs that the distresses of our countrymem in Normandy are not uncared for by those who have the power of alleviating them to a certain extent

The whole subject of this line of railway, and the interests of those connected with it, shall be resumed in our next number.

THE RECEIPTS of the Paris and Rouen railway, from the 26 of December to the 2 of january are as follows:

Passengers	58,544 fr. 05 c.
Goods.	17,946 70
Making a total of	76,490 fr. 75 c.

DESTRUCTIVE FIRE AT SOTTEVILLE. — On Monday night last a fire was discovered to have broken out in one of the outbuildings at the railway station at Sotteville, near to Rouen. Very soon after the alarm was given, the engines belonging to that village were promptly on the spot, and we learn, from good authority, that the officials engaged there in conducted themselves in the most exemplary manner. The tocsin, or fire bell being sounded, the fire brigade from Rouen also repaired to the disastrous scene. — On the arrival of the first engines it was discovered that the fire had occurred in a kind of shed used as the depositary of stores for the locomotive department, which is presided over by MM. Allcard and Buddicom. This building forms two sides of a square, one of which abuts upon the forge belonging to the establishment, and the other adjoins the carriage repository. The part nearest the forge contained a quantity of those combustible materials, oil, grease and cotton for the use of the engines, and the moment they were ignited they accelerated the complete destruction of the building and all it contained, amongst other things some valuable documents and books. — Fortunately that part of the fated building which adjoined the coach house was comparatively empty, a fact which, combined with the exertions of the fire men, contributed to save the valuable property therein contained from destruction; as it was, no further damage was done beyond the entire demolition of the building where the fire occurred, and its contents, if we except a small portion of one of the coach houses, an old carriage used for carrying milk on the line, and the back part of a second class carriage. The damage done altogether is estimated at about 40,000 francs, the greatest part of which is the loss of the railway company, who, we understand, are insured, but to what amount we have not learnt. — Only a very small portion of this loss falls upon MM. Allcard and Buddicom. — The origin of the fire is as yet involved in obscurity, although the police authorities have instituted a rigid enquiry.

DEATH OF THE ARCHBISHOP OF ROUEN. — The Archbishop of Rouen expired in this city on monday morning last at an early hour, in the 70th of year of his age. From the Rouen journals we draw the following particulars respecting this venerable prelate : Gustave-Maximilien Juste, Prince de Croi — belonged to a noble and ancient family, (which numbers among its ancestors Saint Elizabeth of Hungary) and was born on the 12 th. Septembre 1773, at the Chateau of the Hermitage, near to Old Conde. From his earliest years he manifested great piety, and was passionately fond of religious ceremonies. He pursued his studies with great avidity, and, having a prodigious memory, soon acquired a profound erudition. — The abstract sciences appeared to present no difficulty to him; and in the study of the languages he exhibited a marvelous aptitude. He spoke four languages well, and had a tolerable knowledge of four others. His Highness appears to have possesod to great perfection all the qualities that should distinguish a divine — he laboured without ceasing at the work of restoring and decorating sacred monuments — in contributing to the erection of churches and chapels — the establishment augmentation, and embellishment of seminares; and the Hospital at the environs of Rouen, raised for the benefit of

Figure 4.7 *The Norman Times* (6 January 1844).

communities of readers, even local communities. But they sometimes did, especially in the middle class, and they testified to the determination to preserve links as well as shared interests among emigrants.

In many respects, sports and games were supposed to help do the same; that is, to share some common culture so as to preserve and sustain bonds overseas. It is well known that modern sports such as football, rugby, athletics, and cricket were 'invented' in Britain and then diffused to the rest of the world, including Europe.[63] To a degree, some English games and leisure activities were exported even before sports were codified and leagues were set up. From the 1820s, the wealthy Britons who settled in France introduced their model of horse-racing, with clubs and races in Paris, Boulogne-sur-Mer (1835), Pau, Chantilly, Lyon (1839), and Bordeaux (1840).[64] Chantilly also became a centre for horse-racing, when it came of age under the Second Empire. British and French gentlemen had played a key role, though artisans were not totally absent: for instance, the hiring of British smith Richard Taylor and British horse dentists as well as coaches played a key part in the making of a horse-training milieu in Chantilly.[65] The horse-racing milieu also introduced English boxing in France. In September 1838, in Saint-Maur near Paris, a 'boxing prize-fight' between two Englishmen lasted for thirty-eight rounds and eighty-two minutes and led to a trial the following year. It had been illegally organised by British horse-racing entrepreneurs and gamblers such as Lord Seymour, Anthony de Rothschild, and banker Charles Laffitte. Pugilism was prohibited in France, but gradually gained ground, while English boxing only became popular at the turn of the twentieth century.[66] Cricket matches were organised in Chantilly from the 1840s, though the first club, the Chantilly Cricket Club, was not created before 1883. The first ever French regatta took place in Calais in 1836, initiating a tradition which spread to other French harbours.

Such transfers were thus organised by individuals and institutions, from above. Did migrants play a part in transfers 'from below'? Workers and artisans also had their social occasions and their games. Calais lacemakers were keen on gambling, boxing, and cock-fighting, and this allegedly drove up the price of poultry in the local market.[67] Migrants also played trade games, where pride in physical skills could be jointly displayed with professional ones, for example through brick-making or picking up stones as quickly as possible.[68] In 1840, a cricket match between eleven cricketers from Calais and eleven from River, near Dover, was reported, while the return match was to be played in Calais.[69] Similar games were

---

[63] Julien Sorez, 'Le football et la fabrique des territoires. Une approche spatiale des pratiques culturelles', *Vingtième Siècle. Revue d'histoire*, no. 111, 2011, pp. 59–72; François Bourmaud, 'Les Britanniques et le sport en France avant 1914: une histoire de transfert culturel', thesis, Sorbonne Université and Université de Lausanne, 2022.

[64] Daniel Roche, *La culture équestre de l'Occident, XVIᵉ–XIXᵉ siècle. L'ombre du cheval*, 3 vols., Paris, 2008–15.

[65] Bourmaud, 'Les Britanniques et le sport en France avant 1914', ch. 1.

[66] Sylvain Ville, *Le théâtre de la boxe: Histoire sociale de la boxe anglaise professionnelle à Paris (et à Londres) (1880–1930)*, doctoral thesis, Université Paris-Ouest Nanterre-La Défense, 2016; Sylvain Ville, 'Donner la boxe en spectacle: une histoire sociale des débuts de la boxe professionnelle à Paris, à la Belle Epoque', *Actes de la recherche en sciences sociales*, no. 209, 2015, pp. 10–27.

[67] Albert Vion, 'Aspects de la vie calaisienne aux XIXᵉ siècle', p. 531, quoting the *Journal de Calais*,1843.

[68] 'Curious Athletic Feat at Malaunay', *Norman Times*, 2 March 1844; 'Brick-Making', *Norman Times*, 18 May 1844.

[69] 'Cricket match—France v. England', *Northern Star*, 28 June 1840, p. 3.

played between British teams of various towns, such as in Dieppe in 1844 between local players and workers from Malaunay, where the railway line was being built.[70] A correspondent of *The Norman Times* could rejoice that

> it is a peculiar feature in the character of an Englishman, that wherever he takes up his residence, he is sure to indulge himself in those exhiliating [sic] sports that he has been accustomed to in his native land; and, as those sports are calculated to improve health, to give vigour to the frame, and steadiness to the hand and eye, no one can be so churlish as to deny them the enjoyments. Crickets, steeple-chasing, and shooting matches are generally the order of the day where John Bull thinks proper to locate himself.[71]

Games could thus be part and parcel of the national identity kit, alongside the language, traditions, flag, anthem, and so on.[72] But most lasting transfers of standardised sports across the Channel began later. For instance, the first rugby and football club in France, the Havre Athletic Club, was founded only in 1872 by British employees, while the first badminton club was created in Dieppe in 1907.

The migrant workers' cultural practices cannot easily be summarised. After all, the category of migrant worker encompasses very different people, from the navvies or the flax spinners, many of whom were illiterate, to the printers who belonged to the aristocracy of labour. Although much of the cultural environment of the migrants remains elusive, there is evidence to support the idea that they conveyed their domestic reading and leisure habits to continental environments, while also having to adjust. Adjusting also meant negotiating one's food and drink habits in new environments, with different opportunities. And this involved all migrants, regardless of literacy.

4. Meat-Eating and Heavy Drinking

Food and drink were also part of the culture of the British emigrants. Cultural norms were then different from what they are today, and the common cliché about good French food and poor British cooking was not established. But some eating and drinking habits did form part of the national stereotypes and could have political dimensions. In the eighteenth century, it had been common to equate the Catholic, expansionist Frenchmen with their diets. James Gillray and other satirists liked to mock the frogs and snails supposedly eaten by the

---

[70] 'Cricket Match at Dieppe', *The Railway Advocate and Continental Express*, 27 July 1844, p. 2; 10 August 1844, p. 1.

[71] *Norman Times*, 18 May 1844.

[72] Anne-Marie Thiesse, *La création des identités nationales. Europe XVIIIᵉ–XXᵉ siècle*, Paris, 1999.

effeminate Frenchmen, in contrast to the roast beef and ale consumed by the sturdy John Bull. National character and diets were thus intertwined. After the end of the Napoleonic wars, stereotypes were less aggressive but did not vanish. In many respects, they could be more enduring than political shifts. By the 1830s and 1840s, there was a long legacy of texts and pictures in British culture about the proud and inconstant French people. And the same was true among the French about the British. How the stereotypes conveyed by Carlyle, Dickens, or *Punch* were appropriated by workers is another story, which is harder to piece together. As for relations with local communities, one must discard some traditional stereotypes, which originated with the actors themselves. As we shall see (Chapter 5), more migrant workers were probably familiar with the *Northern Star* than with *The Times*. But stereotypes surfaced now and then, especially regarding food and drink, which were often related to work.

Questioned by the 1824 Committee about his two-year-long work as a carder for Schlumberger in Alsace, Adam Young gave straight answers about the French. Although they got up at 4 a.m. and worked until 10 p.m., he said, two or even eight of them would not do the work of a single English worker:

Are all the [French] workmen of that kind?—Yes; they are all of a lazy turn.

...How did you like your residence there?—I did not like it at all.

...What was the obstacle to your quitting when you liked?—I quitted because I did not like the French.

What was the reason you could not get away?—They would not sign my passport.

Did you want to return?—Yes; the day I got there I wanted to return; I did not like the diet, nor the people, nor any thing they had; the Frenchmen seem so fond of an Englishman when they get him among them, I did not like it.

...You were kept in the country contrary to your wishes?—Yes; I could not go out of the town without the permission of the gens d'armes.[73]

It was likely that Adam Young, who infringed on the British prohibition on work on the Continent, overstated his case to convince the committee that he had stayed against his own will. But it is meaningful that he referred to the diet as if it had been a badge of national identity. British workers, especially navvies, were often stereotypically thought to be hard workers, meat eaters, and drunkards. The French press was often positive about the navvies, 'the cleverest and the most hard-working' of their trade, according to a local newspaper.[74] This cliché fed on the stereotype Englishmen had of themselves. As we have seen (Chapter 2),

---

[73] PP. *Report from the Select Committee on Artizans and Machinery*, 1824, pp. 579–82.
[74] *Le Journal du Havre*, 3 April 1841.

engineer Joseph Locke remembered: 'Often have I heard the exclamation of French loungers around a group of navvies—'Mon Dieu, ces Anglais, comme ils travaillent".[75] These characterisations of the Victorian navvy related to some supposedly defining elements of Britishness in the mid-nineteenth century: an Englishman works hard, unlike a Frenchman who is keen on protesting. Links between diets (beef, ale, and plum-pudding), physical strength, and work were often made. Why was the British worker more productive? Rather than finding technical or skill-based explanations, both French and British commentators argued that meat-eating was the clue. The *Journal des débats* discussed at length the merits of the British worker in relation to those of the French one:

> The English worker does more work in a given time. Is it because he is more clever, more supple, brisker, quicker at work? No, but he has more muscular strength and better tools. Put the French worker with the same diet and the same tools as the English worker, and he will be worth him quite immediately. The experiment has been done a hundred times. In the Charenton ironworks... [the French workers] have done the same amount of work as the English from the moment when, like them, they ate beef and mutton, washed down with abundant libations of wine or beer... From this follows once again the need to spread meat-eating by all means possible among the working classes.[76]

Thomas Brassey Jr, remembering his father's enterprise in France, also noted of the British navvies that 'the French held up their hands in amazement at Herculean labours which they were incapable of imitating. The meagre diet of the French labourers rendered them physically incapable of vying with the Englishmen'.[77] And not a meal of English workers was mentioned without a reference to meat.[78] This matched transnational notions about meat-eating. In

---

[75] 'Presidential address of Joseph Locke, M.P., January 12, 1858', *Minutes of the Proceedings of the Institution of Civil Engineers*, vol. 17, 1858, p. 143; Thomas Brassey's time-keeper also noted this: Helps, *Life and Labours of Mr Brassey*, p. 72.

[76] 'L'ouvrier anglais fait plus de besogne dans un temps donné; est-ce qu'il est plus intelligent, plus souple de corps, plus alerte, plus vif à l'ouvrage? non; mais il a plus de force musculaire, et il est mieux outillé. Placez l'ouvrier français dans les mêmes circonstances d'alimentation et d'outillage que l'ouvrier anglais, et presque aussitôt il le vaudra. On en a fait cent fois l'expérience. Aux forges de Charenton, il y a vingt ans, lorsque la coalition força MM. Manby et Wilson d'employer des Français aux plus difficiles opérations du laminage et du puisage, il se trouva que ces ouvriers, jusqu'alors délaissés, faisaient la même quantité de travail que les Anglais du moment où, comme eux, ils se nourrissaient de bœuf et de mouton, arrosés de copieuses libations de vin ou de bière.... De là ressort une fois de plus la convenance de répandre par tous les moyens possibles l'usage de la viande en France dans toutes les classes ouvrières'. *Journal des Débats*, 26 July 1843, p. 2.

[77] Thomas Brassey, *Lectures on the Labour Question*, 3rd ed., London, 1878, p. 230.

[78] 'ENGLISHMEN ABROAD—About 250 Englishmen, foremen and workmen, employed on the Paris and Rouen Railroad, dined together at Vernon, on the 26th ult., off the true English fare of roast goose and plum-pudding. Mr E. Eyre was chairman on the occasion...Mr Brassey was present...

his *Condition of the Working Class in England*, Engels insisted on the scarcity or the poor quality of the meat—'lean, tough, taken from old, often diseased, cattle'— eaten by the workers.[79] A few years later, French engineer Frédéric Le Play investigated four families of British skilled artisans, and he insisted that they all consumed meat, as well as tea, coffee, and sugar.[80] Meat consumption was understood as an index of the standards of living.

Did the British eat more meat than the French? By the middle of the century, bread and potatoes were the staple foods of the British working class. Nutrition historian D. J. Oddy notes that by 1841, in Manchester and Dukinfield, workers ate 1 pound (0.45 kg) of meat a week on average; by 1863, they ate 0.8 pounds (0.36 kg); by 1902–13, this had risen to 1.3 pounds (0.59 kg).[81] He concludes that the diet of the working class probably deteriorated in the early nineteenth century. In France, two major agricultural inquiries, carried out in 1836–8 and 1852, suggested that the average weekly meat consumption was respectively 0.38 kg and 0.44 kg. They also highlighted important differences among regions and between town and country. Gabriel Désert concluded that better incomes may have increased meat consumption but that this was not systematic.[82] And there is no evidence of larger meat consumption among the British migrant workers than among the French. Such stereotypes could conceal other factors like tools, skills, and the organisation of work in accounting for better productivity.

The British taste for alcohol was another commonplace theme. A member of the 1824 Committee wrote: 'The Englishmen abroad, though able workmen, are in general persons of extremely bad character, continually drunk, constantly quarrelling and occasioning most serious complaints'. In Charenton, he added: 'They drink nothing but the most expensive wines, Burgundy and Champagne, and never leave the cabarets till the whole of their wages are exhausted. Two men employed from Chaillot, in setting up a steam engine, drank eighteen bottles of wine in three hours, and a man and boy drank 273 in a fortnight'.[83] The manager

Usual toasts were drunk to the Queen of England, King of the French, etc. Messrs Mackenzie's and Brassey's healths were then proposed...'. *Galignani's Messenger*, quoted in *The Times*, 9 January 1843, p. 6, col. F.

[79] Frederick Engels, *The Condition of the Working Class in England in 1844*, London, 1892, p. 67.

[80] Frédéric Le Play, *Les Ouvriers Européens*, Paris, 1855.

[81] D. J. Oddy, 'Food in Nineteenth-Century England: Nutrition in the First Urban Society', *Proceedings of the Nutrition Society*, vol. 29, no. 1, May 1970, p. 155; J. C. McKenzie, 'The Composition and Nutritional Value of Diets in Manchester and Dukinfield in 1841', *Trans. Lancs. And Cheshire Antiq. Soc.*, p. 72; D. J. Oddy and J. Yudkin, 'An evaluation of English diets of the 1860s', *Proceedings of the Nutrition Society*, vol. 28, no. 1, April 1969, p. 13A.

[82] In 2020, on average, French people ate 1.63 kg of meat/week. Gabriel Désert, 'Viande et poisson dans l'alimentation des Français au milieu du XIXe siècle', *Annales. Economies, sociétés, civilisations*, 30e année, N. 2–3, 1975, pp. 519–36.

[83] Anonymous [Charles Ross], [Anon.] [Charles Ross], "1st, 2nd, 3rd, 4th, 5th, and 6th Reports, from the select Committee on Artizans and Machinery", *Quarterly Review*, vol. 31, March 1825, p. 417. The same argument was repeated in Factory Commission Report, Par I., D. I, p. 123, Edwin Rose, quoted by Andrew Ure, *The Philosophy of Manufactures*, London, 1835, pp. 315–16.

at Fourchambault objected to the recruitment of an English roller: 'a man we would not know [and who] may be a drunkard whom we would find it difficult to control; this defect will not be mentioned to you: it is nearly a quality in Staffordshire'.[84] And a few years later, the press reported the accidental deaths of two wine merchants who successively brought wine to an 'English worker' overnight so that he could avoid paying the tax.[85] In Rasselstein, Remy noted that two puddlers had 'been drinking all night (19 bottles of wine), with both of them getting completely drunk, but [the one] still holding himself up as a true John Bull, whereas [the other] simply behaved boorishly'.[86] Similar evidence was collected in Alsace, as in Mulhouse, where an amusing anecdote was remembered about the early days of the Koechlin works, in the 1820s:

> there was a very active technical foreman, with devouring activity, who soon stood up to the English and overcame their exclusive influence...The English molders had stated that they needed beer to dampen sand, water not being suitable; so everyday, a large cask was introduced into the workshop. Very early one morning, M. Risler hid in an attic, where he had made a hole so as to see without being seen. He easily realised what was done with this beer. From then on, it was no longer brought in.[87]

In Calais, a physician wrote in a memoir on public hygiene in 1829 that 'the English families that have long lived here are made of well-constituted men, women and children, but profligate, drunkards and mostly without probity'.[88] It was also commonly admitted that the navvies were drunkards and, in a picture of the final banquet for the opening of the Paris–Rouen line, the only person drinking is the English roast-spitter (Figure 4.8). In the discussion following the 1844 Queen's

---

[84] Letter from Dufaud to Boigues, 20 June 1820 (AD Nièvre, 22 F), quoted in Guy Thuillier, *Georges Dufaud et les débuts du grand capitalisme dans la métallurgie, en Nivernais, au XIXe siècle*, Paris, 1959, p. 35. Also see 'Mémoire sur la topographie et l'hygiène publique de la ville de Calais, par le docteur Arnaud, transcrit et commenté par Guy Bourel', *Bulletin historique et artistique du Calaisis*, 1990, no. 121, 122, and 123, p. 18.

[85] *Journal du Cher*, 24 March 1835, p. 2.

[86] Beck, 'Die Einführung des englischen Flammofenfrischens in Deutschland durch Heinrich Wilhelm Remy & Co. auf dem Rasselstein bei Neuwied', in C. Matschoss (ed.), *Beiträge zur Geschichte der Technik und Industrie*, vol. 3, 1911, p. 106, quoted in Rainer Fremdling, 'The Puddler: A Craftsman's Skill and the Spread of a New Technology in Belgium, France and Germany', *Journal of European Economic History*, vol. 20, no. 3, 1991, p. 554.

[87] Auguste Lalance, 'Notice nécrologique de M. Henri Thierry-Koechlin (1813–1893)', *Bulletin de la société industrielle de Mulhouse*, 1894, p. 103.

[88] 'Les familles anglaises qui résident ici depuis longtemps sont composées d'hommes, femmes et enfants bien constitués mais débauchés, prodigues, ivrognes et la plupart sans probité. Ils sont en outre orgueilleux et pleins d'amour-propre et de fourberie. Ils ont des habitudes de luxe dont ils se glorifient et nous en font sentir les effets les plus désagréables. Ils mangent, ils boivent sans réserve, font des dettes sans raison et partent sans les payer et encore prétendent-ils nous faire beaucoup d'honneur'. 'Mémoire sur la topographie et l'hygiène publique de la ville de Calais, par le docteur Arnaud, transcrit et commenté par Guy Bourel', *Bulletin historique et artistique du Calaisis*, no. 121, 122, and 123, 1990, p. 18.

; (Rôtissage du bœuf à Maisons. — *Le tourneur de la broche:* un Anglais. — *Les cuisiniers;* Gien, de Paris;
Pons, de Belleville; Flault, de Poissy.)

Figure 4.8 'Rôtissage du bœuf à Maisons', *L'Illustration*, 6 May 1843. ['Beef-roasting in Maisons']. The caption mentions: 'The roast-spitter: an Englishman'.

speech, Lord Brougham raised the issue in the House of Lords: 'Did you find the English sober? was his next question. Not at all, was the answer. He said he was sorry for that, but had heard of such a complaint before'.[89] Despite the indignation, his allegations reflected a view widely shared among the English elite.[90] In the 1846 Select Committee on Railway Labourers, the question also came up: 'Does [the French labourer] drink?' 'No', was the answer of William Reed, the secretary of the Rouen and Paris railway, who often complained about the drunkenness of British navvies.[91]

Most statistics say these converging observations on British intemperance and French sobriety were not well grounded: the British did not drink more. It was true that, as the 1830 Beer Act deregulated the trade, it encouraged consumption and led to a significant increase, which led to a more restrictive act in 1869.[92] In

[89] 'Did you find the English sober? was his next question. Not at all, was the answer. He said he was sorry for that, but had heard of such a complaint before. Well, he asked, surely you got on better with the Irish? Oh, said they, they are a great deal worse; always quarrelling and fighting with each other, and drinking as well as fighting; excellent and good-natured people when they did not fight, but so fond of it that they seemed to beat one another for the mere love of the exercise. He happened to mention this to a gentleman speaking English [from Philadelphia], whom he met saying it was a very painful thing that they could never hear of an Irishman who was not a fighter, or of an Englishman who was not a drinker', *Hansard's Parliamentary Debates*, 3rd series, vol. 72, House of Lords, 1 February 1844, col. 29.
[90] 'Lord Brougham and the Calumniated English and Irish Labourers in France', *Norman Times*, 7, 17 February 1844, p. 1.
[91] PP. Select Committee on Railway Labourers, 1846, question 374, p. 22.
[92] James Nicholls, *The Politics of Alcohol: A History of the Drink Question in England*, Manchester, 2009, p. 122.

1859, annual consumption per head was 107 litres of beer and 3.7 litres of spirits in the UK, while in France, at the same time, annual consumption was 107 litres of wine, 19 of beer, 28 of cider, and 24 of spirits. And the British proportionately had fewer pubs than the French, with one for 186 English, one for 255 Scots, and one tavern for every 122 people in France—a country where, admittedly, the population was more dispersed.[93] British drunkenness was an old French stereotype.[94] It is probably in the uprooting of the migrants, men in particular, away from their family environment that we should look for some explanation for such widespread prejudice. Indeed, British workers were not accused of 'alcoholism'—the disease related to addiction, a notion which emerged only in the 1860s—but of 'drunkenness'—whose circumstances are chosen by the drinker. In Britain, this stereotype also clung to the navvies. And in France, immigrants in general, be they Belgian, Italian, or whatever, were often characterised both as hard-working and as drunkards. In England, Irishmen were also characterised as drunkards.[95] This supposed drunkenness of the workers was a central element of the discourse of the elite and of the temperance leagues about working classes. Anti-drink activity was not new, but the rise of organised temperance societies was, as Brian Harrison has pointed out. Like tuberculosis and venereal disease, drunkenness was supposed to be an illness of the common people, which was a way of associating workers in general with evils which had not been proved to be less prevalent among the elite.[96] According to this convenient habit of thought, English workers ate well, hence their productivity; but they drank too much, hence their poverty and their immorality. Such discourse was central both in Britain among utilitarian social reformers like Edwin Chadwick and in France among hygienists like Villermé.[97] In other words, what was needed to solve the social question was not social and economic change but administrative and legal measures so as to modify the bad habits of the workers.

[93] Brian Harrison, *Drink and the Victorians: The Temperance Question in England 1815–1872*, London, 1971; Thora Hands, *Drinking in Victorian and Edwardian Britain: Beyond the Spectre of the Drunkard*, London, 2018; Didier Nourrisson, *Le buveur du 19ᵉ siècle*, Paris, 1990, p. 321.

[94] Robert Tombs and Isabelle Tombs, *That Sweet Enemy: Britain and France—The History of a Love-Hate Relationship*, London, 2008, p. 100.

[95] Lewis P. Curtis Jr, *Apes and Angels: The Irishman in Victorian Caricature*, Washington, DC, 1997 [1971]; Sheridan Gilley, 'English Attitudes to the Irish in England, 1789–1900', in Colin Holmes (ed.), *Immigrants and Minorities in British Society*, London, 1978, pp. 81–110; Roy Foster, *Paddy and Mr Punch: Connections in Irish and English History*, New York, 1993; Melissa Fegan, *Literature and the Irish Famine, 1845–1919*, Oxford, 2002.

[96] David Barnes, *The Making of a Social Disease: Tuberculosis in Nineteenth Century France*, Berkeley, CA, 1995; Alain Corbin, 'Douleurs, souffrances et mise'res du corps', in Alain Corbin (ed.), *Histoire du Corps*, ii, *De la Révolution à la Grande Guerre*, Paris, 2005, p. 252.

[97] Christopher Hamlin, *Public Health and Social Justice in the Age of Chadwick. Britain, 1800–1854*, Cambridge, 1998; François Jarrige and Thomas Le Roux, '1. Naissance de l'enquête: les hygiénistes, Villermé et les ouvriers autour de 1840', in Eric Geerkens et al., *Les enquêtes ouvrières dans l'Europe contemporaine*, Paris, 2019, pp. 39–52.

As for clues to the higher productivity of the British navvies, the importance of their having eaten beef can be questioned. It could be an explanation, but we should first look to the better tools—not just machines but also wheelbarrows, shovels, spades, and axes (see p. 51). 'The English have perfected tools that could have been believed to have already reached their ultimate shapes', a witty observer noted.[98] Early British industrialisation also meant that the division of labour was more advanced. There was more individual and collective discipline. This difference also related to different uses of the body, something the *Journal des débats* had identified: 'It would be hard to figure out the practical importance of the division of labour and dexterity for works that seem to be most basic'.[99] All this contributed to train a workforce in ways which had no equivalent in France, where in the countryside many textile or construction workers were employed only part-time, while continuing to spend part of the year in farming chores. But the consequences of economic and industrial development on the uses of the body were often concealed from contemporaries by popular theories about national character.

5. Conclusion

In many respects, British workers shared the culture of the countries they went to. Like them, nearly all Europeans were Christians or had a Christian background. In all continental countries, print culture and the civilisation of the newspaper were emerging, though at a different pace. The mechanical steam-powered printing press, the telegraph, the railways, and the steamers contributed to the circulation of information. The revolutions of 1848–9 were truly European, with news circulating between the Continent and Britain at the speed of the telegraph. While fifteen days had been needed before the news of the battle of Trafalgar reached London, the news of the fall of Louis-Philippe on 24 February 1848 reached the British capital overnight; and by the early 1870s, news could be telegraphed from as far as India. There was also now a European world of pictures, which were circulated in the illustrated newspapers, created from the early 1840s onwards, like *The Illustrated London News* and *L'Illustration*, where the same pictures could be seen simultaneously in different nations.[100] An increasing number of books were now being translated into foreign languages, and the flows of both domestic and foreign migrants also involved widespread linguistic

---

[98] 'Les Anglais ont perfectionné les outils qu'on aurait pu croire arrivés à leur dernière forme', *Journal des Débats*, 26 July 1843, p. 2.

[99] 'On se ferait difficilement une idée de l'importance pratique de la division du travail et des tours de mains dans les ouvrages qui semblent le plus élémentaires'. Ibid.

[100] Maurice Agulhon (dir.), *Les Révolutions de 1848: l'Europe des images*, Paris, 1998.

intercourse. As techniques and machines were circulated, so were ideas, authors, political models, concepts, and even fashions.[101]

The stereotypes that applied to the British migrants on the Continent remind us of enduring prejudices about immigrants and about workers. 'They work hard' is a trope that still applies today to immigrants, whether they come from China, from eastern Europe, or from Africa, and which is not incompatible with xenophobic attitudes. Observations on eating and drinking habits are also often part and parcel of national stereotypes—from the French 'froggies' to the English Marmite—that apply to other national groups nowadays. In the case of British migrants, this was made more complex by the fact that many among them were more skilled and literate than their fellow-workers. Although any comparison with Algerians in France being targeted during and after the war in Algeria would be far-fetched, the legacy of the Napoleonic wars was still present in 1815–70 and could resurface, at least in public discourse: migrant workers also embodied their nation's image abroad. And working-class internationalism was still in its nascent stages.

When they moved, many of the working-class migrants found out that there was a world of differences between their background and the culture they were now confronted with. These cultural differences varied widely, between individuals and groups, between illiterate workers and well-read artisans, between those who stayed just a few months and those who stayed permanently. In all cases, migrants had to adjust between the preservation of some of their culture and adaptations to new environments. In the case of lasting moves, children could be the indispensable go-betweens with the natives—something the sociology of modern migration has thoroughly addressed. As for those migrants who were politicised, and who thus went to countries where the freedom of the press and the freedom of expression did not compare with those they had enjoyed in Britain, changing political environments raised other problems.

---

[101] Sylvie Aprile and Fabrice Bensimon (dir.), *La France et l'Angleterre au XIXe siècle: échanges, représentations, comparaisons*, Paris, 2006.

5

'Driven from his native land to seek employment under a foreign despotism'

Unionists, Chartists, and Insurgents

In the Place de la Bastille in Paris, the 50-metre-high July column stands in the centre of the circular square, a few yards from where the hated jail of the *ancien regime* once stood.[1] The 'July column' was erected between 1835 and 1840 as a tribute to those who gave their lives during the Trois Glorieuses, the July 1830 insurrection that toppled the Restoration regime of King Charles X. On top stands a golden statue of the 'Spirit of Freedom' ('Génie de la Liberté'). On the column itself, the names of the 504 victims of the July revolution have been engraved. Beneath the column, a large vault contains their remains. These were excavated from their various burial places and put in groups of ten to fifteen per sarcophagus. On 28 July 1840, when the construction of the column was completed, the sarcophagi were placed in the vault in a public ceremony. Thus, the martyrs could rest in peace together with their brothers-in-arms. Eight years later, on 24 February 1848, another Parisian rising toppled Louis-Philippe, the man who had been made king following the Trois Glorieuses. On 4 March, a funeral march for the deceased insurgents brought together hundreds of thousands of people, from the Madeleine to the Bastille. Their corpses were added into the vault. The plan was then to add their names to the column, but this was never carried out. Among those whose names were not engraved was George Good, a British printer, whose corpse was laid in the vault.

George was born on 6 August 1824 in Brighton, the third son of John Good (c.1791–1860) and Jane Mary Good (1797–1884).[2] John Good was a 'perfumer & haircutter',[3] a prosperous one it would seem: in 1840, he met the £100 qualification to become a Town Commissioner, and he saw himself as a member of the middle class. He had been involved in local politics since at least the late 1820s,

---

[1] The quote in this chapter's title is from the *Northern Star* (hereafter *NS*), 29 August 1846.

[2] England and Wales Baptism Records, 1530–1906. Place: Brighton, Sussex, England; Collection: St Nicholas; Date Range: 1817–27; Film Number: 1067107.

[3] *Pigott's Directory* of Sussex, 1823; see, for instance, 'Withers's Sicilian Bloom, of Youth and Beauty … sold by Mr Good, Perfumer, Brighton', *Brighton Gazette*, 19 July 1839.

Artisans Abroad: British Migrant Workers in Industrialising Europe, 1815–1870. Fabrice Bensimon, Oxford University Press.

working to dislodge the Tories from the control of local affairs.[4] In 1839, John was elected to the General Convention of the Chartists, where he was nominated with two others to canvass the Members of Parliament for the National Petition. Chartism had begun in 1838 as a mass movement for universal manhood suffrage, which was one of the 'six points' demanded by the petition. The Convention acted as the leadership of the movement. It challenged Westminster and saw itself as an alternative parliament. For reasons that remain unclear, John Good resigned from the Convention, a decision for which he was criticised by leader Feargus O'Connor.[5] John Good had made friends with Bronterre O'Brien, the 'school-master of Chartism', who came to Brighton to speak on several occasions and was close to the local Chartists. John was involved in the launching of Bronterre's short-lived *The Southern Star, and London and Brighton Patriot* (1840), an eight-page paper which ended soon after O'Brien was imprisoned.[6] However, in 1842, John did not take part in the conflict between the local supporters of O'Brien and those of O'Connor, and he later attended meetings of the O'Connorite Chartists.[7] Within the Chartist movement, political friendships and leanings were fluid. In the 1840s, John took the chair in local Chartist meetings, though he said little.[8] Again in April 1848, he spoke at a town meeting in favour of the Chartists. And when his son George died, John was referred to by the *Northern Star* as a 'well-known Chartist' of the middle class, one of those who had 'distinguished them-selves by an earnest advocacy of universal freedom' and had 'rendered many pecuniary and other sacrifice'.[9]

Let's return to George. He was the fifth of the eleven recorded children of the Goods, a family size that was not exceptional at the time. According to the 1841 census, he was a 'printer's apprentice' in Brighton.[10] One obituary noted that he was educated at the Collège Royal, in Rouen, where he would have closely followed Gustave Flaubert, who attended the school until 1839.[11] George was also reported to have worked in a 'London printing-office'.[12] But we do not really know where George lived during these 'lost years'. He only resurfaced in the sources in Paris in 1848, when he died. It was not uncommon for British printers

---

[4] 'Parish of Brighton', *Brighton Gazette*, 13 August 1835; 'The Commissioners' Clerk', *Brighton Patriot*, 27 September 1836; 'Brighton Election', *Brighton Patriot*, 11 July 1837; Thomas Kemnitz, 'Chartism in Brighton', PhD, University of Sussex, 1969, p. 251.

[5] 'To the Working Classes', *NS*, 21 September 1839.

[6] Kemnitz, 'Chartism in Brighton', pp. 185–6.

[7] Ibid., pp. 251–4. On John Good we follow this short biography by Kemnitz.

[8] *NS*, 12 June 1841; 27 November 1841; 16 April 1842; 7 April 1846; 23 January 1847.

[9] *NS*, 1 April 1848.

[10] 1841 England Census. HO107. Piece: 1123; Book: 1; Parish: Brightelmstone (Sussex), District 1; Folio 15; p. 22, l. 3; GSU roll: 464167.

[11] *Brighton Herald*, 4 March 1848, p. 3. A small number of the records of Collège de Rouen are kept in the Archives départementales de la Seine-Maritime (formerly Seine-Inférieure). George Good is not mentioned, though no conclusion can be derived. (1T 680 Enseignement—Collège de Rouen—Admissions d'élèves—1815–44; and 1T681 – Bourses).

[12] Percy B. St. John, 'To the Editor of the Brighton Herald', *Brighton Herald*, 4 March 1848, p. 3.

to find work in Paris, as Charles Manby Smith had done in 1826.[13] Like Smith, George may have worked as a compositor for the many cheap books that were printed in his language in France and then smuggled into the British market. But it is more likely that he was a press corrector for *Galignani's Messenger*, the daily English-language newspaper which was published in Paris from 1814 (see Chapter 4).[14] By 1848, George lived at 4 rue Verdelet, in the bustling area around Sainte-Eustache church. Rue Verdelet was a small street, by the post office; it was later destroyed to make way for the construction of rue du Louvre. The address 4 rue Verdelet also housed a bookseller, Rouanet, who was known for publishing communist works by the likes of Théodore Dezamy. Dezamy was related to Cabet, with whom he had fallen out; he was involved in secret societies and took part in the February 1848 insurrection.[15] Rouanet also sold the often ephemeral, communist, neo-Babouvist papers that were published in Paris in the 1840s, such as *L'Humanitaire*. Rue Verdelet was close to 18 rue Vivienne, where *Galignani*'s was based, and to the printer of the paper, Brière, 55 rue Sainte-Anne. And the triangle formed by *Galignani*'s, Brière, and 4 rue Verdelet was close to the Palais Royal, the seat of power (see Map 5.1).

Several historians have shown that, in February 1848 as in July 1830, most insurgents fought near their homes: bonds of solidarity in the neighbourhood proved critical for the revolutionary involvement.[16] In February 1848, 53 per cent of the fighters were mobilised in their neighbourhoods. However, a politicised minority (31 per cent) was ready to fight further away, in strategic places for the conquest of power. As Good lived so close to the Tuileries, his involvement at the Château d'Eau combined some strategic interest and the proximity of his home.

An unnamed friend of George later reported that on 22 and 23 February 1848, 'before the riots had assumed the appearance of a revolution, we managed to keep [George Good] tolerably quiet, although he was greatly excited; but when, on the Wednesday [23 February] evening, the treacherous and cowardly massacre of unoffending people took place, and Paris with one voice raised the cry of "vengeance," nothing could restrain him'.[17] Indeed, on the evening of the 23rd, as

[13] Charles Manby Smith, *The Working Man's Way in the World*, London, 1853.
[14] *Brighton Guardian*, 8 March 1848, p. 3; *Brighton Gazette*, 9 March 1848, p. 8. His hospital admission record states he was a 'correcteur de presse' (press corrector). Archives de l'Assistance publique—Hôpitaux de Paris (APHP). Hôpital de la Charité. Registre des entrées, 24 February 1848, no. 1138. CHARITE 1Q 2/108.
[15] http://maitron-en-ligne.univ-paris1.fr/spip.php?article30026, notice DEZAMY Théodore [DEZAMY Alexandre, Théodore] (orthographié souvent Dézamy). Notice revue et complétée par Jacques Grandjonc, version mise en ligne le 20 février 2009, dernière modification le 3 novembre 2018; Alain Maillard, *La communauté des Égaux. Le communisme néo-babouviste dans la France des années 1840*, Paris, 1999.
[16] Mark Traugott, 'Les barricades dans les insurrections parisiennes: rôles sociaux et modes de fonctionnement', in Alain Corbin and Jean-Marie Mayeur (dir.), *La Barricade*, Paris, 1997, pp. 71–81.
[17] 'DEATH OF MR. GEORGE GOOD, LATE OF BRIGHTON', *Sussex Advertiser*, 14 March 1848, p. 5.

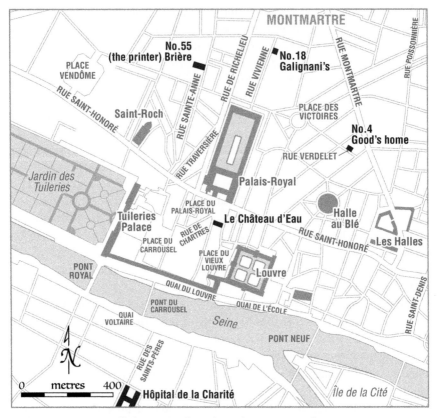

Map 5.1 George Good's home, work, and revolutionary involvement.

thousands had demonstrated on the boulevards, the troops had opened fire, killing dozens. Some of the corpses were laid on a carriage, which was paraded along the boulevards until one o'clock in the morning. 'Vengeance! To arms! To the barricades!' was heard. Overnight, barricades were erected: the insurrection had begun.

On the morning of Thursday 24th, the insurgents attacked the Château d'Eau, which occupied a strategic position, being a stronghold on the way to the Tuileries Palace, where the king, the court, and the army staff were based. Many insurgents were shot by unseen guards from within the Château d'Eau, as Flaubert famously described in *L'Éducation sentimentale*, the novel on 1848 (see Figure 5.1). When it fell, the Tuileries were stormed by the insurgents, the king had to abdicate, and the Republic could be proclaimed. George was involved in the attack. He reportedly 'received a musket ball in the side'. Soon after he had been injured, something amazing happened: among those who 'assisted to remove him to the *Ambulance*', George recognised the English journalist Percy B. St John (1821–89)—according to Good's friends, he even 'fell back into the arms of Percy B. St John, shouting

Figure 5.1 Eugène Hagnauer, *Incendie du château d'eau, place du Palais-Royal, le 24 février 1848*, Musée Carnavalet, Paris, P435, 1848. Oil painting on canvas, 59.5 × 73 cm.

"Vive la Republique!"'.[18] George told St. John they had met in a London print-shop, where he corrected proofs.[19] He was then taken to the Charité, an old hospital on the left bank, where he was admitted with dozens of other wounded insurgents. He died there on 26 February, the death being caused by a 'shot' (coup de feu), according to hospital records (Figure 5.2).[20] Meanwhile, he had managed to dictate one last letter to his parents.[21] They probably received it by the time Louis-Philippe, who had escaped from the Palais Royal after the fall of the Château d'Eau, had crossed the Channel in disguise and was reaching Newhaven, not far from Brighton.

Some of George's friends wrote that they applied 'for leave to bury him by himself; but the Government Commissary, although he did not refuse, begged them to desist from their demand and allow him to be buried with his fellow

[18] *Sussex Advertiser*, 14 March 1848, p. 5.
[19] 'Death of Mr Good, Jun., in the attack of the Palais Royal', *Brighton Herald*, 4 March 1848, p. 3; Percy B. St John, *French Revolution in 1848. The Three days of February 1848. By Percy B. St John. An eye-witness of the whole revolution*, London, Richard Bentley, New Burlington Street, 1848, pp. 215–16.
[20] Archives de l'APHP. Hôpital de la Charité. Registre des décès, 1848. CHARITE 3Q 2/44—No. 179.
[21] *Brighton Herald*, 4 March 1848, p. 3.

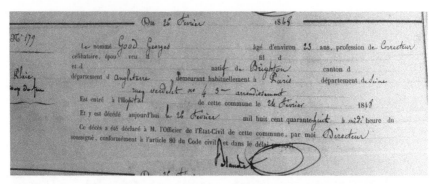

Figure 5.2 George Good's death certificate, 26 February 1848, at the Hôpital de la Charité. To the left, the cause of death: 'Plaie. Coup de feu' ('Wound. Gunshot').

martyrs at the foot of the column of July'.[22] On 4 March, hundreds of thousands attended a funeral march for the victims of the rising, from the Madeleine to the Place de la Bastille. George's corpse, along with about 200 other victims, was carried along the boulevards, and buried under the column.[23] 'Glory to them who die in this great cause', the *Northern Star* mourned, while the Brighton newspapers gave details. George's heroic death could feed into a heroic legend—for instance, his last letter on his deathbed insisting on the fact that 'Louis Philippe has abdicated'.[24] 'His name is one which should not be forgotten', the French Fourierist paper *La Démocratie pacifique* also counselled.[25]

But Good was part of what Carlo Ginzburg described as the 'normal exceptional': he briefly emerged out of the archive after a life in obscurity and then remained an unsung hero. This is partly because he was a migrant and died not at home but in another country. But this was also the result of his absence from the records—those who died in February 1848 largely remained unknown, unless their families applied for compensation, which meant that they were recorded, alongside those who were injured and who applied on their own behalf. No relative applied on behalf of George for a reward from the French government.[26] We will probably never know how the Chartist activism of his father translated into George's revolutionary involvement. Some radical education could have played a part. But it could also be that in Paris, Good was an integral part of a local or trade community which took part in the uprising.[27] Among the rare

---

[22] *Brighton Herald*, 4 March 1848, p. 3.
[23] *Brighton Gazette*, 9 March 1848, p. 8; *La Démocratie pacifique*, 17 March 1848; *NS*, 1 April 1848.
[24] *Brighton Herald*, 4 March 1848, p. 3.   [25] *La Démocratie pacifique*, 17 March 1848.
[26] Archives nationales. F 1d III 83 à 98. Récompenses honorifiques insurgés de 1848.
[27] Louis Hincker, *Citoyens-combattants à Paris, 1848–1851*, Villeneuve d'Ascq, 2008; Maurizio Gribaudi, *Paris ville ouvrière. Une histoire occultée. 1789–1848*, Paris, 2014.

references to his personality, one Brighton paper reported that he 'was of a very excitable temperament',[28] while an older friend wrote:

> Galand and myself were almost his only companions, and we were deeply attached to him, for he possessed a warm and generous heart, a fervid imagination, and all those good qualities which render the friendship of young persons so endearing to those more advanced in life than themselves.[29]

The Brighton press reported his death, including a reprint of a letter sent by Percy B. St John and another by an anonymous friend of George.[30] The reaction of his family was not reported, but on 3 April, just a week before the handing over of the third Chartist petition and the famous gathering on Kennington Common, John Good took part in a Chartist meeting in Brighton's town hall. Neither of the two press reports that were published mentioned his speaking of the recent death of his son George. However, from the platform, John was quoted denouncing the Whigs and the Tories and celebrating the revolutions on the Continent: 'Look at the bright example of the Milanese where the women threw their pianos out on the troops. Look at the Germans—look at Italy, Sicily'.[31] Another report stated: 'He gloried in seeing the advance of the French, and that they had adopted all the points of the People's Charter'.[32] In other words, John Good the Chartist celebrated the revolutions in which his son George had died. Another speaker praised communism. A few months later, George became a character in a serialised fiction written by Percy B. St John, where he emerged as a revolutionary Chartist who chose to go to France and die in a revolution.[33] There is firm reason to believe that George was fondly remembered by family and friends, maybe for a few decades— his mother Jane died in 1884—maybe even more—his younger sister Sophia, born in 1836, died as late as 1921. After 1848, however, George was never mentioned again in any known source.

George's trajectory raises the question of how, when they emigrated, politicised artisans and labourers adjusted to their new environment. We know that Chartism was very much a family commitment, as Malcolm Chase has argued.[34] However, we know neither whether George Good was a Chartist nor how his father's involvement impacted upon his son's beliefs. In any case, once in France,

---

[28] 'Funeral of the Victims of the Revolution', *Brighton Guardian*, 8 March 1848, p. 3.

[29] *Sussex Advertiser*, 14 March 1848, p. 5.

[30] *Brighton Herald*, 4 March 1848, p. 3; 11 March 1848, p. 3; *Sussex Advertiser*, 14 March 1848, p. 5.

[31] *Brighton Gazette*, 6 April 1848, p. 5.

[32] 'Extension of the Suffrage', *Brighton Guardian*, 5 April 1848, p. 3.

[33] 'Literature. Julia Le Roo; or, the Demagogue's wife. A tale of the Passing time', *Westmeath Independent*, 1 July, 5 August, 12 August 1848.

[34] Malcolm Chase, '"Resolved in Defiance of Fool and of Knave"?: Chartism, Children and Conflict', in Dinah Birch and Mark Llewellyn (eds.), *Conflict and Difference in Nineteenth-Century Literature*, London, 2010, pp. 126–40.

it would have been difficult for George to campaign for the People's Charter actively. As far as we know, there were no signatories for the Charter on the Continent. Chartist meetings were held in some places, where there were clusters of British workers, and where some subscribed to the Land Plan, but no trace of this survives in Paris. However, when Chartists, radicals, trade-unionists, or later socialists emigrated, their actions in their new homes often reflected previous commitments. As with viruses, ideas do not easily travel on their own, but they do cross borders, seas, and oceans with the men and women who carry them. This chapter aims to study how the British workers, when they moved to Europe, conveyed their ideas and adjusted politically to their new environments. It addresses five different dimensions of this transnational political activism. It first considers the struggles of British workers to get better wages and sometimes to create trade unions (section 1). It then examines early practices of internationalism (section 2). It then focuses on Chartism on the Continent (section 3). It tries to shed light on the practice of collective reading in the workshop (section 4). Last, starting from the case of George Good, it considers migrants' involvement in revolutionary events in Paris (section 5). Section 6 concludes.

1. Bargaining Wages, Setting Up Unions

No comparative history of trade unions has been written, but in some respects the British were ahead of the others. In the period under study, although the Combination Acts were repealed in 1824, there were still many restrictions: many were still prosecuted for union membership, as the transportation of the Tolpuddle farm workers in 1834 or the Plug Rioters in 1842 showed. In the workplaces, when manufacturers dictated their terms to the workers, when they forced them to work in unsafe conditions, or when they prevented them from looking for another job, they were protected by the master and servant legislation, and by complacent magistrates.[35] At the same time, in the 1830s and 1840s, several unions were created and several strikes were organised, sometimes successfully.[36] From 1829 onwards, some attempts were made to create general unions. This early activity meant that there was a long period of trade-union militancy, which was sometimes interwoven with radicalism—as during the Chartist period—but sometimes was not, such as at the time of Peterloo or in the 1850s.[37] On the Continent, the legal position of the unions was very different.

---

[35] Christopher Frank, *Master and Servant Law: Chartists, Trade Unions, Radical Lawyers and the Magistracy in England, 1840-1865*, Farnham, 2010.

[36] Malcolm Chase, *Early Trade Unionism: Fraternity, Skill and the Politics of Labour*, Aldershot, 2000.

[37] Robert Poole, *Peterloo: The English Uprising*, Oxford, 2019, ch. 8.

France authorised 'coalitions' (meetings and strikes) only in 1864 and trade unions only in 1884, though it experienced universal manhood suffrage earlier than Britain. Its early 'coalitions' were probably more closely assimilated to republican and socialist politics, perhaps in the 1860s. In Germany they became legal in 1871. The Belgian legislation was more ambivalent: on the one hand, the constitution in 1831 preserved the right to form unions; at the same time, coalitions were forbidden until 1866. By 1876, France boasted 31,700 union members, while Britain could claim 1.6 million.[38] While the first attempts to create national unions across the country date from the early 1830s in Britain, the French General Confederation of Labour (Confédération Générale du Travail, CGT) was founded only in 1895. These differing practices and political cultures were noted by some of the migrants and their employers. The British workers also had more experience in terms of friendly societies and Oddfellows.[39] 'Sociétés de secours mutuel' did exist in France, but they were periodically under the close surveillance of the authorities, for instance in the 1850s.

British migrant workers knew how to market their skills in individual or collective negotiations. We have seen how in iron or machinery, ironmasters complained about their tough bargaining on the length of their employment and of the working day, on their wages and the refund of their travel expenses, and on the quality of housing for them and their families. These demands were sometimes accompanied by different forms of conflict, especially against discipline, rules, or shrinking wages. Iron workers were used to this and well versed in such negotiation practices. In Wales a series of strikes and riots took place in the first decades of the century, culminating in the Rebecca Riots of 1839–43.[40] Such experience may have influenced strategies in France. In Charenton in 1824, Manby and Wilson wrote to the mayor with alarm:

> the workers of our factory who have been in a mutiny for two weeks are now using extremities. Two among them have threatened to scratch one of our foremen named Benj. Hodgets. The names of those persons who have used threats were John Davies and John Rodgers. We beg you to order the commander of the gendarmerie to arrest them so as to prevent their threats from being carried out.[41]

---

[38] Keith Laybourn, *A History of British Trade Unionism, c. 1770–1990*, Stroud, 1992, p. 39.

[39] Simon Cordery, *British Friendly Societies, 1750–1914*, London, 2003.

[40] David J. V. Jones, *Before Rebecca: Popular Protests in Wales, 1793–1835*, London, 1973; Rhian E. Jones, *Petticoat Heroes: Gender, Culture and Popular Protest in the Rebecca Riots*, Cardiff, 2015.

[41] 'Les ouvriers de notre fabrique qui ont été en mutine depuis quinze jours ont maintenant recours à des extrémités. Deux d'entre eux ont menacés d'égratigner un de nos contremaitres nommé Benj. Hodgets. Les noms de ces personnes qui ont employés des menaces sont John Davies et John Rodgers. Nous vous prions monsieur de donner un ordre au commandant de la gendarmerie de faire arrêter ces deux hommes afin d'empêcher que leurs menaces aient lieu. Nous enverrons demain matin de bonne

The outcome of this episode is unknown and such a source conceals the voice and the motivations of the workers as much as it reveals the fears of the employers. We do not know more about the organisation of the Charenton workers, yet it appears that the prior traditions of the British workers were re-enacted on French soil and led to their becoming a bane for French employers and authorities. The Fourchambault ironworks master thus wrote about the recruitment of English puddlers:

> I suggest you deal with them before they leave Paris, if you haven't yet; otherwise once here these people could, as well as William, have ridiculous demands that I would find it difficult to comply with; whereas if they come with a deal, we'll hold them firmly.[42]

One of the Fourchambault puddlers, Richard Will, rebelled against the rules and the working hours that he laboured under, and left his employment as early as 1822. In October 1823, another worker, Rollins Haddock, organised the first union in the Fourchambault forges.[43] He could well have been the Rawlings Haddock(s) who had been sentenced to eighteen months' imprisonment for his role as one of the three leaders of the South Wales strike of 1816, when he was only twenty-two. 'We consider [him] to be the worst case', the Merthyr magistrates wrote to the Home Office magistrates at the time.[44] All trace of Rollins Haddock— a 'rebel without a pause'—and Richard Will unfortunately disappears from the sources after 1823, although it is not impossible that Will was the 'R. Wills' listed in the staff of the Remy brothers at the Rasselstein works in Germany in 1824–5. As Rainer Fremdling has shown, puddlers often went from one ironworks to another, from Britain to France, Belgium, and Germany in search of employment.[45]

In textiles, trade-union activity was also vibrant. As early as 1825, the *sous-préfet* of Saint-Quentin (Aisne), where Heathcoat had set up a lace factory, wrote to the director general of the police in Paris:

---

heure une personne pour les indiquer. Nous avons monsieur le maire l'honneur de vous saluer avec bien de considération. Manby Wilson'. Archives municipales de Charenton. 5 I 3. Manby et Wilson au maire de Charenton, 12 December 1824.

[42] 'Je vous engage à traiter avec eux avant leur départ de Paris, si cela n'a pas été fait, car ces gens une fois rendus ici pourraient, ainsi que William, élever des prétentions ridicules qu'il me serait difficile de régler, au contraire s'ils arrivent avec un traité, nous les tiendrons fermes'. Lettre de Dufaud à Boigues, 28 September 1820, AD Nièvre 22 F, quoted in Guy Thuillier, *La vie quotidienne...*, p. 36.

[43] On Richard Will and Rollins Haddock: AD Nièvre, série M. 'Journal de Dufaud', quoted in Jean Maitron (dir.), *Dictionnaire biographique du mouvement ouvrier*.

[44] TNA. HO 42/154, f. 244: Letter from Benjamin Hall, 31 October 1816. David J. V. Jones, 'The South Wales Strike of 1816', *Morgannwg Transactions of the Glamorgan Local History Society*, vol. 11, 1967, p. 39; Jones, *Before Rebecca*, p. 78.

[45] Rainer Fremdling, 'The Puddler: A Craftsman's Skill and the Spread of a New Technology in Belgium, France and Germany', *Journal of European Economic History*, vol. 20, no. 3, 1991, p. 566.

Early in August, agitation in a spinning mill of the town. The authorities held firm. But the workers have been affected by the spirit of English workers, who 'are trying to draw our own [French] workers into making claims they had never even thought of, to get them to draw up petitions, to hold meetings to demand an increase in the prices of work, to sign agreements whereby the workers consent to a deduction from their wages to provide compensation to those who fall ill or become victims of their devotion in making claims against their masters. A commitment on the latter point was signed by workers, who then ended up in prison'. Nothing has happened yet, but one cannot wish that English workers increase in number, for one fears they may propagate 'principles of liberty that our workers don't understand enough not to abuse them', all the more as Saint-Quentin has no garrison.[46]

It was reportedly agreed at a Nottingham meeting of the bobbin-net hand-workers in support of the eight-hour day 'that a copy of the above resolutions be transmitted to the Bobbin Net Committee at Calais, Lisle and St-Quentin, requesting their assistance in case of need'.[47] Not long after the Combination Acts had been repealed in Britain, some unions may have been set up by the lace migrants. This alarmed the French Ministry of the Interior, who unsuccessfully sought further information from the local authorities.[48] Possibly, the *sous-préfet* had blamed the British workers as scapegoats for some industrial unrest.

Despite the difficulty of getting organised at an itinerant workplace, railway-building sites were affected by labour disputes: 150 went on strike on the Paris–Rouen line in April 1842; fifty-five bricklayers and labourers who went on strike in June 1842 had 'their names circulated along the line on a blacklist', a practice which was then common.[49] And, again on Saturday 13 April 1844, 'about four or five hundred' on the Rouen to Le Havre building site, 'feeling dissatisfied with the wages they were receiving, refused to return to their work'.[50] Such 'turnouts' are under-documented and available sources were usually produced by the authorities or by the employers. What emerges is that in most cases migrant workers did not strike for better wages but to defend existing conditions. In his diary, railway

---

[46] Le sous-préfet de Saint-Quentin au directeur général de la police, 25 September 1825, AN F7 9786.3, reproduced in Georges and Hubert Bourgin (dir.), *Le Régime de l'industrie en France de 1814 à 1830. Recueil de textes publiés pour la Société d'histoire de France*, Paris, 1941, vol. 3, p. 120.

[47] *Nottingham Mercury*, 23 September 1825.

[48] See letters in AN, F7 9787.10, reproduced in Bourgin, *Le Régime de l'industrie en France*, pp. 121–4.

[49] Service historique de l'armée de terre, E5 (April 1842), cited in Pierre-Jacques Derainne, 'Les perceptions sociales des travailleurs migrants britanniques en France dans la première moitié du XIXe siècle », in Sylvie Aprile and Fabrice Bensimon (eds.), *La France et l'Angleterre au XIXe siècle. Echanges, représentations, comparaisons*, Grâne, 2006; list of the men who struck for higher wages, June 1842, A5L6:9, quoted in David Brooke, *William Mackenzie: International Railway Builder*, London, 2004, p. 127.

[50] *Norman Times*, 20 April 1844, p. 1.

entrepreneur William Mackenzie mentioned in passing: 'I went to the office and lowered rate of Wage 20 Pr Cent on Smiths and Carpenters'.[51] And on 16 April 1842, he wrote: '19 Scotch came and were dissatisfied with wages I told them to go home again they went away grunting'.[52] Such excerpts testify to the agency and resistance of British workers when bargaining with employers in foreign land.

The employment of several thousand British navvies in France also led to a confrontation on the issue of safety at work. This question and that of different judicial practices were soon drawn to the attention of Mackenzie and Brassey. The activity of navvies and miners, in particular the digging of tunnels, was intrinsically unsafe; the construction of four British lines caused forty deaths and seventy-six serious injuries in 1840 alone.[53] Relief granted to widows and to invalids was dependent on the good will of the employers, who paid minimal contributions to the hospitals. For the Paris–Le Havre line, the death toll was similar to that seen in Britain. In May and June 1844 alone, three deaths and several serious injuries were recorded.[54] The village of Pissy-Pôville (Seine-Inférieure) alone accounted for ten deaths of male adults, nine of them British, when a long tunnel was dug nearby (1844–6).[55] In France, although work accidents became the legal responsibility of the employers only in 1898, and although in the 1840s many workers failed to claim full damages for injuries they had received, some maimed workers received compensation through the courts, which was far beyond what contractors were used to granting in Britain.[56]

This outraged Mackenzie and Brassey, and the matter became the subject of public debate during the hearings of the 1846 Select Committee on Railway Labourers. The secretary of the Paris–Rouen line complained that the widow of a French worker killed in the building had obtained £200. As for a 'stupid Irishman' who had lost both eyes and both arms in an explosion, his behaviour 'was not merely carelessness, but ignorance', 'a positive act of folly', and the company also regretted having had to grant him £200 rather than risk a costly trial.[57] Famous railway entrepreneur Isambard Kingdom Brunel also insisted on the worker's sole liability.[58] But utilitarian reformer Edwin Chadwick argued for the liability of the employer: he contended that the number of accidents would diminish if they shouldered a legal burden. Different interpretations of the

[51]   27 October 1843, The Diary of William Mackenzie, p. 209.
[52]   16 April 1842, The Diary of William Mackenzie, p. 121.
[53]   David Brooke, The Railway Navvy: 'That Despicable Race of Men', London, 1983, p. 146; PP. Select Committee on Railway Labourers, hearing of Edwin Chadwick, 16 June 1846, p. 148.
[54]   Norman Times, 27 April 1844 and 18 May 1844; archives municipales, Malaunay.
[55]   Archives municipales de Pissy-Pôville (Seine-Maritime). État-civil.
[56]   Alain Corbin, 'Douleurs, souffrances et misères du corps', in Alain Corbin, Jean-Jacques Courtine, and Georges Vigarello (dir.), Histoire du Corps, vol. 2. De la Révolution à la Grande Guerre, Paris, 2005, p. 257. Caroline Moriceau, Les douleurs de l'industrie. L'hygiénisme industriel en France, 1860–1914, thesis, EHESS, 2002.
[57]   PP. Select Committee on Railway Labourers, William Reed, 19 May 1846, p. 21.
[58]   PP. Select Committee on Railway Labourers, William Reed, 16 June 1846, p. 140.

political economy thus opposed each other: that of the capitalist, trying to minimise the costs of his business, versus that of social reformers, who deemed it necessary, to improve safety in the workplace, for employers' neglect of their workers' welfare to make them liable to financial penalties. In line with this, the committee recommended that the provisions of the French 'code civil' should be grafted onto English law. But the report was not even debated in Parliament, and only with legislation in 1880 and 1897 were workers empowered to claim money in the case of an accident. As for the British navvies and miners in Normandy, it seems that most of them only belatedly understood that French legislation did not apply to Frenchmen only, and as a result they did not claim the compensation they may have obtained.[59]

Taken together, these various examples show that the multiplying industrial struggles which marked the British social landscape could also be observed in overseas British ventures. Such attempts at combination and strike were not always successful, and lasting trade unions were not created, because of the local legislation, and because migrant workers were limited in numbers and moved from place to place. But British migrant workers were ready to engage not just in tough bargaining but also in labour disputes with their employers. Whether or not this translated into politically structured exchanges is another question.

2. Early Internationalism

The issue of regular political exchange and transfers between continental and British radicals in the 1830s and 1840s has already been raised.[60] We should not think in terms of systematic, regular, and structured exchange before the exile of participants in the 1848–9 revolutions and probably not even before the foundation of the International Working Men's Association (IWMA) in London in 1864. However, without going as far back as the important intercourse between French, British, and Irish republicans during the French Revolution, exchanges had been numerous since the end of the Napoleonic wars. In 1817, Thomas Savage, a machine breaker who was later executed, declared in his depositions that there was a colony of Luddite refugees in Calais; E. P. Thompson considered this to be a possibility, but it has not been substantiated.[61] Because of the shadow of revolution and because of the war, France, the French, and Napoleon were often claimed by Luddites or their enemies to be behind the unrest.[62] Arthur Thistlewood, the chief of the 1820 Cato Street Conspiracy in London, had allegedly spent time in revolutionary France.[63]

---

[59] Brooke, *The Railway Navvy*, p. 126.
[60] Arthur Lehning, *From Buonarroti to Bakunin: Studies in International Socialism*, Leiden, 1970, ch. 6; Henry Weisser, *British Working-Class Movements and Europe*, Manchester, 1975.
[61] TNA. HO 79/3/21, 31–2: Letter from J Beckett to Lewis Allsopp, Nottingham, 21 April 1817; E. P. Thompson, *Making*, 628, n. 1.
[62] Kevin Binfield (ed.), *Writings of the Luddites*, Baltimore, MD, 2015.
[63] Vic Gatrell, *Conspiracy on Cato Street. A Tale of Liberty and Revolution in Regency London*, Cambridge, 2022, pp. 175–6.

Connections are better documented for 1819 and 1820. After the saddler Louvel, who had murdered the duke of Berry, the heir to the throne, was guillotined on 7 June 1820, there was widespread agitation in working-class Paris. On 9 June, a currier was killed by the troops on boulevard Bonne Nouvelle in Paris; as the cavalry slashed and trampled upon other workers, the main cry was that of 'Long live our Manchester brothers!'.[64] This echo of Peterloo could well have been conveyed by the press rather than by direct contact between French and British workers. However, such contact did exist. By June 1820, migrant British workers in Cambrai, Lyon, and Rouen had made contact with French republicans. The English end of the exchange of letters was a Lancashire weaver, James Lang, and a certain Tootall, an ex-soldier and 'violent Radical' from Bolton. Resolutions were adopted in France: 'They will join all Europe in over-turning Tyranny and an impatient anxiety for the above results pervades a great part of the enlightened community. These resolutions are drawn at Calais from correspondents at Lyons Rouen and Cambray and forwarded to William Tootall by his Post Office friend'.[65] Lang and Tootall were arrested on suspicion of planning a rising and resurfaced again in the spring of 1820.

In the early 1830s, Irish reformer Bronterre O'Brien visited Paris several times and met and conversed with 'old revolutionary' Buonarroti, who was Babeuf's surviving companion. O'Brien later translated *Buonarroti's History of Babeuf's Conspiracy* and celebrated Robespierre as well as Babeuf in the Chartist movement and beyond.[66] But this was part of cross-Channel radicalism rather than working-class activism. In the 1830s and 1840s other political contacts existed, and these two decades can be understood as the prehistory of working-class internationalism. *The Poor Man's Guardian* in London (1831–5) and *L'Écho de la fabrique* (1831–4), the newspaper of the Lyon silk workers, the 'canuts', showed some interest in workers' struggles overseas. In 1832, *L'Écho* published a manifesto entitled 'To our brothers in England'.[67] The broker was François Barthélemy Arlès-Dufour, a Saint-Simonian who went for business to England, and who was in close contact with British radicals George Porter and John Bowring. A Benthamite, Bowring visited Lyon for several weeks in 1832 and became a stakeholder in the newspaper.[68] In 1834, some workers in Nantes sent an address to the English trade unions which called for a union between English and French workers and which began: 'The

[64] 'Vive nos frères de Manchester!', Rémi Gossez (éd.), *Un ouvrier en 1820. Manuscrit inédit de Jacques Étienne Bédé*, Paris, 1984, p. 13.

[65] TNA. HO 40/14 fols 131 [letter from Bolton, 21 June 1820, here quoted], 13–12, 135, 137. (I owe these references to Malcolm Chase, *1820*, p. 84.)

[66] Bronterre O'Brien, *Buonarroti's History of Babeuf's Conspiracy for Equality*, London, 1836; Michael J. Turner, *Radicalism and Reputation: The Career of Bronterre O'Brien*, East Lansing, MI, 2017, p. 124.

[67] *L'Écho de la fabrique*, 9 September 1832.

[68] Ludovic Frobert, *Les Canuts ou La démocratie turbulente: Lyon, 1831–1834*, Paris, 2009, pp. 33–9.

working classes of all countries are sisters...'.[69] In this case, the link may be a group of British iron workers employed by the Compagnie des Forges de Basse-Indre, near Nantes, who subscribed for a plaque to celebrate the July 1830 revolution (see pp. 147–8). In 1836 William Lovett's 'London Working Men's Association' drafted an *Address to the Belgian Working Classes* which may have been the first written statement of working-class internationalism, and which began: '*Fellow Producers of Wealth—*, We are of opinion that those who produce the real wealth of any country (by which terms we mean the food, clothing, habitations, and all the great essentials of human happiness) have in reality but *one great interest*'.[70]

In 1842, the newspaper *L'Atelier* (*The Workshop*), edited in Paris by Christian socialists, issued a manifesto urging a 'permanent alliance between workers from France and England'. Direct contacts are likely to have prompted this call.[71] Some travellers, such as Flora Tristan, played their part: when she crossed the Channel in 1839, she became interested in British labour and Chartism, and this led her in her book *Union ouvrière* to call for an international organisation of workers.[72] Between 1842 and 1844, the Scottish surgeon and leading Chartist Peter McDouall went to France after several warrants had been issued against him.[73] We do not know much about McDouall's activities in France, and it seems that no account by him is extant, but it is likely he was in contact with French communists, in particular with utopian socialist Cabet, whom he had met in 1839 at the end of Cabet's own exile in London. In 1843, Cabet's *Le Populaire* published a letter purportedly written by McDouall. He argued that he subscribed to Cabet's ideal and supported the communists at the time of the trial of a so-called communist plot in Toulouse:

> As a Chartist, I want universal suffrage. But I see in it only a *means* and not an ultimate *goal*. This universal suffrage and the other principles of Chartism are to me the key of the garden, the tool to devise a better social organization, the wall to protect the organizers. This is why, after having read, read and again and pondered on your *Voyage en Icarie*, I perfectly adopt the principles of Democracy and Community the book exposes. In my eyes, it is a masterpiece; and

---

[69] 'Address of the Workmen of Nantes to the English Trades' Unions', *The Pioneer*, 7 June 1834. In the 14 June issue, 'The Reply of *The Pioneer* to the Address of the Workmen of Nantes' was published, as quoted in Arthur Lehning, *From Buonarroti to Bakunin*, p. 152.

[70] *The Working Men's Association of London to the Working Classes of Belgium* (London, 1836). This was published in *The Constitutional* (London, 12 November 1836), and is reproduced in an appendix in Lehning, *From Buonarroti to Bakunin*, pp. 210–14.

[71] *L'Atelier*, 13 October 1842.

[72] Flora Tristan, *Promenades dans Londres,* Paris, 1978 [1840 and 1842]; *Union ouvrière*, Paris, 1986 [1843 and 1844].

[73] Owen R. Ashton and Paul A. Pickering, *Friends of the People: Uneasy Radicals in the Age of the Chartists*, London, 2002, ch. 1, pp. 7–28. Most of the following on McDouall is derived from this.

I am convinced the workers in England would adopt it as well if they had a translation.[74]

McDouall wanted to translate Étienne Cabet's book into English. No copy of the *Adventures of Lord William Carisdale in Icaria* has survived, but in 1845 the book was advertised as serialised by Hetherington, the author of the translation being identified as Peter McDouall 'at the author's especial request'.[75] In his publications, Cabet himself spoke of the '8 million Chartists...who were communists', and he had English followers who created an Icarian Committee for England in the mid-1840s.[76] When McDouall returned to London in 1844, he was in touch with French refugees and a republican meeting was convened in September 1844 to celebrate the 1792 First French Republic. This 'banquet'—a strategy used by republicans in France to escape the 1834 ban on meetings of more than twenty people—was chaired by McDouall.[77]

Another Chartist interested in Cabet was George Julian Harney, who was instrumental in forming the Fraternal Democrats. From 1845 to 1848, this group introduced several Chartists to refugees from the Continent and has a claim to be the first internationalist workingmen's association, some twenty years before the IWMA.[78] 'All men are brethren', its membership card claimed in twelve languages. It harboured British Chartists, French and Polish refugees, and German workers. The German artisans belonged to the Deutscher

---

[74] 'Comme Chartiste, je veux le suffrage universel: mais j'y vois seulement un *moyen* et non pas un *but* définitif. Ce suffrage universel et les autres principes du Chartisme sont pour moi la clé du jardin, l'instrument pour faire une meilleure organisation sociale, le mur pour protéger les organisateurs. C'est pourquoi, après avoir lu, relu et médité votre *Voyage en Icarie*, j'adopte parfaitement les principes de Démocratie et de Communauté qui sont exposés dans cet ouvrage. C'est à mes yeux, un chef-d'œuvre; et je suis convaincu que les ouvriers en Angleterre l'adopteraient également s'ils en avaient une traduction'. *Le Populaire*, 19 August 1843, p. 106. A translation of this letter was published in the Owenite newspaper *The New Moral World*, 25 November 1843, p. 176. It was also commented upon by McDouall, who denied the postscript which stated he had subscribed 100 francs to Cabet's movement: 'the statement respecting the subscription has been added by some enthusiast merely to give the cause a stimulus', McDouall added. *NS*, 9 December 1843, p. 5, col. 1. See also Étienne Cabet, *Procès du communisme à Toulouse*, Paris, 1843, pp. 28–30.

[75] The book was advertised as published by Hetherington in 1845, e.g., in *Morning Star, or Herald of Progression*, vol. 1, no. 19 (17 May 1845). This was the journal of the Tropical Emigration Society, of which Chartist Thomas Powell was secretary. The advert appeared only once. It seems it was published in twenty instalments, as advertised in the *Northern Star*, 1 November 1845, p. 3; 25 November, p. 4. No known copy has survived. I owe much of this information to Malcolm Chase.

[76] Étienne Cabet, *Etat de la question sociale en Angleterre, en Ecosse, en Irlande et en France*, Paris, June 1843, pp. 18–25; Ashton and Pickering, *Friends of the People*, p. 17; W. H. G. Armytage, *Heavens Below: Utopian Experiments in England 1560–1960*, London, 1961, pp. 205–7.

[77] Iorwerth Prothero, *Radical Artisans in England and France, 1830–1870*, Cambridge, 1997, p. 217.

[78] Albert Schoyen, *The Chartist Challenge: A Portrait of George Julian Harney*, London, 1958; Frank Gees Black and Renee Métivier Black (eds.), *The Harney Papers*, Assen, 1969; Lehning, *From Buonarroti to Bakunin*; Weisser, *British Working-Class Movements*, pp. 134–78; Fabrice Bensimon, 'The IWMA and Its Precursors in London, c. 1830–1860', in Fabrice Bensimon, Quentin Deluermoz, and Jeanne Moisand (eds.), *'Arise Ye Wretched of the Earth': The First International in a Global Perspective*, Leiden, 2018, pp. 21–38.

Bildungsverein für Arbeiter (German Workers' Education Society), whose under-cover organisation was the Communist League which later issued the *Manifesto of the Communist Party*.[79] From late 1844, when the *Northern Star* moved to London, the editors met in the Red Lion public house, Great Windmill Street, in Soho, where the German and French democrats also met. The Fraternal Democrats, set up at the latest in 1845, and possibly earlier, campaigned publicly for the cause of Poland. They opposed the possibility of war between Britain and the United States in the Oregon question in 1846—'No vote! No musket!!' they claimed. They advocated the gathering of a Congress of Nations to settle inter-national disputes.[80]

In 1847, Harney tried to set up an international organisation with democratic branches abroad, but he managed to do so through the German workers rather than through the British ones, among whom the Land Plan Company (LPC) was the most successful. The Fraternal Democrats did take hold in Brussels, where the Association démocratique was created. Its members were mostly Belgian, but it also attracted foreigners, including German artisans. Marx was one of those running the association to which Engels also belonged.[81] In other parts of the Continent, these early internationalist attempts proved less successful, although various radical newspapers (*The Northern Star*, *La Réforme* in Paris, *Deutsche-Brüsseler Zeitung* and *Le Débat social* in Brussels) worked as a transnational network of democrats, radicals, and socialists. The 1848 revolutions changed this. In Britain, the Chartists petitioned for the Charter for the third time; in a series of meetings that peaked between March and June, they claimed 'The French have the Republic, the British need the Charter'—and sometimes 'If we don't have the Charter, we'll have a Republic'. In March 1848, several Chartist delegations went to Paris, including one from the National Charter Association, which included Harney, Ernest Jones, and Philip McGrath, and probably met Louis Blanc, Ledru-Rollin, and others. Robert Owen spent several months in Paris in the spring of 1848 and was in contact with several French socialists, including Cabet whom he had met in London and at whose club he spoke.

Many more contacts could be mentioned. The impact of internationalism at this stage should not be overestimated in either of the two countries, however: those involved were radicals and communists whose influence was limited, and who possessed diverging expectations. Their common ground was fraternity and comradeship against oppressors, rather than solidarity in disputes and against

---

[79] Christine Lattek, *Revolutionary Refugees: German Socialism in Britain, 1840–1860*, London, 2005.

[80] *Address to the Working Classes of Great Britain and the United States on the Oregon Question*, printed in *NS*, 7 March 1846; *Address of the Fraternal Democrats assembling in London to the working classes of Great Britain and the United States*, 4 July 1846. These tracts are in the British Library, shelfmark 1852.e.4.

[81] See [Friedrich Engels], 'The Free Trade Congress at Brussels', *NS*, 9 October 1847 with an editorial note: 'From Our German Correspondent'.

strike breaking. It was only from 1864 that the rise of working-class organisations and struggles changed the impact and the nature of such transnational connections, through the influence of the IWMA. However, within these early connections in the 1830s and 1840s among British, French, Belgian, and German activists, some methods were devised that would go on to be useful in later international organisations. The Fraternal Democrats had a set of rules, membership cards, conditions for membership, and an international committee with representatives of affiliated national sections: this was new and later reproduced by the IWMA. Although by 1864 Harney had emigrated to the United States, Marx, Engels, Karl Schapper, Friedrich Lessner, and Ludwik Oborski had this early experience which they drew upon for the IWMA. And, like Friedrich Sorge, J. G. Eccarius, G. E. Harris, J. B. Leno, and several of those who were involved in the 1850s in the International Association and the International Committee, two short-lived London-based organisations which were in certain ways descendants of the Fraternal Democrats, also took part in the IWMA.

3. Chartist Artisans

Did economic migrants play a part in transnational political encounters? We know that the distinction between economic migration and political exile can be misleading. For example, in the 1830s, 1840s, and 1850s, tens of thousands of German workers emigrated to France, Belgium, Britain, or the United States, for reasons that were partly economic and partly political.[82] Many of the Irish who emigrated to the United States also saw themselves as 'exiles', the victims of an evil foreign power.[83] The same was true of some French workers, after the defeat of the 1848 revolution and Louis-Napoléon Bonaparte's coup in December 1851. The same person could also experience various types of migration or exile. Martin Nadaud (1815–98), a mason from the Creuse, famously remembered how, in the 1830s, with his fellow-villagers, they tramped to Paris to work during the 'season' before returning home, where they had left their parents and sometimes their wives and children.[84] Nadaud, who was involved in the Second Republic, had to leave France after the coup d'état and spent eighteen years in Britain. As for the British workers, they were less likely to go into exile than most of their continental counterparts: after all, Britain was a free country and to some extent a land of asylum for many political refugees.[85] But in the first half of the century thousands

---

[82] Heléna Tóth *An Exiled Generation: German and Hungarian Refugees of Revolution, 1848–1871*, Cambridge, 2014.

[83] David Brundage, *Irish Nationalists in America: The Politics of Exile, 1798–1998*, New York, 2016.

[84] Martin Nadaud, *Mémoires de Léonard, ancien garçon maçon*, Bourganeuf, 1895.

[85] Bernard Porter, *The Refugee Question in Mid-Victorian Politics*, Cambridge, 1979.

of Britons were transported for political reasons, and many others left the country so as to avoid prosecution and prison.

Though British workers did not have a 'revolutionary tradition', so to speak, they may be said to have been, overall, better organised than continental workers. This was partly because they could exert some rights which other Europeans generally lacked. In Britain, meeting was not a legal right but it was a liberty. There were restrictions on the right to meet, like the 1838 and 1839 Royal Proclamations against Chartist meetings, and still in 1866 meetings in London for electoral reform were clamped down upon.[86] But thousands of meetings were held by the Chartists and others afterwards, while in France meetings of more than twenty people were prohibited until 1868—except during the Second Republic—and even when they were made legal, political and religious issues were not to be mentioned. Whereas, despite the remaining 'taxes on knowledge', the freedom of the press existed in Britain, in France it was tightly controlled. An 1835 Act made it risky for newspapers to criticise the regime, and several papers were closed down in the following years. Under Napoleon III, things were even worse, and a Sheffield worker who visited Paris in 1867 typically contrasted French despotism with British freedom:

> Who would not rather have the right to 'assist' at a political meeting, with free discussion, than be cajoled by an Emperor's fêtes? Who would barter the right to criticize the Government's last blunder, and show clearly how he could rectify it, for the privilege to walk in straight boulevards, or saunter through palaces, however grand they may be? Who would not rather read the unfettered daily paper than have that article cut and dried even by an imperial cook?[87]

As previously mentioned, the right to create combinations or trade unions, which was granted in Britain in 1824, only became legal in France in 1884. As for the right to vote, which most workers were deprived of, it was more common in the UK, where more than 800,000—that is, 7 per cent of the adult population, from the upper echelons of the middle classes—were enfranchised after 1832, whereas in France only 171,000, less than 1 per cent, had the vote in 1834. And this was under a liberal regime. In Britain at the time, the despotisms of Russia, Prussia, and Austria were commonly castigated, and the cause of Poland, Italy, or Hungary could mobilise hundreds of thousands. Differences were not just legal but were also framed in terms of experience: British workers had early working knowledge of the creation of political associations, unions, and newspapers. In the German states, on the other hand, for example, the first significant working-class party,

---

[86] Katrina Navickas, *Protest and the Politics of Space and Place, 1789–1848*, Manchester, 2016.
[87] Jehoida Alsop Rhodes, 'A Sheffield Workman's Week Excursion to Paris and Back for 70 Shillings', *Saint Paul's Magazine*, November 1867, p. 205.

ADAV, was created in 1863, twenty-five years after the Chartists, whose impact it did not match. In France, it was only in the 1880s that significant working-class parties were formed. In all these respects, the British workers had more experience than their continental counterparts; but they did not have the revolutionary tradition which proved so powerful on the Continent, especially in France between 1830 and 1871. Once overseas, migrants had to comply with local legislation and custom. Organisation was made more difficult, especially among temporary or itinerant migrants like the railway navvies, whose involvement in Chartism was limited even in Britain.

Migrants were aware of the more repressive legal framework on the Continent. After all, the British press and politicians boasted of British freedoms, which they contrasted with 'foreign despotism',[88] and Chartists like Feargus O'Connor insisted on the fact that the British constitution was the most liberal. There is evidence that migrants established an associational and political tradition in France. In Britain, the collective tradition outside the trade unions had played an important part: a large part of the male population had some experience in friendly societies, Oddfellows, and trade societies or clubs. Unsurprisingly, migrants created friendly societies, like a 'British Benefit Society of Rouen and its environs' in 1836.[89] In Boulogne and Calais, several Oddfellows societies were also set up. In Saint-Pierre-lès-Calais, two societies of British workers were founded in 1834 and met on a weekly basis (Figure 5.3). Eight similar French Oddfellows societies were then created, which included only French workers. Such societies brought together certain republicans and served as cover for political activities, prompting the authorities to monitor them, especially under Louis-Napoléon Bonaparte's presidency (1848–52). 'The friendly societies of the Boulogne district are allegedly led by men belonging to the anarchist party', the local *procureur* (state prosecutor) wrote in September 1851.[90] And after Bonaparte's coup on 2 December, all the friendly societies of Saint-Pierre, both French and British, were disbanded.

Migrants also set up in France the only branches of the Chartist Land Plan known outside Britain and Jersey. The Land Plan was set up by Feargus O'Connor in 1845. In return for weekly subscriptions, one could expect to be eventually granted a plot of land on a Chartist estate. With this smallholding, workers could also meet the qualification requirement and be enfranchised. Only five estates were eventually set up, while the Land Company got into financial difficulties and was eventually wound up in 1851. Most shareholders were not allocated a plot, but the registers of the Chartist Cooperative Land Company (renamed the National

---

[88]   *NS*, 29 August 1846, p. 8.   [89]   AD Seine-Maritime, 4X 207.
[90]   AD Pas-de-Calais, M7427, September 1851, quoted in William Mauffroy, 'Les Odd Fellows de Saint-Pierre-lès-Calais ou la première rencontre de la mutualité et du mouvement ouvrier dans le Pas-de-Calais au XIXᵉ siècle', *Bulletin de la commission départementale d'histoire et d'archéologie du Pas-de-Calais*, vol. 15, 1997, p. 281.

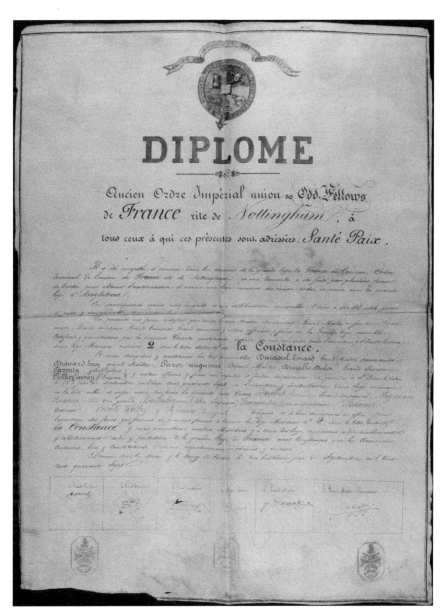

Figure 5.3 By 1844, a French lodge of the Oddfellows had been created in Saint-Pierre-lès-Calais by the British. This 1847 'diplôme' was produced by this lodge, which could only gather French members. Such lodges were friendly societies that provided support in the case of disease or accident. They were also the only legal associations of workers under the July Monarchy. In December 1851, following the coup by Louis-Napoléon Bonaparte, they were dissolved ('Diplôme. Ancien Ordre Impérial union des Odd Fellows de France rite de Nottingham'. AD Pas-de-Calais, 1 J 1652 1, Loges maçonniques).

Cooperative Land Company) listed some 43,000 subscribers.[91] Subscribing could appeal to migrants, many of whom saw themselves as exiles who had had to emigrate to make a living and who partook in the ideal of communal living in one of the future Chartist Land plan villages. In December 1846 the land conference that decided each colony would build a school with teachers answerable to the settlers, and the colony would be devoid of pubs and beer shops.[92] The files reveal 105 names of subscribers overseas, including 104 workers in France and a stoker in Antwerp.[93] This is admittedly a small proportion. But again, Chartism was a domestic movement and while its impact could be felt in different settler societies like Australia, New Zealand, or the United States, no Chartist sections were created in these countries. The geography of the Land Plan subscribers mirrored that of British working-class emigration: Calais (twenty-three names), Boulogne-sur-Mer (twenty-five), and Rouen-Sotteville (thirty-six) were the main branches. In the Chartist press, sections of the LPC were also mentioned in Mantes (Seine-et-Oise) and Evreux (Eure), but it is doubtful whether they persisted, whereas the Boulogne and Rouen sections were represented at the 1845 conference of the Land Plan.[94] Little is known about their real activity, or their links with the National Charter Association (NCA). Ten of the 104 French subscribers (i.e. 9.6 per cent) were women—a high proportion in comparison with the total, for which only 4 per cent of the LPC subscribers were women.[95] But their distribution was uneven. The Calais lacemakers numbered no female subscribers, but out of the twenty-five Boulogne-sur-Mer subscribers, eight were women (32 per cent): they were flax workers, most likely from Dundee, all of them unmarried, which suggests a greater agency among these wage-earning spinners (see pp. 108–16).

One of the main activists in France was John Sidaway, who lived in Rouen with his father Thomas. 'A Radical of the Old school, and a disciple of Henry Hunt', involved in radical initiatives since Peterloo, Thomas Sidaway (1796–1848), a nail and chain manufacturer who also ran a pub, had been an active Chartist speaker since 1838 and had become secretary of the Gloucester branch of the NCA.[96] He was compelled to leave Gloucester and go to France, reportedly because, as a Unitarian, he was prosecuted for non-payment of taxes to the Church of England.[97] In Rouen, John and Thomas Sidaway opened the 'Nailors' Arms Inn', where the Chartist press was available, and where contributions to funds

[91]   TNA. BT 41/474/2659; BT 41/476/2659.   [92]   Chase, *Chartism*, p. 34.
[93]   Thanks to Peter Cox and the U3A for compiling the handwritten records of the LPC.
[94]   *NS*, 13 December 1845, 29 August 1846, 29 May 1847.
[95]   Peter Cox, 'Transcribing the Chartist Land Company Registers', Chartist Ancestors Blog (Mark Crail), 7 July 2017, https://chartist-ancestors.blogspot.com/2017/07/transcribing-chartist-land-company.html.
[96]   'Death of a Patriot', *NS*, 15 January 1848, p. 7.
[97]   *The London Gazette for the year 1839*, vol. 1, p. 279.

to help those persecuted for their involvement were collected.[98] In 1845 John formed a local branch of the LPC which numbered six shareholders, including four Sidaways, and he was appointed the agent for France.[99] Deemed a 'talented' 'lecturer',[100] John toured the country, lecturing in praise of the Land Plan, notably in Mantes (Seine-et-Oise) or in Navarre, near Evreux (Eure), where some British workers were employed by Mackenzie and Brassey in an iron foundry:[101]

> Several meetings have been held and addressed by Mr John Sidaway. Navarre is a small village, surrounded by small allotments, which afford practical proof of the value of the land. Navarre some time since was a dark spot, but within the last few months it has been illumined with NORTHERN STARS, and consequently the inhabitants have become alive to the value of co-operation for the obtainment of the land, and have this day (25th of August) remitted £12 9s. 2d. for shares in the Chartist Co-operative land Society. The office of Mr John Sidaway, N° 2, Navarre Press, Evereux [Evreux], is continually besieged for prospectuses, rules, cards and Northern Stars.[102]

Interestingly, in the absence of a Chartist organisation in France, the *Northern Star* could fulfil this rallying and intermediary function. It could help to create networks of salesmen and buyers, preserve links, and take on the roles of various spaces of sociability, like clubs and meetings, where Chartists met and discussed domestic issues. As James Epstein has argued, the *Star* 'was more than a political paper. It was part of a much larger Chartist cultural experience'.[103] This was a role which, in a context where large meetings were forbidden, was also taken on by some French papers, like Cabet's *Populaire*, and which would later be taken on by anarchist newspapers, in the absence of parties, as Constance Bantman has shown.[104] Thomas Sidaway died early in 1848.[105] His daughter took on his Land Plan plot in Snig's End, in Corse (Gloucestershire). John

---

[98] 'Advertisements: Mr SEDAWAY, Nailer's Arms ... He hopes his Brother Odd fellows will support him. They will find the *Norman Times*, the Dispatch and Northern Star'. *Norman Times*, 13 July 1844, p. 4; 'Received by Mr O'Connor.... From a few friends at the Nailors' Arms, Rouen, France, per John Sidaway', *NS*, 8 March 1845.

[99] *NS*, 19 July 1845, p. 6. John Sidaway was allocated four acres of land at Snig's End in April 1846 (*NS*, 25 April 1846).

[100] *NS*, 15 January 1848.

[101] The Eure département, which was crossed by the Paris–Rouen line, was one in which many British had settled. An official document mentioned the presence of 592 'Anglais' in the Eure département in November 1846 (Archives nationales, F/7/12338: Etats numériques du mouvement des étrangers). Also see Jean Vidalenc, *Le département de l'Eure sous la monarchie constitutionnelle, 1814–1848*, Paris, 1952, pp. 541–3.

[102] [John Sidaway?], *NS*, 29 August 1846, p. 8.

[103] James Epstein, *The Lion of Freedom: Feargus O'Connor and the Chartist Movement, 1832–1842*, London, 1982, p. 73, and the whole of ch. 2.

[104] Constance Bantman, *Jean Grave and the Networks of French Anarchism, 1854–1939*, London, 2021, p. 63.

[105] *NS*, 15 January 1848.

Sidaway returned to his earlier job as a smith, and was apparently the Secretary of the NCA for Gloucestershire and Worcestershire in 1848. According to the 1851 census, he lived in Barton St Mary in Gloucestershire where he was 'employing 3 men'.[106]

Boulogne-sur-Mer and its district also had a branch of the Land Company.[107] Most of the members probably worked for Hopwood, a linen company based there since 1837, and which had hired about a hundred Scottish workers on to its books. In August 1846, a 'soirée' gathered 'upwards of 130...to partake of the good things of this life and to hear the speeches of Messrs O'Connor and Jones read from the *Star*'; 'the song "The People's first estate" was sung in fine style and enthusiastically chorused by the whole company. A number of other appropriate songs were sung by the female part of the company, and also a number of the most patriotic and soul-stirring recitations were delivered'.[108] Chartist sociability in France mirrored what was practised in Britain when members gathered to sing songs and listen to speeches.

Calais was also a hotbed of Chartism where East Midlands lacemakers went to work, as we have seen. The movement was strong in Nottinghamshire. It was in Nottingham that Feargus O'Connor, the only Chartist MP, was elected to Westminster in 1847. Women's participation in the local industries was reflected in the strong tradition of local female Chartism.[109] The presence of Chartists among the Calais lacemakers is not surprising, although evidence only exists from December 1845, when O'Connor's Land Plan was set up.[110] From then on, at least twenty-three Calais and Saint-Pierre inhabitants subscribed to the Chartist Co-operative Land Company.[111] O'Connor celebrated his Plan's transcending of national borders: 'my little work upon "Small Farms" has crossed the seas; and is, I believe, destined to proclaim the triumph of labour'.[112] On several occasions, he quoted letters from Calais, such as 'from a frugal and honest working man, an Englishman earning his bread in France', so as to inspire 'all at home and abroad with home and consolation'.[113] O'Connor may have been interested in Calais because it was the destination of many workers from Nottingham, for which he was MP. Although he seldom showed much interest in foreign affairs, he went to France for a week in September 1849 and spent a day in Calais. When he asked to

---

[106] Class: *HO107*; Piece: *1962*; Folio: *385*; Page: *39*; GSU roll: *87362* 1851 census records for Barton St Mary (Gloucestershire), where John Sidaway is listed living with his family including a niece, Maria, aged seven, born in France (I owe this reference to Mark Crail); NS, 18 March 1848, p. 5.

[107] Thomas Blyth, 30 rue du Moulin à Vapeur, Capecure, Boulogne. NS, 19 July 1845.

[108] NS, 29 August 1846, p. 8.   [109] Epstein, 'Chartist Movement in Nottingham'.

[110] On Calais: NS, 6 December 1845, p. 4.

[111] TNA. National Land Company Register, BT 41/136/790. Also see NS, 6 December 1845; 24 January, 7 and 14 February, 4 and 25 April, 11 July, 1 August, 24 October, 21 November, 5 and 12 December 1846; 23 January, 20 February, 13 March, 3 April, 29 May, 14 August 1847; 1 January 1848; 22 April 1848, p. 5; 17 February 1849; 10 March; 15 September 1849. Also see 'James Guilward, Calais, £2 12 6 d in Receipts of the Chartist Co-Operative Land Society', NS, 6 December 1845, 4.

[112] NS, 24 January 1846, p. 1.   [113] NS, 20 February 1847.

be allowed to address the lacemakers, a Chartist friend told him: 'You do not understand our Republic; a body of police would have you before you spoke three words'.[114] In a similar vein to British workers in France, O'Connor thus contrasted the freedom granted by the British constitution, which he often praised, with the absence of liberties allowed on the Continent. The involvement of some Calais workers in the Land Plan confirms that they saw themselves as temporary migrants, identifying themselves as British and longing to return to their native land. Economic migration and political exile were therefore not always separate. This is exemplified by Ralph Kerfoot, who had left his native Chowbent, near Manchester, following the Lancashire demonstrations of September 1839 and was also a member of the Rouen first section; though Ralph died too early to get his plot, he had been granted two acres in Heronsgate (renamed O'Connorville), alongside artisans from Wigan, Northampton, Halifax, and Edinburgh.[115] Like the Irish emigrants in the United States after the Great Famine, the migrants sometimes used the word 'exile', blaming 'that system which has driven honest and industrious artizans to seek that subsistence abroad which has been denied them at home'.[116]

All of this suggests that the Chartists tried to reproduce, as much as possible, modes of organisation which they were accustomed to in Britain: itinerant agitation, meetings, and public reading of newspapers.[117] At the same time, they had to adjust to the different usages and legal constraints operating in France, where for example a procession would have been hard to imagine. Meetings of more than twenty were illegal, and it was significant that the Boulogne soirée took place in a 'British' factory. The Oddfellows were also used as a cover by, for example, those attending Chartist meetings in Rouen.[118]

When they emigrated to Australia, Chartists set up organisations that adapted the Chartist programme to the local political context. In France, this was not possible strictly speaking, but the case of George Good is a telling example of how one individual could try and adapt his 'British' commitment in a different political environment. We are dependent on scarce sources to ascertain the precise nature of this tendency, the main one being the *Northern Star*. It seems that the French police were not especially interested in Chartism, which was something alien, and not considered a domestic threat.

---

[114] 'To the Working Men of England', *NS*, 15 September 1849, p. 1.
[115] *NS*, 25 April 1846; his allotment number is mentioned in *NS*, 1 August 1846; his death in *NS*, 18 December 1847.
[116] 'Death of a Patriot', *NS*, 15 January 1848.
[117] Humphrey Southall, '"Agitate, Agitate! Organise!": Political Travellers and the Construction of National Politics, 1839–1880', *Transactions of the Institute of British Geographers*, new series, vol. 21, 1996, pp. 177–93.
[118] *Norman Times*, 13 July 1844, p. 4.

The migrant Chartists hoped they could return to Britain, which may explain why one of the main forms their commitment took in France was subscription to the Land Plan. Chartist William Peddie described the Boulogne meeting of 13 August 1846 in a way that may have captured the mood of the most politicised of these British emigrants to France:

> At half-past eleven the company dispersed, every face radiant with joy at the success that has already attended the Land Society, and full of high hopes that the time will soon come where every man will have a home which he can call his own, and not as now be driven from his native land to seek employment under a foreign despotism.[119]

This echoed Chartist assumptions about English liberties. When French 'despotism' was brought down in February 1848, this provoked widespread excitement in Chartist circles.[120]

Does the experience of the Chartists in France add to our knowledge of Chartism, about which so much has already been written? In some ways, the Chartist agenda did not spread to the Continent, and the emigrant Chartists were temporary migrants. At the same time, this facet adds a transnational dimension to the history of a movement thought to be insular. It has long been known that when Chartists emigrated, they conveyed their ideas to their destinations, and that in the United States, Australia, or New Zealand, they played a part in the local democratic, union, or land reform movements.[121] The specificity of the French branches is that the Chartist forms of organisation were exported to the Continent, in a different political context. Land Plan subscribers also show that many emigrants nurtured hopes that returning to Britain would imply some form of emancipation. Toiling on the Continent did not prevent Chartists from dreaming of a life where they could enjoy both political and economic freedom, without having to emigrate for work purposes.

---

[119] NS, 29 August 1846, p. 8.

[120] See John Saville, 1848: The British State and the Chartist Movement, Cambridge, 1987; Fabrice Bensimon, Les Britanniques face à la révolution française de 1848, Paris, 2000.

[121] Ray Boston, British Chartists in America 1839–1900, Manchester, 1971; Jamie L. Bronstein, Land Reform and Working-Class Experience in Britain and the United States, 1800–1862, Stanford, CA, 1999; Paul Pickering, 'The Oak of English Liberty: Popular Constitutionalism in New South Wales, 1848–1856', Journal of Australian Colonial History, vol. 3, 2001, pp. 1–27; Paul Pickering, 'A Wider Field in a New Country: Chartism in Colonial Australia', in Marian Sawer (ed.), Elections Full, Free and Fair, Sydney, 2001, pp. 28–44; Andrew Messner, 'Chartist Political Culture in Britain and Colonial Australia, c. 1835–60' (unpublished PhD thesis, University of New England (Australia), 2000); John Griffiths and Vic Evans, 'The Chartist Legacy in the British World: Evidence from New Zealand's Southern Settlements, 1840s–1870s', History, vol. 99, no. 5 (338), December 2014, pp. 797–818.

4. Collective Readers and the Hearing Public

The year 1848 was not the end of Chartism, as is sometimes argued. The *Northern Star* was published until 1852 and, as late as 1858, a Chartist conference gathered forty-nine delegates representing seventy-one localities.[122] French sources testify to the continued politicisation of British migrants, for instance those of the Société linière du Finistère in Landerneau (Brittany). In 1849, a report, probably by Max Radiguet, a publicist who happened to be the son of the manager of the plant, was published in *L'Illustration*. The pictures of the factory included the public reading of a Chartist newspaper (Figure 5.4).

> Today, all [Scottish, English, Bretons] are mixed together. Thus, in our drawing representing the linen hackling workshop, you can see the Breton with his wide-brimmed hat working alongside the English worker. This workshop presents a rather curious feature. About 50 Englishmen who are cool, phlegmatic and as hard-working as one can imagine, divide their attention between their work and the reading of an English Chartist newspaper done by one of their comrades who is paid by them to do this. These men, who have left their country for the lure of a high wage, seem to attach a religious significance to this piece of paper that comes from their country and is read by one of their fellow-citizens. This is a touching remembrance of their homeland which thus is never absent.[123]

Radiguet commented elsewhere:

> Not a single syllable is uttered during the twelve hours of the working day; only in the centre of the room, a reader, concealed behind the broadsheet format of the *Times*, with a powerful voice which seems to borrow its notes from the voice of a locomotive, declaims to his fellow-workers, all of them being fervid Chartists, the content of the gigantic newspaper from the date to the name of the publisher.[124]

This exceptional illustration of the Chartist practice of public reading, probably of the *Northern Star*, points to the circulation of the Chartist press in France, which could be traced back to 1841 at least.[125] The collective reading of radical or

---

[122] Chase, *Chartism*, p. 395.

[123] [Max Radiguet?], 'Grands établissements industriels de la France (1). Filature de lin', *L'Illustration*, 27 October 1849, p. 141.

[124] Max Radiguet, *A travers la Bretagne. Souvenirs et paysages*. Paris, 1865, p. 247. The quotation does not imply Radiguet was confusing the *Northern Star* with *The Times*, but probably that the broadsheet format of the latter was known.

[125] In 1841, an editorial in the Scottish *Chartist Circular* noted that the paper circulated in France 'whither a number of our countrymen have gone to fill situations' (18 September 1841).

Figure 5.4 'Atelier de sérançage [heckling workshop], d'après un dessin de M. Puyo' [Max Radiguet?], 'Grands établissements industriels de la France (1). Filature de lin', *L'Illustration*, 27 October 1849, p. 140.

Chartist newspapers was common in families, public houses, and on other occasions.[126] It was also common in those workplaces where machinery had not yet been introduced: among printers, wool combers, tailors, and the famous 'political shoemakers' studied by Eric Hobsbawm and Joan Scott.[127] In the Dundee linen and jute industry, the hecklers were also keen on getting one of them to read a newspaper aloud to the others during work. Most of the Landerneau workers came from Dundee from where they had imported the practice. This also prevailed among artisans in France. Frédéric Le Play reported that tailors were intent on subscribing to pay an invalid soldier to read aloud in the workshop.[128] Martin Nadaud remembered reading Cabet's *Populaire* aloud. *L'Atelier* was also read in some workshops.[129]

---

[126] James Epstein, *The Lion of Freedom. Feargus O'Connor and the Chartist Movement, 1832–1842*, London, 1982, p. 68; Chase, *Chartism*, p. 45.

[127] Hobsbawm and Scott, 'Political Shoemakers'.

[128] Frédéric Le Play, *Les ouvriers européens. Étude sur les travaux, la vie domestique et la condition morale des populations ouvrières de l'Europe*, 2nd ed., Paris, 1878, vol. 6, pp. 438–9.

[129] 'Faits divers', *L'Atelier*, December 1840, no 4, p. 30.

The reading of newspapers or books in the workshops could, in some ways, be branded as 'rational', insofar as it fitted an economic and productive framework which impeded individual reading. When in Landerneau fifty British workers paid their mate to read the newspaper aloud, they reaped benefits in a number of ways. First, they could benefit from the reading skills which they did not necessarily have. Although two thirds of British men and half of British women signed marriage registers by 1850, reading a newspaper like the *Northern Star* was another matter. On top of that, finding the time to read the eight pages of a weekly newspaper on top of a fifty-five-, sixty-, or seventy-hour working week was difficult. If one supposes that the reading of eight pages of the *Northern Star*, 'the content of the gigantic newspaper from the date to the name of the publisher', *L'Illustration* mentioned,[130] required some six hours, each worker then had to contribute 0.2 per cent of his weekly wage to pay the reader.[131] Buying the newspaper (4.5 d.) would have cost about 3 per cent of a weekly wage—that is, fifteen times as much, not to mention the cost of postage. One should probably also take into account the issue of light, which was scarce in the autumn and winter in Brittany; in Dundee, daylight exceeds twelve hours for only six months in the year, fourteen hours only for 4.5 months. And although the cost of candles shrank, they still put a price on domestic reading. The rationality of collective reading had not escaped some reformers like Henry Brougham who, in the mid-1820s, had unsuccessfully tried to spread the practice.[132] Still, in 1844, as mechanisation was speedily progressing, *Chambers's Journal* argued that 'the introduction of reading aloud to each other in turn would be productive of incalculable benefit. Singing for the million is cried up on all hands—why not reading aloud?'[133] However, more than rationality, it seems that political militancy and radicalism were the critical stimulus to reading aloud. Promoters of collective reading were often advocates of workers' education and emancipation. This was true in France as well as in Britain. It was observed among cigar-makers transnationally.[134]

To come back to the Landerneau picture, if one supposes the reader was one of the local correspondents of the *Northern Star*, a few names can be suggested: James Robertson, Peter Forrester, Brown or James Forbes,[135] all of whom were flax carders. Nothing else is known about them, except an anecdote about Forrester.

---

[130] Max Radiguet, *A travers la Bretagne. Souvenirs et paysages*, Paris, 1865, p. 247.

[131] One tenth of one fiftieth.

[132] See Henry Brougham, *Practical Observations upon the Education of the People*, London, 1825, p. 8.

[133] 'Reading Aloud', *Chambers's Journal*, 19 October 1844, p. 243.

[134] Ad Knotter, 'Transnational Cigar-Makers: Cross-Border Labour Markets, Strikes and Solidarity at the time Of the First International (1864–1873)', *International Review of Social History*, vol. 59, December 2014, p. 419.

[135] *NS*, 27 April 1850, p. 4; 10 August 1850, p. 5; 22 November 1851, p. 4; Archives municipales de Landerneau, registres d'état-civil.

He was born in Kinghorn, near Dundee, and in September 1848 when he was twenty-four he married Jeannette Henry, an eighteen-year-old Blairgowry spinner who worked in the Landerneau mill. Among other documents, the consent of the parents was requested and the mayor wrote to the local authorities that this was difficult to obtain because 'her father being a Chartist had been compelled to run away from his house'.[136] Chartism was very much a family involvement, as we have seen. This was also true of migrants, including among several women, often the wives of Land Plan contributors.

As for collective reading, it seems that it declined in the 1850s and 1860s. In France, the Bonapartist regime left little scope for this. In Britain, Chartism and radicalism declined. In both countries, mechanisation went on, undermining the culture of the artisan. By the late nineteenth century, reading had become more individual. And when in Europe mechanisation made progress and the culture of the artisan declined irretrievably, other areas took over. In cigar-making, collective reading went on. In colonial and slave-holding Cuba, from 1865 cigar-makers started reading aloud from books and periodicals, as they then did in Tampa in Florida and in New York, Puerto Rico, Mexico, the Dominican Republic, and Spain.[137] Samuel Gompers, born in London in 1850, was a public reader in New York tobacco making in his youth, before becoming a trade-union leader. Collective reading also existed among German cigar-makers in the 1860s and 1870s. As for western Europe, the progress of a culture of print, which had first stimulated collective reading, eventually hindered it. The declining cost of the paper and the increasingly silent and private nature of reading marginalised collective practices. The noise of the machines and the discipline of work gradually chased this practice away from the factory.[138]

5. Insurgents?

What we have seen so far are forms of political activity among Chartist migrants. What about the involvement of British exiles in continental revolutionary politics? During the French revolution, a group of British radicals went to Paris to take part in events, and Thomas Paine was elected to the 1792 Convention where he sat

---

[136] 'Quant à la future, son père étant chartiste a été obligé de fuir de son domicile'. Archives municipales de Landerneau, 13 D 6, no. 788, 29 October 1848, lettre du maire au procureur.

[137] Joan Casanovas, *Bread, or Bullets! Urban Labor and Spanish Colonialism in Cuba, 1850–1898*, Pittsburgh, PA, 1998; Araceli Tinajero, *El Lector: A History of the Cigar Factory Reader*, Austin, TX, 2010.

[138] Fabrice Bensimon and François Jarrige, 'Lire les socialistes et les radicaux dans l'atelier. Esquisses sur les pratiques ouvrières de lecture collective (France et Grande-Bretagne, 1780–1860)', in Nathalie Brémand (dir.), *Bibliothèques en utopie: les socialistes et la lecture au XIXe siècle*, Lyon, 2020, pp. 93–113.

before being jailed.[139] For nineteenth-century revolutions, sources don't say much. Although we now know the names of eighteen individuals who died at Peterloo on 16 August 1819, we do not even know how many died in the Parisian uprisings of June 1832, February and June 1848, and the crushing of the Commune in May 1871, let alone their names and nationalities. However, several sources testify to the strong involvement of foreigners in revolutions. As in the settler colonies, where emigrants like Paine and Garibaldi played a critical part in local politics, in Europe German migrants or Polish refugees were well represented in insurrectionary events.[140] This may be related to the fact that these groups were usually politicised, and they adjusted their commitment to their new environments. In Paris, for instance, the numerous German workers set up associations and were involved in insurrectionary episodes such as the 12–13 May 1839 rising of the secret societies.

The participation of British workers in continental uprisings was far more limited. After the Belgium revolution of 1830, John Hodson was listed among those who were rewarded for their participation. He was one of the sons of James (Jacques) Hodson (1768–1833), an English mechanic who had married Nancy Cockerill (1782–1817), a daughter of the famous entrepreneur. After the Napoleonic wars, James had first bought steam machines in London for Cockerill, and by 1806 he had set up a machine-making factory in Verviers, before shifting to spinning.[141] By the end of his life he ran several factories, while his son John led some Verviers volunteers, who successfully fought in Sainte-Walburge against the Dutch on 30 September 1830. But John Hodson was more Belgian than British.

As for the Paris revolutions, we have tried to quantify the involvement of British subjects in three episodes: the June days in 1848; the rebellion against the 2 December 1851 coup; and the 1871 Paris Commune (Table 5.1). The results do not confirm that British migrants played a significant role in revolutionary episodes. For example, among the 11,662 who were charged in June 1848, 718 (6.16 per cent) were born abroad; that is, a proportion that compared with the share of foreign-born residents in the population of Paris. But whereas 221 were born in Belgium, 138 in Germany, 120 in Savoy, 69 in Switzerland, 45 in Italy and Luxemburg, and 25 in Holland, only a tiny 8 (0.07 per cent of those charged) came

[139] Rachel Rogers, *Friends of the Revolution: The British Radical Community in Early Republican Paris 1792–1794*, London, 2021.

[140] Jacques Grandjonc, 'Les émigrés allemands sous la monarchie de Juillet. Documents de surveillance policière 1833–février 1848', in *Cahiers d'Études Germaniques*, Aix-en-Provence, 1972, no. 1, pp. 115–249; Delphine Diaz, '"J'ai fait mon service comme un brave citoyen français". Parcours et récits de combattants étrangers sur les barricades parisiennes en février et juin 1848', unpublished paper, conference 'Les acteurs européens du "printemps des peuples" 1848', Paris, 1 June 2018; Emma Harris, *Bartlomiej Beniowski 1800–1867: Cosmopolital Chartist and Revolutionary Refugee*, Warsaw, 2019; Lattek, *Revolutionary Refugees*.

[141] Liste nominative de 1031 citoyens proposés pour la Croix de Fer par la Commission des récompenses honorifiques (p. 1–129) dans *Bulletin officiel des lois et arrêtés royaux de Belgique*, no. 807, 1835, vol. 11, pp. 56–7.

from the UK, including a tin-worker, a Charenton roller, two English teachers, an annuitant, a servant, and an army captain. All were released but one: Thomas Boylan, a thirty-nine-year-old book gilder born in Dublin, who was transported for his involvement. He spent three months on a pontoon in Lorient before being pardoned on Christmas Day. This was a scant contribution, especially in comparison with the rumours that British money was instrumental in fostering the June insurrection. While foreign-born nationals were involved in proportion to their share of the population (11 per cent were charged), the British-born were less likely to be involved, while Belgians and Italians were more likely to be involved. More in-depth analysis would be needed, but it might be possible to hazard the suggestion that while those born in Belgian, Italian, and German states were mainly working-class, most of those born in Britain were middle class and therefore not involved in the uprising. In December 1851, overall, foreigners were proportionately slightly more charged than the average population (1.03 per cent vs. 0.7 per cent), which may be related to their larger presence in the towns, but the underrepresentation of the British is even more obvious than for June 1848: only one British participant was prosecuted out of a total of 26,848.

As for the 1871 Paris Commune, the underrepresentation of the British is also striking: they were proportionally ten times less likely to be charged than other foreigners. Whereas Belgian, Swiss, or Polish nationals played prominent roles, the British were underrepresented, with only eighteen prosecuted. It could be argued that by 1871, most of the British who lived in Paris were not workers and were therefore less involved in the insurrection. According to the 1866 census, 50 per cent of the 8,015 'English' lived in the well-off 8th, 9th, and 16th arrondissements of the capital.[142] And the accusation, by the Versailles government, that the IWMA, allegedly leading the Commune, 'put our working-class masses under the leadership of English and German communists' was not substantiated.[143]

However, two isolated figures emerge from the French revolutions. Both were printers, which may not be a coincidence. Like the 'political shoemakers' studied by Scott and Hobsbawm, compositors were particularly politicised and featured prominently among radicals in Britain (James Watson, W. E. Adams, Thomas Frost, J. B. Leno...) and republicans in France (Pierre Leroux, Proudhon).

The life of the first figure is known thanks to his lively autobiography.[144] Charles Manby Smith (1804–80) had come to Paris in 1826, when there was a shortage of work in London, and stayed there until 1830 (see pp. 138–41). Smith also worked as a language teacher in Paris, but he was above all a

---

[142] Sylvie Aprile and Jacques Rougerie, 'Introduction', 'La Commune et les étrangers', *Migrance*, no 35, premier semestre 2010, p. 6.

[143] *Enquête parlementaire sur l'insurrection de 1871*, Paris, 1872, p. 72, col. 3, quoted by Robert Tombs, 'Les Versaillais et les étrangers', *Migrance*, no 35, premier semestre 2010, p. 40.

[144] Charles Manby Smith, *The Working Man's Way in the World: Being the Autobiography of a Journeyman Printer*, London, 1853.

Table 5.1 The involvement of the British and other foreigners in the risings of June 1848 in Paris, December 1851 in France, and the 1871 Paris Commune

Born in	Charged (inculpés) in June 1848	Population in 1851 (Paris)	Charged 1848/census 1851	Prosecuted (poursuivis) in December 1851 (France)	Population in 1851 (France)	Prosecuted in December 1851/population (France)	Prosecuted in 1871	Population in 1866 (Paris)	Prosecuted 1871/population 1866
Belgium	221	12,156	18.1‰	61	128,103	0.47‰	641	28,430	22.5‰
Italy and Savoy (except 1871)	165	9,562	17.2‰	156	63,307	2.45‰	181	7,398	24.5‰
Germany	138	13,584	10.1‰	44	57,061	0.77‰	71	30,456	2.3‰
Spain	9	1,321	6.81‰	17	29,736	0.57‰	29	2,359	12.2‰
Switzerland	69	6,030	11.4‰	42	25,485	1.64‰	187	9,939	28.8‰
Poland	16	2,600	6.15‰	15	9,338	1.61‰	104	4,100	25.3‰
Luxemburg							175	?	
Britain	**8**	**5,781**	**1.38‰**	**1**	**20,357**	**0.05‰**	**18**	**8,015**	**2.2‰**
Total foreign-born	718	63,812	11.2‰	391	379,289	1.03‰	1,554	105,887	14.7 ‰
Total French + foreign-born	11,662	1,053,263	11‰	26,848	35,783,170	0.75‰	41 375	1,825,274	22.7‰

Methodology: Columns 1–3 compare, in Paris, the involvement of foreign-born in the June days of 1848 in relation to their numbers in the capital in 1851; columns 4–6 do the same comparison for France for resistance to the December 1851 coup; columns 7–9 compare the numbers of prosecuted following the Paris Commune and the Paris population of 1866. It is supposed that population numbers had not changed between 1848 and 1851 (whereas they had). It is also supposed that nationality (in the 1851 census) and place of birth (in the judicial records) can be equated, which was indeed not the case as many listed as born abroad in June 1848 had obtained French nationality. It is also supposed that involvement in insurrection (June 1848) or resistance (December 1851) was fairly reflected by judicial procedures: 'inculpation' ('charge') in 1848 and 'poursuites' ('prosecution') in 1851. For the 1871 Paris Commune, a difficulty is that no census was carried out between 1866 and 1872, and it is ascertained that the Franco-Prussian war, the Commune itself, and its bloody repression led many foreigners to leave the town, especially Germans.

'Inculpés des insurrections de juin 1848', database by Jean-Claude Farcy and hosted by Centre Georges Chevrier (université de Bourgogne, http://inculpes-juin-1848.fr/index.php). 'Poursuivis à la suite du coup d'Etat de décembre 1851', database by Jean-Claude Farcy and hosted by Centre Georges Chevrier (http://poursuivis-decembre-1851.fr); 'La repression judiciaire de la Commune de Paris: des pontons à l'amnistie (1871–1880)', database by Jean-Claude Farcy and hosted by LiR3S (Université de Bourgogne/CNRS); 1851 and 1866 censuses: Insee, 'Données historiques de la Statistique générale de France'.

compositor, working twelve hours a day since completing his Bristol apprentice-ship. He happened to be in Paris when the 'revolution of the Three Days of July' 1830 broke out. Although he sincerely despised Charles X, he did not take part in the 'Trois Glorieuses', which 'burst upon [him] like a thunder-clap, and overthrew all [his] previous ideas of Parisian society', and described himself as 'one who had little or nothing but a whole skin to take care of'.[145] He disparagingly wrote of his 'almost perfect indifference' and his 'decided aversion to close intimacy with cold steel or hot lead, especially when nothing was to be got by it'. He refused to gather fellow-Britons to 'render good service in the cause of freedom' and was just an eyewitness to the Trois Glorieuses, wishing he was a Frenchman, or that he 'was a hundred miles away'. It is hard to confirm Smith's narrative: his memoirs were published for a middle-class British audience in the mid-1850s, and Smith admit-ted briefly helping with the building of a barricade.[146] However, his text was a rare first-hand account of the insurrection, from street level, wandering around with an insurgent, from the working-class districts of Saint-Antoine and the quai de Grève to the Pont-Neuf and the Palais Royal, the seat of power. His narrative of the Revolution was written from the viewpoint of an onlooker, someone placed at the heart of a tremendous battle he was not involved in, a 'bloody game', as he called it:

> Under the direction of the grim and grizzled old soldiers of the Empire, and animated by the example of the students and well-dressed youth of the capital, they dug and hewed, and sawed and hammered, and piled and built in decorous order by the light of flaming torches without parley or questioning.[147]

After the abdication, Smith was out of work. On 10 August, he left Paris for London.

Another known involvement of a British printer in a Parisian revolution was that of George Good in February 1848, which we saw earlier. Smith's and Good's involvement could not have been more different. This reminds us that revolutions don't just have fighters, but also observers. Between them, Smith and Good illustrate two attitudes which have been noted in the rare studies on foreigners in revolutions: Smith did not consider Charles X as his king and therefore saw no point in risking his life; although he had been in touch with a radical printer who told him about Paine, his conservative stance distanced him from the revolution-ary involvement of some of his mates. Smith narrated the revolution, while Good made it. For some reason, Good thought it worthwhile to take those risks that Smith rejected. Maybe the reasons for these diverging attitudes were to be found in their respective backgrounds, and the radicalism of George's father in Brighton.

---

[145] p. 107.   [146] p. 121.   [147] p. 126.

6. Conclusion

What emerges from these sketchy individual or collective itineraries is that when on the Continent British workers were far from disengaged. They tried to adjust their political beliefs to changing circumstances. Unlike the emigrants to the United States or to the settler colonies, such as the former Chartists who struggled for democracy in Australia or land reform in New Zealand, in Europe they seldom tried to modify the local political structures. They mostly prepared for an auspicious return to the mother country, following what they sometimes labelled their 'exile'.

In 1864, radical artisans were to play an essential part in the making of the IWMA. The creation of this association again originated in transnational encounters, rather than in the circulation of newspaper articles, pamphlets, or books. It emerged, on the one hand, from the dramatic growth of industrial output and of world trade, the intensifying transnational circulation of labour, the integration of the economies of western Europe and North America. A second important change was the development of strikes and of trade unions not just in Britain but also in France, Belgium, and German states.[148] Another important dimension was that in Britain, which was the most industrialised country of the Continent, there was a lively interest in international matters, such as Poland, Italy, and the US Civil War. In the years that followed the creation of the IWMA in 1864, and especially until 1871, contacts and exchanges between the British activists and their continental counterparts multiplied. By then, British workers no longer played an important part in the industrial take-off of western Europe. However, two later anecdotes that testify to this enduring legacy can be mentioned as postscripts to this story.

In July 1873, during the cantonalist revolution in Spain, two mechanics, Samuel Price and Samuel Leighton, were involved in a mutiny in Carthagena, where the fleet was based: 'Samuel Price, an English internationalist, is in command of one of the insurgent frigates in Carthagena', the British press reported.[149] That's all we know about them. In certain ways, this elusive appearance reminds us of the old radicalism and agency of the British artisans. For more than half a century, mechanics had been among the most skilled and most politicised of the workers. Like the puddlers, like the shoemakers or the printers, they were often at the forefront of struggles.

Far more substantiated is the later solidarity between workers across the Channel. In 1890, a strike broke out in Calais among the lacemakers. One of them, Georges Hazeldine, was sent to curry support in Nottingham, possibly

---

[148] Marcel van der Linden, 'The Rise and Fall of the First International: An Interpretation', in Frits Van Holthoon and Marcel van der Linden (eds.), *Internationalism in the Labour Movement, 1830–1940*, 2 vols., Leiden, 1988, vol. 1, pp. 323–35.

[149] E.g., *London Evening Standard*, 22 July 1873, p. 6. I owe this information to Jeanne Moisand. See her *Se fédérer ou mourir. Carthagène, 1873. Une Commune espagnole et ses mondes*, Paris, to be published in 2023.

because he was related to a British trade-union activist based there: £257 was collected in Nottingham, where the local press daily reported on the strike. This was repeated in 1900–1 when a strike occurred in Calais in favour of the eight-hour day, at a time when lacemakers still toiled more than twelve hours, and the Amalgamated Society of Lace Makers supported the strike. Three years earlier, in 1897, the Calais lacemakers supported the Nottingham mechanics.[150] In the heyday of labour internationalism, the practices that had been initiated in the 1860s were now pursued with more organisation, commitment, and force.

[150] Michel Caron, *Trois âges d'or de la dentelle. Calais, 1860–1905*, Roubaix, p. 57; Magali Domain, 'Jaurès et la grève des tullistes calaisiens (12 novembre 1900–7 février 1901)', *Cahiers Jaurès*, 2014/1, no. 211, pp. 53–75; Nicolas Delalande, *La Lutte et l'entraide. L'Âge des solidarités ouvrières*, Paris, 2019, pp. 187–9.

6

'À bas les Anglais!'

Integration and Rejection

The destiny of John Leavers (1786–1848) is odd.[1] On the one hand, his name is famous worldwide: the Leavers, by far the best lace machines, were sold from the early nineteenth century until the 1960s. Leavers lace received a prize at the Brussels International Exhibition in 1910. At the zenith of the industry after World War I, around 2,000 Leavers machines in Britain and 2,400 in France were recorded.[2] By 1947, there were still, in the United States alone, 730 Leavers machines in fifty-four factories employing 5,000 workers.[3] And if the technology is now outdated, a few firms, including Cluny Lace in Ilkeston, UK, still produce Leavers lace, a luxury item. At the same time, John Leavers himself is an unknown figure. Neither the *Oxford Dictionary of National Biography* nor even Wikipedia has an entry on him. Not much is known about him, in Nottingham or elsewhere. There is even more uncertainty about what he looked like (Figures 6.3 and 6.4). Let us try and find his trace, through the billions of meshes that have been knitted by the machines that bore his name.

John Leavers was born John Levers in 1786 at Sutton-in-Ashfield, in Nottinghamshire, to John Levers and his wife Ann, née Walker.[4] He had two brothers and a sister: Joseph Levers (born c.1796, who married Anne Mila in 1815), a lacemaker and lace mechanic; Mary Levers (born 1797), a lace runner; and Thomas Levers (born 5 December 1800 in Nottingham), a machine-maker. Little is known about the early part of his life in Nottinghamshire, which was the heart of the English hosiery industry, and where machine-made lace first developed, as we have seen. Historiography has insisted on the upward social mobility afforded by the industrial revolution when many inventors from a humble background made a fortune. In fact, most inventors hailed from an artisan,

---

[1] The quote in this chapter's title is from TNA, FO 146 350. Letter of the consul in Calais to Palmerston, Foreign Secretary, 21 March 1848, on the cries heard in Calais.

[2] D. E. Varley, *A History of the Midland Counties Lace Manufacturers' Association, 1915–1958*, Long Eaton, 1959, p. 113.

[3] Vittoria Rosatto, *Leavers Lace: A Handbook of the American Leavers Lace Industry*, Providence, RI, 1948, p. 15.

[4] He was christened on 12 March 1786. Baptism Register of Sutton-in-Ashfield, deposited in the Southwell Diocesan Record Office, County House, Nottingham. In the registers of Grand-Couronne, Leavers was said to be thirty-seven in July 1821 (i.e. two years' error), but was indeed thirty-nine on 1 February 1826, and sixty-two and a half when he died in September 1848.

Artisans Abroad: British Migrant Workers in Industrialising Europe, 1815–1870. Fabrice Bensimon, Oxford University Press.
© Fabrice Bensimon 2023. DOI: 10.1093/oso/9780198835844.003.0007

manufacturing, professional, or well-off background.[5] John Heathcoat, who had
patented the 'Old Loughborough', became very wealthy during this era. The first
historian of machine-made lace, William Felkin, insisted on the fact that Leavers,
himself a 'frame smith and setter up', thanks to his 'mechanical genius and skill',
which 'proved to be very great, as was shewn by the extraordinary results', had
improved Heathcoat's machine in 1813–14.[6] The improvement, upon which
Leavers had worked 'secretly' in a garret on the edge of Nottingham, made it
possible to produce good-quality machine-made lace in great quantity, with
bobbins 'as thin as requisite' (less than one millimetre each) and in one tier. For
reasons that remain unclear, neither Leavers nor his client patented the improvements. Leavers worked in another workshop where he improved his machine
again and built several each year. Felkin did not know Leavers personally but
relied on first-hand evidence to describe him as

> a friendly, kind-hearted man, and a great politician; fond of company and song,
> being himself band-master of the local militia, in which also one of his brothers
> was a member...A free-liver and irregular in his application to his business.
> He sometimes worked day and night if a mechanical idea or contrivance struck
> him, and would then quit all labour for days of enjoyment with chosen boon
> companions.[7]

In retrospect, Felkin insisted on the discrepancy between Leavers's inventiveness,
his machine being 'by far the most delicate',[8] and his financial misfortune:

> By his invention, he was in reality greatly assisting to lay the foundation of the
> machine lace trade, the annual English transactions have at times amounted to
> £5,000,000, and of which the share arising from the adaptations of Levers'
> beautiful machine, has not been less than £3,000,000 a-year. By the exercise of
> self-command, energy, and even a moderate amount of ambition, Levers'
> advance to eminence and fortune was inevitably secure. But stimulants at the
> work-bench by day, and each evening the acknowledged supremacy amongst his
> brother mechanicians and politicians, stole away his incomings and energies
> together, so that he was not unfrequently without a sixpence, and had to borrow
> the money wherewith to purchase the next morning's supply for his family.[9]

---

[5] Donald Cardwell, *The Development of Science and Technology in Nineteenth-Century Britain*,
Farnham, 2003; B. Zorina Khan and Kenneth Sokoloff, 'The Evolution of Useful Knowledge: Great
Inventors, Science and Technology in British Economic Development, 1750–1930', Working Papers
7005, Economic History Society, 2007.
[6] William Felkin, *A History of the Machine-Wrought Hosiery and Lace Manufactures*, London, 1867,
p. 271.
[7] Ibid., pp. 274–5.   [8] Ibid., p. 277.   [9] Ibid., p. 275.

In the early days of the industrial revolution, such a gap was not uncommon: the wealthiest factory owners were not always the most talented ones, but those who had made the greatest profit based on the mechanical skills of others. However, some caution is needed in accepting Felkin's account: he was a staunch evangelical, always ready to castigate artisans who went to the public house after the long hours at the stocking frame and early lace machines. The chapels were the alternative for men like Heathcoat, whom Felkin, the son of a Baptist preacher, admired without reservation.

In 1821, the Levers brothers (John, Joseph, Thomas), their sister Mary, their mother, John's and Joseph's wives and Mary's future husband, and possibly other members of the family emigrated to Grand-Couronne (Seine-Inférieure) in France. On 10 July 1821, Mary married 'Jean Sallis', a Nottingham-born mechanic.[10] The 'Levers' then became the 'Leavers', probably for phonetic reasons. But while in the local registers John was called 'Jean', his first name being typically Frenchified, he now signed 'John Leavers' (Figure 6.1). The reasons for this family departure, at a time when emigration was still not legal for artisans from Britain, are not documented, but several hypotheses can be put forward. John, aged thirty-five, was a brilliant artisan and a recognised inventor, but he had scarcely benefited from the unprecedented boom of machine-made lace in Britain. It seems that Heathcoat's monopoly on bobbin lace played its part in this.[11] The first historian of French lace, Samuel Ferguson, wrote that Heathcoat and Lacey 'prosecuted so much those who used [their frame] without a patent that the three Leavers, who were peaceful by nature, and more musicians than lawyers, left Nottingham c. 1821'.[12] In the early 1820s, departures from the Nottingham area to France, Calais especially, were multiplying, as we have seen. In 1824, framework knitter, lace maker and trade-unionist Gravener Henson, returning from a tour in France, and giving evidence to a parliamentary committee, mentioned that Leavers was 'now in Grande Carron [sic], near Rouen', a place that Henson had not visited.[13] The presence in Grand-Couronne of several other British artisans suggests that the Leavers kept ties with their native region, as many migrants did. One of Leavers's nephews, John, remained in Nottingham where he worked as a lace mechanic in the 1820s and 1830s.

Why did the Leavers go to Grand-Couronne, rather than Calais, which was the main centre of French lacemaking? Grand-Couronne is located on the river Seine,

---

[10] Sallis was born on 30 January 1798. État-civil de Grand-Couronne.

[11] Felkin, *A History of the Machine-Wrought Hosiery*, p. 275.

[12] 'Ils poussèrent si loin leurs poursuites contre ceux qui s'en servaient sans licence, que les trois Leaver, qui étaient d'une nature pacifique, et plus musiciens que plaideurs, quittèrent Nottingham, vers 1821, pour la Grande-Couronne, près de Rouen, où ils établirent des métiers de leur système pour le compte de M. Lefort, récemment décédé', Samuel Ferguson fils, *Histoire du tulle et des dentelles mécaniques en Angleterre et en France*, Paris, 1862, p. 92.

[13] PP. *Report from the Select Committee on Artizans and Machinery*, 1824; Gravener Henson, 23 March 1824, p. 274.

some 6 miles downstream from Rouen, which was then the centre of a dynamic cotton and wool manufacturing industry, but mostly still a cottage industry. Between 1815 and 1817, a Norman entrepreneur, Chauvel, had created a lace workshop in Grand-Couronne. One of his partners, Louis-Paul Lefort, often went to England for bleaching, and there met the Leavers whom he hired, which was common practice.[14] When Chauvel died in 1827, his workshop was taken over by Lefort, then twenty-four, who turned the workshop into a factory. John and Thomas Leavers then played a key part in the development of the factory. In 1833, they patented a new frame for ten years in France (Figure 6.1).[15]

Figure 6.1 A frame patented in 1833. John Leavers's signature can be seen below the design (Archives du Conservatoire des arts et métiers. Métier Leavers breveté en 1833. Planche no. 1).

[14] Ferguson, *Histoire du tulle et des dentelles mécaniques*, p. 92; Lefort is mentioned by Felkin as 'M. Le Forte' (*A History of the Machine-Wrought Hosiery*, p. 276); Georges Dubosc, 'Une industrie peu connue: la fabrique de tulle de Grand-Couronne', *Journal de Rouen*, 31 December 1907.

[15] Métier Leavers breveté en 1833. Archives du Conservatoire des arts et métiers. Sheila Mason (*Nottingham Lace, 1760s–1950s*, p. 46, n. 44) mentioned patent 6423 of Louis Paul Lefort, 1833. Ministère du commerce, *Catalogue des brevets d'invention*, Paris, 1843, p. 524. Leavers is described in it as a 'fabricant de tulle à Grand-Couronne' (lace manufacturer).

It seems that in the 1830s, the technical reputation of Leavers, who ran the factory, was established.[16] The departmental jury for the Exposition publique nationale des produits de l'industrie et de l'agriculture (Public National Exhibition of the Produce of Industry and Agriculture) noted in 1834:

> The works of Mister Lefort, run by Mister Leavers, is one of those the jury of the department of Seine-Inférieure is happy to introduce to the central jury, as worth its attention for the great improvement in the making of net by circular frames, which has gained even more importance thanks to the changes made by Mister Leavers.[17]

In 1839, the same jury stated:

> This manufacturer, whose reputation for this type of produce has been made, manages frames that deliver large quantities of lace at prices worthwhile for consumers.

> Mister Leavers who runs this works is a distinguished artist to whom great improvements to the frames imported from England are owed, and who skilfully makes them rival the best frames. The imitation of Mechlin lace and Brussels lace is a fortunate result of the system produced by Mister Leavers which has been patented. The beauty and the relative solidity of these products justify all the valuable thoughts of the jury on them.[18]

It is very likely that the Leavers kept on working for Lefort until the 1840s. In the 1836 and 1841 censuses, 'Jean Leavers' was still listed as a mechanic. The Leavers frame, now combined with the Jacquard system, was very successful. However, Grand-Couronne did not ensure Leavers the wealth he had failed to get in Britain. In 1831, he was admittedly listed among the 105 people who qualified for the vote

---

[16] In 1835, a patent was delivered to 'Messrs Leavers and Houston' ('MM. Leavers et Houston'), 32 route de Caen in Rouen, for a 'new kind of steam engine appropriate for fire engines' ('un nouveau genre de Boite à Vapeur propre aux Pompes à Feu'). However, it is not proven that this Leavers was a member of the same family (Claude Pouillet, *Portefeuille industriel du Conservatoire des arts et métiers*, Paris, 1836, p. 41).

[17] 'L'établissement de Monsieur Lefort, dirigé par Monsieur Leavers, est un de ceux que le jury du département de Seine-Inférieure se plait à présenter au jury central, comme digne de son attention la grande amélioration, introduite dans la fabrique des tulles par les métiers à rotation, a acquise encore plus d'importance par les modifications qu'y a apportées Monsieur Leavers'. AD Seine-Maritime. 8 M 40. Annotations du jury départemental, 1834.

[18] 'Ce fabricant, dont la réputation est faite pour ce genre de produit, a en activité des métiers qui livrent à la consommation de grandes quantités de tulle dans des prix avantageux aux consommateurs. Monsieur Leavers qui dirige cet établissement est un artiste distingué à qui on doit de grandes améliorations aux métiers emportés d'Angleterre et qui les fait habilement rivaliser avec les meilleurs métiers. L'imitation des points de Malines et Bruxelles est un heureux résultat obtenu par le système de Monsieur Leavers qui a été breveté. La beauté et la solidité relative de ces produits justifient tout ce que le jury en pense d'avantageux'. AD Seine-Maritime, 8 M40, Annotations du jury départemental, 1839.

in the village (which then numbered about 1,100), but in a modest eighty-ninth position, behind many farmers and shopkeepers.

In 1813 in Nottingham, John had married Hannah Wheeldon, who was born c.1784.[19] It seems that they had no children. Hannah came with him to France and died in Grand-Couronne on 25 July 1824. On 1 February 1826, the widowed Leavers married Françoise Massiotty, thirty-four, who was born in Brussels, the natural daughter of a Belgian woman, and who lived in Grand-Couronne, where he probably met her.[20] Three of the witnesses to the wedding were lace mechanics. John had at least four children with Françoise: Guillaume Jean, born on 5 November 1826 in Grand-Couronne, Saara Elisabeth, born c.1828, Edouard Alphonse, born c.1829, and Marie Stéphanie Ambroise, born on 4 April 1835—John was then forty-eight and Françoise forty-three.[21] In 1836 and 1841, the couple housed the four children as well as a nephew, Jean Sallis (Figure 6.2).[22] Jean Sallis was most likely one of John's sister Mary's children—she had died on 17 April 1822 giving birth to twins.[23]

Even if sources are scarce, the Leavers seem to have been fully accepted in the local community. By the mid-1830s, they remained the only British family in a

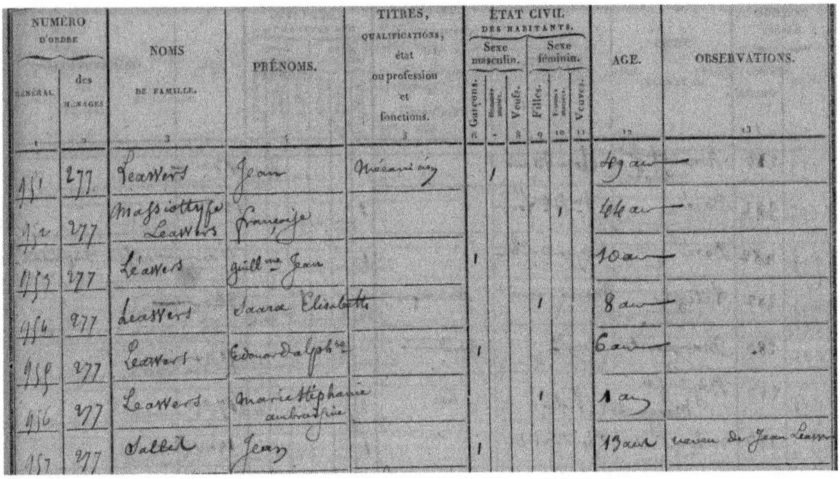

Numéro d'ordre général	des ménages	Noms de famille	Prénoms	Titres, qualifications, état ou profession et fonctions	Garçons	Hommes mariés	Veufs	Filles	Femmes mariées	Veuves	Age	Observations
151	277	Leavers	Jean	Mécanicien		1					49 ans	
152	277	Massiotty femme Leavers	Françoise						1		44 ans	
153	277	Leavers	guill^me Jean		1						10 ans	
154	277	Leavers	Saara Elisabeth					1			8 ans	
155	277	Leavers	Edouard alphonse		1						6 ans	
156	277	Leavers	marie Stéphanie ambroise					1			1 an	
157	277	Sallet	Jean		1						13 ans	neveu de Jean Leavers

Figure 6.2 The Leavers family in 1836 in Grand-Couronne, including his wife Françoise Massiotty, their four young children, and John's nephew, 'Jean Sallis'. 'Jean Leavers' is listed as a mechanic (AD Seine-Maritime. 6M0004. Recensement de 1836. Grand-Couronne p. 41).

[19] Marriages. *Nottingham Gazette*, 3 December 1813.

[20] AD Seine-Maritime. $2^{E}3$ 163. Contrat de mariage. 29 janvier 1826. Lefèvre notaire.

[21] État-civil de Grand-Couronne (Seine-Maritime).

[22] AD Seine-Maritime. 6M0004. Recensement de 1836. Grand-Couronne (p. 41). See also AD Seine-Maritime. 6M0046. Recensement de 1841. Grand-Couronne (p. 18).

[23] État-civil de Grand-Couronne.

village which only boasted a handful of foreigners. In 1848, when riots targeting British workers occurred in Rouen, John Leavers and his family escaped injury. By 1838, Joseph Leavers was the chair of a friendly society based in Rouen, the 'British benefit of society': for a franc a month, members could get 14 francs a week in case of illness, and their families got 100 francs for their burials. This apolitical society was sponsored by the vice-consul and the pastor of the Reformed Church in Rouen: 'Politics, profane language, or the introduction of any subject foreign to the business of the Meeting shall be strictly prohibited'.[24] In 1848, the Leavers brothers created the Société musicale de Grand-Couronne.[25] Little is known about this early local club, except that it took part in regional competitions in the following years.[26] The talents of the Leavers, 'more musicians than lawyers', were deep-rooted, Felkin noted, since in Nottingham Leavers had been a master in the band of the local militia.[27]

On 24 September 1848, 'Jean Leavers, 62 ans et demi', died in Grand-Couronne.[28] A Nottingham paper reported his death, probably based on information from a member of the family. He was remembered as the 'sole inventor of the Leavers machine', and the obituary mentioned his being a 'band master to the National Guards'; this earned him military honours for his funeral, which was attended by the mayor and guards of his regiment.[29]

After their sibling's death, the trace of John's brothers vanishes. While they appear to have left Grand-Couronne, John's widow and their children remained there for a while.[30] In 1912, when the municipality had to name local roads, a street was named 'Jean Leavers' to honour him. Calais (since 1883) and Caudry, which both built their fortunes on lace machines, also have their 'rue Leavers' (see p. 248). If John Leavers thus still features in the history of French lacemaking cities, he is largely forgotten in Nottingham, the world capital of machine-made lace, except for a grey plaque on the site of the house in which he lived in 1813, in St Helen's Street, Canning Circus. Leavers's fall into obscurity belies the fact that Victorian

---

[24] AD Seine-Maritime. 4X 207. Association des ouvriers anglais. Sociétés de secours mutuel. *Articles of the British benefit society of Rouen and its environs; authorised by the minister of the Interior and the prefet of the department of the Seine-Inférieure*, 1838, Paris, 16 pp.

[25] AD Seine-Maritime. 4M 460. Sociétés de musique.

[26] Société d'histoire de Grand-Couronne, *Le frais et charmant village de Grand-Couronne. Une commune rurale à l'aube du XXe siècle (1890–1914)*, Grand-Couronne, 1997.

[27] Felkin, *A History of the Machine-Wrought Hosiery*, pp. 274–5.

[28] État-civil de Grand-Couronne.

[29] 'DIED. On the 24th of September last, at Grand Corrounne [sic], near Rouen, France, Mr. John Leavers, aged 62: he was sole inventor of the Leavers machine, and resided formerly on Sion-hill, New Radford. He was band master to the National Guards, and was attended with military honors to his grave, by the mayor and National Guards of his regiment; and was honored and respected by all who knew him'. *Nottingham Review*, 6 October 1848, p. 3.

[30] AD Seine-Maritime. Recensement de 1851. Grand-Couronne, p. 34. Françoise Leavers née Massioty, aged fifty-four, is listed as 'fabricant' (manufacturer) and lived with Guillaume Jean (twenty-four), Saarah Elizabeth (twenty-three) and Edouard Alphonse (twenty-one). Marie, who would have been sixteen, is not mentioned.

society generally celebrated inventors, who had generated so much wealth for the country and who were national heroes in the same vein as political leaders and military chiefs. Inventors were now famous figures, like James Watt, whose statue was erected at Westminster Abbey in 1834. In his best-selling *Self-Help* (1859), Samuel Smiles drew a hagiographical portrait of John Heathcoat, who had become a wealthy capitalist and a Liberal MP, but he did not mention Leavers. As for Felkin, who was close to Heathcoat, he insisted on 'the almost entire forgetfulness in which his memory [was] now enveloped', despite his mechanical genius.[31] And even today's historical literature ignores Leavers.[32] In contrast, Heathcoat is a local celebrity in Tiverton and, thanks to the efforts of Smiles and Felkin, in the manufacturing history of the country, whereas Leavers is only mentioned in specialised works.[33] The contrast between both legacies can be explained by the differing fortunes the two men accrued, but it was also due to the emigration of Leavers who, when he left, withdrew from a British technical pantheon which was then in the making, without really entering the French one. After his death, John Leavers became as anonymous as his invention was famous.

What did John Leavers (1786–1848) look like? There are two known portraits, and one at least is not of him. The first is a glamorous portrait (Figure 6.3) which was donated in 1970 to the Nottingham Castle Museum and Art Gallery, who have identified Sylvanus Redgate (1827–1907), who painted several portraits of Nottingham notables, as the artist. The second portrait is part of a set of two miniatures (Figures 6.4 and 6.5), one supposedly of John Leavers and the other of his second wife, Françoise Massiotty, posing as if facing each other. The miniatures made of painted ivory with a lead frame are more modest than the portrait. Both miniatures are in the hands of descendants of John Leavers who live in Seine-Maritime and firmly believe them to represent their glorious ancestor and his second wife. So, which one is John Leavers? No first-hand evidence can give a clue. From a historical viewpoint, the modest miniature made in France makes more sense than the glamorous portrait made in Nottingham: John Leavers was not rich, and the Nottingham press did not mention him either after he left in 1821, which suggests that he did not spend long periods there after emigrating. But the portraits are still shrouded in mystery.

In France, John Leavers was as integrated a migrant as one could be. He worked for a French manufacturer in whose company he obviously secured a prominent

[31] Felkin, *A History of the Machine-Wrought Hosiery and Lace Manufactures*, p. 276.

[32] E.g. Christine MacLeod, *Heroes of Invention: Technology, Liberalism and British Identity, 1750–1914*, Cambridge, 2007.

[33] Sheila Mason, *Nottingham Lace 1760s–1950s: The Machine-Made Lace Industry in Nottinghamshire, Derbyshire and Leicestershire*, Stroud, 2010 [1994]; Stanley. D. Chapman, 'The Life and Work of William Felkin (1795–1874)', in Felkin, *A History of the Machine-Wrought Hosiery and Lace Manufactures*, pp. v–xxxviii; S. D. Chapman, 'Felkin, William (1795–1874)', *ODNB*, Oxford, 2004; Roy A. Church, *Economic and Social Change in a Midland Town: Victorian Nottingham 1815–1900*, London, 1966.

Figure 6.3 John Leavers—oil on canvas (76.2×63.5 cm). Nottingham Castle Museum and Art Gallery (NCM 1970-109).

position, while his mechanical skills were acknowledged across the country. He married a local woman and had several children with her. He was involved in the local community, and when he died, he was buried with local honours. How representative was his case and that of his brothers? How did British migrant workers interact with the local populations? Were they mostly welcomed, rejected, or just treated on a par with other workers? This is a complex issue, and no single answer can be offered. We have seen that in many circumstances, British workers had a role in the local community, as John Leavers did. They worked in workshops with other workers of different nationalities, they lived in the same streets and houses as fellow French workers, and many migrant workers even married local people, as was the case in Calais where male lace workers married women from the area. In linen, it was not uncommon for Scottish and Irish women to marry local men and it even seems that some itinerant workers occasionally married local women. However, on several occasions, British migrant workers were specifically targeted for abuse because of their nationality. Such incidents may challenge our understanding of the sociability and solidarity that existed between workers of different nationalities. Still, episodes of conflict and confrontation,

Figures. 6.4 and 6.5 John Leavers and Françoise Leavers née Massiotty, c.1826—painted China miniatures—private collection of Bénédicte Meurice and Carmen Molins.

especially in 1848, did occur, and this chapter aims to address them, disturbing though they may be.

In studies of collective protests against foreigners in France, those targeting the British occupy a somewhat marginal place, commensurate with their relative neglect in the history of immigration to the country. The works of Michelle Perrot, Gérard Noiriel, Laurent Dornel, and Bastien Cabot focus on the period of greatest intensity, the 1880s and 1890s, when dozens of foreign workers were killed, and possibly thousands had to leave.[34] However, the golden age of British labour immigration spanned the period from 1815 to the fall of the July Monarchy in 1848, a period which has received less attention from historians of social conflict between workers; the main source on the topic is Pierre-Jacques

---

[34] Michelle Perrot, 'Les rapports entre ouvriers français et étrangers (1871–1893)', *Bulletin de la Société d'histoire moderne*, 1960, pp. 4–9; Laurent Dornel, *La France hostile. Socio-histoire de la xénophobie (1870–1914)*, Paris, 2004; Gérard Noiriel, *État, nation, immigration. Vers une histoire du pouvoir*, Paris, 2001; Gérard Noiriel, *Le massacre des Italiens: Aigues-Mortes, 17 août 1893*, Paris, 2010; Bastien Cabot, 'À bas les Belges!'. *L'expulsion des mineurs borains (Lens, août-septembre 1892)*, Rennes, 2017; Delphine Diaz and Hugo Vermeren (dir.), 'Éloigner et expulser les étrangers au xixe siècle', special issue of *Diasporas. Circulations, migrations, histoire*, no 33, 2019.

Figures. 6.4 and 6.5 Continued

Derainne's unpublished PhD.[35] In addition, while migrants from Belgium, Italy, or Germany mainly provided low-skilled and cheap labour, the British were largely skilled migrants, as we have seen, sometimes well paid, especially in metallurgy, and most had come to the Continent on a temporary basis. The fact they often did not settle may also explain the relative paucity of studies.[36]

British workers could be subject to hostility and even targeted in riots. This was particularly the case during the broader upheavals of 1848. Such outbursts of animosity towards British workers, without any apparent link between them, are perplexing. How can we account for the fact that these workers were targeted by others, whose work and neighbourhood they shared? What motivated these actions at a time when the second Republic had just been proclaimed and the

---

[35] Pierre-Jacques Derainne, *Le travail, les migrations et les conflits en France. Représentations et attitudes sociales sous la monarchie de Juillet et la seconde République*, thesis under the direction of Serge Wolikow, Université de Bourgogne, 1998–9.

[36] Fabrice Bensimon, 'British Workers in France, 1815–1848', *Past and Present*, no. 213, November 2011, pp. 147–89.

brotherhood of peoples was being widely celebrated? These events must be understood both in the *longue durée* and in terms of the immediate industrial crisis and February revolution. The cases used for study in the following section highlight some similarities in the nature of such attacks and the way they were justified by perpetrators, but also show that many incidents were isolated or had specific characteristics which do not indicate a broader trend. Here we will focus on a few documented cases, to try and make sense of these manifestations of hostility towards fellow-workers. The sources, while contradictory, are relatively abundant since such riots appear to have alarmed the authorities, sometimes on both sides of the Channel. In addition to the local press, which often covered the topic extensively, the police and justice archives, as well as consular archives, contain evidence of these incidents. Yet, as these sources do, they also raise problems of their own. The next section of the chapter starts with a review of incidents over the 1815–48 period; that is, the Restoration and the July Monarchy (section 1). It then focuses on different 'riots'/protests against the British in 1848 which can be viewed as a flashpoint of xenophobia (section 2), including the flax workers at La Foudre (section 3) and the Calais lacemakers (section 4), before trying to make sense of these collective actions (section 5).

1. 1815–48: An Imperfect Integration?

In this period, as we have seen, thousands of British workers and technicians worked in France, mainly in the north: Picardy, Normandy, Brittany, and Paris. There is evidence of daily interactions between British migrants and other work- ers, and we know that in many circumstances British migrant workers worked alongside French workers and migrants of other nationalities. It is also clear that many married French people, and usually had French witnesses at their wedding ceremonies. All of those who stayed settled into the local community and were accepted in French society. Many young British workers, both male and female, married local people, often their workmates, although they usually had to convert to Catholicism (see p. 155). When, for example, a lethal tornado struck Montville near Rouen on 19 August 1845, killing seventy-five, the local press celebrated the navvies, while the mayor praised in his report 'some brave Englishmen, employed in the building of the railway to Le Havre' who had 'been as zealous and courageous as the French workers' in the rescue operations.[37]

However, despite such evidence of harmonious communal living, the relation- ship between British migrants and the local population should not be idealised,

---

[37] 'Quelques braves anglais, employés aux travaux du chemin de fer du Havre; ils ont rivalisé de zèle et de courage avec les travailleurs français', B . . ., Maire de Monville, au préfet, 29 août 1845, in Placide Alexandre, *La Trombe de Monville et de Malaunay. 1845*, Rouen, 1920, p. 59.

since a variety of xenophobic incidents took place across this period. People working together or having a drink, getting into an argument, and eventually throwing xenophobic insults at each other is nothing new. Some incidents were benign and did not lead to violence, while others, as in 1848, could be far more dramatic. After all, despite the advent of peace and some 'cordial understanding' between the states/nations of Britain and France from the 1830s onwards, the Napoleonic Empire loomed large in national memory. In the 1840s there were also several episodes of colonial tension such as the Pritchard affair in Tahiti in 1844. National pride could easily be offended, and xenophobia had not vanished in the intervening period since the end of the war. To illustrate this, we could point to one incident which exercised the local authorities. On 11 May 1842 the préfet of Eure was alerted to the fact that a meal had been organised by British workers building the railroad at a British innkeeper's in Villers-sur-le-Roule (Eure). The mayor and the sous-préfet feared the repercussions of 'letting the Union Jack float in France, on the rumours this would cause, on the brawl that could result'.[38] The préfet soon concurred that the event represented a risk to public order. But the public works engineer, a Frenchman named Lemoine, protested that banning the dinner 'could result in trouble instead of preventing it', arguing that the British workers had hoisted French colours on May Day, and that there was 'neither rivalry, nor opposition' in hoisting theirs.[39] The sous-préfet himself admitted that 'the colours of a nation at peace with us could be seen without any inconvenience in Villers, as they were on the ships in the port of Rouen'.[40] The meal was eventually held in an orderly manner with 150 workers in attendance, and 'the French flag was hoisted, as a badge of unity'.[41]

In Paris, where foreigners were proportionately numerous, a rare source is available to historians. Every day, the Paris police chief sent a report to the Minister of the Interior, the 'Bulletin de Paris'.[42] Several thousand reports were drafted, from 1819 to 1848, primarily focused on workers, furnished houses, the pawnshops, games, general surveillance, foreigners, and so on. Jacques Grandjonc analysed this series and reported in total six incidents against foreigners, a comparatively low figure.[43] British workers were targeted on two of these occasions.

---

[38] 'À laisser flotter le drapeau anglais en France, sur les rumeurs que cela causera, sur les rixes qui peuvent s'en suivre'. Lettre du sous-préfet de Louviers au préfet, 11 mai 1842; A.D. Eure, 1M 243. Surveillance de l'ordre et de l'esprit public sous la monarchie de Juillet, 1842.
[39] 'La crois de nature à susciter des embarras au lieu de les prévenir'.
[40] 'L'on pouvait sans inconvénient voir à Villers les couleurs d'une nation qui est en paix avec nous, comme on les voit par exemple sur les navires du port de Rouen'.
[41] 'Il y a eu repas et tir de pigeon. 150 ouvriers étaient de la fête. Le drapeau français avait été arboré comme signe de réunion, tout s'est bien passé avec un ordre parfait'.
[42] Archives nationales, Bulletin de Paris, F/7/3874 à F/7/3893.
[43] Jacques Grandjonc, 'Les étrangers à Paris sous la monarchie de Juillet et la Seconde République', in *Population*, vol. a.29, special issue, March 1974, pp. 61–88.

IMPRIMERIE IMPÉRIALE. — Salle des presses mécaniques.

Figure 6.6 The room of mechanical presses in the imperial print, in 1860 ('Imprimerie impériale. Salle des presses mécaniques'. Turgan, *Les Grandes usines*, vol. 1, Paris, 1860, p. 104).

In 1830, a series of incidents, which François Jarrige has charted, occurred in the printing sector in the wake of the Trois Glorieuses.[44] On 29 July, at the height of the uprising, mechanical presses, then made in Britain, from nine printing plants and the Royal Printing House were destroyed by workers (Figure 6.6). The following day, the provisional government posted a poster 'urging workers not to destroy the mechanical presses anymore'.[45] On 14 August, an ordinance provided for the reinstatement of mechanical presses at the Imprimerie Royale and, on 2 September, this ordinance was inserted in the 'Bulletin des Lois', again prompting protests by typographic workers, 2,000 to 3,000 of whom gathered at the gates of the city.[46] They elected a commission tasked with relaying the workers' demands and which '[undertook] and [urged] their colleagues not to work in the houses where machines are in operation'.[47] The authorities soon dispatched troops to monitor the main printing plants. On 7 September, the préfet wrote:

[44] François Jarrige, *Au temps des 'tueuses de bras'. Les bris de machines à l'aube de l'ère industrielle (1780–1860)*, Rennes, 2009, pp. 91–3.
[45] 'Engageant les ouvriers à ne plus détruire les presses mécaniques'. 'Avis contre la destruction des presses mécaniques', in P. Chauvet, *Les Ouvriers du livre en France de 1789 à la constitution de la fédération du livre*, Paris, 1964, ch. 4. Quoted by Jarrige, *Au temps des 'tueuses de bras'*, p. 92, whom we're following here.
[46] AN, F/7/3884: bulletin de police, 1830.
[47] 'S'engage et engage ses confrères à ne pas travailler dans les maisons où des mécaniques seraient en activité'. Bibliothèque historique de la Ville de Paris (Na 154), papiers Odilon Barrot. Proclamation de la commission typographique, feuille imprimée, s.d.

There are no signs of restlessness among the typographers. Yesterday morning, however, the English compositors did not dare to print Galignany's Messenger. Mr. Galignany himself begged the printer, Mr. Delaforest, to use hand presses, but this example of condescension could have had unfortunate results; the authority opposed Mr Galignany's request, the English workers returned to their mechanical presses and no one thought of disturbing them. It was the same elsewhere. The royal printing works have resumed their usual activity and I do not know that the composition of the newspapers has experienced any obstacle.[48]

By the 9th, the incidents were over and the eight printers of the typographers' commission were due to be prosecuted for gathering for illegal purposes. The attacks seem to have had less to do with workers' Anglophobia than with machine breaking, though the fact remains that the machines themselves were British. As a matter of fact, Charles Manby Smith, who worked for Galignani from 1826 to 1830, did not point out any animosity between nationalities in his memoirs (see pp. 138–41).

Another incident reported by the head of the Paris police occurred at the Charenton ironworks in May 1837 and centred on the question of wages:

The French workers of the Charenton ironworks today threatened the English workers of the same factory to bully them, because of some inequalities in the hours of work. Quarry workers from the surroundings and founders from Paris, have added to the already very considerable number of French workers. Some preventative measures prevented a collision, and the order was not disturbed.[49]

Wage inequality between workers of different nationalities was indeed a bone of contention, as we shall see in other circumstances. However, all in all, the Anglophobic incidents in Paris and its surroundings seem to have been, during this period, few and far between.

---

[48] 'Aucun symptôme d'agitation ne se manifeste parmi les ouvriers typographes. Hier matin, néanmoins, les compositeurs anglais n'osaient point imprimer le Galignany's Messenger. Mr Galignany lui-même priait l'imprimeur, Mr Delaforest, de se servir de presses à bras, mais cet exemple de condescendance eût pu avoir de fâcheux résultats; l'autorité s'est opposée à la demande de Mr Galignany, les ouvriers anglais se sont remis à leurs presses mécaniques & personne n'a songé à les troubler. Il en a été de même ailleurs. Les travaux de l'imprimerie royale ont repris leur activité accoutumée et je ne sache pas que la composition des journaux ait éprouvé le moindre obstacle'. Archives Nationales, Bulletin de Paris, F/7/3884. 7 September 1830.

[49] 'Les ouvriers français des forges de Charenton ont menacé aujourd'hui les ouvriers anglais de la même manufacture de leur faire un mauvais parti, à cause de quelques inégalités dans les heures de travail. Des ouvriers carriers venus des environs et des fondeurs de Paris, ont grossi le nombre déjà très considérable des ouvriers français; quelques dispositions préventives ont prévenu toute collision, et l'ordre n'a pas été troublé'. Archives nationales, Bulletin de Paris, F/7/3889, 17 July 1837.

More violent episodes took place in the provinces. In Fourchambault, riots occurred on 15, 19, and 20 August 1837 against British blacksmiths. According to ironmaster Dufaud and the king's prosecutor in Nevers the French workers were convinced that the British were receiving preferential treatment. A brawl began at the foundry, resumed in a tavern, and two British workers were soon threatened and chased, the hostility against them extending to 'those who refused to deliver them defenseless to their enemies'. A woman named Gardiennent testified that 'she and her husband were threatened *with bleeding like pigs* if they were *to receive wolves* (Englishmen)'.[50] On 19 August, the authorities reported that 'the exasperation was brought to its peak' and, from a group of workers, 'escaped words such as these: "I will kill an Englishman, I will kill two"'.[51] 'Two houses inhabited by foreigners were besieged', the manager of the forge reported, 'all the windows were broken and one of the English workers was stabbed in the arm. They even announced the intention to kill the other'.[52] On the morning of 20 August, the troops arrived and seven men were arrested. The locals successfully negotiated for the right to escort the men themselves—rather than have the gendarmes take them—to Nevers, where they were to be incarcerated. Quiet was thus restored in Fourchambault.[53] The 'English' workers targeted in the incident were actually from South Wales and usually had better wages because they were more productive than their French counterparts (see pp. 47–53). Wage inequality was a common reason for hostility towards foreigners.

In March 1844, during the building of the Paris–Le Havre line, in Maromme and Déville (Seine-Inférieure), workers made redundant by the factories in the neighbourhood gathered and 'demanded to be hired on the railway sites . . . They expressed great dissatisfaction that the English were employees while they are out of work'.[54] In this case as in others, it was the shortage of jobs that was at the root of the conflict. Local newspapers also reported brawls in rural communities along the construction site, between Irish, Scottish, and English workers, who, however, '[knew] how to make the sacred union on Sundays to go to fight with the young

---

[50] 'Ceux qui ont refusé de les livrer sans défense à leurs ennemis; témoin encore la femme Gardiennent qu'on a menacée, elle et son mari, de *saigner comme des cochons* s'ils s'avisaient de *recevoir des loups* (des anglais)'. AD Nièvre, 3 U5 1633. Rapport du procureur du roi, 27 August 1837. This document and others about this riot can be found in Guy Thuillier (ed.), *Les ouvriers des forges nivernaises. Vie quotidienne et pratiques sociales*, Paris, 2002.

[51] Le 19 août, rapportent les autorités, 'l'exaspération a été portée à son comble' et, d'un groupe d'ouvriers, 's'échappaient des propos tels que ceux-ci: "Moi, je tuerai un anglais, moi j'en tuerai deux"'. Ibid.

[52] 'Deux maisons habitées par les étrangers ont été assiégées, rapporte le directeur de la forge, toutes les fenêtres ont été brisées et l'un des ouvriers anglais a été blessé d'un coup de couteau au bras. Ils annonçaient même l'intention de tuer l'autre'. AD Nièvre, 22 F 6, Fonds Dufaud-Martin, Journal de Georges Dufaud.

[53] 'Troubles dans les départemens', *Le Siècle*, 27 August 1837; also see 'Assault on English Workmen in France', *Morning Post*, 27 September 1837, p. 2.

[54] *Norman Times*, 30 March 1844, p. 1.

Normans of Pays de Caux'.[55] In April 1845, a fight 'between English and French workers' was also reported.[56] In these sporadic incidents, latent xenophobia, ready to be tapped into, openly manifested itself.

In other circumstances, protests targeted those—business leaders, subcontractors, engineers, foremen—who were accused of introducing new machines that caused unemployment.[57] The rioting against British presses in Paris in 1830 has already been discussed. In a similar vein, in Montrouge, in 1842, during work on the city wall of Paris, French navvies stopped working when two British subcontractors used four pulley machines to mount the barrows of rubble, and they urged the twenty or so British excavators to join them.[58] In Elbeuf in May 1846, the arrival of an English mechanic hired by a sheet manufacturer to install a wool sorter provoked the anger of the women responsible for sorting wool in the home. The machine was attacked and the owner's house besieged before troops intervened and made thirty-three arrests.[59]

Apart from wage inequality and modern machinery resulting in job losses, two other motivations may have stirred anger against British workers. First, as historian David Todd has pointed out, 'economic nationalism' was strong under the July Monarchy, with influential advocates such as minister Adolphe Thiers, Roubaisian industrialist Auguste Mimerel, and engineer and economist Charles Dupin. Workers' newspapers like L'Atelier also defended economic Anglophobia. Men of the republican left such as Philippe Buchez, Louis Blanc, Proudhon, Pierre Leroux, and left-wing newspapers, Cabet's Populaire apart, were mainly protectionist and anti-English.[60] Second, under the July Monarchy, the employment of women in the textile industry was often a bone of contention among workers. As mentioned earlier, when, in 1847, Scottish female workers were hired by the Société linière du Finistère, located in Landerneau, L'Atelier was indignant (pp. 114–15). It had no correspondent on the ground and its comments were xenophobic and possibly misogynistic. While criticising the young workers, it also argued against the political economists, the free traders, and those who admired British manufacturing in France. Such arguments help us understand some of the ingredients of the collective anti-British protests that broke out in 1848.

---

[55] 'Savent faire l'union sacrée le dimanche pour aller en découdre avec les jeunes Normands du Pays de Caux', Journal du Havre, 17 October 1844, quoted in Jean Le Guen, '1847, l'arrivée du chemin de fer au Havre', Cahiers havrais de recherche historique, no. 54, 1995, p. 23.

[56] 'On annonce qu'une rixe vient d'éclater entre les ouvriers anglais et français occupés aux travaux du chemin de fer de Rouen au Havre. L'autorité aurait rétabli l'ordre'. Le Globe, 2 April 1845.

[57] Jarrige, Au temps des 'tueuses de bras'.

[58] Service historique de la Défense, E5 100, quoted in Derainne, 'Les perceptions sociales des travailleurs britanniques', p. 364.

[59] A substantial set of documents can be found in the Archives nationales, BB 18/1442. Also see Journal de Rouen, 23 May 1846.

[60] Derainne, Le travail, les migrations et les conflits en France; Bensimon, 'British Workers in France, 1815–1848'.

2. The Manufacturing Crisis, the 1848 Revolution, and Anglophobia

The main actions against the British took place after the revolutionary days of February 1848 and the fall of the July Monarchy. In Decazeville (Aveyron), Welsh iron workers and their families, thirty-eight people in total, were forced to leave.[61] In Paris, French servants organised against the employment of the British, heckling them and threatening to attack the horses of those who employed them. French coachmen promised to dislodge British ones from their cars.[62] Elsewhere, Anglophobia was expressed differently. The British consul in Granville (Manche) reported that the 'populace', assembled on the quay, prevented the loading of food towards England, because they were convinced that meat prices resulted from cattle exports.[63] A similar incident occurred in May in Calais, a city where anti-British demonstrations may also have occurred.[64] In Rouen, in March, Scottish and Irish flax workers were forced to leave, as discussed later. As early as 9 March, the issue of anti-British actions against migrant workers was raised in the House of Commons by Tory MP Augustus Stafford, who considered 'retaliation' against the French. Home Secretary George Grey was informed of the plight of the workers of La Foudre (see pp. 227–30) and he replied that 'the Government did not entertain the slightest notion of retaliation' but that the British ambassador had called on Lamartine, the French head of government, to 'prevent a repetition of similar scenes'.[65] By early April, such evictions, which were reported by the press, had become a public scandal. British newspapers were indignant:

Upwards of 500 English mechanics and workmen of different descriptions have arrived from France, since Sunday, many of them in a destitute state, without money, scarcely any clothing, and the loss of their tools, in consequence of the violence they have experienced from the combined French operatives who have made their masters and foremen completely submit to their will and cry 'A bas les Anglais!'... Others are quitting daily not only Paris but nearly every part of the country, as most serious disturbances are looked forward in the departments during the approaching elections from outbreaks of the populace and it is

---

[61] 'Expulsion of Welsh Workmen from France', *North Wales Chronicle* (Bangor), 16 May 1848, no. 1105.

[62] 'Antipathy to English Servants', *Hull Packet*, 17 March 1848, p. 6.

[63] TNA, FO 146 350. Letter of the Consul in Granville, John Turnbull, to Lord Normanby, British ambassador in Paris, 4 March 1848.

[64] 'Calais. Notre ville, si calme jusqu'ici, a été troublée mercredi dernier. Quelques groupes d'ouvriers ont essayé de s'opposer à un embarquement de bestiaux sur le paquebot de Londres', *L'Industriel calaisien*, 27 May 1848, p. 3.

[65] HC. Deb. 9 March 1848, vol. 97, cc336–8. Also see HC Deb. 13 March 1848, vol. 97, c458; HC Deb. 20 June 1848, vol. 99, c879.

dreaded that the military may take a prominent part in the movement, several regiments being in an absolute state of mutiny.[66]

Although no railway workers were targeted, the British press mostly represented those forced to flee as hard-working navvies, rather than flax workers or lace-makers (Figures 6.7 and 6.8). The technical capacities of the French were derided in comparison to those of the British (Figure 6.9). Russell's government created a 'Committee for the Relief of the British Workmen, Refugees from France', to which Queen Victoria and Prince Albert donated £200. These visible efforts on the part of the ruling Whig ministry were primarily intended to garner domestic support. France and Europe were in revolution and the British authorities feared the effects on two groups: the Chartists and the Irish nationalists. The Chartists were engaged in collecting signatures for a third giant petition for the six points and tried to build on the upsurge of popular support in the aftermath of the continental revolutions. 'The Republic for France, and the Charter for England', the Chartists said at the March 1848 meetings. Some added: 'We will have the Charter; otherwise, we will impose the Republic'. Wasn't their monster meeting, due to be held on 10 April on Kennington Common, to turn sour? In Ireland,

Figure 6.7 'The Generous Youth of the Glorious Republic', *The Man in the Moon*, vol. 3, 1848, no. 16, p. 220.

---

[66] 'Arrival of English Operatives from France', *Shipping and Mercantile Gazette*, 6 April 1848, p. 4.

Figure 6.8 'A Specimen of French "Fraternité": English Labourers driven out of France', *Punch*, 11 March 1848, vol. 14, p. 120.

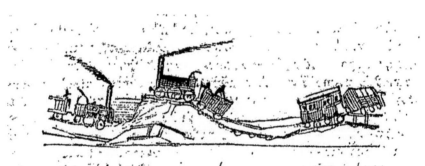

Figure 6.9 'Train on a French railway, constructed by themselves after the departure of English workmen', *The Man in the Moon*, vol. 3, 1848, p. 333.

Daniel O'Connell had died and the nationalists of the Irish Confederation were making claims for the repeal of the Act of Union, also building on the momentum created by the continental revolutions. In Great Britain, therefore, the expulsions by a Republic which publicly proclaimed international 'Fraternité' were even more vilified and they were addressed by the British ambassador in his discussions with the provisional government of Lamartine.[67] Lamartine, who wanted a smooth

---

[67] Fabrice Bensimon, *Les Britanniques face à la révolution française de 1848*, Paris, 2000, ch. 10.

relationship with the British government, gave instructions so that the local authorities firmly opposed and sanctioned anti-English protest.

Now, what were the reasons for and the circumstances of the riots against foreigners? In at least two cases—the linen factory in Petit-Quevilly and the lacemakers in Calais—several sources are available, providing interesting case studies from which to offer some tentative answers.

3. The Scottish and Irish Flax Workers at La Foudre

The presence of British workers in Norman textiles dated back to the eighteenth century, and in 1848 some 2,000 of them lived in and around Rouen. La Foudre in Petit-Quevilly (Seine-Inférieure) was one of the many flax factories where manufacturers imported British machines and employed British workers (see pp. 64–72 and 108–16). As we have seen, many of these workers initially came from Ulster, especially Belfast, and went to France after a spell in Dundee. In a sample of twenty-five workers from the La Foudre factory, fourteen of them gave addresses in Belfast and eleven in Scotland, including eight in Dundee.[68] The majority of these women had therefore migrated at least twice. By late 1848, the economic crisis left the textile factories in and near Rouen in dire straits, with at most three working days out of six per week. As early as 25 February, improvised processions of French workers celebrating the fall of the July Monarchy shouted, 'Vive la République, à bas les Anglais!'.[69] British machines were denounced by the protestors, and the railway bridge across the Seine was burnt. On 28 February 1848, British and Irish workers were the target of demonstrations, and dozens, 238 of them according to a newspaper, had to quit in a hurry, often leaving their personal belongings and clothes behind.[70] Betsy Houston, for instance, a spinner from Dundee, 'left in her hotel 3 gowns, 3 petticoats, a pair of boots, a hat and a shawl'; John McGivern, a heckler from Belfast, 'left his clothes, trousers and jacket in the mill'; Alexandre Smire, a heckler from Belfast, 'left a bed, bedsheets, chairs and clothes in the manufacture'; Jessie Young, a spinner from Dundee, left '25 francs'.[71] The British consul in Le Havre met them a few days later:

---

[68] AD Seine-Maritime, 10 M 324, 'Mouvement et émigration de la main-d'œuvre...Renvoi d'ouvriers étrangers 1848'. A table dated 6 March 1848 gives details about the reparations some of the expelled workers demanded.

[69] *Mémorial de Rouen*, 27 April 1848.

[70] 'Ce matin, le bateau à vapeur *Louis-Philippe*, qui a pris nom de *Sésostris*, est entré dans le port, ayant à son bord 238 ouvriers irlandais, qui viennent prendre passage au Havre pour retourner dans leur pays. Ces hommes étaient employés dans la grande filature rouennaise *La Foudre*'. *L'Impartial de Rouen*, 5 March 1848, p. 2, col. 3.

[71] AD Seine-Maritime, 10 M 324.

I had to go at 7 O'clock this morning to the shore to see near three hundred British Subjects male and female work people in the Flax manufactory of Messieurs Le Bandy of Petit Quevilly near Rouen, whom I found in a most desolate condition. The French workmen in the same manufactory had bullied and driven them on board a steamer without giving them time to receive their wages, to go home and get clothes and effects and in this state of destitution they have reached this place. Some of them I have forwarded to England already, and a deputation of them has gone to Rouen to endeavour to recover the clothes of the Females.[72]

This episode was the most violent of the anti-British demonstrations of 1848. Its roots are complex, and we lack the testimony of the rioters themselves. Moreover, little is known about the trajectories of the British and Irish La Foudre workers. On 13 March, the question was raised in Parliament, and Home Secretary George Gray mentioned an exchange with the mayor of Portsmouth, where 'ninety-seven persons, men, women and children, all flax-workers, or somehow connected therewith arrived': 'They came here very bare of clothes, and it became necessary to provide the greater part of the women with bonnets, shawls and shoes'.[73] These workers were preparing to leave the port for Dundee and Glasgow, and especially for Dublin and Belfast, which confirms their Irish and Scottish backgrounds. Their subsequent trajectories remain unknown, however. The episode supports the hypothesis of a latent xenophobia, which would have been expressed in the wake of the fall of the July Monarchy. But other sources cast these events in a different light.

In Rouen, the riot of La Foudre was criticised by the French authorities. The republican and socialist Rouen activist Charles Cord'homme (1824–1906), depicted by his nephew Maupassant in the famous short story 'Boule de Suif' (1880) in the guise of Cornudet, 'the terror of respectable people', later remembered:

[72] TNA FO 146 350. Letter of the British consul in Le Havre, Featherstonehaugh, to the British ambassador in Paris, Normanby, on 4 March 1848.

[73] Letter of the Portsmouth mayor: 'Sir—I have the honour to report that two vessels, the Brighton and the Dieppe, have arrived at this port, bringing together ninety-seven persons, men, women and children, all flax-workers, or somehow connected therewith. Have taken an account of their names, the places to which they belong, their trades—where they have been employed and by whom—what wages, if any, remain unpaid—what goods they have left behind—and where they desire to be sent to. They will all leave the ships this evening, and arrangements have been made for conveying them to their destination as early as possible. They will all leave Portsmouth tomorrow; several for Dundee and Glasgow, but the greater number for Dublin and Belfast. They came here very bare of clothes, and it became necessary to provide the greater part of the women with bonnets, shawls and shoes. I am unable yet to state the cost that may be incurred. The arrangements have been made with a proper consideration for economy, and they have expressed themselves as very thankful for the attention which has been shown to them.—I have the honour to be Sir, your very obedient servant. T.E. OWEN'. *Banner of Ulster*, 14 March 1848, p. 4. Also see *Parliamentary Debates*, House of Commons, 13 March 1848, vol. 97, col. 458.

The Foudre flax mill...was invaded to drive out the English workers who worked there, forgetting that the worker must be an internationalist; isn't his homeland where he finds work, life, and existence?[74]

Local historian André Dubuc, who studied this case using French sources, noted that afterwards, a number of the workers returned, and 'attended at the beginning of April, in a group, the planting of Liberty trees in Petit-Quevilly, where they were even honoured, which says a lot about the change in the public mind'.[75] During the various disturbances culminating in the Rouen riots of 27–29 April 1848, anti-English slogans were no longer noted, and Anglophobia was no longer mentioned as one of the motives of the mobilisation. Furthermore, the motives of the workers' petitions addressed in March 1848 in Rouen to the Commissioner of the Republic and to the Provisional Government are instructive in this regard.[76] Dozens of them came from spinners, dyers, 'sheet manufacturers, Indian Cloth and Rouenneries manufacturers', and weavers, as well as carpenters, cabinet-makers, bakers, plasterers, masons, and soap makers. Among the subjects giving rise to grievances (and demands) were job guarantees, prices, wages, the removal of fines, and working hours. Some suggested 'that, given the scarcity, the farmers supply them, and then be paid by the government'[77]; others called for industrialists to respect their commitments to their employees. Fifty-seven carpenters from Buddicom in Sotteville (the factory making railway carriages and employing British workers) petitioned for a ten-hour working day. Plasterers and masons also asked for a ten-hour day, on the premise 'that every day they are exposed to some accident and even death; because someone who leaves home in the morning in good health, sometimes does not return there, or returns with a few broken limbs'.[78] But none of the petitions mentioned British machines, workers, or manufacturers. Anti-English hostility was never prevalent or the sole reason behind protests, but it could be used occasionally in times of job and food scarcity.

---

[74] 'C'était la filature de lin La Foudre qui était envahie pour chasser les travailleurs anglais qui y étaient occupés, oubliant que l'ouvrier doit être internationaliste, sa patrie n'est-elle pas où il trouve travail, vie et existence?'. Yannick Marec, 1848 à Rouen. Les Mémoires du Citoyen Cord'Homme, oncle de Maupassant, Luneray, 1988, p. 55; this was first published in Le Réveil social, 22 April 1894.

[75] André Dubuc, 'Les émeutes de Rouen et d'Elbeuf en 1848 (27, 28 et 29 avril 1848)', Etudes d'Histoire Moderne et contemporaine, vol. 2, 1948, p. 249.

[76] AD Seine-Maritime, 10 M 330: Coalitions, grèves, manifestations, an XI-1848.

[77] 'que, vu la disette, les fermiers les fournissent, et soient ensuite payés par le gouvernement'. Ibid.

[78] 'sur ce que tous les jours ils sont exposés à quelqu'accident et à la mort même; car tel qui part le matin bien portant de chez lui, n'y rentre quelquefois pas, ou y revient avec quelques membres fracturés'. Ibid.

However, from late 1847, Rouen's textile industry was in a state of perpetual crisis and the working week was curtailed. It was this broad climate of industrial crisis which prompted workers to address their grievances to the authorities, rather than any widespread anti-English sentiment.

Historian Charles Tilly distinguished between an old repertoire of collective action (charivari, blocking, seizure of grains, coalitions, riots, destruction of machines...) and a modern one, shaped in the nineteenth century (electoral and public meetings, demonstrations, social movements...). This has been contested by other historians such as John Walter, who has argued that riots should be read as 'political protest' rather than spontaneous and apolitical outbursts of anger.[79] Walter also writes that actions such as food and agrarian riots, intercepting grain, and attacking middlemen were sometimes the culmination of the long-term breakdown of community relations. Tilly argues that in Britain, where several essential freedoms were secured before 1830, the modern repertoire settled sooner than in France.[80] It can be maintained with Tilly that, in Rouen in 1848, the two repertoires somehow coexisted; the La Foudre riot was from an old repertoire, while the petitions or planting of freedom trees belonged to a more modern one. It can also be argued with Walter that even the riot against the British workers was essentially part of a political tradition, if politics is defined as people's relationship with and attempts to influence those in authority. Other cases of xenophobic outbursts may help us understand such episodes.

4. The Calais Lacemakers

In Calais, British lacemakers had been working and selling their products on the French market since 1817. As we have seen, unlike flax workers or blacksmiths, they were primarily artisans, small entrepreneurs, and workers who worked for themselves and their families. At the time of the 1846 census, there were over 1,500 British workers in Saint-Pierre-lès-Calais, the southerly town bordering Calais, and where most of the lace industry was based.

On 21 March 1848, the British consul reported to the Foreign Office:

On Sunday the cries of 'A bas les Anglais' were first heard in the Basse ville, these were redoubled yesterday and accompanied by much occasional abuse towards English workmen in the streets on the part of the lowest rabble. Some placards were posted, calling a meeting for last night to petition for work, bread and the

---

[79] John Walter, *Crowds and Popular Politics in Early Modern England*, Manchester, 2013.
[80] Charles Tilly, 'Les origines du répertoire de l'action collective contemporaine en France et en Grande-Bretagne', *Vingtième Siècle*, vol. 4, October 1984, pp. 89–108.

expulsion of the English workmen: this meeting was attended by about 200 of the lowest of the mob.[81]

The sources documenting the Calais riot are inconsistent. The local newspaper *L'Industriel calaisien* did not report actions against the British, and was critical of the 'exaggeration and serious insults' that were 'the habit of the English press'.[82] Curiously, in the French municipal and departmental archives, there are no records attesting to the manifestations of xenophobia mentioned by the consul. The explanation may be found by considering the aftermath of the events rather than what preceded them. Indeed, on 21 March, the British consul conveyed to his government a request from several hundred lacemakers in Calais to help them leave for Australia. Such journeys were costly at the time, and assistance for emigration was mainly financed by the Australian colonies, which sought farmers or craftsmen in certain trades, though not lacemakers. In addition, these colonies, still sparsely populated by Europeans and marred by their reputation as penal colonies, were unattractive to prospective migrants. In this context, while neither staying in Calais nor returning to the Midlands was possible, going to Australia was a heart-breaking outcome for these lacemakers, who maintained close links with their region of origin. In London, the Colonial Land and Emigration Commission (CLEC) was responsible for deciding on the eligibility of Anglo-Calais lacemakers for assisted emigration and for organising their departure. CLEC dispatched an officer to the site to 'inspect' them. The latter reported to his administration, which informed the government on 27 April:

> it appears that for more than a year there has been great distress among the lace-makers in that town, and that recent events have brought the trade of lace-making, like almost every other trade in France, to a stand-still. But there has been no attempt to force the people in question out of employment, or out of France, because they are English, nor have the employers been exposed to any annoyance on that account.[83]

---

[81] TNA, FO 146 350. Letter of the consul in Calais to Foreign Secretary Lord Palmerston, 21 March 1848.

[82] 'Un de nos compatriotes, à la lecture de cette lettre, crut devoir se présenter chez le consul anglais, lui donner sur les faits qui s'étaient passés à Saint-Pierre des détails bien circonstanciés, et desquels il résulte que loin de s'être montrés hostiles aux ouvriers anglais, les ouvriers français de Saint-Pierre sont allés les trouver et leur promettre aide et protection s'ils étaient inquiétés, et le prier de vouloir bien démentir les faits avancés par le Times. Le consul écouta les explications, les admit comme vraies, mais déclara ne pouvoir pas faire droit à la demande qu'on lui faisait.—Grande fut la surprise de notre compatriote, qui ne pouvait pas comprendre, qu'après avoir une fois reconnu l'injustice de l'attaque, on refusa de protester contre, et de rétablir les faits dans leur vérité'.

'L'explication de ce refus nous semble toute simple: l'exagération et les grosses injures entrent dans les habitudes de la presse anglaise'. *L'Industriel calaisien*, 15 April 1848, p. 3.

[83] Colonial Land and Emigration Office, 27 April 1848, PP. *Papers Relative to Emigration to Australian Colonies*, vol. 47, 1847–8, p. 100.

What is to be made of this? The lacemakers' statements are missing. However, when they wrote to the government to back up their request for immigration assistance, they reported 'feelings of an hostile character on the part of the French towards the English, which [they] hoped had long ceased to exist, thus rendering their position one of both insecurity and destitution'.[84] They knew that returning to the Midlands, which in some cases they had left years earlier, would be difficult because the lace industry itself was depressed there as well. So, was this a strategy, devised by the consul, which consisted in politicising the cause of the Anglo-Calais lacemakers to obtain aid to which they could not claim on the sole ground of their economic distress? The approach succeeded in any case. In the days that followed, the British government accepted the request, filed by several hundred of them. For 642 Britons from Calais, the funding was granted, and they left Europe on a one-way journey. However, as later figures show, the British population in Saint-Pierre did not decline inexorably after this wave of departures. While the number of British inhabitants had been 1,578 in 1841, it had returned to 1,073 in 1851 and 1,597 in 1861 (see p. 42). Although xenophobia regularly resurfaced, no further riots were recorded in later years. We therefore have to probe further to try and understand the 1848 outburst of xenophobia.

5. Making Sense of Riots and Expulsions

We have seen that the words of the rioters are often missing from historical records. However, one phrase/call resurfaces here and there: 'À bas les Anglais!'. Several studies have pointed out that being a foreigner under the July Monarchy first meant coming from a different area, or even from another village.[85] Martin Nadaud evoked in his memoirs the brawls between masons belonging to two villages of Creuse, and Agricol Perdiguier also recalled the violence of the confrontations between the different companionship societies.[86] Certainly, as Gérard Noiriel has pointed out, based on the great public inquiry on agricultural and industrial work which began in 1846, in border regions, the 'national vocabulary [was] regularly used to designate the antagonism between "them" and "us"'.[87] Pierre-Jacques Derainne has shown how, under the July Monarchy and in 1848,

---

[84] TNA, FO 27/817. Letter to the members of the British Government, 21 March 1848.

[85] Laurent Dornel, *La France hostile*; Gérard Noiriel, *État, nation, immigration*; Pierre-Jacques Derainne, *Le travail, les migrations et les conflits en France*.

[86] Martin Nadaud, *Léonard, maçon de la Creuse*, Paris, 1998 [1895]; Agricol Perdiguier, *Mémoires d'un compagnon*, Paris, 1992 [1855].

[87] Gérard Noiriel, *Une histoire populaire de la France. De la guerre de Cent Ans à nos jours*, Marseille, 2018, p. 316.

identities shifted, with the foreigner first becoming that of another nationality. The 1830s and 1840s saw more massive migrations, and the movement towards the national unification of workers' interests was at work, while conversely the protections offered by local communities (such as the restriction of access to work) were weakening. As the working class nationalised, he points out, working-class conflict also nationalised.[88] He has traced numerous outbursts of xenophobia against foreigners—Italians, Germans, Belgians, and British—even if, in total, there were only six demonstrations of more than 100 people against foreigners between 1819 and 1847. In 1848, while the 'English' were targeted in Normandy or in Calais, some inhabitants of Lille attacked the Belgians, some in Lyon the Savoyards, while others in Dauphiné and Auvergne targeted Italians or Belgians.

Another critical explanation for many departures was that while 1848 was a year of revolution in France, a major economic and commercial crisis had begun the year before, resulting in high unemployment and shortages. We have seen that the British press castigated the departure of the British navvies. But when about 200 employees of the Rouen–Dieppe railway building enterprise were also forced to leave, the British ambassador in Paris wrote: 'It does not appear that in this instance there was any injustice or cruelty, the railroad works having now been for some time stopped for want of funds, and all workmen having been alike discharged'.[89]

In March, the Scottish workers at the Colombier, Thiebault, and Bonpain flax factory in Haubourdin, in the north, were dismissed by their employer who refused to pay the money he owed them.

When they asked for help from the British ambassador in Paris, they did not mention any hostility from the other workers, but just their being laid off by an 'unjust company' (see p. 146).[90]

After being hired because of their skills, these workers had trained Flemish workers with whom they were now in competition. And, having obtained some money from the ambassador, they left, without having been victims of animosity.

---

[88] The thesis is summarised in Pierre-Jacques Derainne, 'Le travail, les migrations et les conflits en France: représentations et attitudes sociales sous la Monarchie de Juillet et la Seconde République', mis en ligne en juin 2001: http://barthes.enssib.fr/clio/revues/AHI/articles/volumes/derainn.html#fnB1.

[89] Marquis of Normanby, *A Year of Revolution: From a Journal Kept in Paris in 1848*, London, 1857, vol. 1, p. 266.

[90] TNA, FO 146 350. Letter to Lord Normanby, the British ambassador in Paris, 21 March 1848.

However, we do not need to look for a single cause of workers fleeing from France. Economic distress and the rhetoric of nationality could coalesce. In Saint-Rémy-sur-Avre (Eure-et-Loir), the Waddington factory was also the site of a riot against Scottish workers, as late as June 1848. In 1842 Waddington had brought in eight Scottish workers 'to instruct French workers in mechanical weaving which they knew very imperfectly'. He wrote a letter to the préfet:

> The more uninspired workers of Mocquedieu [the French weavers] discovered a new pretence to impose their will on me: they wanted to expel eight Scottish female workers who had been living in this country for six years, including one or two who have married Frenchmen, because one of the Scots, publicly insulted by a weaver, would have made a dishonest answer. Upon my refusal to sacrifice the foreigners to them, the workers abandoned their frames again and despite my repeated promises to have the culprit make reparation, if it was due, or to send her back if she did not want to submit to it, they remained on permanent strike.[91]

However, without denying the reality of this collective protest, the mayor of the neighbouring town of Nonancourt gave another explanation to the préfet:

> Not only have these Scottish women not perfected mechanical weaving in Mocquedieu, but most of them barely knew how to work. And that Mr Waddington had brought them in to get a drop in the price of labour by threatening to fire them all to replace them with strangers.[92]

The words of the mayor were as dubious as those of Waddington, since the Scottish women had indeed been hired for mechanical weaving. Sources are

---

[91] 'Les ouvriers de Mocquedieu (ou Mocdieu) plus mal inspirés, découvrirent un nouveau prétexte pour m'imposer leur volonté: ils voulurent expulser huit ouvrières écossaises qui résident dans ce pays depuis six ans et dont une ou deux ont épousé des Français parce l'une d'elles, insultée publiquement par un tisserand, aurait fait une réponse malhonnête. Sur mon refus de leur sacrifier les étrangères, ils abandonnèrent à nouveau leurs métiers et malgré mes promesses réitérées de faire faire une réparation par la coupable, si elle était due, ou de la renvoyer si elle ne voulait pas s'y soumettre, ils sont restés en grève permanente'. AD Eure, 1 M 246: Coalitions ouvrières, Lettre de Frédéric Waddington au préfet de l'Eure, 21 June 1848. Geneviève Dufresne-Seurre, *Les Waddington, une dynastie de cotonniers en Eure-et-Loir: 1792–1961*, Chartres, 2011, p. 316; Yannick Marec, 'Un républicain social, député, sénateur, président de la Chambre de commerce de Rouen. Richard Waddington (1838–1913)', *Bulletin de la société libre d'émulation de la Seine-Maritime*, 2002, pp. 3–10.

[92] 'Non seulement ces écossaises n'avaient pas apporté de perfectionnement dans le tissage mécanique de Mocquedieu mais que la plupart savaient à peine travailler. Et que M. Waddington les avait fait venir afin d'obtenir une baisse du prix du travail en les menaçant de les renvoyer tous pour leur substituer des étrangers'. AD Eure, 1 M 246: Coalitions ouvrières, Lettre du maire de Nonancourt, Claude Gros-Fillay, au préfet de l'Eure, 5 July 1848.

contradictory and, again, neither the words of the assailants nor those of their victims have reached us. But in this case as in others, the competition for jobs introduced by the manufacturer in a context when work was scarce may well have accounted for manifestations of hostility against foreigners.

If we summarise the incidents we have reviewed, a variety of motives emerges, as shown in Table 6.1. Most riots seem to have been caused by joblessness, rather than wage inequality. But each situation was specific, and it is essential to appreciate business structures and local contexts. If the professional status of the iron workers or the lacemakers is known, the riots against the 'English' often targeted workers who were supposedly less skilled, like female weavers. In several cases, women were targeted at a time when there was concerted opposition to their employment in manufacturing. At the same time, in 1848, many British workers in other factories, like the Scots of Landerneau who had been castigated by *L'Atelier*, and the workers of Landerneau, Boulogne, Coudekerque, and Fourchambault were not targeted.

However, xenophobia should not be overlooked. In the nineteenth century, collective actions against foreigners were common to all the countries of immigration and were the lot of many migrants. Anti-Chinese riots in California are well known, but US nativism also took violent and politically structured forms on the East Coast, especially against Irish Catholics during the 1830–60 period.[93] At the end of the century, the Australian colonies were also the scene of violent collective actions against the Chinese, the Fijians, and the Melanesians, a prelude

Table 6.1 Some anti-British incidents in France, 1830–48

Date	Place	British target	Motive
29 July 1830	Paris	Mechanical presses	Loss of work
17 July 1837	Charenton	Iron workers	Inequalities in the hours of work
20 August 1837	Fourchambault	Blacksmiths	Employment preference
March 1844	Maromme	Navvies	Employment preference
1842	Montrouge	Pulley machines	Loss of work
May 1846	Elbeuf	Wool-sorting machine	Loss of work
28 February 1848	Petit-Quevilly	Linen workers	Employment preference?
19 March 1848	Calais	Lacemakers	'A bas les Anglais!'?
21 June 1848	Saint-Rémy-sur-Avre	Female cotton weavers	'Dishonest answer'

[93] Katie Oxx, *The Nativist Movement in America: Religious Conflict in the Nineteenth Century*, London, 2013.

to the policy of 'White Australia' which was part of official national policy when colonies were federated in 1901.[94] However, this case, as well as that of the Chinese in the United States, were colonial situations, and therefore different from the French case. Closer to France, Britain was not a large country of immigration in the nineteenth century, being home to only 50,000 foreigners in 1851, while France had 370,000. However, the English had their 'foreigners from within', the Irish, who were the victims of widespread xenophobia, which was exacerbated during the Great Famine (1845–51) and the arrival in Britain of tens of thousands of them.[95] In 1848, some invited those who criticised the French to tend to their own gardens: 'neither in England nor in Scotland, are the "Irish navvies" at all popular', a Liverpool newspaper recalled.[96] Anti-Irish hostility sometimes took violent forms. In February 1846, on the construction site of a line in the northwest of England, 1,500 to 2,000 English people armed themselves and destroyed the Irish workers' huts. Likewise, in Scotland, in the same year, 1,000 Scots and English attacked the Irish, and killed a police officer who intervened.[97] The causes of the riots were unclear: partly religious, partly related to the use of Irish as strike breakers. In June 1852, an English crowd attacked the Irish in Stockport, one of whom was killed while several were seriously injured. In the 1860s, again, following the anti-Catholic diatribes of a Protestant pastor, violent riots targeted the Irish in Lancashire.

*

Did these anti-English riots reflect a long-lasting atavism, inherited from Waterloo, or even the wars of the Old Regime or Joan of Arc, and which we would find later in the time of Fashoda and then under Vichy?[98] The Anglophobia of the republican left under the July Monarchy has been mentioned and the legitimist party was also Anglophobic. However, it is difficult to assess the extent to which this Anglophobia was shared by the working classes since it was unstructured and the Napoleonic wars were fading from memory.[99] Colonial tensions pitted the two countries against each other, but during the 1840s a diplomatic rapprochement took place and, in 1848, Lamartine, the new head of the provisional government, married to an Englishwoman, was an Anglophile. British departures did not result from official expulsions. On the contrary, the authorities opposed these collective actions. For instance, in Petit-Quevilly the national guard was sent in to put down the riot. Lamartine, the head of the provisional government at the time, was questioned by the British ambassador in Paris and, being concerned with maintaining good relations with Britain, he

---

[94] Jane Carey and Claire McLisky (eds.), *Creating White Australia*, Sydney, 2009.
[95] Donald MacRaild, *The Irish Diaspora in Britain, 1750–1939*, London, 2013.
[96] *Liverpool Mercury*, 14 March 1848, p. 6.
[97] David Brooke, *The Railway Navvy: 'That despicable Race of Men'*. London, 1983, p. 113.
[98] Jean Guiffan, *Histoire de l'anglophobie en France: De Jeanne d'Arc à la vache folle*, Dinan, 2004.
[99] Philippe Darriulat, *Les Patriotes: la gauche républicaine et la nation, 1830–1870*, Paris, 2001.

'expressed the deepest concern at what had occurred ... it was only a local quarrel amongst workmen, and did not partake at all of national character; that it was impossible for the government, considering the collision which had so recently taken place between the people and the troops, to attempt, at least for some time, to maintain order through the means of the latter'.[100] Above all, one does not find references to historical Anglophobia in the words of rioters, as they were reported by the authorities or by the press. Nor was British Protestantism, which aroused suspicion from the authorities during the Restoration, mentioned. The Scottish and the Irish were indiscriminately targeted as 'Anglais' by the rioters of Petit-Quevilly or Saint-Rémy-sur-Avre, while Scotland and especially Ireland, traditionally seen as 'allies' of France, did not arouse the hostility England received in the republican discourse. Finally, in Calais, Rouen, and elsewhere, the British worked with the French, lived in their neighbourhoods, or even married them. There were several binational unions in Calais, Landerneau, and small working-class communities, like Saint-Rémy-sur-Avre or Pissy-Pôville. When the British were targeted by French workers, they were also defended by others, as in Fourchambault. Many British migrants who came temporarily to the Continent remained there. In brief, nothing corroborates the hypothesis of a profound and structural Anglophobia. In a context of deep economic crisis, of extreme shortage, and therefore of competition for employment and resources, and when all the political forces exalted the 'nation', to engage in collective violence within the framework of the defence of this very nation could seem to confer legitimacy on such actions.

---

[100] Marquis of Normanby, *A Year of Revolution*, p. 178.

Conclusion

George Stubbs (1806–66), the son of a joiner, was born in Quorndorn (now Quorn), Leicestershire. Apprenticed to become a joiner himself, he married Sarah Mays in the local Baptist Church in 1824. They had seven children who were all baptised in the same church. At some stage, George became a lacemaker, which could have been a strategic change to improve his living, or just to cope with a downturn in family fortunes. Around 1840, the family emigrated to Calais, where George was a lacemaker and the couple had three more children. In 1848, the family were among the 642 Calais British who made it to Australia. They left Deptford on 19 April onboard the *Fairlie*, a ship which had been built in Calcutta in 1810. The *Fairlie* reached Sydney with 296 immigrants onboard on 7 August. On the passenger lists, one can find George, Sarah, and eight of their children, the eldest of whom, Anne, was nineteen. George and Sarah's two eldest sons, who were already in their twenties, joined them later. In Australia, the lace market was non-existent, and there were no machines either. So, George returned to his initial job. He became a foreman joiner at the Australian Steam Navigation Company works in Pymont, not far from Sydney. His children mostly married other British immigrants. For instance, Frances (1832–1913) became a live-in family servant; in 1855 she married Joseph Smeal, a Scottish joiner, with whom she had five children. The Stubbs never returned to Britain. They settled down in the Australian colonies and took part in the peopling and colonisation of the continent.[1]

The destiny of the Stubbs calls for reflection on three further dimensions of this study. One is what happened to the migrants who have been the subject of this book (section 1). Another issue is whether the emigration of British workers and engineers went on after 1870, and how it changed (section 2). Last, this concluding chapter considers how migrants were remembered: how memory of them was preserved, and how it was erased (section 3).

---

[1] 'Funeral', *Empire* [Sydney], 13 June 1866, p. 8; Audrey Carpenter, John Carpenter, and Tony Jarram, *The Lacemakers' Story. Loughborough, Luddites and Long Journeys*, Charnwood, 2007; John Carpenter, 'Les tullistes anglais de l'Est des Midlands à la recherche d'un nouvel avenir à partir de 1816', in Stéphane Curveiller and Laurent Buchard (eds.), *Se déplacer du Moyen âge à nos jours*, Calais, 2009, p. 308.

Artisans Abroad: British Migrant Workers in Industrialising Europe, 1815–1870. Fabrice Bensimon, Oxford University Press.
© Fabrice Bensimon 2023. DOI: 10.1093/oso/9780198835844.003.0008

1. From Calais to Australia

The story of George and Sarah Stubbs was that of hundreds of the Calais lacemakers. We left these artisans in a difficult situation in 1848. Because of the economic and commercial crisis, the lace market had collapsed, and they no longer received orders. Moreover, in the wake of the February revolution, xenophobia had surfaced (see pp. 230–2). To many, leaving appeared to be the best option. However, there was no work available in and around Nottingham. On 31 March, it was reported in the local press that '120 have arrived in Nottingham from Calais, as we are given to understand; and they tell pretty tales of French oppression and cruelty. Others from other ports have reached here, and a few have obtained admission to the Nottingham union workhouse'.[2] This meant that, especially if more came, they were going to be an additional burden on poor relief, something the local middle class could not but oppose. But in Calais, consul Bonham, a central figure in this crisis, had other prospects. On 21 March, he wrote to Foreign Secretary Palmerston:

> a number from whom I shall receive and will tomorrow forward to your lordship a memorial, are most desirous to emigrate to Australia or any other of the British colonies. They are men of respectability now reduced by hard times, and generally with large families. . . . as strong able bodied men in the prime of life, industrious and intelligent they would be well able to turn their hands to any thing.[3]

Compared to the United States and Canada, Australia was not a preferred destination for most British emigrants. It was distant and therefore expensive, the passage costing about £13 per adult, the equivalent of several months of a worker's income. And Australian colonies, where British settlers had so far mostly been convicts, had a poor reputation. However, British colonial authorities favoured the flow of migrants, especially skilled ones. The Colonial Land and Emigration Commission (CLEC) assisted emigration, and they seem to have been central in this case, while three quarters of the funding came from the colonies themselves. The press also campaigned for emigration to the colonies, which was now presented as a way of alleviating poverty in Britain (Figure C.1), while the Chartists condemned such emigration as 'transportation of the poor'.

It is therefore likely that when the distressed Calais migrants wrote that they wanted above all 'emigration to one of the British colonies, South Australia

---

[2] 'English Mechanics from France', *NR*, 31 March 1848, p. 4.   [3] TNA. FO 27/817.

The Needlewoman at Home and Abroad.

AT HOME.   ABROAD.

Figure C.1 John Leech, 'The Needlewoman at Home and Abroad', *Punch*, 12 January 1850.

preferred', this had been suggested to them.[4] A group of several hundred applied to the government for assisted emigration there:

> We, your memorialists... pledge ourselves to be men of good moral characters and industrious habits, in full possession of health and strength, and men whose feelings revolt at the idea of becoming a burden to their native land.
>
> If therefore, you can provide us with the means of free emigration, we shall cheerfully and gratefully accept them.[5]

When the xenophobic riots occurred in France, the British press lambasted the supposedly 'fraternal' claims of the Republic and the distasteful attitude of the French to British workers. To alleviate the distress of these workers, a 'Committee for the Relief of the British Workmen, Refugees from France' was formed in London and sent a representative to Nottingham to raise a subscription. Historian Robin F. Haines has underlined the interweaving of philanthropic and mercantilist interests in such schemes: public and private funding had to be found, while

---

[4] UK Parliamentary Papers. *Papers Relative to Emigration to Australian Colonies*, vol. 47, 1847–8, pp. 97–8.
[5] TNA. FO 27/813.

the skills of the lacemakers were of no value to the Australian colonies.[6] The CLEC rejected an unknown number of applicants, according to clear guidelines. First, some were rejected at once 'as bad characters'.[7] Second, couples had to produce marriage certificates: some were suspected not to be married, and 'some have even wives and families in this country [Britain] whom they have deserted'.[8] This claim may have been substantiated, especially in the context of migration. Ginger Frost has convincingly argued that bigamy and cohabitation were not uncommon in the British working class, and were accepted in most communities, provided those involved conformed to some standards.[9] For the CLEC, the issue was not so much moral as financial: the deserted families might then have requested either to be sent out to Australia or to be assisted. Third, the CLEC objected to families with more than five children aged ten or below. A health-based argument was put forward: the likely spread of 'infantine complaints' onboard resulting in high mortality. The other argument was that the cost of passage would mean that 'the colony is burthened . . . with a heavy charge for emigrants whose labour will not be available until a remote period'—this reminds us that assisted emigration was, in this case as in many others, paid for in the interest of the colony rather than that of the migrants.[10] Eventually, 642 of the Calais applicants embarked on ships to Sydney and Adelaide, which they reached after 110–120 days at sea. While the British lacemakers who had gone to Calais had benefited from greater circulation of people and goods across the Channel and the gradual repeal of state regulations and had emigrated on their own initiative, when they went to Australia their destinies turned out to be largely a product of state policies—not an uncommon combination. Their step migration was not planned but accidental in many ways. What had begun as temporary, middle-distance migration ended as long-term, definitive migration.

The migrants spread across South Australia and New South Wales.[11] Although they shared a common geographical and occupational background, they dispersed and made their lives separately. There was no lace industry in Australia, and like many emigrants, they had to adjust. Some, like George Stubbs, resumed occupations they had abandoned before, which met some need in the colonies. While some took part in the 1849 and 1850 gold rush, most found employment as servants and labourers. The Nottingham press published some of their letters, one of which narrated the perilous and exhausting journey to Goulburn of a migrant who had been hired as a gardener and his wife as a cook. He had to milk cows,

[6] Robin F. Haines, *Emigration and the Labouring Poor Australian Recruitment in Britain and Ireland, 1831–60*, London, 1997, p. 207.

[7] PP. *Papers Relative to Emigration to Australian Colonies*, vol. 47 (1847–8), p. 100.

[8] Ibid., p. 101.

[9] Ginger S. Frost, *Living in Sin: Cohabiting as Husband and Wife in Nineteenth-Century England*, Manchester, 2008.

[10] *Papers Relative to Emigration*, p. 101.

[11] Gillian Kelly, *Well Suited to the Colony*, Queanbeyan, 1998.

fetch wood and water, and shepherd from sunrise to 'sun-down'. He complained about the heat in the summer, about the rain in the winter, about the deadly snakes and the ants 'one or two inches in length' that make you 'suffer four or five days after being bitten by them'. He lamented that 'apples [were] grown only for the rich' and that ale, rum, gin, tobacco, shirts, shoes, and trousers reached 'exorbitant' prices in comparison with Nottingham's. He even missed sitting on chairs, 'a block or stool being generally used instead'. 'What we have endured, were we to attempt to tell you', he concluded, 'would put your faith to the test, and our powers of description to their utmost limit'.[12]

This story reminds us that Britain, the Continent, and the Empire had interwoven histories. While emigrating to France first resulted from economic and social rationales, going to Australia was related to a political, imperial scheme. Relocating Britain's paupers to its colonies while trying to develop these remote territories was on the British government's agenda. The story also shows that emigrating to Nottingham, Calais, or Australia—though of course these choices made significant differences for those who made them—were not intrinsically different. Thanks to the passenger lists of those who went to Australia, we can try to follow some Calais lacemakers and trace their migration patterns.

As we have seen, step migration was common: workers did not always go from A to B, and then possibly from B to A, but also to C, D, and so on. For instance, in 1848, the Johnson family, who emigrated from Calais to New South Wales, consisted of Thomas Johnson (b. 1813 in Loughborough) and Phoebe Roper (b. 1823) and Thomas's three children (b. 1837–41 in Nottinghamshire). When Thomas's first wife Myra (1816–42) had died, Thomas had moved to the Continent with his children. Phoebe Roper (or Rogers or Rodgers) was from Portsea (Hampshire). When she married Thomas Johnson, on 8 September 1846, they both lived in Douai, but they were married in Brussels by the British chargé d'affaires. In 1848, they lived in Calais and the whole family, then emigrated to Australia, where they had nine children.

Thomas Harrison (b. 1800 in Sneinton, near Nottingham) and his wife Maria (b. Stubbs, 1804 in Belper, Derbyshire) had seven children, born in Calais (in 1824, 1825, 1826, and 1827), then Hyson Green (Nottinghamshire, 1833), Calais again (1835), and Douai (1842), suggesting movements between different areas, before they emigrated to Australia onboard the *Fairlie*. Thomas Wells (b. 1803) and his wife Sarah (née Creswell, 1815) were born in Nottingham, while their six children were born in Caen, Le Havre, and Calais between 1831 and 1848, suggesting an itinerant migration in France, another pattern about which much remains to be learned.

---

[12] 'The Anglo-French Emigrants', *NR*, 16 August 1850, p. 4.

The stories of mixed families also suggest a variety of patterns. In 1848, William Brownlow (b. Lenton, near Nottingham, 1821) and his wife Emma Courquin (b. Calais, 1821) emigrated to Australia with their three children born in Calais. Wheelwright Thomas Pettit (b. Dover, 1810) emigrated with Joséphine Mattong (b. Calais, 1808), a house servant, onboard the *Agincourt*. Richard Goldfinch (b. Deal, Kent, 1814–76) went with Eugénie de Sombre (b. Calais, 1820–98) and their four children born in Calais to Port-Adelaide; they settled, had another four children, and died there in 1898.[13] Unsurprisingly, these three mixed couples that decided to emigrate to Australia had British husbands: both for the authorities and in popular assumptions, the nationality of a couple was that of the man. In French law, when husband and wife had different nationalities, the wife adopted her husband's and lost hers, something which prevailed until the twentieth century. Once in Australia, hardly any of the emigrants returned. Their lives there are another story.

Many among those who had just gone to France returned to Britain and died there, as had Charles Manby Smith, William Duthie, Colin, and many others. After all, there was nothing like returning home and being able to make a living in your own country. We lack more longitudinal studies, but it is likely that not just many individuals but also groups of workers moved back to Britain, not necessarily to their hometowns, but to areas where there was work. John Morgan (1811–61), born in Dowlais, was an iron puddler in Decazeville (Averyron), where at least fifty-five iron workers had been recruited in Merthyr between 1830 and 1848. In 1848, following the economic crisis and the revolution, the family returned to Wales. By 1861, one part of the Morgan family lived in Escombe (now Escomb), County Durham. An ironworks had opened there in 1846, and by 1861 six Welsh families lived close to one another, all with children in France, as family historian Rick Lux has found out. This suggests a step migration that had led some of the Morgans and their neighbours from Wales to Decazeville and then to Co. Durham. The nature of the bonds they formed is uncertain, however.[14]

We do not know how many in the other groups we have dealt with made it to other continents after their sojourn in Europe, but there must have been thousands. One son of John Morgan, David Morgan (1846–1935), born in Decazeville, went back to Wales with his parents in 1848, but in 1867 he emigrated to Portsmouth, Ohio, to work in a rolling mill, before going to Ohio University and eventually becoming a minister in St Paul, Minnesota.

[13] New South Wales, Australia, Assisted Immigrant Passenger Lists, 1828–1896. Series: 5317; Reel: 2458; Item: [4/4904].

[14] Rick Lux, 'Welsh Ironworkers in France', *Glamorgan Family History Society*, J137, March 2020, pp. 26–31.

It is ascertained that many navvies went to the Crimea during the Crimean war, or, more permanently, to Canada to build the Grand Trunk Railway between Montreal and Toronto (1853–6).[15] Like Timothy Claxton (see pp. 95–8), many ironworkers, mechanics, and engineers also made it to the United States. These different trajectories illustrate the complexity of migration patterns. Temporary and permanent, short-, long-distance, and step migration could be interwoven in various ways. Crossing the Channel for a few months or years was not so different a choice from that of crossing the Atlantic forever, and such choices could be made based on word-of-mouth information or letters from relatives. By the mid-nineteenth century, most workers migrated several times in their lifetimes, including overseas. Moving to a nearby town, to the Continent, or to the New World was part of the same rationale.

In the history of British labour migration, the Calais connection is a minor but telling one. Flows of lacemakers (overall, a few thousand) were not organised from above, but grew out of a series of economic opportunities and constraints. Regions (the East Midlands, Devon, northern France), rather than national entities, are the crucial units of analysis. Practicalities and the circulation of information are essential to understanding the development of this chain migration. While these migrants were in many respects 'tramping artisans', many mediators (relatives, manufacturers, agents, authorities) played a critical part in providing information, advice, and sometimes relief. The Nottingham–Calais connection was part of a wider network, as most migrants often experienced other moves, including to other towns, and sometimes other countries. They do not easily fit into categories of domestic and short-distance migration, as opposed to overseas and long-distance. In nineteenth-century Europe, many short- or middle-distance migration flows crossed national borders, and such was the case for many across the Channel. Nor do the Calais lacemakers easily fit into categories of temporary/definitive migrants: many saw themselves as temporary migrants, maintained many connections with their homes, and yet ended up as definitive migrants. Studying their movements helps us understand the complexity of the connections between the British and the continental industrial revolutions, the British and European labour markets, Europe and the making of the 'Anglo-world', the local and the global.

---

[15] David Brooke, *The Railway Navvy: 'That Despicable Race of Men'*, London, 1983; Anh-Dao Bui Tran, 'Le Grand Tronc. La construction d'un chemin de fer au Canada britannique (1852–1860)', thesis in preparation, Sorbonne Université.

2. 'To the Dominions of the Czar and the Sultan':
New Horizons

However, neither 1848 nor 1870 was the end of the story of the British workers in continental Europe.[16] Until circa 1870, many more businesses were set up in France and Belgium by British manufacturers. But the technological gap was shrinking. In 1871, in the early years of the Meiji era, after centuries of isolation, a large embassy of Japanese officials, led by Foreign Minister Iwakura, visited Europe. They were impressed by 'the country which bestrides the world': 'Britain has harnessed the power of steam, has thereby multiplied its power to produce, has come to monopolise the profit to be derived from textiles and sea transport'.[17] Then, visiting France, they added that 'while industry in Britain depends on machinery, in France it is balanced between human skills and machines'. But they also noted that 'France ranks foremost in Europe in manufacturing' and that it 'competes with Britain in large-scale engineering works such as steam-powered iron warships, cannon and rifles, and buildings and bridges'.[18] They were also impressed by Belgium, especially 'porcelain, lace, rolling-stock, swords, iron and lumber, all of which have acquired fame in Europe', and they noted: 'The thriving state of railway construction ranks foremost among the countries of Europe'.[19] But when they visited Krupp's ironworks in Essen, with its 20,000 workers and its 50-ton hammer, they wrote 'the spectacular scale of it all was extraordinary', even in comparison with Britain.[20] The Japanese report was quite right. Continental manufacturing gradually acquired its own dynamic with the making of domestic capital, the impetus from the nation-states in terms of protection and public orders, and the training of a local workforce. The part played by the British thus diminished.

Technological transfers had never been unidirectional, as illustrated by the importation of the Jacquard system to Nottingham. Although, as we have seen, the UK was not a large immigration country by the middle of the century, a significant import to British lace manufacturing was, as in other sectors, the development of German international merchant houses. By the mid-nineteenth century, foreign houses conducted three quarters of the exports of Lancashire and Yorkshire. German merchants also played a significant part in lace from the 1830s, for instance Lewis Heymann, a former German Jew, who became a mayor of Nottingham in 1857.[21] Another example was noted by historian Laura Tabili concerning South Shields, with a significant input of French and Belgian

---

[16] The quote in this section's title is from Elizabeth Gaskell, *Mary Barton*, Oxford, 2008 [1848], p. 28.
[17] Kume Kunitake, *Japan Rising: The Iwakura Embassy to the USA and Europe*, Cambridge, 2009, p. 108.
[18] Ibid., p. 215.   [19] Ibid., pp. 260, 258.   [20] Ibid., p. 295.
[21] Stanley Chapman, *Merchant Enterprise in Britain: From the Industrial Revolution to World War I*, Cambridge, 1992, ch. 5.

glass workers as early as 1851, suggesting either a recruitment by a local glassmaking firm or chain migration.[22]

At the same time, while Britain increasingly imported continental know-how and technology, it also expanded its geographical range, with more investments in areas like Russia, where industrialisation began later. By 1848, Elizabeth Gaskell was already celebrating 'the great firms of engineers, who send from out their towns of workshops engines and machinery to the dominions of the Czar and the Sultan',[23] and we have encountered several examples of artisans who had gone to Russia. In 1869, Welsh ironmaster John Hughes (c.1816–89) reached Donbass. Hughes, born in Merthyr in South Wales, set up a huge complex of blast furnaces, collieries, and brickworks in what became Yuzovka (Hughesovka). Hughes was the son of a Cyfarthfa engineer and had worked with him before joining the Milwall Engineering and Shipbuilding Company on Thameside in London where he became director in 1860. At a time when the tsarist Russian regime wanted to develop its heavy engineering, Hughes came to their attention as he produced a successful mounting for heavy naval guns in which the Russian Admiralty was interested. Hughes signed an agreement with the Russian government. The works he set up became the largest in the Russian Empire. Predictably, Hughes had gone not only with wife and family, but also with about a hundred ironworkers and miners from South Wales, who trained local workers. Many of these men settled in Yuzovka, bringing out their wives and families. Over the years, although a Russian workforce was trained by the company, skilled workers from the UK continued to be employed, and many technical, engineering, and managerial positions were filled by British (and especially Welsh) emigrants. When he died in 1889, Hughes's body was returned to London to be buried in the family plot at Norwood cemetery. His four sons, John James, Arthur David, Ivor Edward, and Albert Llewellyn, took over the running of the company in Yuzovka which became Donetsk, the capital city of a major industrial area, today at the heart of the war in Ukraine.[24]

The story of John Hughes was quite exceptional, but overall, the period following 1870 did not witness a decline in the overseas emigration of British technicians and engineers. In the main sectors of industry, more and more of them went to faraway destinations across the Empire, the United States, Latin America, and elsewhere. Engineering is an especially important sector to assess in this context. Overall, the number of professional engineers in Britain rose from

[22] Laura Tabili, *Global Migrants, Local Culture: Natives and Newcomers in Provincial England, 1841–1939*, London, 2011, p. 52.

[23] Gaskell, *Mary Barton*, p. 28.

[24] J. N. Westwood, 'John Hughes and Russian Metallurgy', *The Economic History Review*, vol. 17, no. 3, 1965, pp. 564–9; Susan Edwards, *Hughesovka: A Welsh enterprise in Imperial Russia*, Glamorgan Record Office, 1992; https://glamarchives.wordpress.com/2017/11/03/hughesovka-a-welsh-enterprise-in-imperial-russia.

about 1,000 in 1850 to 40,000 in 1914, and it was common for them to spend at least part of their careers overseas. For instance, in railway building, labour migration to the Continent preceded the exportation of British technology to Canada, Central and South America, the Middle East, Australia, and most of Asia—including non-colonised countries such as Japan—as well as central and southern Africa. The migration of British mechanics to northwestern Europe therefore arguably set a precedent for the global diaspora of British engineering.[25]

The routes the nineteenth-century migrants traced have also survived. The lace sector has now collapsed in Britain, but Cluny Lace, a small firm in Ilkeston (Derbyshire) operating in an economic niche, still relies on old Leavers machines made in the nineteenth century to manufacture lace, as they have since 1845. Because they can no longer dye their produce locally, they make weekly trips to Calais. They also go there to have their bars made, or their bobbins and carriages repaired. In so doing, they are using the route which, from 1816 onwards, lacemakers from the Midlands used when they started migrating to Calais and northern France.

3. A Memory in the Making

As we know, memory is selective and unfair to the deeds of the men and women in the past, especially those who neither wrote nor published about their lives, nor patented their inventions, nor became heroes in their own times. The memory of the British working-class migrants to the Continent is hazy, imprecise, and sometimes even non-existent. In some respects, to use Charlotte Erickson's phrase, they were 'invisible'.[26] We have seen the reasons: they were not counted, and unlike in English-speaking countries such as the United States, Canada, Australia, and New Zealand, where the memory of British immigrants was integrated into narratives of nation-building, or other countries like Argentina and South Africa, where the Welsh and the British constituted specific language groups, they either returned to Britain or dispersed and assimilated. Continental countries could be oblivious to their contributions and each of them produced its own narrative of industrialisation with its own national heroes. As a result, migrants could easily be forgotten in their countries of destination as well as in Britain. Although in the nineteenth and twentieth centuries France was the first European country in terms of immigration, immigrants were not integrated into the narrative of the construction of national identity, in a tradition which

---

[25] R. A. Buchanan, 'The Diaspora of British Engineering', *Technology and Culture*, vol. 27, no. 3, July 1986, pp. 501–24.
[26] Charlotte Erickson, *Invisible Immigrants: The Adaptation of English and Scottish Immigrants in Nineteenth-Century America*, Ithaca, NY, 1972.

extended to Fernand Braudel.[27] Since the 1980s, immigration has increasingly been a subject of public debate, and following a seminal book by Gérard Noiriel, there has been a growing interest in the history of immigration, now a recognised sub-field of the discipline, as illustrated by the opening in 2008 of what is now the Musée de l'histoire de l'immigration in Paris.[28]

We have seen that Nottinghamshire lace workers had played a key part in the take-off of French lace: while their names were forgotten, Joseph Marie Jacquard (1752–1834) became an industrial hero and, although he never went to Calais, he has had his statue in the town centre, outside the municipal theatre, since 1910. Thus, the foreign origins of a luxury industry of which France boasts were concealed. John Leavers, the genius mechanic who improved Heathcoat's bobbin-net machine, gave his name to generations of machines that were exported from Nottingham around the world. A couple of towns have streets that were named Leavers, but otherwise he remains unknown (see pp. 207–17).

Some of the lacemakers' language was adopted in French, although this is now fading with the collapse of the lace industry. Nevertheless, in 2009 Calais opened its Cité internationale de la dentelle et de la mode (International Museum of Lace and Fashion), to preserve its history and possibly appeal to tourists. In Nottinghamshire heritage, the emigration of lacemakers to Calais is virtually unknown: emigrants do not produce sources in their areas of departure, and unless they become famous, their lives are forgotten. One exception is the migration of Heathcoat's workers from Loughborough to Tiverton in 1816: this flow has been remembered by local historians in an exhibition and in festive 200-mile walks.[29] As for Calais, it is now mostly seen in Britain as a passing point for immigrants into Britain, or for British holidaymakers to the Continent—but not as one for their emigration, for which Heathrow airport is a more likely candidate.

At the same time, this memory is still taking shape, 200 years later. It benefits from the development of labour history since the 1960s, and from that of migration history as a field, over the past fifty years. It is also gaining from the developments of local history and heritage and is sometimes preserved in localities, in place names, in the language, and in family histories, as well as in painting or literature. Of course, manufacturers are better remembered than workers. Barentin has its statue of Joseph Locke, the engineer of the Paris–Le Havre railway and of a local viaduct (Figure C.2). Most monuments, however, are probably funerary ones. In Pissy-Pôville, a small village where a railway tunnel was dug between Rouen and Le Havre, local historian Nicole Duboc was instrumental in

---

[27] Fernand Braudel, *L'identité de la France: espace et histoire*, Paris, 1986.

[28] Gérard Noiriel, *Le Creuset français*, Paris, 1988.

[29] *The Lacemaker's Story: Loughborough, Luddites and Long Journey—Souvenirs of an Exhibition by Audrey Carpenter, John Carpenter and Tony Jarram, Friends of Charnwood Museum*, Charnwood Museum, Loughborough, 2007.

Figure C.2 A statue of civil engineer Joseph Locke (1805–60) in Barentin (Seine-Maritime). The statue, which was erected in 1951, is a stone replica of that made in bronze by Carlo Marochetti and erected in Barnsley in 1866. In the background: the viaduct, which was rebuilt after World War II.

bringing about the renovation of a tombstone of two Welsh brothers who died there (Figure C.3). In Rouen, an even older tombstone has been preserved; that of James Barker (Matterson, 1771–Rouen, 1832), who, after working for

Figure C.3 Tombstone of Thomas and William Jones in Pissy-Pôville (Seine-Maritime).
On the other side, the following words are engraved in English: 'Sacred to the memory
of Mʳ Thoˢ Jones, native of Tryddyn in the county of Flint, North Wales, who departed
this life in the Commune of Pissy Poville. April 13th 1845, aged 39 years. Likewise to
the Memory of his brother Mr Wm Jones, native of the same place who died also
in the above named Commune, June 5th 1845, aged 52 years' (photo: the author).

Waddington in Saint-Rémy-sur-Avre, was a founder in Sotteville-lès-Rouen in
1828 and whose tombstone is entirely in cast iron (Figure C.4).[30] It is not surprising that these tombstones, as well as the Barentin monument, should pay tribute
to entrepreneurs rather than to ordinary workers: this is in line with what our
society does with the living. At the same time, some workers are just starting to
have statues erected in their honour, like the Chinese worker of the Great War
whose statue was erected outside the Gare de Lyon in Paris in 2018. Maybe in the
future, the navvies of the Paris–Rouen–Le Havre line will also have their stone
memories. After all, they have been incorporated into literature: in 1996, British

---

[30] Serge Chassagne, 'Les Anglais-en France, et plus particulièrement en Normandie, dans la
"révolution industrielle" (1715–1880)', *Études Normandes*, 62ᵉ année, no. 2, 2013, pp. 121–40.

Figure C.4 Tombstone of James Barker (1771–1832) in the Cimetière monumental de Rouen.

novelist Julian Barnes dedicated a short story to the beef-consuming navvies crossing the Channel in the 1840s.[31]

As shown by historian Angela Moore, William, Thomas, and John Jones of Treuddyn were three brothers involved in railway construction, but they were neither navvies nor miners. John Jones was an agent working for Mackenzie and Brassey; that is, overseeing a particular stretch of the line, like the long tunnel which was built in Pissy-Pôville. They lived there for a while, and Thomas died there, soon followed by his brother William, for unknown reasons. Both deaths occurred at their dwellings and their death certificates did not mention accidents. William was described as an 'entrepreneur du tunnel du chemin de fer' (railway tunnel contractor). In 1852, John started working on Brassey's Mantes–Caen railway. He died on 23 September 1853 in Paris, was embalmed, and his body was brought by railway to his house in Newcastle-under-Lyme, where he was buried following a funeral procession.[32] As John had bought an expensive

[31] Julian Barnes, 'Junction', in *Cross Channel*, London, 1996, pp. 21–42.
[32] Angela Moore, 'John Jones, Railway Contractor of Treuddyn, Newcastle-under-Lyme and Pissy-Pôville, France', *Clwyd Historian*, vol. 67, winter 2012, pp. 2–9.

'perpetual concession' in Pissy-Pôville, the tombstone has survived, unlike the tombstones of the numerous workers who died there. In 2007, following the request of local historian Nicole Duboc, it was restored by the municipality.

In Landerneau, another tombstone, with its epitaph in English, preserves some memory of George Williamson (1823–1908), a flax carder who was already present in 1848, who became a foreman and remained in Landerneau even after most of the British had left after the factory closed in 1892. On 12 January 1852, Williamson declared that Jeanne Noble, a twenty-seven-year-old Scottish spinner, had given birth to their daughter Jeanne Williamson, out of wedlock. Neither Jeanne nor the daughter could be found in later local records, but George stayed until he died. In the same town, the building of the flax mill, which, after it closed in 1891, became a brick factory, has been mostly preserved and the local archivist, Marie-Pierre Cariou, has worked to have it restored, preserved, and transformed into a heritage site.

As we know, memory depends on the needs of the present more than on those of the past. We mentioned the boom in amateur family history and the huge potential it represents for academic history. Over the past decades, some major projects have been carried out relying on local and family historians. For the Reconstruction of the English population, the Cambridge Group for the History of Population & Social Structure founded by Peter Laslett and Tony Wrigley mobilised hundreds of local historians in 550 parishes in the 1970s, making it possible to know more of the pre-census population of England than we do of any other. More recently, a survey carried out by the Family and Community Historical Research Society added greatly to our knowledge of the Swing Riots.[33] One unpredictable location where the memory of the British emigrants to France has been preserved is Australia, where in 1982 an Australian Society of the Lacemakers of Calais was created by the descendants of those who had emigrated in 1848.[34] The society edited a quarterly journal, *Tulle*, from its inception in 1982 to 2018. A book was also published to celebrate the 150th anniversary of the emigration of the lacemakers, and quarterly meetings are still being held online.[35] A lot of what we know about the Calais British lacemakers has been exhumed by this society, without which these migrants would probably have remained in the shadows. The history of these migrants is still in the making, and future years and studies will hopefully help us know their lives and works better.

*

In July 1862, during a parliamentary debate on fortifications, free-trading manufacturer and politician Richard Cobden celebrated British artisans: 'Our strength,

---

[33] E. A. Wrigley and R. S. Schofield, *The Population History of England 1541–1871: A Reconstruction*, London, 1981; Michael Holland (ed.), *Swing Unmasked: The Agricultural Riots of 1830 to 1832 and Their Wider Implications*, Milton Keynes, 2005.

[34] https://www.lacemakersofcalais.com.au.   [35] Kelly, *Well Suited to the Colony*.

wealth, and commerce grow out of the skilled labour of the men working in metals. They are at the foundation of our manufacturing greatness'.[36] Samuel Smiles quoted this when he celebrated a few great inventors as heroes of the nation, alongside Wellington and Nelson.[37] The crucial part played by artisans is now being rediscovered by economic historians. In a comparative study of the forty-one English counties, Morgan Kelly, Joel Mokyr, and Cormac Ó Gráda have recently argued that artisan skill may well have been the crucial factor in the industrial revolution.[38] This is a welcome evolution from the narrative of industrialisation which focused on capital, businessmen, markets, and techniques, while neglecting the workers.

The flows we have studied were multi-faceted. In some ways, these migrant workers resembled the small numbers of eighteenth-century tramping artisans; in other respects, they belonged to the large-scale migrations of the modern industrial era consisting of many low-skilled workers, such as in railway building. Documenting these flows enables us to transcend conventional ideas about the interactions between the British and Europeans. It also helps us change scales, between the local and the global. It shows that regions (the East Midlands, Dundee, South Wales, northern France, Normandy...), and not just national entities or capital cities, are crucial units of analysis. Migrants experienced a world that was often different from that of tourists or books, following trajectories which took them to different urban centres outside the political and cultural capitals of Europe. They experienced interactions that were different from those of the elite, and which diverged markedly from the kinds of cross-cultural encounters depicted in travel literature or guidebooks for tourists.

Last, this book may also contribute to current debates. In Britain and on the Continent, migration is often criticised and denounced as a threat to jobs and standards of living. But the history of humankind and that of migration cannot be dissociated. What this study shows is that workers were recruited overseas not just as a means of lowering wages but also out of a desire to harness their valuable skills and expertise. While today Calais is first associated with being the port of entry for illegal immigrants, it is useful to know that it was long a major gateway to continental Europe for British emigrants. In Britain, while the Empire was expanding, much of the social and economic history of the country was written in constant interaction with the European Continent. On the Continent, where the temptation to transform Europe into a fortress is rampant and where nationalism and anti-migrant policies are gaining ground, this history also reminds us that there is no such thing as a self-sufficient economy and labour market. Without

[36] 'Our wealth, commerce, and manufactures grow out of the skilled labour of men working in metals'. HC Deb. 7 July 1862, vol. 167, cc1557.
[37] Samuel Smiles, *Industrial Biography: Iron-Workers and Tool-makers*, London, 1863.
[38] Morgan Kelly, Joel Mokyr, and Cormac Ó Gráda, 'The Mechanics of the Industrial Revolution', online research paper, 3 June 2020.

inward migration, industrial development would have been impossible. Machines and technology did not travel freely, they had to be conveyed, and without the British artisans, there was no industrialisation. There was never a time when national economies operated in closed circuits. Before generations of Italian, Belgian, German, Polish, southern European, Maghreb, and sub-Saharan African immigrants made their huge contributions to the economic development of western Europe, British migrants played a critical part in its industrial take-off.

Bibliography

1. Manuscript Material

United Kingdom

The National Archives, Kew
FO 27 series: Foreign Office and predecessor: Political and Other Departments: General Correspondence before 1906, France
FO 146 series: Foreign Office and Foreign and Commonwealth Office: Embassy and Consulates, France: General Correspondence
HO 40/14 fols. 131, 13–12, 135, 137
HO 44/10/79: ff. 268–9. Samuel Butler, France, that a person in Nottingham has sent him a lace-making machine supposedly from his friend, and asks if he should prosecute
BT 41/136/790: National Land Company Register

Nottinghamshire County Archives, Nottingham
DD/2081/1e: Miscellaneous correspondence
M351: Agreement for the execution of a restriction of hours deed (1829)
M/5085: Assignment
M/18211: Certificates of Foster family, etc.
M/22861: Specification of machine submitted in application for a patent in France, 1864
M/23175: Release
M/22870: Certificate

Institution of Civil Engineers, London
Mackenzie Archive

Belgium

Archives royales de Belgique à Bruxelles
Inventaire F1075

Archives de l'État à Liège
Fonds Cockerill

Université de Liège
Fonds Ernest Mahaim

France

Archives nationales, Pierrefitte-sur-Seine
BB 18/1442: troubles d'Elbeuf en mai 1846, à la suite de l'introduction d'une trieuse actionnée par un mécanicien anglais

BB 30/365/2: Troubles postérieurs à la Révolution de Février 1848—Cour de Rouen 1848–50
F7 3874 à 3893: Bulletins de Paris
F7 9787: Dossier Patrick et Cooper
F7 12187: Demandes de passeports
F7 12338: Etats numériques du mouvement des étrangers. Classement départemental. 1838–44 and 1846–8

Archives de l'Assistance publique—Hôpitaux de Paris (Le Kremlin-Bicêtre)
CHARITE 1Q 2/108: Registre des Entrées de l'Hôpital de la Charité (1er janvier au 24 juillet 1848)
CHARITE 3Q 2/44—Décès: Registre des déclarations de décès—1848—1er janvier au 24 juillet 1848

Archives départementales de l'Eure (Evreux)
1M 243–245: Surveillance de l'ordre et de l'esprit public sous la monarchie de Juillet
4M 218–220: Surveillance des étrangers
9M1: Industrie: instructions et correspondances an VIII-1858
9M3: Situation industrielle: rapports sur les crises industrielles; enquêtes sur les ouvriers 1837–81
9M12: Industrie textile

Archives départementales d'Eure-et-Loir (Chartres)
6 J 13: Album souvenir des établissements Waddington

Archives départementales du Finistère (Quimper)
4M48: Etrangers
4M 81: 1851 (police judiciaire)
4M 83: Surveillance des étrangers
6M 1039 Salaires industriels—1853–92
7M 247: 1850 (industrie du lin)
10M12: Travail et repos ouvrier—1848–1939
10M 26: Associations ouvrières et industrielles—1848–1940
1Z12: Correspondance du sous-préfet. Transcription de la correspondance active avec les maires
1Z29: Affaires politiques, esprit public: correspondances, rapports 1848–51
1Z63: Rapports de police municipale
1Z74/77: Surveillance des étrangers an XI-1859

Archives départementales du Pas-de-Calais (Arras)
1J 1652: 1 Loges maçonniques
M 2923: Boulogne sur Mer—Etablissements industriels
M 7427: Loges maçonniques

Archives départementales de Seine-Maritime (Rouen)
1M 162: Situation morale et politique
1T 680: Enseignement—Collège de Rouen—Admissions d'élèves—1815–44
1T 681: Bourses
2E3 163: Contrat de mariage de John Leavers (29 janvier 1826)
4M117: Rapports de police, 1828–54
4M158: Rapports des brigades de gendarmerie, 1816–82
4M 197–198: Morts et blessures accidentelles, par arrondissement
4M203: Mendicité

4M640: Librairie étrangère: importations (1848–60)
4M671: Anglais (statistique départementale), 1827
4M685: Etat numérique des étrangers par commune, 18 déc. 1881
4X207: Association des ouvriers anglais
6M850: Rapports et stats: mouvement des voyageurs dans les ports de Dieppe et du Havre, 1825–1906
6M1052: Répertoire des noms des étrangers naturalisés avec mention de leur nationalité et de la date du décret de naturalisation (1817–1920)
8M26: Dossiers individuels des consuls, vice-consuls et agents commerciaux dans le dpmt, classés par pays Angleterre
8M40: Exposition des produits de l'industrie française
10M108: Secours aux ouvriers sans travail, 1811–89
10M324: Mouvement et émigration de la main-d'œuvre … Renvoi d'ouvriers étrangers 1848
10M330: Coalitions, grèves, manifestations, an XI-1848

Archives départementales de la Somme (Amiens)

4M 1220: Surveillance des étrangers—Britanniques, Anglais, Ecossais, Irlandais
4M 1317: Transfuges français réfugiés en Angleterre 1824
6M11: Recensement de la population d'Ailly-sur-Somme
99M 106987/5: 1841–57 Travail des enfants dans les manufactures
99 M 94/5: Enquêtes sur les grèves … filature Carmichaël d'Ailly-sur-Somme

Archives départementales de la Seine-et-Oise (Saint-Quentin-en-Yvelines)

4MI41: Rapport sur la construction et l'exploitation des chemins de fer, 1842–5
Série S: Chemins de fer

Archives municipales

Archives municipales de Boulogne-sur-Mer (Pas-de-Calais)
Archives municipales de Calais (Pas-de-Calais)
Archives municipales de Charenton-le-Pont (Val-de-Marne)
Archives municipales de Coudekerque-Branche (Nord)
Archives municipales de Dunkerque (Nord)
Archives municipales de Grand-Couronne (Seine-Maritime)
Archives municipales de Landerneau (Finistère)
Archives municipales de Le Havre (Seine-Maritime)
Archives municipales de Malaunay (Seine-Maritime)
Archives municipales de Petit-Quevilly (Seine-Maritime)
Archives municipales de Pissy-Pôville (Seine-Maritime)
Archives municipales de Rouen (Seine-Maritime)
Archives municipales de Sotteville-lès-Rouen (Seine-Maritime)

Archives privées

Archives privées de la famille Wood-Maxton (Calais)
Archives privées de la famille Michaud-Carmichael
Archives privées de la famille Meurice-Molins (Seine-Maritime)

Canada

Private records of Nancy Adams (Mattawa)

2. Official Publications

UK Parliamentary Papers

Report from Select Committee on Artizans and Machinery (1824)

Report from the Select Committee on Manufactures, Commerce, and Shipping (1833)

Supplementary Report of the Central Board on the employment of Children in Factories (1834)

Report from the Select Committee on Import Duties (1840)

Report from the Select Committee appointed to inquire into the Operation of the Existing Laws affecting the Exportation of Machinery, 1841

Royal Commission on Children's Employment in Mines and Manufactories. Second Report (Manufactures). Appendix, 1843, vol. 13 and 14

Report from the Select Committee of the House of Lords on the Management of Railroads (1846)

Report from the Select Committee on Railway Labourers (1846)

Emigration Papers relative to Emigration to the Australian Colonies. 1847–8. Vol. 47, 481 p. (1847–8)

Report addressed to Her Majesty's Principal Secretary of State for the Home Department upon the Expediency of Subjecting the Lace Manufacture to the Regulations of the Factory Acts. London, 1861

Report from the Select Committee on Postage (1837–8)

Hansard's Parliamentary Debates

France

Ministère du commerce et des manufactures. *Enquête sur les fers*, 1829

Mémoire et extraits de délibérations des Chambres de commerce et des chambres consultatives des arts et manufactures, Paris, 1834

Ministère des travaux publics, de l'agriculture et du commerce. *Statistique de la France, Industrie*, Paris, 1847

Chambre de commerce et d'industrie de Paris, *Statistique de l'industrie à Paris résultant de l'enquête faite par la Chambre de commerce pour les années 1847–1848*, Paris, 1851

Enquête sur les lins

Conseil supérieur de l'agriculture, du commerce et de l'industrie, *Enquête: traité de commerce avec l'Angleterre*, Paris, vol. 5, 1860–2

Enquête parlementaire sur l'insurrection de 1871, Paris, 1872

Recensements de la population française

3. Newspapers

Annuaire de Brest et du Finistère
Boulogne Gazette [Boulogne News and Boulogne Gazette]
Brighton Gazette
Brighton Herald
Brighton Patriot
Bristol Temperance Herald
Calais Messenger
Courrier de l'Eure
Galignani's Messenger

Hampshire Telegraph and Sussex Chronicle
Illustrated Exhibitor
Illustrated London News
Journal de Calais
Journal de l'arrondissement du Havre, industriel, commercial, littéraire et d'annonces [then:
   Journal de l'arrondissement du havre, industriel, commercial, politique, littéraire et d'annonces]
Journal de la Somme
Journal de Rouen [et des départements de la Seine-Inférieure et de l'Eure]
Journal des chemins de fer et des progrès industriels
Journal des débats politiques et littéraires
Journal du Havre
L'Annotateur (Boulogne)
L'Atelier
L'Écho de la Fabrique (Lyon)
L'Illustration
L'Impartial de Rouen
L'Industriel Calaisien
La Colonne et l'Observateur. Journal politique de Boulogne et de l'arrondissement.
La Démocratie pacifique
La Démocratie pacifique
La Presse
Le Beffroi (Amiens)
Mechanics' Magazine
Mechanics Magazine and Journal of Science, Arts and Manufactures
Mémorial de Rouen
Midland Counties' Illuminator
Norman Times
North Wales Chronicle
Northern Star
Nottingham Gazette
Nottingham Journal
Nottingham Review
Nottingham Review and General Advertiser for the Midland Counties
Paris Sun
Penny Magazine
Punch
Quarterly Review
Railway Advocate and Continental Express
Railway Magazine
Sheffield Iris
Sussex Advertiser
Sydney Morning Herald
The Times

4. Digital Primary Sources

Legacies of British slave-ownership (Centre for the Study of the Legacies of British Slavery—UCL): https://www.ucl.ac.uk/lbs

'Inculpés des insurrections de juin 1848', database created by Jean-Claude Farcy and hosted by LiR3S (UMR, 7366 CNRS-université de Bourgogne): http://inculpes-juin-1848.fr/index.php

'Poursuivis à la suite du coup d'Etat de décembre 1851', database created by Jean-Claude Farcy and hosted by LiR3S (UMR 7366, CNRS-université de Bourgogne): http://poursuivis-decembre-1851.fr

'La répression judiciaure de la Commune de Paris: des pontons à l'amnistie (1871–1880)', database created by Jean-Claude Farcy and hosted by LiR3S (UMR 7366, CNRS-université de Bourgogne)

'Données historiques de la Statistique générale de France' (Insee)

5. Other Contemporary Works

Aftalion, Albert, *La crise de l'industrie linière et la concurrence victorieuse de l'industrie cotonnière*, Paris, 1904.

[Anon.], 'Autobiography of a navvy', *Macmillan's Magazine*, vol. 5, 1861–2.

[Anon.], 'Obituary. William Barber Buddicom, 1816–1887', *Minutes of the Proceedings of the Institution of Civil Engineers*, vol. 91, 1888, pp. 412–21.

[Anon.] [Charles Ross], "1st, 2nd, 3rd, 4th, 5th, and 6th Reports, from the select Committee on Artizans and Machinery", *Quarterly Review*, vol. 31, March 1825, p. 391–419.

Arnaud, docteur, 'Mémoire sur la topographie et l'hygiène publique de la ville de Calais, par le docteur Arnaud, transcrit et commenté par Guy Bourel', *Bulletin historique et artistique du Calaisis*, 1990, no. 121, 122, and 123, pp. 1–68.

Bailey, Mary, *Poems, Humorous and Sentimental*, Nottingham, 1826.

Blount, Edward, *Memoirs of Sir Edward Blount*, edited by Stuart J. Reid, London, 1902.

Bourgin, Georges and Hubert Bourgin, (dir), *Le Régime de l'industrie en France de 1814 à 1830. Recueil de textes publiés pour la Société d'histoire de France*, Paris, 1941, vol. 3.

Bowdler, T., *Observations on Emigration to France, on account of health, Economy, or the Education of Children, being a postscript to the Letters written in France in 1814*, London, 1815.

Brassey, Thomas (junior), *Lectures on the Labour Question*, 3rd ed., London, 1878.

Brougham, Henry, *Practical Observations upon the Education of the People*, London, 1825.

Cabet, Étienne, *Etat de la question sociale en Angleterre, en Ecosse, en Irlande et en France*, June 1843.

Claxton, Timothy, 'Memoirs', in his *Hints to Mechanics on Self-Education and Mutual Instruction*, London, 1839.

Cobbett, William, *A Grammar of the English Language*, New York, 1818.

Colin [pseud.], John, *The Wanderer Brought Home: The Life and Adventures of Colin—An Autobiography*, London, 1864.

Devey, Joseph, *The Life of Joseph Locke, Civil Engineer*, London, 1861.

Devlin, James Dacres, *The Boot and Shoe Trade of France*, London, 1838.

Devlin, James Dacres, *The Shoemaker*, 2 vols., London, 1839–41.

Devlin, James Dacres, *Critica Crispiana; or the Boots and Shoes British and Foreign of the Great Exhibition*, London, 1852.

Devlin, James Dacres, *Strangers' Homes; or, the Model Lodging Houses of London*, London, 1853.

Devlin, James Dacres, *Contract Reform*, 1856.

Dictionnaire de l'Académie française.

Duthie, William, *A Tramp's Wallet; stored by an English Goldsmith during his Wanderings in Germany and France*, London, 1858.

Engels, Friedrich, *Die Lage der arbeitenden Klasse in England* [*The Condition of the Working Class in England*], Leipzig, 1845.

Engels, Frederick, 'On the History of the Communist League', *Sozialdemokrat*, 12–26 November 1885, in Karl Marx and Frederick Engels, *Collected Works*, London, vol. 26, 1990.

Faucheur, Narcisse, *Mon Histoire à mes chers enfants et petits-enfants*, Paris, 1886.

Felkin, William, *A History of the Machine-Wrought Hosiery and Lace Manufactures*, London, 1867.

Ferguson, Samuel fils, *Histoire du tulle et des dentelles mécaniques en Angleterre et en France*, Paris, 1862.

Garnett, Elizabeth, *Our Navvies: A Dozen Years Ago and To-Day*, London, 1885.

Gaskell, Elizabeth, *Mary Barton*, Oxford, 2008 [1848].

Gossez, Rémi (ed.), *Un ouvrier en 1820. Manuscrit inédit de Jacques Étienne Bédé*, Paris, 1984.

Helps, Arthur, *Life and Labours of Thomas Brassey, 1805–1870*, London, 1888.

Henson's History of the Framework Knitters, a reprint with a new introduction by S. D. Chapman, London, 1970.

Hopkinson, Arthur W., 'Home industries in Nottingham', *The Economic Review*, vol. 13, London, July 1903, pp. 334–9.

Howitt, Mary Botham, *Little Coin, Much Care; or How poor men live—A tale*, London, 1842.

Hugo, Victor, *Choses vues*, Paris, 1887 [1845].

Hugo, Victor, *Le Rhin. Lettres à un ami*, vol. 1, Paris, 1906 [1842].

Jackson, F. W., *James Jackson et ses fils*, Paris, 1893.

James, G. P. R., 'Some observations on the book trade, as connected with the literature in England', *Journal of the Statistical Society of London*, vol. 6, 1843, pp. 50–60.

Janin, Jules, *Voyage de Paris à la mer*, Paris, 1847.

Jones, Ernest, 'Woman's wrongs', *Notes to the People*, 1 November 1851 to 25 April 1852 [republished as *Women's Wrongs: A Series of Tales*, London, 1855].

Jowett, William, *Diary of Sergeant William Jowett, of the Seventh Fusiliers. Written during the Crimean War. To which is added, a Brief Memoir*, Beeston (Nottinghamshire), 1856.

Lalance, Auguste, 'Notice nécrologique de M. Henri Thierry-Koechlin (1813–1893)', *Bulletin de la société industrielle de Mulhouse*, 1894.

Lefrançais, Gustave, *Souvenirs d'un révolutionnaire*, Paris, 1972.

Le Play, Frédéric, *Les ouvriers européens. Étude sur les travaux, la vie domestique et la condition morale des populations ouvrières de l'Europe*, vol. 6, 2nd ed., Paris, 1878.

Leroux, Pierre, *La Grève de Samarez, poème philosophique*, Paris, 1863.

Levers, John, 'Description de divers perfectionnements ajoutés aux métiers destinés à la fabrication du tulle connu sous le nom de bobin-net', *Bulletin de la Société d'Encouragement pour l'Industrie Nationale*, Paris, 1830, pp. 379–383.

Locke, Joseph, 'Presidential address of Joseph Locke, M.P., January 12, 1858', *Minutes of the Proceedings of the Institution of Civil Engineers*, vol. 17, 1858, pp. 128–53.

Marchant, James, *Dr John Clifford, C.H.: Life, Letters and Reminiscences*, London, 1924.

Marec, Yannick, *1848 à Rouen. Les Mémoires du Citoyen Cord'Homme, oncle de Maupassant*, Luneray, 1988.

Marx, Karl, *Das Kapital. Kritik der politischen Oekonomie*, Hamburg, 1867.

Molard, Jeune, 'Rapport sur les fonderies et établissements d'industrie de MM. Manby et Wilson à Charenton près de Paris', *Bulletin de la société d'encouragement pour l'industrie nationale*, April 1825, pp. 123–6.

Nadaud, Martin, *Léonard, maçon de la Creuse*, Paris, 1998 [1895].

Normanby, Marquis of, *A Year of Revolution: From a Journal Kept in Paris in 1848*, London, 1857.

Notice historique et statistique sur l'industrie tullière à Calais et à Saint-Pierre les Calais présentée avec un album des échantillons de ses produits à monsieur le ministre de l'agriculture et du commerce, sur sa demande, par la chambre de Commerce de Calais, Paris, February 1851.

O'Brien, Bronterre, *Buonarroti's History of Babeuf's Conspiracy for Equality*, London, 1836.

Owen, Robert, *The Revolution in the Mind and Practice of the Human Race*, London, 1850.

Pigott's Directory of Sussex, 1823.

Perdiguier, Agricol, *Mémoires d'un compagnon*, Paris, 1992 [1855]

Radiguet, Max, *A travers la Bretagne. Souvenirs et paysages*, Paris, 1865.

Renouard, Alfred, *Etudes sur le travail des Lins, chanvres, jutes, etc. Tome Premier. Histoire de l'industrie linière*, Lille, 1879.

Salavy du Fresnoy, *Une analyse raisonnée des langues française et anglaise: moyen facile pour apprendre l'une ou l'autre*, Paris, 1806.

Smiles, Samuel, *Industrial Biography: Iron-Workers and Tool-Makers*, London, 1863.

Smith, Charles Manby, *The Working Man's Way in the World: Being the Autobiography of a Journeyman Printer*, London, 1853.

Tennent, James Emerson, *Belgium*, London, 1841.

Tristan, Flora, *Promenades dans Londres,* Paris, 1978 [1840 and 1842].

Tristan, Flora, *Union ouvrière*, Paris, 1986 [1843 and 1844].

Turgan, *Les grandes usines. Etudes industrielles en France et à l'étranger*, Paris, vol. 8, 1868.

Turgan, *Les grands usines*, vol. 3, Paris, 1874.

Ure, Andrew, *The Philosophy of Manufactures*, London, 1835.

Verne, Jules, *The Begum's Fortune*, translated by W. H. G. Kingston, Philadelphia, PA, 1879.

Villermé, Louis-René, *Tableau de l'état physique et moral des ouvriers employés dans les manufactures de coton, de laine et de soie*, Paris, 1840.

Warden, Alexander J., *The Linen Trade, Ancient and Modern*, Dundee, 1864.

6. Later Works

Addis, J. P., *The Crawshay Dynasty: A Study in Industrial Organisation and Development, 1765–1867*, Cardiff, 1957.

Agnès, Benoît, *L'appel au pouvoir. Les pétitions aux Parlements en France et au Royaume-Uni (1814–1848)*, Rennes, 2018.

Agulhon, Maurice (dir.), *Les Révolutions de 1848: l'Europe des images*, Paris, 1998.

Alexandre, Alain, 'L'évolution industrielle de la vallée du Cailly (1850–1914)', *Études normandes*, vol. 84, 3ᵉ trimestre, 1972, pp. 1–31.

Alexandre, Alain, and Michel Croguennec, *Histoires d'usines. 180 ans de vie industrielle dans l'agglomération rouennaise*, Nolléval, 2013.

Alexandre, Placide, *La Trombe de Monville et de Malaunay. 1845*, Rouen, 1920.

Allen, Robert C., *The British Industrial Revolution in Global Perspective*, Cambridge, 2009.

Altick, Richard, *The English Common Reader: A Social History of the Mass Reading Public 1800–1900*, Chicago, IL, 1957.

Anderson, Clare, *Subaltern Lives: Biographies of Colonialism in the Indian Ocean World, 1790–1920*, Cambridge, 2012.

Anderson, Olive, 'Emigration and Marriage Break-Up in Mid-Victorian England', *The Economic History Review*, vol. 50, no. 1, February 1997, pp. 104–9.

Aprile, Sylvie, and Fabrice Bensimon (dir.), *La France et l'Angleterre au XIXe siècle: échanges, représentations, comparaisons*, Paris, 2006.

Aprile, Sylvie, and Jacques Rougerie, 'Introduction', 'La Commune et les étrangers', *Migrance*, 35, premier semestre 2010.

Armytage, W. H. G., *Heavens Below: Utopian Experiments in England 1560–1960*, London, 1961.

Ashton, Owen R., and Paul A. Pickering, *Friends of the People: Uneasy Radicals in the Age of the Chartists*, London, 2002.

Awty, Brian G., 'French immigrants and the iron industry in Sheffield', *Yorkshire Archaeological Journal*, vol. 53, 1981, pp. 57–62.

Bade, Klaus, *Migration in European History*, Oxford, 2003.

Baines, Dudley, 'The use of published census data in migration studies', in E. A. Wrigley (ed.), *Nineteenth-Century Society: Essays in the Use of Quantitative Methods for the Study of Social Data*, Cambridge, 1972, pp. 311–35.

Baines, Dudley, *Migration in a Mature Economy: Emigration and Internal Migration in England and Wales, 1861–1900*, Cambridge, 1985.

Balachandran, Gopalan, *Globalizing Labour? Indian Seafarers and World Shipping, c. 1870–1945*, New Delhi, 2012.

Bantman, Constance, *Jean Grave and the Networks of French Anarchism, 1854–1939*, London, 2021.

Barnes, David, *The Making of a Social Disease: Tuberculosis in Nineteenth Century France*, Berkeley, CA, 1995.

Barnes, Julian, 'Junction', in *Cross Channel*, London, 1996, pp. 21–42.

Barzman, John, *Dockers, métallos, ménagères. Mouvements sociaux et cultures militantes au Havre, 1912–1923*, Rouen, 1997.

Bayly, Chris, *Imperial Meridian: The British Empire and the World, 1780–1830*, Harlow, 1989.

Becchia, Alain, *La draperie d'Elbeuf (des origines à 1870)*, Rouen, 2000.

Beckert, Sven, *Empire of Cotton: A New History of Global Capitalism*, London, 2015.

Belhoste, Jean-François, 'Les forges de Charenton', in *Architectures d'usines en Val-de-Marne (1822–1939), Cahier de l'inventaire*, vol. 12, 1988, pp. 22–31.

Belhoste, Jean-François, and Denis Woronoff, 'The French iron and steel industry during the industrial revolution', in Chris Evans and Göran Ryden (eds.), *The Industrial Revolution in Iron: The Impact of British Coal Technology in Nineteenth-Century Europe*, Aldershot, 2005, pp. 75–94.

Belich, James, *Replenishing the Earth: The Settler Revolution and the Rise of the Anglo-World, 1783–1939*, Oxford, 2009.

Bensimon, Fabrice, *Les Britanniques face à la révolution française de 1848*, Paris, 2000.

Bensimon, Fabrice, 'British workers in France, 1815–1848', *Past and Present*, no. 213, November 2011, pp. 147–89.

Bensimon, Fabrice, 'Calais: 1816–2016', https://www.historytoday.com/calais-1816-2016, 24 October 2016.

Bensimon, Fabrice, 'The IWMA and its precursors in London, c. 1830–1860', in Fabrice Bensimon, Quentin Deluermoz, and Jeanne Moisand (eds.), *'Arise Ye Wretched of the Earth': The First International in a Global Perspective*, Leiden, 2018, pp. 21–38.

Bensimon, Fabrice, and Christopher A. Whatley, 'The thread of migration: A Scottish-French linen and jute works and its workers in France, c. 1845–c. 1870', *Journal of Migration History*, vol. 2.1, 2016, pp. 120–47.

Bensimon, Fabrice, and François Jarrige, 'Lire les socialistes et les radicaux dans l'atelier. Esquisses sur les pratiques ouvrières de lecture collective (France et Grande-Bretagne, 1780–1860)', in Nathalie Brémand (dir.), *Bibliothèques en utopie: les socialistes et la lecture au XIXe siècle*, Lyon, 2020, pp. 93–113.

Berg, Maxine, 'What difference did women's work make to the industrial revolution?', *History Workshop*, vol. 35, 1993, pp. 22–44.

Berthoff, Rowland, *British Immigrants in Industrial America, 1790–1850*, Cambridge, MA, 1953.

Biernacki, Richard, *The Fabrication of Labor: Germany and Britain, 1640–1914*, Berkeley, CA, 1995.

Binfield, Kevin (ed.), *Writings of the Luddites*, Baltimore, MD, 2015.

Black, Frank Gees, and Renee Métivier Black (eds.), *The Harney Papers*, Assen, 1969.

Blackburn, Sheila, *A Fair Day's Wage for a Fair Day's Work? Sweated Labour and the Origins of Minimum Wage Legislation in Britain*, London, 2016.

Blanc-Chaléard, Marie-Claude, *Histoire de l'immigration*, Paris, 2001.

Blavier, Yves, *La société linière du Finistère. Ouvriers et entrepreneurs à Landerneau au XIXe siècle*, Rennes, 1999.

Bocard, Hélène, *De Paris à la mer. La Ligne de chemin de fer Paris-Rouen-Le Havre*, Paris, 2005.

Bodinier, Bernard, 'La révolution industrielle par les Anglais à Pont-Audemer', *Les Anglais en Normandie*, Louviers, 2011, pp. 473–85.

Bonte, Odette, 'Coudekerque-Branche, les Dickson et la colonie d'Ecossais', *Revue de la Société dunkerquoise d'histoire et d'archéologie*, no. 26, November 1992, pp. 155–84.

Borde, Christian, *Calais et la Mer, 1814–1914*, Villeneuve d'Ascq, 1997.

Borde, Christian, 'Les dentelliers de Calais sous le Second Empire: l'ouverture au monde', in Bruno Bethouart (ed.), *Napoléon III, Boulogne et l'Europe. Les cahiers du Littoral*, vol. 2, 2002, pp. 205–17.

Borde, Christian, 'Le contrebandier, le tulliste et le négociant: Calais, relais européen de l'industrie dentellière, 1802–1832', in Stéphane Curveiller and Laurent Buchard (eds.), *Se déplacer du Moyen âge à nos jours*, Calais, 2009, pp. 291–302.

Borde, Christian, and Xavier Morillion, *La Grande usine à tulle. Histoire de l'usine Boulart, site de la Cité Internationale de la Dentelle et de la Mode à Calais*, Calais, 2014.

Boston, Ray, *British Chartists in America 1839–1900*, Manchester, 1971.

Bourmaud, François, 'Les Britanniques et le sport en France avant 1914: une histoire de transfert culturel', thesis, Sorbonne Université et Université de Lausanne, 2022.

Brandt, André, 'Travailleurs anglais dans le Haut-Rhin dans la première moitié du XIXe siècle', *Actes du 92ème congrès national des sociétés savantes, Strasbourg, Colmar, 1967*, vol. 2, *Le Commerce et l'industrie*, 1970, pp. 297–312.

Braudel, Fernand, *L'identité de la France: espace et histoire*, Paris, 1986.

Bret, Patrice, Irina Gouzévitch, and Liliane Pérez (dir.), 'Les techniques et la technologie entre la France et la Grande-Bretagne XVIIe–XIXe siècles', *Documents pour l'histoire des techniques*, 2010, n° 19.

Brettell, Caroline B., and James F. Hollifield (eds.), *Migration Theory: Talking across Disciplines*, London, 2000.

Bronstein, Jamie L., *Land Reform and Working-Class Experience in Britain and the United States, 1800–1862*, Stanford, CA, 1999.

Brooke, David, *The Railway Navvy: 'That Despicable Race of Men'*, London, 1983.

Brooke, David, 'Brassey, Thomas (1805–1870)', *ODNB*, Oxford, 2004.

Brooke, David, *William Mackenzie: International Railway Builder and Civil Engineer*, London, 2004.

Bruland, Kristine, *British Technology and European Industrialization: The Norwegian Textile Industry in the Mid-Nineteenth Century*, Cambridge, 1989.

Brundage, David, *Irish Nationalists in America: The Politics of Exile, 1798–1998*, New York, 2016.

Buchanan, R. A., 'The British contribution to Australian Engineering', *Historical Studies*, Melbourne, 20, 1983, pp. 401–19.

Buchanan, R. A. 'Institutional proliferation in the British engineering profession, 1847–1914', *Economic History Review*, 2nd ser., vol. 38, February 1985, pp. 42–60.

Buchanan, R. A., 'The diaspora of British engineering', *Technology and Culture*, vol. 27, no. 3, July 1986, pp. 501–24.

Buchanan, R. A., *The Engineers: A History of the Engineering Profession in Great Britain, 1750–1914*, London, 1989.

Bui Tran, Anh-Dao, 'Le Grand Tronc. La construction d'un chemin de fer au Canada britannique (1852–1860)', thesis in preparation, Sorbonne Université.

Burgess, Greg, *Refuge in the Land of Liberty: France and Its Refugees, from the Revolution to the End of Asylum, 1787–1939*, Basingstoke, 2008.

Burnett, John, David Vincent, and David Mayall (eds.), *The Autobiography of the Working Class: An Annotated Critical Bibliography*, Brighton, 3 vols., 1984–9.

Burnette, Joyce, *Gender, Work and Wages in Industrial Revolution Britain*, Cambridge, 2008.

Cabot, Bastien, *'À bas les Belges!' L'expulsion des mineurs borains (Lens, août-septembre 1892)*, Rennes, 2017.

Cahn, Susan, *Industry of Devotion: The Transformation of Women's Work in England, 1500–1660*, New York, 1987.

Callite, Anne, *Alexis Hallette. Ingénieur et industriel en Artois, 1788–1846*, Roubaix, 2003.

Cardwell, Donald, *The Development of Science and Technology in Nineteenth-Century Britain*, Farnham, 2003.

Carey, Jane, and Claire McLisky (eds.), *Creating White Australia*, Sydney, 2009.

Caron, François, *Histoire des chemins de fer en France*, vol. 1, 1740–1883, Paris, 1997.

Caron, Michel, *Du tulle à la dentelle, Naissance d'une industrie, 1815–1860*, Baie-du-Tombeau, 1997.

Caron, Michel, *Trois âges d'or de la dentelle. 1860–1905*, Lille, 2003.

Carpenter, Audrey, John Carpenter, and Tony Jarram, *The Lacemakers' Story: Loughborough, Luddites and Long Journeys*, Charnwood, 2007.

Carpenter, George W., revised by Mike Chrimes, 'Buddicom, William Barber (1816–1887)', *ODNB*, 2004 and 2006.

Carpenter, John, 'Les tullistes anglais de l'Est des Midlands à la recherche d'un nouvel avenir à partir de 1816', in Stéphane Curveiller and Laurent Buchard (eds.), *Se déplacer du Moyen âge à nos jours*, Calais, 2009.

Carrier, N. H., and J. R. Jeffery, *External Migration: A Study of the Available Statistics, 1815–1950*, London, 1953.

Carrothers, W. A., *Emigration from the British Isles*, 2nd ed., London, 1965 (1929).

Casanovas, Joan, *Bread, or Bullets! Urban Labor and Spanish Colonialism in Cuba, 1850–1898*, Pittsburgh, PA, 1998.

Chaline, Jean-Pierre, 'Modèle ou rivale? L'Angleterre vue par les Rouennais du XIXe siècle', *Etudes Normandes*, vol. 1, 1983, pp. 53–9.

Chapman, Stanley D., 'The life and work of William Felkin (1795–1874)', in William Felkin, *A History of the Machine-Wrought Hosiery and Lace Manufactures*, Newton Abbot, 1967, pp. v–xxxviii.

Chapman, Stanley D., *Merchant Enterprise in Britain: From the Industrial Revolution to World War I*, Cambridge, 1992.

Chapman, Stanley D., *Hosiery and Knitwear: Four Centuries of Small-Scale Industry in Britain c. 1589–2000*, Oxford, 2002.

Chapman, Stanley D., 'The first generation of Nottingham lace makers: The Restriction of Hours Deed of 1829', in J. B. Bailey (ed.), *Nottinghamshire Lace Makers: The First Generation of Nottingham Lace Makers—Including 700+ Names of Lace Machine Owners in 1829*, Melton Mowbray, 2003.

Chapman, Stanley D., 'Felkin, William (1795–1874)', *ODNB*, Oxford, 2004.

Chase, Malcolm, *Early Trade Unionism: Fraternity, Skill and the Politics of Labour*, Aldershot, 2000.

Chase, Malcolm, *Chartism: A New History*, Manchester, 2007.

Chase, Malcolm, '"Resolved in defiance of fool and of knave"?: Chartism, children and conflict', in Dinah Birch and Mark Llewellyn (eds.), *Conflict and Difference in Nineteenth-Century Literature*, London, 2010, pp. 126–40.

Chase, Malcolm, 'Labour history's biographical turn', edited by Fabrice Bensimon, *History Workshop Journal*, vol. 92, 2021, pp. 194–207.

Chassagne, Serge, 'Les Anglais en France, et plus particulièrement en Normandie, dans la "révolution industrielle" (1715–1880)', *Études Normandes*, 62e année, no. 2, 2013, pp. 121–40.

Châtelain, Abel, *Les migrants temporaires en France de 1800 à 1914*, 2 vols., Villeneuve d'Ascq, 1976.

Chevalier, Jean-Joseph, 'La Compagnie des Toiles de l'ouest et ses promoteurs (1839–1862): l'échec d'une entreprise capitaliste choletaise...', *Annales de Normandie*, vol. 38, no. 2–3, May to July 1988, pp. 105–23.

Chrimes, Michael, Mary K. Murphy, and Georges Ribeill (eds.), *Mackenzie—Giant of the Railways: William Mackenzie (1794–1851) and the Construction of the Early European Railway Network*, London, 1994.

Church, Roy A., *Economic and Social Change in a Midland Town: Victorian Nottingham 1815–1900*, London, 1966.

Church, Roy A., and S. D. Chapman, 'Gravener Henson and the making of the English working class', in E. L. Jones and G. E. Mingay (eds.), *Land, Labour and Population in the Industrial Revolution*, London, 1967, pp. 131–61.

Clark, Alice, *Working Life of Women in the Seventeenth Century*, London, 1919.

Cockburn, Cynthia, *Machinery of Dominance: Women, Men and Technical Know-How*, London, 1985.

Coffin, Judith G., *The Politics of Women's Work: The Paris Garment Trades, 1750–1915*, Princeton, NJ, 1996.

Coleman, Terry, *The Railway Navvies*, Harmondsworth, 1981 [1965].

Collins, Brenda, and Philip Ollerenshaw, 'The European linen industry since the Middle Ages', in Brenda Collins and Philip Ollerenshaw (eds.), *The European Linen Industry in Historical Perspective*, Oxford, 2003.

Commission on Emigration and Other Population Problems, 1948-1954: Reports, Dublin, 1956.

Conway, Stephen, *Britain, Ireland, and Continental Europe in the Eighteenth Century. Similarities, Connextions, Identities*, Oxford, 2011.

Cooper-Richet, Diana, 'La librairie étrangère à Paris au XIXe siècle. Un milieu perméable aux innovations et aux transferts', *Actes de la recherche en sciences sociales*, vol. 12, March 1999, pp. 60-9.

Cooper-Richet, Diana, 'La diffusion du modèle victorien à travers le monde. Le rôle de la presse en anglais publiée en France au XIXe siècle', in Marie-Eve Thérenty and Alain Vaillant (dir.), *Presse, nations et mondialisation au XIXe siècle*, Paris, 2010, pp. 17-32.

Cooper-Richet, Diana, *La France anglaise. De la Révolution à nos jours*, Paris, 2018.

Cooper-Richet, Diana, and Emily Borgeaud, *Galignani*, Paris, 1999.

Corbes, H., 'L'immigration anglaise dans les Côtes du Nord au XIXe siècle', *Société d'émulation des Cotes du Nord*, 1962, pp. 118-30.

Corbin, Alain, 'Douleurs, souffrances et misères du corps', in Alain Corbin, Jean-Jacques Courtine, and Georges Vigarello (dir.), *Histoire du Corps*, vol. 2. *De la Révolution à la Grande Guerre*, Paris, 2005.

Cordery, Simon, *British Friendly Societies, 1750-1914*, London, 2003.

Cotte, Michel, *De l'espionnage industriel à la veille technologique*, Besançon, 2005.

Cotte, Michel, *Le choix de la révolution industrielle: les entreprises de Marc Seguin et de ses frères, 1815-1835*, Rennes, 2007.

Cunningham, Hugh, and Viazzo, P. P. (eds.), *Child Labour in Historical Perspective, 1800-1985: Case Studies from Europe, Japan and Colombia*, Florence, 1996.

Curtis, Lewis P. Jr, *Apes and Angels: The Irishman in Victorian Caricature*, Washington, DC, 1997 [1971].

Cuthbert, Norman H., *The Lace Makers' Society: A Study of Trade Unionism in the British Lace Industry, 1760-1960*, [Nottingham?], 1960.

Dambron, Gérard, *La construction de la ligne de chemin de fer de Paris-Rouen-Le Havre. Analyse des premières années d'exploitation jusqu'à la fusion en Compagnie de l'Ouest*, mémoire pour le Diplôme d'études supérieures d'histoire, sous la direction de Jean Vidalenc, Université de Rouen, 15 December 1970.

Darriulat, Philippe, *Les Patriotes: la gauche républicaine et la nation, 1830-1870*, Paris, 2001.

Daumalin, Xavier, and Olivier Raveux, *Philippe de Girard ou l'invention de l'Europe industrielle (1775-1845)*, Avignon, 1999.

Delalande, Nicolas, *La Lutte et l'entraide. L'Âge des solidarités ouvrières*, Paris, 2019.

Delavignette, Robert, *Birama*, Paris, 1955.

Denéchère Yves, and Jean-Luc Marais (dir.), 'Les étrangers dans l'Ouest de la France (XVIIIe-XXe siècle). Actes du Colloque de Cholet, 25-26 juillet 2002', *Annales de Bretagne et des Pays de l'Ouest*, vol. 109, no. 4, Rennes, 2002.

Derainne, Pierre-Jacques, *Le travail, les migrations et les conflits en France. Représentations et attitudes sociales sous la monarchie de Juillet et la seconde République*, thesis, Université de Bourgogne, 1998-9.

Derainne, Pierre-Jacques, « Les perceptions sociales des travailleurs migrants britanniques en France dans la première moitié du XIXe siècle », in Sylvie Aprile, Fabrice Bensimon (eds.), *La France et l'Angleterre au XIXe siècle. Echanges, représentations, comparaisons*, Grâne, Créaphis, 2006, pp. 351–367.

Désert, Gabriel, 'Viande et poisson dans l'alimentation des Français au milieu du XIXe siècle', *Annales. Economies, sociétés, civilisations*, 30e année, no. 2–3, 1975, pp. 519–36.

Diaz, Delphine, '"J'ai fait mon service comme un brave citoyen français". Parcours et récits de combattants étrangers sur les barricades parisiennes en février et juin 1848', unpublished paper, 'Les acteurs européens du "printemps des peuples" 1848', Paris, 1 June 2018.

Diaz Delphine, and Hugo Vermeren (dir.), 'Éloigner et expulser les étrangers au xixe siècle', special issue of *Diasporas. Circulations, migrations, histoire*, no 33, 2019.

Domain, Magali, 'Jaurès et la grève des tullistes calaisiens (12 novembre 1900–7 février 1901)', *Cahiers Jaurès*, vol. 1, no. 211, 2014, pp. 53–75.

Dornel, Laurent, *La France hostile. Socio-histoire de la xénophobie (1870–1914)*, Paris, 2004.

Downs, Laura Lee, *Manufacturing Inequality: Gender Division in the French and British Metalworking Industries, 1914–1939*, Ithaca, NY, 1995.

Drummond, Diane K., *Tracing Your Railway Ancestors: A Guide for Family Historians*, Barnsley, 2010.

Dubosc, Georges, 'Une industrie peu connue: la fabrique de tulle de Grand-Couronne', *Journal de Rouen*, 31 December 1907.

Dubuc, André, 'Les émeutes de Rouen et d'Elbeuf en 1848 (27, 28 et 29 avril 1848)', *Etudes d'Histoire Moderne et contemporaine*, vol. 2, 1948.

Duché, Elodie, 'L'otium des captifs d'honneur britanniques à Verdun sous le Premier Empire, 1803–1814', in Nicolas Beaupré and Karine Rance (eds.) *Arrachés et déplacés. Réfugiés politiques, prisonniers de guerre, déportés (Europe et espace colonial 1789–1918)*, Clermont-Ferrand, 2016, pp. 117–44.

Dufresne-Seurre, Geneviève, *Les Waddington, une dynastie de cotonniers en Eure-et-Loir: 1792–1961*, Chartres, 2011.

Durbec, A., 'Contribution à l'histoire du chemin de fer de Paris à la mer', in *Actes du 81ème congrès national des sociétés savantes, Rouen-Caen, 1956*, Paris, 1956.

Durie, Alastair J., *The Scottish Linen Industry in the Eighteenth Century*, Edinburgh, 1979.

Edwards, Susan, *Hughesovka: A Welsh Enterprise in Imperial Russia*, Glamorgan, 1992.

Epstein, James, 'Some organisational and cultural aspects of the Chartist Movement in Nottingham', in James Epstein and Dorothy Thompson (eds.), *The Chartist Experience: Studies in Working-Class Radicalism and Culture, 1830–60*, London, 1982, pp. 221–68.

Epstein, James, *The Lion of Freedom. Feargus O'Connor and the Chartist Movement, 1832–1842*, London, 1982.

Erickson, Charlotte, *Invisible Immigrants: The Adaptation of English and Scottish Immigrants in Nineteenth-Century America*, Ithaca, NY, 1972.

Erickson, Charlotte, *Leaving England: Essays on British Emigration in the Nineteenth Century*, Ithaca, NY, 1994.

Evans, Chris, 'Crawshay, William (1764–1834)', *ODNB*, Oxford, 2004.

Extermann, Blaise, 'The teaching of modern languages in France and francophone Switzerland (1740–1940): A historiographical overview', *The Language Learning Journal*, vol. 46, no. 1, 2018, pp. 40-50.

Fegan, Melissa, *Literature and the Irish Famine, 1845–1919*, Oxford, 2002.

Fennetaux, Ariane, and John Styles (eds.), *Album Holker. The Holker Album*, Paris, 2022.

Fewkes, Anne V. 'Protestant families extracted from the 1841 Census of St Pierre, Calais, France', *Nottinghamshire Family History Society*, vol. 121, December 1998.

Finkelstein, David, *Movable Types: Roving Creative Printers of the Victorian World*, Oxford, 2018.

Fitzgerald, Patrick, and Brian Lambkin, *Migration in Irish History, 1607–2007*, Basingstoke, 2008.

Foster, Roy, *Paddy and Mr Punch: Connections in Irish and English History*, New York, 1993.

Fourn, François, *Étienne Cabet ou le temps de l'utopie*, Paris, 2014.

Frank, Christopher, *Master and Servant Law: Chartists, Trade Unions, Radical Lawyers and the Magistracy in England, 1840–1865*, Farnham, 2010.

Fremdling, Rainer, 'The puddler: A craftsman's skill and the spread of a new technology in Belgium, France and Germany', *Journal of European Economic History*, vol. 20, no. 3, 1991, pp. 529–67.

Fremdling, Rainer, 'Transfer patterns of British technology to the continent: The case of the iron industry', *European Review of Economic History*, vol. 4, 2000, pp. 197–220.

Fremdling, Rainer, 'Foreign trade—transfer—adaptation: British iron making technology on the continent (Belgium and France)', in Chris Evans and Göran Ryden (eds.), *The Industrial Revolution in Iron: The Impact of British Coal Technology in Nineteenth-Century Europe*, Aldershot, 2005.

Frobert, Ludovic, *Les Canuts ou La démocratie turbulente: Lyon, 1831–1834*, Paris, 2009.

Frost, Ginger S., *Living in Sin: Cohabiting as Husband and Wife in Nineteenth-Century England*, Manchester, 2008.

Gallagher, John, *Learning Languages in Early Modern England*, Oxford, 2019.

Gatrell, Vic, *Conspiracy on Cato Street. A Tale of Liberty and Revolution in Regency London*, Cambridge, 2022.

Gayot, Gérard, 'La classe ouvrière saisie par la révolution industrielle à Verviers, 1800–1810', *Revue du Nord*, vol. 4, no. 347, 2002, pp. 633–66.

Geerkens, Éric, 'Avant-propos', in Nicole Caulier-Mathy and Nicole Haesenne-Peremans (eds.), 'Inventaire des archives Ernest Mahaim', Université de Liège, 2011, https://orbi.uliege.be/bitstream/2268/108622/1/Mahaim.pdf.

Gille, Bertrand, *La Sidérurgie française au XIXe siècle*, Geneva, 1968.

Gilley, Sheridan, 'English attitudes to the Irish in England, 1789–1900', in Colin Holmes (ed.), *Immigrants and Minorities in British Society*, London, 1978, pp. 81–110.

Goodway, David, *London Chartism 1838–1848*, Cambridge, 1982.

Gordon, Eleanor, *Women and the Labour Movement in Scotland, 1850–1914*, Oxford, 1991.

Grandjonc, Jacques, 'Les émigrés allemands sous la monarchie de Juillet. Documents de surveillance policière 1833–février 1848', in *Cahiers d'Études Germaniques*, Aix-en-Provence, no. 1, 1972, pp. 115–249.

Grandjonc, Jacques, 'Les étrangers à Paris sous la monarchie de Juillet et la Seconde République', *Population*, special issue, vol. a.29, March 1974, pp. 61–88.

Greenlees, Janet, *Female Labour Power: Women Workers' Influence on Business Practices in the British and American Cotton Industries, 1780–1860*, Burlington, VT, 2007.

Gribaudi, Maurizio, *Paris ville ouvrière. Une histoire occultée. 1789–1848*, Paris, 2014.

Griffiths, John, and Vic Evans, 'The Chartist legacy in the British world: Evidence from New Zealand's southern settlements, 1840s–1870s', *History*, vol. 99, no. 5 (338), December 2014, pp. 797–818.

Guiffan, Jean, *Histoire de l'anglophobie en France: De Jeanne d'Arc à la vache folle*, Dinan, 2004.

Guilbert, Madeleine, *Les fonctions des femmes dans l'industrie*, Paris, 1966.

Guin, Yannick, 'Au cœur du libéralisme: La loi du 22 mars 1841 relative au travail des enfants employés dans les manufactures, usines et ateliers', in Jean-Pierre Le Crom (ed.), *Deux siècles de droit du travail: L'histoire par les lois*, Paris, 1998, pp. 29–44.

Haines, Robin F., *Emigration and the Labouring Poor Australian Recruitment in Britain and Ireland, 1831–60*, London, 1997.

Hall, Catherine, Nicholas Draper, Keith McClelland, Katie Donington, and Rachel Lang, *Legacies of British Slave-Ownership: Colonial Slavery and the Formation of Victorian Britain*, Cambridge, 2014.

Hamlin, Christopher, *Public Health and Social Justice in the Age of Chadwick. Britain, 1800–1854*, Cambridge, 1998.

Hands, Thora, *Drinking in Victorian and Edwardian Britain: Beyond the Spectre of the Drunkard*, London, 2018.

Hardach, Gerd H., 'Les problèmes de main-d'œuvre à Decazeville', *Revue d'histoire de la sidérurgie*, vol. 8, no. 196, 1967.

Harper, Marjory, and Stephen Constantine, *Migration and empire*, Oxford, 2010.

Harris, Emma, *Bartlomiej Beniowski 1800–1867: Cosmopolitical Chartist and Revolutionary Refugee*, Warsaw, 2019.

Harris, John R., *Industrial Espionage and Technology Transfer: Britain and France in the Eighteenth Century*, Aldershot, 1998.

Harris, John R., 'John Holker (1719–1786)', *ODNB*, Oxford, 2004.

Harrison, Brian, and Patricia Hollis (eds.), *Robert Lowery: Radical and Chartist*, London, 1979.

Harrison, Brian, *Drink and the Victorians: The Temperance Question in England 1815–1872*, London, 1971.

Harzig, Christiane, and Dirk Hoerder, with Donna Gabaccia, *What Is Migration History?*, Cambridge, 2009.

Headrick, Daniel, *The Tools of Empire: Technology and European Imperialism in the Nineteenth Century*, New York, 1981.

Headrick, Daniel, *The Tentacles of Progress: Technology Transfer in the Age of Imperialism, 1850–1940*, Oxford, 1988.

Henderson, W. O., *Britain and Industrial Europe*, Liverpool, 1954.

Hill, Bridget, *Women, Work and Sexual Politics in Eighteenth-Century England*, London, 1993.

Hincker, Louis, *Citoyens-combattants à Paris, 1848–1851*, Villeneuve d'Ascq, 2008.

Hobbs, Andrew, *A Fleet Street in Every Town: The Provincial Press in England*, Cambridge, 2018.

Hobsbawm, E. J., 'The tramping artisan', *Economic History Review*, vol. 3, no. 3, 1951, pp. 299–320.

Hobsbawm, E. J., and Joan Wallach Scott, 'Political shoemakers', *Past and Present*, no. 89, November 1980, pp. 86–114.

Hoerder, Dirk, *Cultures in Contact: World Migrations in the Second Millennium*, Durham, NC, 2002.

Holland, Michael (ed.), *Swing Unmasked: The Agricultural Riots of 1830 to 1832 and Their Wider Implications*, Milton Keynes, 2005.

Honeyman, Katrina, *Women, Gender and Industrialisation in England, 1700–1870*, New York, 2000.

Honeyman, Katrina, 'Holden, Sir Isaac, first baronet (1807–1897)', *ODNB*, Oxford, 2004.

Honeyman, Katrina (ed.), *Childhood and Child Labour in Industrial England: Diversity and Agency, 1750–1914*, Aldershot, 2013.

Honeyman, Katrina, and Jordan Goodman, *Technology and Enterprise: Isaac Holden and the Mechanisation of Woolcombing in France, 1848–1914*, Aldershot, 1986.

Hoppit, Julian, *Britain's Political Economies: Parliament and Economic Life, 1660–1800*, Cambridge, 2017.

Horrell, Sara, and Jane Humphries, '"The exploitation of little children": Child labor and the family economy in the industrial revolution', *Explorations in Economic History*, vol. 32, no. 4, 1995, pp. 485–516.

Horrell, Sara, and Jane Humphries, 'Women's labour force participation and the transition to the male-breadwinner family, 1790–1865', *Economic History Review*, 2nd ser., vol. 48, 1995, pp. 89–117.

Howatt, A. P. R., and Richard Smith, 'The history of teaching English as a foreign language, from a British and European perspective', *Language & History*, vol. 57, no. 1, 2014, pp. 75–95.

Humphries, Jane, *Childhood and Child Labour in the British Industrial Revolution*, Cambridge, 2010.

Humphries, Jane, 'The lure of aggregates and the pitfalls of the patriarchal perspective: A critique of the high wage economy interpretation of the British industrial revolution', *Economic History Review*, vol. 66, no. 3, 2013, pp. 693–714.

Humphries, Jane, and Benjamin Schneider, 'Spinning the industrial revolution', *Economic History Review*, vol. 72, no. 1 (2019), pp. 126–55.

International Organization for Migration, *World Migration Report 2020*, Geneva, 2019.

Jackson, Gordon, and Kate Kinnear, *The Trade and Shipping of Dundee, 1780–1850*, Dundee, 1990.

Jackson, James H. Jr., 'Alltagsgeschichte, social science history, and the study of migration in nineteenth-century Germany', *Central European History*, vol. 23, no. 2/3, June to September 1990, pp. 242–63.

Jarrige, François, *Au temps des 'tueuses de bras'. Les bris de machines à l'aube de l'ère industrielle (1780–1860)*, Rennes, 2009, pp. 91–3.

Jarrige, François, and Thomas Le Roux, '1. Naissance de l'enquête: les hygiénistes, Villermé et les ouvriers autour de 1840', in Eric Geerkens et al. (eds.), *Les enquêtes ouvrières dans l'Europe contemporaine*, Paris, 2019, pp. 39–52.

Jay, Elizabeth, *British Writers in Paris, 1830–1875*, Oxford, 2016.

Jeremy, David J., 'Damming the flood: British governments' efforts to check the outflow of technicians and machinery 1780–1843', *Business History Review*, vol. 51, 1977.

Jones, David J. V., 'The South Wales strike of 1816', *Morgannwg Transactions of the Glamorgan Local History Society*, vol. 11, 1967.

Jones, David J. V., *Before Rebecca: Popular Protests in Wales, 1793–1835*, London, 1973.

Jones, Rhian E., *Petticoat Heroes: Gender, Culture and Popular Protest in the Rebecca Riots*, Cardiff, 2015.

Jousse, Emmanuel, 'Les traducteurs de l'Internationale', *Cahiers Jaurès*, no. 212–13, 2014, pp. 181–94.

Kéfer, Fabienne, 'Ernest Mahaim: 1865-1892-1919-1938', February 2019. https://www.news.uliege.be/upload/docs/application/pdf/2019-02/ernest_mahaim.pdf

Kelly, Gillian, *Well Suited to the Colony*, Queanbeyan, 1998.

Kelly, Morgan, Joel Mokyr, and Cormac Ó Gráda, 'The mechanics of the industrial revolution', online research paper, 3 June 2020.

Kemnitz, Thomas, 'Chartism in Brighton', PhD thesis, University of Sussex, 1969.

Kerr, Ian, *Building the Railways of the Raj, 1850–1900*, Delhi, 1995.

Khan, B. Zorina, and Kenneth Sokoloff, 'The evolution of useful knowledge: Great inventors, science and technology in British economic development, 1750–1930', Working Papers 7005, Economic History Society, 2007.

Kiernan, Michael T., *The Engineers of Cornwall at the Mines of Pontgibaud in France*, Redruth, 2016.

Kirby, Peter, *Child Labour in Britain 1750–1870*, London, 2003.

Kirk, Neville, *Comrades and Cousins: Globalization, Workers and Labour Movements in Britain, the USA and Australia from the 1880s to 1914*, London, 2003.

Kunitake, Kume, *Japan Rising: The Iwakura Embassy to the USA and Europe*, Cambridge, 2009.

Lattek, Christine, *Revolutionary Refugees: German Socialism in Britain, 1840–1860*, London, 2005.

Laurant, Annie, *Des fers de Loire à l'acier Martin*, vol. 1, *Maîtres de forges en Berry et Nivernais*, Paris, 1995.

Laybourn, Keith, *A History of British Trade Unionism, c. 1770–1990*, Stroud, 1992.

Leboissetier, Léa, 'Les colporteurs étrangers et perçus comme étrangers au Royaume-Uni (années 1820–années 1970)', thesis, Lyon, Ecole normale supérieure/Sorbonne Université.

Lebrun, Pierre, Marinette Bruwier, Jan Dhondt, and Georges Hansotte, *Essai sur la révolution industrielle en Belgique, 1770–1847* (*Histoire quantitative*, 1ère série, t. II, vol. 1), Brussels, 1979.

Lee, J., 'Labour in German industrialization', in P. Mathias and M. Postan (eds.), *Cambridge Economic History of Europe*, vol. 7, part 1, Cambridge, 1978.

Lehning, Arthur, *From Buonarroti to Bakunin: Studies in International Socialism*, Leiden, 1970.

Le Maitron. Dictionnaire biographique. Mouvement ouvrier. Mouvement Social, https://maitron.fr.

Lemire, Beverly, and Giorgio Riello (eds.), *Dressing Global Bodies: The Political Power of Dress in World History*, London, 2020.

Lenman, Bruce, Charlotte Lythe, and Enid Gauldie, *Dundee and Its Textile Industry*, Dundee, 1969.

Light, Alison, *Common People: The History of an English family*, London, 2014.

Linant de Bellefonds, Xavier, 'Les techniciens anglais dans l'industrie française au 18e siècle', thesis, Paris, 1971.

Locke, Robert R., 'Drouillard, Benoist et Cie (1836–1856)', *Revue d'histoire de la sidérurgie*, vol. 8, 1967.

Lown, Judy, *Women and Industrialization: Gender at Work in Nineteenth Century England*, Cambridge, 1990.

Lux, Rick, 'Welsh ironworkers in France', *Glamorgan Family History Society*, J137, March 2020, pp. 26–31.

Mackay, Brian, 'Overseeing the foundations of the Irish linen industry: The rise and fall of the Crommelin legend', in Brenda Collins and Philip Ollerenshaw (eds.), *The European Linen Industry in Historical Perspective*, Oxford, 2003, pp. 99–122.

MacLeod, Christine, *Heroes of Invention. Technology, Liberalism and British Identity, 1750–1914*, Cambridge, 2007.

MacRaild, Donald, *The Irish Diaspora in Britain, 1750–1939*, London, 2013.

Maddison, Angus, *The World Economy: A Millennial Perspective*, Paris, 2001.

Mahaim, Ernest, 'Les débuts de l'établissement John Cockerill à Seraing. Contribution à l'histoire des origines de la grande industrie au Pays de Liège', *Vierteljahrschrift für Social- und Wirtschaftsgeschichte*, 1905, pp. 627–48.

Maillard, Alain, *La communauté des Égaux. Le communisme néo-babouviste dans la France des années 1840*, Paris, 1999.

Marec, Yannick, 'Un républicain social, député, sénateur, président de la Chambre de commerce de Rouen. Richard Waddington (1838–1913)', *Bulletin de la société libre d'émulation de la Seine-Maritime*, 2002, pp. 3–10.

Maréchal, Virginie, 'La construction des lignes de chemin de fer de Paris à Rouen et de Rouen au Havre (1839–1847)', *Revue d'histoire des chemins de fer*, no. 14, 1996, pp. 64–89.

Mason, Sheila, *Nottingham Lace 1760s–1950s: The Machine-Made Lace Industry in Nottinghamshire, Derbyshire and Leicestershire*, Stroud, 2010 [1994].

Mauffroy, William, 'Les Odd Fellows de Saint-Pierre-lès-Calais ou la première rencontre de la mutualité et du mouvement ouvrier dans le Pas-de-Calais au XIXe siècle', *Bulletin de la commission départementale d'histoire et d'archéologie du Pas-de-Calais*, vol. 15, 1997.

McKee, Denis, 'Jonathan Holden. 1828–1906. Industriel du peignage de la laine', in Gracia Dorel-Ferré and Denis McKee (dir.), *Les Patrons du Second Empire. Champagne-Ardenne*, Paris, 2006, pp. 141–4.

McKee, Denis, '"L'usine des anglais" de Reims et Jonathan Holden (1828–1906): un succès industriel, un patron philanthrope', *Travaux de l'Académie nationale de Reims*, vol. 186, 2019, pp. 113–34.

McKenzie, J. C., 'The composition and nutritional value of diets in Manchester and Dukinfield in 1841', *Transactions of the Lancashire and Cheshire Antiquarian Society*, vol. 72, 1962.

McKitterick, David, 'Introduction', in *The Cambridge History of the Book in Britain*, vol. 6, *1830–1914*, Cambridge, 2009.

McLelland, Nicola, 'The history of language learning and teaching in Britain', *The Language Learning Journal*, vol. 46:1, 9.2, 2018.

Messner, Andrew, 'Chartist political culture in Britain and Colonial Australia, c. 1835–60', unpublished PhD thesis, University of New England, 2000.

Meyering, Anne, '*La Petite ouvrière surmenée*: Family structure, family income and women's work in nineteenth-century France', in Pat Hudson and W. R. Lee (eds.), *Women's Work and the Family Economy in Historical Perspective*, Manchester, 1990, pp. 132–56.

Miller, Kerby A., *Emigrants and Exiles: Ireland and the Irish Exodus to North America*, Oxford, 1988.

Minard, Philippe, *La France du colbertisme*, Paris, 1998.

Minoletti, Paul, 'The importance of ideology: The shift to factory production and its effect on women's employment opportunities in the English textile industries, 1760–1850', *Continuity and Change*, vol. 28, no. 1, 2013, pp. 71–90.

Miskell, Louise, and C. A. Whatley, '"Juteopolis" in the making: Linen and the industrial transformation of Dundee, c. 1820–1850', *Textile History*, vol. 30, no. 2, 1999, pp. 176–98.

Miskell, Louise, Christopher A. Whatley, and Bob Harris, 'Introduction: Altering images', in Louise Miskell, Christopher A. Whatley, and Bob Harris (eds.), *Victorian Dundee: Image and Realities*, East Linton, 2000.

Moch, Leslie Page, *Moving Europeans. Migration in Western Europe since 1650*, Bloomington, IN, 2003.

Moisand, Jeanne, *Se fédérer ou mourir. Carthagène, 1873. Une Commune espagnole et ses mondes*, Paris, to be published in 2023.

Moore, Angela, 'John Jones, railway contractor of Treuddyn, Newcastle-under-Lyme and Pissy-Pôville, France', *Clwyd Historian*, vol. 67, winter 2012, pp. 2–9.

Moriceau, Caroline, *Les douleurs de l'industrie. L'hygiénisme industriel en France, 1860–1914*, thesis, EHESS, 2002.

Morieux, Renaud, 'Diplomacy from below and belonging: Fishermen and cross-channel relations in the eighteenth century', *Past and Present*, vol. 202, 2009, pp. 83–125.

Nardinelli, Clark, *Child Labor and the Industrial Revolution*, Bloomington, IN, 1990.

Navickas, Katrina, *Protest and the Politics of Space and Place, 1789–1848*, Manchester, 2016.

Nicholls, James, *The Politics of Alcohol: A History of the Drink Question in England*, Manchester, 2009.

Noël, Benoît, 'Les Anglais et l'origine de la dentelle de Calais', *Revue du Nord*, 2006/1, no. 364, pp. 67–88.

Noël, Benoît, 'Outsiders. Petites entreprises et petits entrepreneurs anglo-calaisiens dans le marché français des tulles et dentelles mécaniques de la première moitié du XIXème siècle', in Anne-Sophie Bruno, Claire Zalc (eds.), *Actes de l'histoire de l'immigration*, numéro spécial, vol.5, 2005, pp. 161–180.

Noiriel, Gérard, *Le Creuset français*, Paris, 1988.

Noiriel, Gérard, *État, nation, immigration. Vers une histoire du pouvoir*, Paris, 2001.

Noiriel, Gérard, *Le massacre des Italiens: Aigues-Mortes, 17 août 1893*, Paris, 2010.

Noiriel, Gérard, *Une histoire populaire de la France. De la guerre de Cent Ans à nos jours*, Marseille, 2018.

Nourrisson, Didier, *Le buveur du 19ᵉ siècle*, Paris, 1990.

Nuvolari, Alessandro, 'Collective invention during the Industrial Revolution: the case of the Cornish pumping engine', *Cambridge Journal of Economics*, 2004, 28, pp. 347–63.

Oddy, D. J., 'Food in nineteenth century England: Nutrition in the first urban society', *Proceedings of the Nutrition Society*, vol. 29, no. 1, May 1970, p. 155.

Oddy, D. J., and J. Yudkin, 'An evaluation of English diets of the 1860s', *Proceedings of the Nutrition Society*, vol. 28, no. 1, April 1969, p. 13A.

Oxx, Katie, *The Nativist Movement in America: Religious Conflict in the Nineteenth Century*, London, 2013.

Payton, Philip, *The Cornish Overseas: The Epic Story of Cornwall's Great Emigration*, Exeter, 2019.

Peltola, Jarmo, 'The British contribution to the birth of the Finnish cotton industry (1820–1870)', *Continuity and Change*, vol. 34, 2019, pp. 63–89.

Perrot, Michelle, 'Les rapports entre ouvriers français et étrangers (1871–1893)', *Bulletin de la Société d'histoire moderne*, 1960, pp. 4–9.

Phillips, Anne, and Barbara Taylor, 'Sex and skill: Notes towards a feminist economics', *Feminist Review*, vol. 6, 1980, pp. 56–79.

Pickering, Paul, 'A wider field in a new country: Chartism in colonial Australia', in Marian Sawer (ed.), *Elections Full, Free and Fair*, Sydney, 2001, pp. 28–44.

Pickering, Paul, 'The oak of English liberty: Popular constitutionalism in New South Wales, 1848–1856', *Journal of Australian Colonial History*, vol. 3, 2001, pp. 1–27.

Pinchbeck, Ivy, *Women Workers and the Industrial Revolution, 1750–1850*, London, 1930.

Poole, Robert, *Peterloo: The English Uprising*, Oxford, 2019.

Pooley, Colin, 'Using life histories to explore the complexities of internal and international migration', *Continuity and Change*, vol. 36, no. 1, May 2021, pp. 111–31.

Pooley, Colin, and Jean Turnbull, *Migration and Mobility in Britain since the Eighteenth Century*, London, 1998.

Porter, Bernard, *The Refugee Question in Mid-Victorian Politics*, Cambridge, 1979.

Prados de la Escosura, Leandro, ed. *Exceptionalism and Industrialisation: Britain and Its European Rivals, 1688–1815*, Cambridge, 2004.

Prothero, Iorwerth, *Radical Artisans in England and France, 1830–1870*, Cambridge, 1997.

Raffiee, Leila, 'A study of British slave owners in Boulogne-sur-Mer based on the records of the Slave Compensation Commission following the abolition of slavery in 1833', Master's thesis 2, Université Paris-Sorbonne, September 2016.

Ravenstein, E. G., 'The laws of migration', *Journal of Statistical Society*, vol. 48, June 1885, pp. 167–235.

Raveux, Olivier, 'Les ingénieurs anglais de la Provence maritime sous la monarchie de Juillet', *Provence historique*, no. 177, 1994, pp. 301–320.

Raveux, Olivier, 'Un technicien britannique en Europe méridionale: Philip Taylor (1786–1870)', *Histoire, économie et société*, 19(2), 2000, pp. 253–266.

Redford, Arthur *Labour migration in England: 1800–1850*, 2nd ed., revised by W. H. Chaloner, Manchester, 1964 [1926].

Rediker, Marcus, *The Slave Ship: A Human History*, New York, 2007.

Richards, Eric, *Britannia's Children: Emigration from England, Scotland, Wales and Ireland Since 1600*, London, 2004.

Richardson, Christopher, *Socialism, Chartism and Co-operation: Nottingham 1844*, Nottingham, 2013.

Riello, Giorgio, *Cotton: The Fabric That Made the Modern World*, Cambridge, 2015.

Robinet, René, 'Les premiers fours à puddler dans les Ardennes. Techniciens anglais et lorrains aux forges de Jean-Nicolas Gendarme (1822–1826)', *Actes du 89ᵉ congrès national des sociétés savantes. Lyon, 1964*, Paris, 1965.

Roche, Daniel, *La culture équestre de l'Occident, XVIᵉ–XIXᵉ siècle. L'ombre du cheval*, 3 vols., Paris, 2008–15.

Rogers, Rachel, *Friends of the Revolution: The British Radical Community in Early Republican Paris 1792–1794*, London, 2021.

Rosatto, Vittoria, *Leavers Lace: A Handbook of the American Leavers Lace Industry*, Providence, RI, 1948.

Rose, Sonya O., *Limited Livelihoods: Gender and Class in Nineteenth-Century England*, London, 1992.

Rosental, Paul-André, *Les sentiers invisibles : espace, familles et migrations dans la France du 19ᵉ siècle*, Paris, 1999.

Ruer, Philippe, 'Les métiers populaires et la naissance du monde ouvrier à Charenton de 1625 à 1875', Université Créteil Paris 12, 1987.

Samuel, Raphael, 'The workshop of the world: Steam power and hand technology in mid-Victorian Britain', *History Workshop Journal*, vol. 3.1, spring 1977, pp. 6–72.

Saville, John, *1848: The British State and the Chartist Movement*, Cambridge, 1987.

Schoyen, Albert, *The Chartist Challenge: A Portrait of George Julian Harney*, London, 1958.

Schwarzkopf, Jutta, *Unpicking Gender: The Social Construction of Gender in the Lancashire Cotton Weaving Industry, 1880–1914*, Aldershot, 2004.

Sharpe, Pamela, *Adapting to Capitalism: Working Women in the English Economy, 1700–1850*, Basingstoke, 2000 [1996].

Sharpe, Pamela, and Stanley D. Chapman, 'Women's employment and industrial organisation: Commercial lace embroidery in early nineteenth-century Ireland and England', *Women's History Review*, vol. 5, 1996, pp. 325–50.

Siméon, Ophélie, *Robert Owen's Experiment at New Lanark: From Paternalism to Socialism*, London, 2017.

Sinclair, Bruce, 'Canadian technology: British traditions and American influences', *Technology and Culture*, vol. 20, January 1979, pp. 108–23.

Smith, Richard, and Nicola McLelland, 'Histories of language learning and teaching in Europe', *The Language Learning Journal*, vol. 46, no. 1, 2018.

Société d'histoire de Grand-Couronne, *Le frais et charmant village de Grand-Couronne. Une commune rurale à l'aube du XXᵉ siècle (1890–1914)*, Grand-Couronne, 1997.

Sorez, Julien, 'Le football et la fabrique des territoires. Une approche spatiale des pratiques culturelles', *Vingtième Siècle. Revue d'histoire*, no. 111, 2011/3, pp. 59–72.

Southall, Humphrey, '"Agitate, agitate! Organise!": Political travellers and the construction of national politics, 1839–1880', *Transactions of the Institute of British Geographers*, new series, vol. 21, 1996, pp. 177–93.

Spenceley, G. F. R., 'The English pillow lace industry 1840–80: A rural industry in competition with machinery', *Business History*, vol. 19, 1977.

St Clair, William, *The Reading Nation in the Romantic Period*, Cambridge, 2004.

Strachey, Lytton, *Eminent Victorians*, London, 1918.

Stromquist, Shelton, 'Railroad labor and the global economy: Historical patterns', in Jan Lucassen (ed.), *Global Labour History: A State of the Art*, Bern, 2006, pp. 623–47.

Sugier, Fabrice, 'L'immigration européenne dans le bassin houiller de la Grand'Combe', *Causses et Cévennes, Revue bimestrielle du Club Cévenol*, no. 4, 1992, p. 266.

Tabili, Laura, *Global Migrants, Local Culture: Natives and Newcomers in Provincial England, 1841–1939*, London, 2011.

Thiesse, Anne-Marie, *La création des identités nationales. Europe XVIIIe–XXe siècle*, Paris, 1999.

Thompson, E. P., *The Making of the English Working Class*, Harmondsworth, 1968 [1963].

Thuillier, Guy, *Georges Dufaud et les débuts du grand capitalisme dans la métallurgie, en Nivernais, au XIXe siècle*, Paris, 1959.

Thuillier, Guy (ed.), *Les ouvriers des forges nivernaises. Vie quotidienne et pratiques sociales*, Paris, 2002.

Tilly, Charles, 'Les origines du répertoire de l'action collective contemporaine en France et en Grande-Bretagne', *Vingtième Siècle*, vol. 4, October 1984, pp. 89–108.

Tilly, Louise A., and Joan W. Scott, *Women, Work and Family*, New York, 1987 [1978].

Tinajero, Araceli, *El Lector: A History of the Cigar Factory Reader*, Austin, TX, 2010.

Todd, David, *Free Trade and Its Enemies in France, 1814–1851*, Cambridge, 2015.

Tombs, Robert, and Isabelle Tombs, *That Sweet Enemy: Britain and France—The History of a Love-Hate Relationship*, London, 2008.

Tóth, Heléna, *An Exiled Generation: German and Hungarian Refugees of Revolution, 1848–1871*, Cambridge, 2014.

Traugott, Mark, 'Les barricades dans les insurrections parisiennes: rôles sociaux et modes de fonctionnement', in Alain Corbin and Jean-Marie Mayeur (dir.), *La Barricade*, Paris, 1997, pp. 71–81.

Van der Linden, Marcel, 'The rise and fall of the First International: An interpretation', in Frits Van Holthoon and Marcel van der Linden (eds.), *Internationalism in the Labour movement, 1830–1940*, 2 vols., vol. 1, Leiden, 1988, pp. 323–35.

Varley, D. E., 'John Heathcoat (1783–1861): Founder of the machine-made lace industry', *Textile History*, vol. 1, no. 1, 1968, pp. 2–45.

Varley, D. E., *A History of the Midland Counties Lace Manufacturers' Association, 1915–1958*, Long Eaton, 1959.

Verley, Patrick, *L'Echelle du monde. Essai sur l'industrialisation de l'Occident*, Paris, 2013.

Vidalenc, Jean, *Le département de l'Eure sous la monarchie constitutionnelle, 1814–1848*, Paris, 1952.

Ville, Sylvain, 'Donner la boxe en spectacle: une histoire sociale des débuts de la boxe professionnelle à Paris, à la Belle Epoque', *Actes de la recherche en sciences sociales*, vol. 4, no. 209, 2015, pp. 10–27.

Ville, Sylvain, *Le théâtre de la boxe: Histoire sociale de la boxe anglaise professionnelle à Paris (et à Londres) (1880–1930)*, doctoral thesis, Université Paris-Ouest Nanterre-La Défense, 2016.

Vincent, David, *Bread, Knowledge and Freedom: A Study of Nineteenth-Century Working Class Autobiography*, London, 1981.

Vion, Albert, 'Aspects de la vie calaisienne aux XIXe siècle: la communauté britannique', *Bulletin historique et artistique du Calaisis*, vol. 80, December 1979.

Walter, John, *Crowds and Popular Politics in Early Modern England*, Manchester, 2013.

Weisser, Henry, *British Working-Class Movements and Europe*, Manchester, 1975.

Westwood, N., 'John Hughes and Russian metallurgy', *The Economic History Review*, vol. 17, no. 3, 1965, pp. 564–9.

Wright, Thomas, *The Romance of the Shoe: Being the History of Shoemaking in All Ages, and Especially in England and Scotland*, London, 1922.

Wrigley, E. A., and R. S. Schofield, *The Population History of England 1541–1871: A Reconstruction*, London, 1981.

Index

For the benefit of digital users, indexed terms that span two pages (e.g., 52–53) may, on occasion, appear on only one of those pages.